Personal Problems

HOUGHTON MIFFLIN COMPANY

Personal Problems

★ ★

HOUGHTON MIFFLIN COMPANY

and Morale

BY JOHN B. GEISEL, *Formerly Principal
of Alpena High School, Alpena, Michigan*

UNDER THE EDITORSHIP OF

FRANCIS T. SPAULDING, *Dean of the School of
Education, Harvard University. At present, Colonel,
Army of the United States, Chief of the Education
Branch, Special Service Division, War Department.*

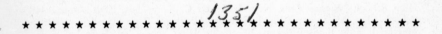

1351

Boston · New York · Chicago · Dallas · Atlanta · San Francisco
𝔗𝔥𝔢 ℜ𝔦𝔳𝔢𝔯𝔰𝔦𝔡𝔢 𝔓𝔯𝔢𝔰𝔰 ℭ𝔞𝔪𝔟𝔯𝔦𝔡𝔤𝔢

ACKNOWLEDGMENTS

The author acknowledges his indebtedness to Dr. Laurance F. Shaffer, Associate Professor of Psychology, Carnegie Institute of Technology (at present, Major, United States Army Air Corps), for many suggestions and for critical reading and checking of both manuscript and proof; to Gove Hambidge, U.S. Department of Agriculture, Washington, D.C., for valuable editorial help; and to Grace B. Rinard, Supervisor of Home Economics, Lansing, Michigan, Public Schools, who read proof on Unit VI.

During six years of classroom experimentation in Alpena High School, practical help was generously given by Perry D. Chatterton, who also taught the course; Harriet K. Foley, who helped to improve the materials during these years; Ella M. White, Business Secretary to the Board of Education, whose counsel proved repeatedly invaluable; Russell H. Wilson, Superintendent of Schools, under whose administration this experimentation was possible; and Clifton E. Lutes, who supplied many of the literary references for the present book.

Appreciation is also due the following for helpful suggestions: M. G. Batho, West Bend High School, West Bend, Wisconsin; Catherine Beachley, Hagerstown High School, Hagerstown, Indiana; Dr. Floyd Cromwell, Supervisor of Educational and Vocational Guidance, Department of Education, State of Maryland, Elkton, Maryland; Howard Cummings, Clayton High School, Clayton, Missouri; Wilbur Devilbiss, Frederick High School, Frederick, Maryland; Herbert Espy, Professor of Education, Western Reserve University, Cleveland, Ohio; Mrs. Lester C. Furney, High School, Radford, Virginia; Thomas S. Gwynn, Jr., Oxon Hill High School, Oxon Hill, Indiana; Mrs. Grace F. Harrison, Chapman Technical High School, New London, Connecticut; Helen Hawkins, Elkton High School, Elkton, Maryland; Ethel M. Henry, Senior High School, Altoona, Pennsylvania; J. G. Hickox, Harding Senior High School, Warren, Ohio; Arthur A. Hitchcock, Bristol High School, Bristol, Connecticut; Dorothy Ellen Jones, Supervisor of Home Economics, Cleveland Public Schools, Cleveland, Ohio; C. A. Meter, Menominee High School, Menominee, Michigan; Evelyn F. Miller, Fort Hill High School, Cumberland, Maryland; Ola Day Rush, Home Economics Department, Washington, D.C.; Mrs. Gladys G. Saur, Godwin Heights High School, Grand Rapids, Michigan; Louise Scott, East Haven High School, East Haven, Connecticut; M. L. Smith, High School, Springfield, Pennsylvania; Robert C. Smith, High School, Beaver Dam, Wisconsin; Lyndon H. Strough, Niagara Falls High School, Niagara Falls, New York; D. C. Snoyenbos, Flint Central High School, Flint, Michigan; Mary J. Swerby, Alleghany High School, Cumberland, Maryland; Kate R. Steichmann, Shortridge High School, Indianapolis, Indiana; Mrs. Rose T. Stelter, Supervisor, Curriculum Office, Los Angeles Schools, Los Angeles, California; J. F. Towell, Lyons Township High School, LaGrange, Illinois; Louise Welch, Springfield High School, Springfield, Illinois; Winfield M. Wickham, Berkeley, California; M. V. Zimmerman, Easton High School, Easton, Maryland.

The Riverside Press

CAMBRIDGE · MASSACHUSETTS

PRINTED IN THE U.S.A.

CONTENTS

Unit IX · A HOME OF YOUR OWN

PART THREE. MAKING YOUR WAY IN TIME OF WAR

Unit X · WHAT IS MORALE?

Unit XI · THE WAR EFFORT AND YOUR FUTURE

CONCLUSION

WHAT KIND OF PERSON DO YOU WANT TO BE?

> *What kind of person do you want to be? Describe someone who seems to be quite satisfied with himself just as he is. Can you explain his actions? Is a bad habit easier to acquire than a good one? Explain. Would you say that making personal improvements is a gradual process or a rapid one? Why?*

"I LIKE MYSELF just the way I am."

Did you ever hear anyone say that and really mean it? You may have seen someone act as if he thought as much, but deep down, of course, he did not approve of his own actions and was not fully satisfied with himself. Most of us, in fact, are not satisfied with ourselves as we are, but are building and rebuilding for the future.

Before a carpenter builds a house, he asks himself, "What kind of house do I want to build?" Then he spends a good deal of time making plans. Once the blueprints are finished, he builds according to his plan, though he may find that some changes are necessary. Certain materials may not be available, or he may not be able to secure the site for which he had designed the house, so he modifies his plans according to circumstances that cannot be foreseen. A good carpenter does not build a house in hit-or-miss fashion; he thinks it through in advance and builds according to plan.

Each one of us spends a lifetime building the sort of person he finally becomes. Too many of us go at it in a hit-or-miss fashion and do not think it through in advance. What we need is a plan for our building.

Deep down, most of us have a plan — an ideal self — which we should like to see in action more of the time. For our ideal self we usually think of a person who has our personality at its best, successful in work and in love, able to get along with others, and well liked by them. In other words, our ideal self — the house we are building — is a likable person in the broadest sense of the term.

WORKING OUT YOUR PERSONAL PROBLEMS

A person who is too often upset, uneasy, worried, nervous, restless, irritable, or extremely dissatisfied does not see his ideal self in action very much of the time. Can a person learn any ways to keep his thinking and feeling straight, so that he does not get "down in the dumps" too often or too long? — so that his personality and behavior are not warped by jealousy? — so that he does not feel too inferior to mingle freely with his fellows? — so that he is not apt to act like a fool when he wants to be the reverse? Are there any ways and any rules that might help a person develop his personality?

Yes, there are. There is a great deal of information that can help you in working out your personal problems.

What are the causes of your problems? In order to solve the problems of life, it is necessary to know what causes them. For this reason the question "Why?" will constantly be repeated or implied in this book. *Why* is a person jealous? *Why* does he gossip? *Why* does he sacrifice himself for someone else? *Why* does he become angry? *Why* does he quarrel with his brother or sister? *Why* does he have trouble with his boss? *Why* does he succeed at his work? You have to know *why* you do the things you do before you can go about improving or correcting yourself. Furthermore, the most important person for you to understand is yourself. Until you understand yourself, you cannot really understand other people.

The first step toward solving a problem is insight. Working out your personal problems begins with a willingness to look squarely at the causes, whether they are complimentary to you or not — and some of them are bound to be uncomplimentary. The first step is to become willing and able to see through the make-believe of life. If you are willing and able to understand the causes behind your own behavior, you are said to have insight. You need insight before real improvement can take place.

Insight is a word that means practically just what it says — internal sight. Internal sight, or insight, is understanding. It is the ability to see through the make-believe into the real causes of a situation — the ability to understand yourself and catch the hidden or inner nature of things — the ability to recognize your own strength and weakness. Before you can go about developing your personality in an efficient manner, you should understand the causes of or the reasons for your behavior.

Who can see himself as others see him? It is, however, especially hard for a person to see his own faults or even to see his own virtues in their true light. We are inclined either to overestimate or to underestimate our strong points and also to overestimate or underestimate our weak points. It would be well if each of us had a personal friend with whom we could talk about ourselves. Then, through helpful criticism and suggestion, we might improve more rapidly. This is not just a general suggestion; it is sound psychology. But not everyone has an intimate friend who dares to act the part of a mirror for him and tell him those facts about himself which he needs in order to improve.

We have "blind spots." There seems to be a tendency in everyone to forget or close his mind to his own faults and weaknesses. Although we know how John Jones looks when he smiles or when he is angry, we do not know how we ourselves look when we smile or are angry. Although we can see how Mary Jones treats her brother, we do not see how we treat our own brother. There is a tendency for each of us to put his best foot forward, not only in dealing with others, but perhaps even more in dealing with himself. We are inclined to try to forget our own shortcomings. In fact, it is probably natural for us to be unwilling to think about our own shortcomings. We should, however, be eager to learn more about ourselves, more about the underlying reasons for our behavior, whether the reasons are flattering or unflattering. As our knowledge of human nature grows, we find that there is a good deal of deceit in every personality, including our own. We all "kid ourselves along" much more than we think we do.

Working out our personal problems is a long-time process. It is impossible for anyone suddenly to develop complete insight into his own behavior or anyone else's. That is an art to be developed over many years. Moreover, though guiding principles can be presented and studied in such a book as this, it is up to you personally to make your understanding of human behavior real and worth while by constant, daily use of these principles.

Socrates, the great teacher of ancient times, is said to have taught that "knowing is doing"; that if a person fully knew how to behave, he would behave that way. Although it is not necessary to agree entirely with Socrates, we can agree to some extent. Knowing how to do a certain thing may not mean that we will do it, but at least it is a necessary first step. If a person fully knew how to make a football tackle, it would be much easier for him to do it right than if he knew little or nothing about it. Similarly, knowing what your problems are and understanding their causes is a necessary first step toward solving them.

Case One. James, a sixteen-year-old boy, was jealous of his younger brother, John. John was his only brother, five years younger than James. When John was born, the parents' attention naturally turned to the baby of the family, and practically all attention was taken away from James. The older brother would strike the baby and be mean to him in many ways. As the years passed, this behavior continued. When James was sixteen, however, one of his high-school teachers talked with him about the matter and explained to him why he felt unkindly toward his younger brother. When James understood that it was jealousy (for John had apparently taken the place of importance in the family which James had formerly held securely for five years), a new understanding came to him. In the course of the year he talked with his teacher two or three times again and gained a fuller understanding of his own behavior. He developed an insight into his own problem and was thereafter better able to improve his relations with the younger brother. Two years later the relations between these two boys had changed a great deal.

James was no longer jealous of John, and this brought a great change in the home atmosphere. James no longer aroused the anger of his father and mother by his treatment of John; both boys received an equal affection from their parents; and James became truly the "big brother" in his attitude toward John. Insight into his own behavior had enabled James to solve a difficult personal problem.

Case Two. Celia M—— was one of the brightest girls in her class. She was talented in dramatics and public speaking. She was successful in a part-time job. She dressed well. She had many friends in school. Yet during her last semester in high school she confided in one of her teachers the following extraordinary story: Every class was another hour of fear to her — fear that she would be called upon and not know the answer. She hardly slept at all when a test was on the program for the next day. Every time she thought she was sure to fail. School life was very difficult — a long series of fearful experiences. As for dramatics and debating, she was certain she had no ability. She did not like to buy clothes because she thought she had poor taste, and the pretty suit she was wearing seemed to her to be a misfit. She felt sure she hadn't a friend in school and wondered when they would tell her what they thought of her.

The part-time job was a daily unhappy experience to her; she was afraid everything she did was wrong, that she did not do enough, and that she would be discharged any day. She felt certain that she would be without a job after graduation, and this fear for the future was perhaps her keenest fear.

Naturally, Celia's teacher listened to all this with surprise, but she did not interrupt except to give her own and others' opinions that might inspire confidence. Among the things she told Celia was the fact that teachers often spoke well of her work and that her high average of 94.3 was worthy of pride instead of worry. As for her clothes, they were becoming. Teachers and students alike thought well of Celia. She also told Celia that she knew her employer was planning to give her a full-time position after graduation; that he was very well pleased with her work.

Toward the end of the long visit, Celia began to feel better. She became more confident about the future and gained an honest insight into her many high qualities.

Case Three. Elizabeth S—— was a senior in high school. At the end of her junior year she had successfully completed all the commercial subjects offered in her school. She was one of the brighter girls in her class and had been working at part-time stenographic positions since the middle of her junior year. Her difficulty was that she never held a position more than a few weeks. Why was it, she often wondered, that she did not keep her positions?

When her counselor had a heart-to-heart talk with her, Elizabeth listened with an honest desire to know the truth. The counselor told her, in as kindly and helpful a manner as possible, that all of her four previous employers had made the same comment about her work. Summed up, it was simply that Elizabeth was slovenly. She made too many erasures; she was not careful about punctuation and divisions; she frequently soiled the paper with finger marks; her desk was not orderly; her own appearance was not that of a well-groomed stenographer; and so on. If Elizabeth would try, at her present position, to develop habits of neatness in her work and her appearance, she would probably have no trouble keeping the job. But if she did not succeed in solving this problem of neatness, she would again be laid off or discharged.

Elizabeth was willing to listen to criticism and suggestion, so the counselor helped her make a list of specific things to watch every day at the office. During the next few weeks Elizabeth carefully checked herself at work according to this list. Gradually she was able to remove the cause of her employment problem, for she now had insight as to what it was, as well as a willingness to do something about it. The reward was not long in coming: she received a small salary increase and a promise of full-time employment after graduation.

These illustrations show how it helps a person to have insight into his problem. Cases like them could be multiplied many times. Whatever the difficulty may be — whether it is in emotional life, in choosing a life work, in getting along with people, in making the most of a job, or in any activity — the solution of the difficulty begins with an understanding of its causes. When you know what the causes are, you have a better chance to solve the problem to which these causes lead.

All behavior is symptomatic. *Symptomatic* is a term of importance in the study of behavior. It comes from the word *symptom,* used as a doctor uses it. Take measles as an example. Red circular spots are the most common symptom for measles, but a doctor can recognize the disease by still other symptoms — the appearance of the eyes and the condition of the throat, for instance. All the symptoms together tell the doctor what is going on in the patient's body. They are outward signs symptomatic of an inner struggle. Likewise, in behavior there are outward signs that are symptomatic of inner struggles.

The millionaire's son who steals (and there are such cases on record) may not be stealing just to get things, as a beggar boy would steal a loaf of bread. Then why should the rich boy steal? It has been found that punishment for stealing in such a case does little good, and we are forced to regard the stealing as a symptom of some deeper sickness in the personality. Perhaps the boy's father is too busy with his business to pay any attention to the son. Perhaps his mother is too busy with bridge clubs and social affairs to give the boy any mother-love. Perhaps the boy is not satisfied with his governess or nurse and does not receive the affection that other normal boys at his age receive. In order to force his parents to pay some attention to him, he may go to extremes and steal, so that something must be done about it, so that his parents will talk with him, spend some time with him, perhaps show him that they care for him. Stealing in such a case is a symptom of loneliness or lack of affection.

A summary. For everything we do, even in everyday living, there exists some underlying reason. We sleep because we are tired; we eat because we are hungry; we cry because we are sad; we fight because we are angry. There is always some reason for what we do. Our actions are symptoms revealing the inner nature of the personality. In order to solve our personal problems, we always try to discover causes.

Being able and willing to look at these causes is the first step in working out your problems. After that it is a question of constant, conscious effort and gradual change. And, peculiarly enough, once you have solved one problem others arise. Life is a series of problems which we meet more or less successfully. As we solve the simple ones, we are able to recognize more difficult ones and work them out. The problems of a high-school student are much more complex than those of a small child.

You have your problems, and your fellows have theirs. Everyone must solve his problems in one way or another. The solving of problems continues while there is life. The right solutions help you grow up; the wrong solutions keep you from growing up.

How will you make the right start in the solution of your problems? You will try to face the facts as they are, whether favorable or unfavorable, and deepen your insight into each problem. You may get some friend to help you see yourself, for you know that another person's point of view may show you what you yourself do not see. And, in your efforts to improve, you will have patience, remembering that it is a long-time process.

FOR CLASS DISCUSSION

1. Abraham Lincoln is an historical personage whom we all know. He was not "good-looking." He dressed carelessly. He was inclined to be untidy in his habits. Personality traits like these are not generally found in people who have a great many friends. Although Lincoln had some enemies, he did have a great many friends.

Why is Lincoln thought of as a likable person?

If you do not remember very much about his personality, look up an account of his life in a United States history book or in an encyclopedia and come to class prepared for discussion.

2. Booth Tarkington, in telling the story of his own childhood and youth, recalls how he had been pampered by his parents and relatives. He had been made the center of attraction at all times until, in a certain grade schoolroom, he clashed with a teacher who did not pamper him. From that time on, continuing through grade school and high school, he regularly was tardy and often absent. Finally he played "hooky" for two months and then dropped out of school.

Why did Booth Tarkington develop the habit of tardiness and poor attendance?

What was his problem?

What would have been a good way for him to begin the solution of his problem?

3. Think of some other historical figure, literary character, or per-

son you know, whose difficulties were overcome after he had gained an understanding of the causes leading to them, and be prepared to report on him for class discussion.

4. If everything we do has a cause, what is the cause for some people's crossness when they first get up in the morning?

READINGS

In Literature

In literature you can find an endless number of illustrations for the personal problems discussed in this book, because literature is the artist's way of describing life with all its emotions, ambitions, and actions. Present study will undoubtedly sharpen your understanding of literature, while literature (since it deals with personal problems) will enrich your understanding of the principles studied in this book. The titles suggested provide a ready reference to reading that is both interesting and revealing, chosen especially to fit the sections they follow.

AUTOBIOGRAPHY

Tarkington, Booth. "As I Seem to Me"; in *The Saturday Evening Post* (July 5 to August 23, 1941).

> This series of articles contains part of the author's life story, from birth to the publication of his first book, and is of special interest to students in Personal Problems.

NOVELS

Bennett, Arnold. *Clayhanger.* Doubleday, Doran.

> Edwin Clayhanger's life becomes understandable in the light of his father's dominating influence upon him.

Dickens, Charles. *David Copperfield.*

> The early chapters deal with Dickens's childhood, giving a host of details that explain his conduct, not only in childhood, but also as an adult.

Johnson, Owen. *Tennessee Shad.* Little, Brown.
> *The Varmint.* Little, Brown.

> The spirit of youth is in these books because they deal with the interests, activities, and problems of young people who are still in school.

Wells, H. G. *The History of Mr. Polly.* Dodd, Mead.
   An interesting and amusing story showing causes and effects in
   the life story of a haberdasher.

For Further Information

Many people supplement their reading in one book with selections
from others because they get additional points of view and information, provided the selections are carefully made. In the titles for
further information given here and elsewhere throughout this book
you will find handy references to chapters or pages which bear directly
upon the thoughts discussed in the sections.

Bliss, Walton B. *Personality and School,* Chapter 29. Allyn and
   Bacon.
Fedder, Ruth. *A Girl Grows Up,* Chapter 5. McGraw-Hill.
   Equally interesting for boys and girls.
Goodrich, Laurence B. *Living with Others,* Chapters 1 and 12. Amer-
   ican Book.
McKown, H. C., and Le Bron, Marion. *A Boy Grows Up,* Chapter 2.
   McGraw-Hill.
Morgan, John J. B. *Keeping a Sound Mind,* Chapter 13. Macmillan.
Webb, Ewing T., and Morgan, John J. B. *Strategy in Handling People,*
   Chapter 2. Boulton Pierce. Also published by Garden City.
Wright, Milton. *Getting Along with People,* Chapters 1 and 5. Mc-
   Graw-Hill. Also published by Garden City.

PART 1

KNOWING MORE
ABOUT YOURSELF

Everyone Has Certain Powerful Wants

ALL LIVING THINGS seem to have desires. Even the paramecium, a minute single-celled animal, can be seen under a microscope taking in food particles or swimming away from iodine placed in the water. It seems to desire food and safe water in which to live. The behavior of this tiny animal shows that it wants to live.

The earthworm, a more complex animal, made up of thousands of cells, can be seen feeding on small bits of decayed vegetable matter, withdrawing from sunlight or dry objects, and mating with another earthworm. It too apparently desires to eat, to be comfortable, and to mate.

The wants of a dog are more complex. It eats, sleeps, fights, mates, and can carry on various more or less complicated activities, depending partly on its training. Although a dog cannot tell us about its wants in words, we think its behavior indicates, for example, that it too desires to live, to love and be loved by human beings, and to be with other dogs.

Human beings understand one another by means of language and their ability to reason. Our insight into human behavior may be more correct than our insight into the behavior of lower animals, such as the dog, the earthworm, or the paramecium, because they cannot tell us what they feel or think. When we study the behavior of human beings, we are on surer ground because we ourselves are human beings, and our own behavior is like the behavior of those whom we study. Hence it is possible to get a sound understanding of our own behavior and that of others. This understanding we have called insight.

Insight involves not only the willingness to face facts, as is explained in Section 1, but also the ability to understand oneself

and to catch the hidden meanings of behavior. While it is impossible for any teacher or any book to give you the willingness
to improve yourself by facing the facts of your personality, it is
possible to present a body of knowledge which you may use if you
so desire.

If you want to know why people do what they do, you must
understand the deep longings, urges, or desires that drive them to
action. Careful study has shown that we are all alike in having
a number of basic desires. Five of the most important are: the
desire to live, the desire to love, the desire to be with people, the
desire to excel or be important, and the desire to believe in something lasting.

Psychologists are not all agreed as to the relative importance of
these five desires, or master drives, as we shall call them. It might
be argued that there are many other drives, some important and
some trivial. These five, at any rate, represent a group of the
most important human desires, but not necessarily all of them.
The five will be considered one by one in the following sections.

EVERYONE WANTS TO LIVE

> *Why do people who cannot swim avoid going into deep water? In case of fire in a crowded hall, why do people become panic-stricken? If you were starving, would you have any desire to read or play or work before your hunger had been satisfied?*

JOHN JONES was on his way to Centerville, a small city seventy-six miles from home, where he was to begin a job as a garage mechanic's helper. He was seventeen years old and had just been graduated from the industrial course in high school. He had no friends or acquaintances in Centerville except the garage owner, who had hired him. John had left home with twenty-five dollars and sufficient clothing for his immediate needs.

Can you figure out, from your present knowledge of psychology, what his immediate wants would be when he arrived in Centerville, and what he would be most likely to do first?

Here is what he actually did: As soon as he arrived, he went to a restaurant and had dinner. After dinner he telephoned his employer and asked for information about rooms and living accommodations. Then he spent two or three hours securing a room, and remained there for some time, arranging his clothes in the wardrobe, taking a shower, and dressing. Evening came and John went to a restaurant for supper. Here he purchased a five-dollar meal ticket. He then strolled up and down Main Street, looking over the town. It was Saturday and the stores were open, so he bought a coverall before closing time. Then he returned to his room and went to bed.

Figure out for yourself what desires led him to each of these actions.

Life and desire go together. A human being is always wanting something; at a given time it may be an education, twenty-five cents for a movie, an invitation to a formal party, a new bicycle, a big Irish stew with dumplings — or all of them together. Strange though it seems, as soon as one desire is fulfilled, he wants something else. As long as he lives this will continue, for desire is in the very nature of life. It may be said of human beings that there is no life without desire.

Certain desires are more important and more deeply rooted than others. For example, the desire to live is more deeply rooted and more important than, say, the desire to read the funny paper. Probably the will to live is the first and most fundamental of all wants. Most of us are not conscious of this desire because such needs as food, clothing, and shelter are taken for granted in our lives, but the desire to live was evident before any other in our behavior as infants. It shows itself in the actions of all animals and always remains at the root of what they do.

Self-preservation. Self-preservation is the term usually given to this desire. It is self-preservation that drives one to get food. The desire is evident in its most primitive and naked form in people who are starving or who hardly know from day to day where they will get their next meal. The things these people do are a direct outcome of their need to preserve life itself. Hunger constantly reminds them of this need, and they are consciously striving to keep alive. Again, people who are so poorly clothed and live in such miserable dwellings that disease and exposure threaten their existence consciously struggle for clothing and shelter in order to keep alive. Their behavior can be understood in the light of the urge toward self-preservation.

It is easy to understand the behavior of a starving man who snatches food from refuse cans. Fortunately, the great majority of people in our country do not have to struggle for mere existence on any such primitive level. Most of us take the simplest needs of life — food, clothing, and shelter in some form — for granted. Men and women work, of course, to have money for food, clothing, and shelter, but the struggle for existence does not occupy most people's minds at every moment. There is time, opportunity, and a certain amount of money for satisfying other desires.

Self-preservation in reverse. People who commit suicide are not trying to preserve life; they are ending it. This extreme behavior is the result of an extreme inner conflict with life's problems. A person who commits suicide gives up the fight, and his action is a symptom of acute mental illness. His behavior is abnormal.

The mere thought of committing suicide, however, is not rare among normal people. In fact, most people have occasionally thought about "ending it all" or have wished, when they went to sleep, that they would not wake up again. This is especially true of young people, and if you have had such thoughts, you need not think that you are peculiar. Surveys of high-school students show that more than half of them have at one time or another toyed with the idea of suicide as a means of escaping from the problems of life. As they grow older, they become better able to meet their problems and face them as a matter of habit. Escaping, running away, is not a healthful or courageous way to deal with difficulties and of course does not lead to solving them.

Is self-preservation the source of all desires? So important a force is self-preservation, driving men to many different kinds of action, that some people regard it as the source of all other desires. It might be argued, for example, that love is self-preservation, because a person who loves another thinks of that person as something more important than himself, if not actually as a part of himself, that he wishes to protect and preserve. Likewise, the desire to be with people might be thought of as a form of self-preservation, because, in getting along with other people, a person is more secure than he would be alone. The desire to excel might be called self-preservation in the sense that it drives a person toward successes that make him more secure. Finally, the desire to believe in something might be thought of as self-preservation because standing in awe or reverence of the Good, the Beautiful, the Great, and the Eternal shows a desire to be in touch with and partake of those things that last a long time.

Direct and indirect selfishness. If every act of ours were to

be explained in terms of self-preservation, or, to put it in a word
that is not flattering, selfishness, then we should perhaps think of
two kinds of selfishness, direct and indirect. Direct selfishness
would apply to actions planned directly for your own good, as,
for example — if you are a girl — helping your mother with the
dishes so that she will have time to do some sewing on your
dress. Indirect selfishness would apply to actions directly for
another's good, as, for example, giving money to someone who
needs it or helping your mother with the dishes because she is
tired. It might be argued that actions such as these are selfish
because they return advantages even though they are intended
for the advantage of others without any obvious return. Thus,
giving money to someone who needs it gives the giver a feeling of
satisfaction and security; washing dishes to help your tired
mother gives you a feeling of satisfaction, because you have been
kind and thoughtful of someone else.

Whether or not you think of self-preservation as the desire basic
to all other desires, studies of human behavior have shown that,
once the question of supplying the fundamental needs of life is
answered, new desires arise; and the first of these is the desire to
love and be loved.

FOR CLASS DISCUSSION

1. Two high-school girls, whom we shall call Mary and Jane, lived
near the foothills of the Cascade Mountain Range in northern Oregon.
They decided to pack a lunch and spend a day hiking. During the
afternoon they lost their way. They were not familiar with wood-
craft, had brought no matches or camping equipment, and could do
nothing but try to retrace their path. Darkness fell before they found
any clue in the surroundings as to where they were. They were seized
with fright and began to run wildly, shout for help, and cry by turns.
They also became irritable and quarreled with each other, though they
had been devoted friends of long standing. They became separated,
each wandering alone, frightened and weeping. Some time later they
met again in the dark and clung together. Every sound now intensi-
fied their fears. They became hysterical, and, while running wildly,
they often stumbled, bruising themselves, and spending their strength.
Finally, too tired to go on, they sat down to rest briefly; but soon they

fell asleep. Even then a searching party was within hearing, but Mary and Jane were not found until early morning when, wakened by the cold, they heard distant calls and made off swiftly in the direction of the sounds.

How can you explain their irritableness and their quarreling?

How can you explain their fear? Their falling asleep?

What was their strongest desire from the time they first discovered that they had lost their way?

2. Suppose you had been hiking or skating from two o'clock in the afternoon until six without refreshment of any kind. Would you then prefer to sleep, pick a quarrel with someone, eat, read a book, or go after a new job? Explain the reason for your choice.

3. Study the advertisements in a health or physical culture magazine and see if any of them appeal to the reader's desire to live. If permissible, clip them and bring them to class.

4. Is it at all times right to try to preserve your own life? If not, when not?

READINGS

In Literature

NOVELS

Defoe, Daniel. *Robinson Crusoe.*

> The adventures of Robinson Crusoe are, of course, the experiences he has in his effort to keep alive after having been shipwrecked.

Ellsberg, Edward. *Hell on Ice.* Dodd, Mead.

> Men in open boats fight their way across the icy Arctic Ocean to Alaska, bleak but inhabited.

Nordhoff, Charles, and Hall, James Norman. *Men Against the Sea.* Little, Brown.

> What chance do men have when they are suddenly thrown out of their customary way of life into a situation where only courage and intelligence coupled with endurance can win?

Rawlings, Marjorie. *The Yearling.* Scribner.

> The main task was to keep a shelter for the family and the few farm animals, to provide needed clothing, and to get food for the long dry seasons. It was very hard to meet these needs; therefore a yearling deer that nibbled out the new corn shoots had to be killed.

SHORT STORIES

Connell, Richard. "The Most Dangerous Game"; in *Variety*. Minton.
> An island, deserted except for General Zaroff and his servant, is the setting for a game in which man stalks man in the jungle.

London, Jack. "To Build a Fire"; in *Lost Face*. Macmillan.
> The Yukon Trail was not for the tenderfoot.

Mansfield, Katherine. "The Fly"; in *Doves Nest*. Knopf.
> The boss, snug in his office, it seems, faces again the why of life.

Poe, Edgar Allan. "The Pit and the Pendulum"; in any collection of Poe's stories.
> A story depicting a man's struggles against death by torture.

For Further Information

McLean, Donald. *Knowing Yourself and Others*, Chapters 24-27. Holt.

Overstreet, H. A. *Influencing Human Behavior*, Chapter 2. Norton.

Starch, Daniel, Stanton, Hazel M., and Koerth, Wilhelmine. *Controlling Human Behavior*, Chapter 2, pp. 27-34. Macmillan.

Webb, Ewing T., and Morgan, John J. B. *Strategy in Handling People*, Chapter 9. Garden City.

EVERYONE WANTS TO LOVE AND BE LOVED

Which comes first in the life of a human being, the desire to live or the desire to love? Does the desire for affection lead to jealousy? Does it lead to actions of self-denial or of selfishness? Is there any similarity between the affection of a man for a woman and the affection of a brother for a brother?

Case One. Right after graduating from high school, Leslie D—— joined the Marines. He left his home in the Middle West for San Diego, where he went through the usual rigid training given to recruits in "boot camp." He was, of course, very busy and was usually tired at the end of the day, but he found time to write home regularly to his parents and his sister. He sent all his letters by air mail and frequently sent small gifts to the family. Occasionally, when writing to his sister, he reminded her that he was going to buy her that wrist watch he had promised her before he left home. His sister wrote him emphatically not to do it. How could he buy her a wrist watch from his meager monthly pay? But when her birthday came, she did receive a beautiful wrist watch, which Leslie had bought for thirty-five dollars saved from his small wages.

Case Two. In a small village one night a widow was roused from her bed by the noise of a fireman who was knocking down the door of her room. As soon as she was out of the burning house, she immediately looked around for her three children. Arthur she saw, and Helen. They were standing in the glare of the fire, amazed, watching the house burn. She paid no attention to them except to ask where Jimmy was. They said nothing. She asked four or five others, but none had seen him. Suddenly she turned from the staring crowd to enter the burning frame house. But a fireman stopped her.

"It's too bad, Bess," he said, "but you can't go in any more. It's too late."

"But Jimmy! He's still in the little room!" She tried to pull away from him.

"Too bad, Bess. Take it easy, now. We'd of gone in, if it could be done."

With a quick, desperate struggle, she tore loose from the fireman and dashed into the flaming building. Some moments later she staggered out carrying little Jimmy covered with a blanket which was burning. Then she collapsed in the yard in front of the steps, her night clothing in flames. After three days of painful suffering she died. Jimmy recovered.

Case Three. One of the most famous stories of ancient times is that of the friendship between Jonathan and David. Jonathan was heir to the throne, for he was King Saul's first son; but his friendship for David was stronger than his desire for the crown. Although this friendship interfered with his chances to become king, he nevertheless stayed loyal to David.

Case Four. Marian D——, a junior, and Roger A——, a senior, had been "steadies" during their high-school years. As often happens in such cases, Marian managed to pass in her school work, but Roger did not. At the beginning of his senior year, it became evident that he would not graduate with his class. The reason? He just had to be with Marian all the time. Neither his family nor hers objected to their keeping company, but when they discussed Roger's graduation, they all realized that something had to be done. Marian and Roger also realized that there was a problem, and they knew from previous experience that trying to limit their meetings did not work in their case. Finally Marian agreed to transfer to another high school in a city more than two hundred miles distant, where she could stay with an aunt. This change did bring about the desired results: Roger had more time for study and really did graduate. After a somewhat lonely semester, Marian returned in time for Roger's graduation.

These four illustrations indicate that affection leads to or causes certain actions, just as does the will to live. Whether the love be between parents and children, between brothers and sisters, or between friends, it is a strong drive toward action.

The need for affection is shown early in life. A newborn baby seems to be concerned at first only with nursing and being comfortable; everyone knows how a baby cries when he is hungry or in discomfort. Later, however, in a matter of weeks or months, the baby will begin to show affection by smiling and hugging his mother or other persons whom he recognizes and with whom he feels safe.

It is natural for a baby to show affection and a need for affection soon after its first needs, food and comfort, are regularly provided. Perhaps no baby ever lived who did not show affection for its mother (or the person who took care of it) and a need for mother-love. In fact, the failure to receive mother-love so strongly influences an infant that his personality shows it for years, or ever afterward. Without understanding why, the child who has not had the love of a mother or foster mother may feel rejected and act as if no one loves him, as if he does not fit into his group, as if he is alone. On the other hand, it should also be mentioned that an infant can be given too much love of the demonstrative kind so that he cries whenever he is not the center of attention. Some moderation is needed, but affection is necessary to the normal development of a baby.

What is the nature of affection? Up to this point we have been going along as if we knew what love really means. We do not, and perhaps we never shall. It is an extremely complex thing. According to Thorndike's dictionary, love is a fond, deep feeling; a high appreciation, as for music, art, trees; but this does not really tell us very much. We can say that love is tenderness, pity, admiration, devotion, family loyalty; that it expresses itself in giving to those who need and in being equally gracious in receiving; but this does not tell the whole story. The infant shows pleasure in response to food, drink, and coddling. Is this the first manifestation, the early beginning, of love, as a bud is the begin-

ning of a leaf? In early childhood, it is said, the first likings are
for parents and toys. Later there is a desire to be close to other
people. Are these too the early stages of what will develop into
the thing called love?

The common denominator in all affection. In all forms of affection there exists to some extent a coming together of two or more
personalities into one. A father, in his love for a son, makes the
interests of the son his own interests. The father himself is to
some extent lost in his concern for the son. If the affection between them is deep and strong, each in certain ways is more concerned with the other than with himself. Their separate selves
are to some extent lost in a unity or a coming together of mind
and emotion. In a situation involving danger, the father would
prefer to die rather than lose his son; the son would prefer to die
rather than lose his father. The person loved becomes part of the
one he loves. Wherever there is any degree of affection, no matter how little or how much, a person to some extent identifies his
own desires with those of the other person.

Perhaps this quality of love — the losing or denying of oneself
in another self — is the quality that makes it Godlike. The quality
is present in the love of a mother or father for a child, of a
brother for his sister, of a man for a woman. When this quality
is not there, the emotion is not love. The actions then are symptoms of some other basic drive — perhaps to excel, to be important
— but not of love.

Affection should be cultivated. Love is not born full-grown in
the child, but rather, like the child himself, needs care and attention so that it may grow as the child grows. The growth of
this emotion is just as natural as the growth of body tissue. A
person may be said to pass through several states in the development of his desire to love and be loved.

Stages in the development of affection. These stages in the
average person can be explained as follows:

First, a child naturally shows love for his mother. She provides
food when the baby is hungry. She keeps his body warm. She
takes care of him when he is ill. After a time, he learns that his
mother is different from the things around him, including his
toys. She does much more for him than these things can do. His

Rittase

The will to live remains at the root of all we do, whether we work as farmers to wrest a living from the soil (*above*) or fight as soldiers in uniting against a common enemy (*below*).

Galloway

People like company (*above*), so it is more fun for this boy and girl to fish together than to fish alone.

The desire to excel (*below*) spurs us on, whether it be to win a race or to raise a prize pig for the 4–H Club contest.

mother becomes a person to be observed. He watches her and finds that she responds to his feelings with feelings of her own.

Second, a child learns to return, or reciprocate, love. He learns, after a while, to satisfy the desires of other people. He reciprocates, or meets people halfway, because he learns that situations are happier if he considers the other person's wants and does what the other person desires. If the child does not learn to do this, he becomes selfish, and later this will influence his chance of making friendships.

This development continues gradually up to the third stage in the growth of affection, which may be called romantic love. As the child grows to be a man, he becomes interested in the opposite sex. Eventually the time comes when he wants a home of his own. Perhaps without consciously realizing it, he has a desire to give back the love that was given to him when he was a small boy. The man or woman who does not desire a family and its responsibilities is likely to be a lonely and unhappy human being.

Finally, a man arrives at full social maturity, the fourth stage in the development of love. He then not only wishes to help and protect his own family, but is interested in the welfare of others around him. He does not give up his own happiness by helping others; in fact, he gains more happiness by this means than he could in any other way.

It is normal to pass through all the stages. It is natural and necessary for one to undergo gradual changes in the development of one's affection. Little by little a child should become more independent of his mother's intimate care and should desire the friendship of other children his own age. Later he should become interested in the opposite sex. It is natural for him, at the right stage, to have an urge to marry. And finally, by the time he is an adult, he should be interested in the welfare of many others besides himself. These changes are gradual and extend over many years, but they should take place.

Symptoms of retardation in the growth of affection. A small boy who cries every day when his mother leaves him at the kindergarten shows that he wants to continue the habits of his babyhood and be with his mother all day long. Both the mother and the kindergarten teacher know that it is time for him to leave the cradle stage and pick up friendships with other boys and girls. They will carefully, kindly insist that he remain at school. Usually the boy can make the change.

A seventeen-year-old girl who rarely goes on a date with a boy, who always prefers the company of girls, and who, though she has chances, always refuses a date unless her chum is dated with her, shows that she has not entered the stage of romantic love that would be natural for her. It would be well for her to accept a date occasionally even if she does not strongly desire to do so.

A young man of twenty-four who pays more attention to his mother than to any other woman — always taking her to movies and to and from club meetings, for instance — and who in fact rarely or never pays any attention to another woman is said to be "tied to his mother's apron strings." If such a man does marry, he may try to find a wife who reminds him of his mother, and his attitude toward his wife will be like the attitude he had toward his mother. The love urge in his life never outgrew the stage of childhood.

An eighty-year-old man who marries a very young woman does so either because he has not left the stage of romantic love or because he is in his second childhood, and foolish.

The behavior of the four persons used in these illustrations must be understood in the light of their desire for affection. In each case behavior is symptomatic of a sickness in the personality. Improvement for any one of them would begin with insight into and understanding of the causes of his or her actions and would continue by constant, daily effort to change.

FOR CLASS DISCUSSION

1. When Anna L—— had definitely decided to get married, her mother told her that it was only right for her and her future husband to know that Anna was an adopted daughter. Naturally, Anna was curious to know more about her real mother and began to correspond with her. The letters did not seem to be fully satisfying, so at the first opportunity she paid her mother a visit. During the visit she found that, although her mother was a good woman and treated her hospitably and kindly, the mother-daughter feeling just wasn't there.

They were strangers at heart. It was the adopted mother that Anna really loved.

How can you account for the feeling of strangeness between Anna and her real mother?

Would it be possible in time for a strong affection to develop between them? If so, what could bring this about?

2. Why do people who are separated over long periods of time have to become acquainted all over again when they meet?

3. Can a person love someone who makes no effort to return his affection? Could this go on indefinitely, or, say, for a period as long as ten years?

4. Which is better, to show affection to others or to receive affection from others?

INDIVIDUAL ACTIVITIES

1. In order to study how affection influences another person's behavior, try for three days to refrain from finding fault with someone whom you frequently criticize. At the same time, show as much interest in this other person as you can. Describe the results.

2. Since desiring the desires of another person is basic to affection in all of its forms, try to help someone get what he wants and see what happens to your relationship at that time. Study his reaction to your help and your own feeling about helping him.

READINGS

In Literature

SHORT STORIES

Crane, Stephen. "A Dark-Brown Dog"; in *Midnight Sketches.* Knopf.
     There must be affection; man cannot live without it. Nor can a boy. The dog is the center of his existence.

Henry, O. "The Gift of the Magi"; in *The Four Million.* Doubleday, Doran.
     A story of how infinite riches were lost and gained in a shabby, one-room slum apartment.

For Further Information

Fedder, Ruth. *A Girl Grows Up,* Chapter 4. McGraw-Hill.

McLean, Donald.   *Knowing Yourself and Others*, Chapter 12.   Holt.

Morgan, John J. B.   *Keeping a Sound Mind*, Chapter 6, pp. 183-189. Macmillan.

Overstreet, H. A.   *Influencing Human Behavior*, Chapter 2.   Norton.

Starch, Daniel, Stanton, Hazel M., and Koerth, Wilhelmine.   *Controlling Human Behavior*, Chapter 2, pp. 27-34.   Macmillan.

Webb, Ewing T., and Morgan, John J. B.   *Strategy in Handling People*, Chapter 9.   Garden City.

EVERYONE WANTS TO BE WITH PEOPLE

Can you have friends without having affection for them? How do people show that they want to have friends? Do people go to a Big Ten football game just for the game? Why does a mere acquaintance from back home suddenly seem to be a welcome friend when met in a large city far from home? Why is solitary confinement one of the most dreaded of punishments?

JUST AS THERE ARE TIMES when your actions can be explained in terms of your desire for affection, there are other times when they can best be explained in terms of your desire to be with people. This is one of the master drives of personality and is sometimes known as the social urge.

This social urge is also called gregariousness, from the Latin word *grex, gregis,* meaning herd; hence the word means *herdness,* or the tendency to herd together. If you have ever read Kipling's *Jungle Books,* you will remember how the different animals herded and hunted with their own kind; Kipling gave a vivid picture of gregariousness. This urge is responsible for some of the best things in human nature, as found in fellowship, and also for some of the worst, as found in the actions of gangs and mobs.

Sometimes, when things are going wrong, we may have daydreamed of going off to a desert island or of being alone in a sort of earthly paradise where we could be masters of our fate, could do exactly as we pleased, and need not be bothered with people.

Every now and then someone actually pops off and tries to live on such a desert island. But, in due course, he is mighty glad to get back to civilization and his own kind.

The truth is that very few people are able or willing to be continuously and completely alone for any great length of time. Most of us need the society of our fellows a good part of the time or our personalities become warped. If we do not need it, or think we do not — if we habitually withdraw from people and prefer to be alone all the time — it is a sign that there is something wrong with us. The urge to be with people is one of the most powerful master drives, and it explains much of our conduct. It explains, for instance, why solitary confinement has always been one of the most terrible punishments that could be given a man in prison.

The desire to be with people begins early in childhood, when it is shown in play with brothers, sisters, parents, or playmates. Some children can amuse themselves alone for a long time, but sooner or later they will show a need for companionship, preferably with other children. When his playmate moves away from the neighborhood, a child may become cross; he may whine or be unusually restless, or show other signs that something is wrong. What is wrong is loneliness; the child wants to be with people. When he has found another friend or a group of friends, he will be satisfied again.

Normal people have friends. Among older children it is hard to find a single happy individual who does not have a circle of friends. The individual who regularly shuns company — and there are some who do, in the teen age and even later — does not do so because he really dislikes to be with people. His hermit-like behavior is the result of some unhappy experience with others in the past. He may have been brought up by parents who shun people, or he may have been bullied and frightened by other children, or he may have found other children far more capable of doing things than he himself was. In order to protect himself from such experiences, he does not try to satisfy his desire to be with people. In fact, he may go to the other extreme and try to convince himself that he finds more satisfaction in not being with them.

Gerald was an only child. His family lived in a beautiful house set in a grove on a large piece of land. The nearest neighbors were blocks away. Few children ever came to the house, and none came every day. The older people with whom Gerald came in contact did not like to have youngsters around. At an early age he learned to play by himself, sometimes all day long, for even his parents had no time for him. He usually ate in the kitchen with the nursemaid. No duties were assigned him. Few obstacles ever confronted him. If any trouble arose, Gerald got what he wanted. At the age of five he attended kindergarten for the first time. He stood in a corner by himself, refusing to move, until the teacher pulled him into a group of boys and girls who were playing. It was not long before Gerald wanted something he could not have. He went into a temper tantrum. He repeated these tantrums every day until finally he was taken out of school for a year. In the following years he made adjustments to groups with great difficulty, and at the age of fifteen he had a nervous breakdown.

This is an extreme case of lack of adjustment due to loneliness in childhood. In other cases the symptoms might not be so marked, but they might make the individual more or less unhappy in certain everyday situations for many years.

Social life requires give and take. The normal boy and girl of high-school age enjoys group activity, team work, and friendships. In such gatherings life is interesting because there is an interplay among the individuals of the group. Moreover, even if it were not enjoyable, group activity is necessary. In a sense, the dependency of a child at birth continues throughout life. Even a hermit must occasionally deal with other people for the necessaries of life. Not only are human beings born with relations to others; they are brought up in a world where everyone depends upon thousands or even millions of other people. Just trace one industry on which you depend for some necessity like shoes, and you will see how true this is.

As an illustration of normal social development, there is the life of Jim D——, a statesman, inventor, and philosopher. He was an only child, born in a poor family, but one that had good ideals of home life. His parents gave him small duties to perform when he was a child. Although he had few toys, most of them home-made or given to him by friends of the family, Jim was glad to share them with the neighbor boys. He learned how to make the most of things and how to take the bumps of life. At six he began to peddle papers and at twelve he was a delivery boy for a grocery store. He enjoyed meeting people, but he was also interested in many other things — for example, reading, music, dancing, and writing. Most of his spare time was taken up with these interests. Later in life he became a business leader, a statesman, and an author. That his social urge always remained strong was shown by the active help he gave to youth movements and his ability in politics and business.

Extremes in gregariousness should be avoided. Some people have a problem in controlling their social urge, for they can never be content unless they are with other people. They would not go to a movie alone, for instance, or would not walk alone to a club meeting; they would prefer to be late to school than to go without Susie and Jane; they cannot eat lunch or study or enjoy reading a book alone. People who require company to such an extent show that their desire to be with people rules them too much. Everyone is forced to spend some time alone, and he should be able to enjoy his own company when the occasion arises. For every personality there is a happy medium, and everyone should find his own balance.

The story of Arnold T——, who could not do anything alone with pleasure shows how excessive sociability may affect a man's work. Arnold grew up with three brothers and two sisters in a moderately well-to-do home. His life both at home with the other five youngsters and outside of it with their many companions was such that he never knew what it was to be alone. As he grew older, he seldom did any work entirely by himself. When he became a man, he decided to be a farmer, but after three years of farming he had lost everything. He would work in the field for a short time and then quit and go to town to visit. He frequently spent hours visiting with the neighbors when he should have been getting in hay or doing some other urgent work. When he did his chores he wanted his wife with him. The loneliness of the farm was not the kind of life for him.

Timidity. Timidity is a symptom of fear of failure and is closely related to the social urge. Timidity shows that one is afraid to deal with others. It can usually be traced back to early childhood. For example, the individual's first experiences in mingling with other children may have been very unsatisfactory or even unpleasant and painful, so that he tried to shun them afterward and turned to experiences more satisfying to him. The excessively timid person may build up a whole set of satisfying experiences to make up for his lack of social contacts; he may be successful in writing, for instance, but not in talking to people, or get a great deal of satisfaction from reading books, but little from games and sports. Although the social urge is stronger in some people than in others, and few of us feel sociable all the time, it is safe to say that the person who shuns almost all sociability is not well rounded in his personality. Usually he has poor mental health, at least in respect to the underlying fear of failure that has caused him to suppress the normal human desire to be with people.

If you feel very little desire to be with people at any time, it would be well for you to study yourself and try to find out why. Timidity in human relationships is not overcome by running away from people or shunning them. It can be overcome by practice in dealing with people. Do the best you can when you are with them; listen, show interest in them, make yourself feel friendly; above all, take your mind off yourself, and try to think only of the other person. After a while you will overcome your timidity and begin to enjoy your associations.

Loneliness. Loneliness is the feeling we experience when the master drive to be with people is not satisfied. It often leads to symptomatic behavior. It may cause one to lose his appetite. But it may also make one hungry all the time, as is the case with some college freshmen who have not accustomed themselves to college, or have not acquired new friends, or have been unable to make the break with their old home life successfully. Students thus affected will eat huge meals and constantly munch peanuts and candy between meals. When they cannot satisfy their desire to be with people, they try to get other satisfactions.

Loneliness is the cause of more personality difficulties than most people realize. Moving from one home to another, from one city

11-29

"I'm not cold. Can't I set here 'til the newsboy comes? We always argue a bit about politics and world affairs."

HINTS FOR DISCUSSING THE CARTOON

What is the real reason the elderly gentleman is waiting for the newsboy? What in his relations with the family may have forced him to sit alone on the front porch and to seek companionship elsewhere? If you were a member of this family, what could you do to make his life pleasanter?

to another, from one school to another, would naturally give rise to loneliness because new friends must be made, and the interplay of personalities enjoyed in the previous place will not immediately be enjoyed in the new one. It is natural that everyone should experience some loneliness as a result of these changes, but it is also normal to go about making new contacts and new friends and establishing social relations that will make up for those lost.

We want to belong. We wish to feel that we fit in with the group, that we "belong." This accounts for a remarkably wide range of our actions, good and bad, wise and foolish. A woman will wear a queer hat because most women are wearing them; it's the "style." A man will feel uneasy in evening clothes when the majority of the group are dressed in business suits. People use the slang of whatever group they happen to belong to, say "stooge," "twerp," "jeepers" if the group does. They smoke if the group does, drink if the group does, "neck" if the group does. They do the thing "that's done" and refrain from doing the thing "that isn't done." These instances, and many others, are evidences of giving in readily to the desire to fit in.

Just where to draw the line between losing our individuality for the sake of belonging and keeping it at the cost of not belonging would be hard to say. No doubt most people go too far in their effort to belong. But some, who so clearly stand out as queer, rejected, misfit, should make a study of their actions and try to do more things that other people do. People who feel that they do not fit in can improve themselves by daily effort and study.

FOR CLASS DISCUSSION

1. Ellen D—— said Rosedale was an unfriendly town — even more unfriendly than Centerville, where she used to live. Ellen did not go to the high-school dances because (she said) if you didn't belong to a clique, you were simply out of it. A few girls had asked her to join a club when she first enrolled in Rosedale high school, but she had decided against it because (she said) the clubs at Rosedale were too dull. She had attended one or two football games, but since (she told herself) she did not know the players, she was not interested; besides, they didn't put on a real show at Rosedale as they did at

Centerville. Ellen wished her father would be transferred again so they would be able to go to a more friendly town.

Did Ellen really want friends?

Did she know how to make friends?

Why didn't she have any friends at Rosedale?

What might she have done to make friends there?

What are her chances for friendships in the next town?

2. Can a timid person overcome his timidity? Make a plan that might be followed by some apparently timid fellow student in his daily living — or by yourself if you think you are inclined to be timid.

3. Explain why younger brothers and sisters often want to go along with older brothers and sisters. Can they be blamed for this desire?

4. What do you consider the most important thing in Jim D——'s childhood that helped to lay the foundation for a successful career? Why?

5. What recommendations could you make to parents like those of Gerald?

INDIVIDUAL ACTIVITIES

1. As a means to getting acquainted with people, try listening to them. Make it a point to sit down and chat with three or four of your fellow students and check your ability to listen to them. Also study the effect of your listening. Do this not once but six times at least. Does the other person like to have you interested in what he has to say? Do you enjoy listening?

2. If you do not belong to a club, join one and plan to take an active part. Arrange for a report at some later date.

3. When you are with others, do you follow their suggestions a good share of the time, or do you usually do the suggesting? If the latter, during one whole evening with a group of your friends try to be agreeable, following the suggestions of others and helping them carry out their plans. Check the results of this experiment with your instructor.

4. Cartoons are a rich source of materials for the study of human relations, for the cartoonist is a keen observer of human nature. From your newspaper clip cartoons which are concerned with personal problems treated in this book, and bring them to class for discussion.

One of the best cartoonists to help us "see ourselves as others see us" is George Clark whose "Our Neighbors" appears in many daily papers.

For several of the Clark cartoons included in this text, hints are given for class discussion. What questions would you suggest for the others?

READINGS

In Literature

NOVEL

Hudson, W. H. *The Crystal Age*. Dutton.

A prophecy for the life of the future, especially as regards human relations.

SHORT STORIES

Andersen, H. C. "The Emperor's New Clothes"; in *Emperor's New Clothes*. Parker.

A hoax story that shows how people tend to think, feel, and act like the rest of the group.

Chekov, Anton. "The Bet"; in *The School Mistress*. Macmillan.

The story of the urge and need for being with other people is illustrated by this account of a man who bet he could live in solitary.

Davis, Richard H. "Gallegher"; in *Boy Scout*. Scribner.

The criminal felt safe in the crowd.

For Further Information

Bliss, Walton B. *Personality and School*, Chapter 29, p. 205. Allyn and Bacon.

Groves, Ernest R. *Personality and Social Adjustment*, Chapter 9. Longmans, Green.

Overstreet, H. A. *Influencing Human Behavior*, Chapter 2. Norton.

Starch, Daniel, Stanton, Hazel M., and Koerth, Wilhelmine. *Controlling Human Behavior*, Chapter 2, pp. 27-34. Macmillan.

Trilling, Mabel B., and Nicholas, Florence Williams. *The Girl and Her Home*, Problem 1, pp. 8-10. Houghton Mifflin.

Webb, Ewing T., and Morgan, John J. B. *Strategy in Handling People*, Chapter 9. Garden City.

SECTION 5

EVERYONE WANTS TO EXCEL

Why do people enter contests? Do you think a man known as Public Enemy Number One enjoys his distinction? Why is it worth while to discover your abilities while you are young? Why do some people read success stories? Which is the stronger desire, to be with people or to excel? Which of these leads to more personal problems?

NOT ALL OF OUR ACTIONS by any means are the results of a single strong desire. The desire to love and be loved, for example, is not at the root of everything we do. Neither is the desire to live, nor the desire to be with people. Sometimes one drive dominates and sometimes another. One of the drives not yet discussed is the desire to excel or be superior. It accounts for many of our actions.

The child who wanted to stay superior. Walter, Junior, a three-year-old boy, has a fifteen-months-old sister, June, who has lately begun to walk, and this has been responsible for some curious actions on Walter's part. When June first came into the family, Walter did not like her at all. He was caught throwing a rattle at her several times and he also used to slap her. Little by little, however, he became used to his baby sister, began to do things for her, and would talk about her to his mother and father. As the older child, of course, he was able to run through the house, eat at the table, play with large toys, and do a great many things that June could not do. He seemed to feel that he was pretty important in the house, whereas June was a helpless little baby who could not do much of anything. Finally the time came when June began to creep around the living room. Walter watched

her, not knowing just what to make of it. Now that June is beginning to walk, Walter looks at her with a frown on his face and
says, "Sit down, June. Sit down." Sometimes he actually pushes
her and says, "Sit down, will yuh?"

Why doesn't Walter want June to walk?

The boy who wanted to excel. Several years ago the author
had a boy in one of his classes, Eldred K——, who came to school
every day from the farm where he lived. He had no social life at
school whatever, talked to no one, and took no part in extra-
curricular activities. He recited when called upon and occasionally volunteered information. He was always quiet. In fact, he
went through his school day without calling attention to himself
in any way, except one. He was the most brilliant student, not
only in that class but in the whole school. It was in his written
work that he excelled, and he excelled to such a degree that he
was never known to write less than an A test or composition.

The girl who found herself. Jessica C—— was graduated from
high school fourth from the lowest in her class. She had spent
five and a half years in high school, and it was all the teachers
could do to get her through even then. Her record was spotted
with a large number of absences, tardinesses, and minor difficulties. Although she had some friends, she was not especially popular either with boys or with girls. She seemed to lack interest
in them as well as in school and life in general. She was not a
troublesome girl and could listen to reason when a teacher coun-
seled with her; but she simply could not get down to diligent
study.

During her last semester she elected a course in freehand drawing, and at graduation time she had decided to enroll in a commercial art school in Detroit. When September came, she moved
to Detroit, her parents and teachers alike wondering how long
she would remain. At the end of six weeks, reports from the
studio manager showed that Jessica was not only doing promising work, but was working all the time, had never been absent or
tardy, and was, in fact, one of the most promising students in the
school. She had found something in which she could excel. She
continued her art study for two years and then took a position in
an advertising department. Since then she has continued to ad-

vance until now she is considered one of the best commercial artists in her field and draws a large salary.

The desire to excel is natural. The desire to excel or to be important, like all the other basic drives we have been considering, is a natural part of our personality. It is a source of power that drives some persons to extreme heights and some to extreme depths and keeps others on a middle course. Everyone is entitled to do something well, even if he does not do it better than anyone else. He is not only entitled to this achievement, but should be encouraged in it. It is through success of some kind that life becomes worth while and satisfying.

As the three cases described above show, the desire to excel is easily recognized as a force motivating or causing certain actions. Many similar cases might be given, but you can find them everywhere, in your home, classroom, church, and community. Everyone wants power, and power comes to people for their superiority or their ability to excel in something. One person gets his power from popularity in school, another from his dependability in his family, another from a keen mentality, another from skill in athletics, another from wealth, and so on. There are a great many sources of power. The desire to excel is often called the will to power, on the theory that what we really desire is the power that superiority brings rather than the superiority itself.

How should the will to power be applied in life? We should ask three questions about the desire to excel in any given situation:

(1) Does this desire drive the individual toward excellence or superiority in something for the good of others or for purely selfish gains?

(2) Does it make him act in a manner that is acceptable to society or the reverse?

(3) Does it make him work in a direction suited to his own ability and conducive to his happiness?

A person who has good mental health uses his power for the good of others. Although he may become a great artist partly because he wants the feeling of strength that comes from superiority, he will use his work as a means of service. In childhood and youth the emphasis may be more selfish than it will be later in life, but even then, if the individual entirely forgets about other people's interests, his actions are purely selfish and do not reflect good mental health.

A genius is often described as the most selfish of individuals because he permits nothing to interfere with his work. Not all geniuses are like this, but many of them are, and those who are could hardly be said to have good mental health, even though the world needs them. A genius should be thought of as an exception to the rule, and we can pass him by in our study of the will to power. Although the world cannot do without geniuses, surely a world made up of nothing but geniuses would be a strange place, indeed.

Your efforts should not be too extreme. A bully, whose desire for power is shown by a display of physical superiority over smaller boys, is not using his strength for the good of others, but for purely selfish reasons. If he protected the smaller boys instead of beating them, he would use the same physical strength in a better way. His superiority, if he really has superior strength, would still be shown, but his behavior would be unselfish; it would be of service to others. Like many abnormal actions, however, those of the bully really show a hidden sense of inferiority somewhere. He tries to compensate for it by showing superiority in an easy way.

The high-school beauty, whose desire for importance is shown in beguiling first one then another boy friend away from other girls, is not behaving in an acceptable manner. She may be superior because of her technique with boys, and she may like to show her power with them, but she is not using her abilities in such a way as to get the approval of her group. The same ability might be used in influencing the boys, let us say, to cooperate in social plans and school activities. Her superiority would still be shown, but in a more unselfish way.

The "A" student who pays no attention to the social life of school is not only withholding his support where it is needed; he is also hindering his own full development. His desire for importance is being satisfied at the cost of a narrow education, for he does not take time to learn how to deal with other people. He might find, after trying it, that social relations increased his

superiority, made him more of an all-round person, and gave him
additional chances for leadership.

The same kind of behavior that we have seen in the bully is
sometimes seen in a more extreme form in the actions of the
gangster. The will to power, or the desire to excel, can drive man
toward evil as well as toward good.

Selection of one's abilities. It is important for everyone to
understand his own abilities, while he is young if possible, so that
he may cultivate those that have a fair promise of success for him.
People usually enjoy the activities in which they are successful,
and they render the greatest service in their most successful work.
The world is full of misfits resulting from incorrect choice of occupation. Although most people are perhaps able to achieve a good
deal of success in more than one activity, there are some who will
be happy in only one kind of work.

This was the case with Ron L——, whose greatest interest in
school had been in mathematics. After graduation he went to a
trade school and then worked in a local factory. Because he had
a keen mind, it was generally considered that he would be able
to advance rapidly. What actually happened was that he did not
enjoy the work, did not get along with fellow workers, and was
not interested in advancement. For one thing, the work was too
strenuous for his health; he lost weight, became ill, and finally
had to quit the job. Then he decided to prepare himself for the
one kind of work that had always fascinated him — the teaching
of higher mathematics. Several years later, in his first teaching
position, he was extremely happy. He was devoting himself to
the one work for which he was really suited both in interest and
in ability.

People who have a special ability and a keen interest in some
one thing will always be more or less unhappy unless they can
make use of that ability, because this alone will satisfy their desire
to excel. Unit III deals more fully with information about
abilities.

FOR CLASS DISCUSSION

1. Jenny Lee, aged fourteen, considered herself an accomplished
pianist. She was rarely called upon to play, because of her irritable

disposition. On one occasion she walked up to the platform with an air of indignation, and, standing at the piano, defiantly faced the audience, and said, "Now I have spent a great deal of time practicing for this performance and I want it quiet or I won't play a note." There she stood for a moment, glaring and frowning at an audience suddenly become quite still. Then she played her piece and tripped back to her seat. There was some scattered applause; no encore.

Why did Jennie Lee make her remark?

How would her acquaintances be likely to feel about it?

When Jennie Lee played, did she do so for her own pleasure or for the pleasure of the audience?

2. Helen H—— did not go into the sixth grade with a perfect record. Miss Jones, the sixth-grade teacher, was told that Helen was mischievous, that she was a bright youngster, but that she used her wits far too often in thinking up rascality in the classroom. Nevertheless, Helen was a likable child, and the new teacher had no difficulty in feeling kindly toward her. As soon as Miss Jones discovered that Helen was an excellent penman, she asked her to write certain English sentences on the blackboard, and regularly thereafter Helen did much of the blackboard writing for Miss Jones. One day another girl, who also was good at writing on the blackboard, wrote out the English sentences during the lunch hour. Helen arrived, early as usual, to do the writing; but when she saw that it had been done by someone else, she began to cry and scold. Finally she erased the writing and rewrote the sentences herself.

Why did Miss Jones ask Helen to help with the blackboard writing?

Did Helen like to do it? How can you tell?

Why did the other girl write the sentences?

Explain Helen's behavior when she found the sentences had been written.

3. Which is better, to try to improve upon your own record, as, for example, in typing, or to try to improve upon someone else's record? Why?

4. What would you do in the case of Walter, Junior, if you were his mother or father?

5. What would you recommend to Eldred by way of helping him develop a better-rounded personality?

INDIVIDUAL ACTIVITIES

Make a list of the things you do during a certain day and check the actions that spring from the desire to excel or be important.

READINGS

In Literature

BIOGRAPHY (almost any)

Lane, Margaret. *Edgar Wallace.* Doubleday, Doran.
   This biography is especially recommended.

NOVEL

Spring, Howard. *Fame Is the Spur.* Viking.
   A best seller that describes the rise of a man to fame and power.

SHORT STORIES

Galsworthy, John. "Quality"; in *Inn of Tranquility.* Scribner.
   Is it good business to cheat the buying public? Suppose one can get away with it?

Lewis, Sinclair. "Young Man Axelbrod"; in *Short Stories,* edited by H. C. Schweikert. Harcourt, Brace.

O'Flaherty, Liam. "Irish Pride"; in *Contemporary Literature,* edited by Russell Blankenship, R. L. Lyman, and H. C. Hill. Scribner.
   An Irish chieftain, a fight, and a picture of how integral a part of a man is his pride in himself.

For Further Information

Goodrich, Laurence B. *Living with Others,* Chapter 9. American Book.

McLean, Donald. *Knowing Yourself and Others,* Chapter 4. Holt.

Overstreet, H. A. *Influencing Human Behavior,* Chapter 2. Norton.

Starch, Daniel, Stanton, Hazel M., and Koerth, Wilhelmine. *Controlling Human Behavior,* Chapter 2, pp. 27-34. Macmillan.

Webb, Ewing T., and Morgan, John J. B. *Strategy in Handling People,* Chapters 7 and 13. Garden City.

EVERYONE WANTS TO BELIEVE IN SOMETHING

Why do some people refuse to walk under a ladder? Do you believe in any such superstitions? Do you think they are silly or sensible? Why? What is magic? Is magic like religion?

What is an ideal? People believe in ideals. They have faith and confidence in ideals. Why? Because ideals are dependable; they do not change rapidly; they last a long time. Suppose honesty is one of your ideals. You give it a high place in your thought and striving because you believe honesty is a virtue that will always be good — not this week or this year only, but throughout your life. You can have faith in such an ideal; you can devote yourself to it. An ideal is something toward which you aim your life. You aspire toward it; you place your trust in it.

The word *ideal* is also used to apply to persons as well as to ideas, like honesty. But the two are the same in the long run. Suppose you know some person who seems to you an ideal man or an ideal woman. It is the *ideas* summed up or represented by this person that you admire — his (or her) appearance, his way of handling himself, his spiritual qualities — strength, courage, loyalty, generosity, sportsmanship. These are qualities in which you can put your faith. As they are expressed in the other person, you would like to see them expressed in yourself. They are permanent values that do not change — though, to be sure, your understanding of them may grow, and also your understanding of people. The person we think ideal today may not seem so ideal to us ten years from now, not because our ideals have changed, but because our understanding has increased.

When people talk about ideals, religion, faith, and worship, they are talking about belief in something that endures. That something is usually a spiritual thing, usually permanent, usually good wherever it is found.

The need for faith comes after childhood. Broadly considered, then, the desire to believe in something is a regard for that which lasts. But thinking about ideas or abstractions — Truth, Beauty, Goodness, and God — is not something that happens to us in childhood; it comes later in life. A small child's actions usually spring from interest in things, not ideas, whereas the desire to believe in something lasting leads eventually to interest in ideas as well as things. Religion, which has to do with man's relation to a Supreme Being or Idea, is not very deeply understood by a small child, and he is not strongly moved to think about it. He is busy learning about his relation to the things around him — the things he can see, touch, hear, taste, and smell. Only after his first curiosity about the surrounding world has been satisfied to a large degree does his attention begin to shift to the principles, ideas, and meanings ruling that world. Although there may be exceptions, it is safe to say that the desire to believe in something — unless it is the father or mother or big brother or sister — does not exist as a ruling force in personality much before adolescence — before, say, one is twelve or fourteen years of age.

We want to believe in something that does not change. In normal persons the desire to believe in something lasting — or to worship, in its broader meaning — grows as the years go by. When adulthood is reached in body and mind, this desire has an important influence on our actions. As we grow older, we are likely to become more curious about the reasons behind the universe, about the nature of Beauty, Truth, and Goodness, and about the nature of God and our relation to Him. We learn — or we should learn — to shift our attention away from ourselves to others, and away from material things to spiritual things.

Sooner or later, we are faced with the great truth that apparently all things change. Plants die and decay; friends pass away. Even our own body, it is said, is completely replaced by new tissue every seven years. New, strange things happen to society. Nothing seems to last forever.

Isn't there anything that remains unchanged? After childhood is left behind, people think about these things and search for what is changeless in a world of change. Ideals sum up what seems to be permanent in all the changing forms of society, with its wars and revolutions. Religion sums up what seems to be permanent in a changing universe.

Religion is an individual matter. No two people have exactly the same religion. They may subscribe to the same creed, belong to the same church group, or go to the same church; but they do not have identical beliefs. Every person adds to his religion a worship of his own. The thoughts and feelings of one are not the same as the thoughts and feelings of another. It is as impossible to find two identical believers as it is to find two identical leaves or flowers.

In certain respects we all believe alike. Perhaps all believing aspires or looks up to the Good, the True, the Beautiful, and the Eternal, whether this be in a friend, an idea, or in God. All faith contains reverence, curiosity, or wonder for something greater than ourselves. All worship brings a feeling of acceptance toward life and the world. The poet Keats made Beauty his object of worship, and this religion was shown in his life and his poetry. Thoreau and Bryant worshiped nature; they saw in nature the answers to many questions about the meaning of life. Their worship of nature led them to solitary walks in the woods and fields away from crowds. The majority of people worship God, some knowing better than others what they mean by God. Some worship the life of an idealized human being. But whatever it is that a man worships, he usually worships something that seems to him to endure forever, something that is greater than himself and all men, something that reminds him of Truth, Beauty, Goodness, and something that helps him understand the riddles of life. Out of this worship grows the feeling of acceptance toward life.

Religion gives meaning to everything else. It is good to have a desire to believe in something, for your religion gives meaning to everything else that you know, however impossible it may be to prove its soundness to someone else. Through it you can better understand sorrow, failure, and change, as well as joy, success, and permanence. All things come to have a broader meaning, for the happenings of life are seen in relation to bigger things. For instance, it is easier for a person to accept the loss of his mother when he fully realizes that such tragedies do not happen to him alone but to all men — when he realizes that death, like birth, is a part of the same big plan of life. Religion should give one a spiritual support in times of stress or uncertainty and a sane point of view in times of success.

We all need a faith or a religion. Without it, life is burned up with conflict. As we grow older, we become ever more aware of the conflict of life and for the sake of mental health, if for no other reason, we must learn to accept many unpleasant and even tragic events. Religion helps us to accept because it gives us an understanding of evil in the midst of good.

Believing helps us to accept life's problems. A little boy of eight had just finished the second grade. Every night during the summer vacation he prayed before going to bed that the Lord would make the next day bright and that it would not rain. When it rained, he had to play indoors, and he much preferred the outdoors. Occasionally, despite his prayers, it rained. Then he would sulk all day. One week in August it rained every day. Friday night his mother overheard his prayer, which had the following sentence in it: "And if it rains tomorrow again, Lord, I'll never pray again. There!" This little fellow was using his religion as a means to control the weather to his advantage. Grownups might think of the parched earth that needed rain; he thought of rain only in relation to himself. In a small child, of course, this is natural. The point is that his prayer sprang, not from a desire to worship, but from a desire to control things, to have them his own way.

At a speed skating meet one day a skater dashed out of place for a moment and said to a pastor standing by, "Pray for me." He then quickly dashed back to the mark and was off with the gun. At the finish he came in second and was next seen arguing with the judges. He was angry and shouted that someone had pushed or fouled him. Now, why did this young man ask the pastor to pray for him? Was it because he wanted help from some greater source to do his best and be a good sport? Or was it because he wanted help to win the race and satisfy his desire to excel?

These illustrations are given to show that religion is used by some as a way to get something, to control events, rather than to help them accept events. This is not true worship; it is magic. It is like trying to cast a spell over people or things in order to have them work to one's advantage. There is little value in such religion for our mental health. Religion should help us to do our best, to be unselfish, and to accept things as they are when they cannot be changed. When your religion does not help you in this way, think it through again, for it is not the result of your desire to believe in something lasting, but the result of your desire to excel.

FOR CLASS DISCUSSION

1. Look up the following words in a dictionary and an encyclopedia: *superstition, magic, animism, religion.* Bring to class for discussion one illustration of each of these words.

2. Is there any difference between science and religion? Should there be a conflict between them?

3. Why is religion an individual matter?

4. Why do some people go to fortune tellers?

5. Why do some people believe in superstitions? Is a superstition worthy of faith?

INDIVIDUAL ACTIVITIES

1. Write a paragraph explaining your own religion. This is not for class discussion unless you desire it.

2. If you have not been to church for some time, go next Sunday and try to understand why some people do go regularly. What do they get out of church services that satisfies them?

READINGS

In Literature

ADVENTURE

Byrd, Richard E. *Alone.* Putnam.

Admiral Byrd has strange thoughts as he is alone in the Antarctic.

NOVELS

Byrne, Donn. *Messer Marco Polo.* Appleton-Century.

Golden Bells, beautiful daughter of the Khan of China, finds something lasting in Christianity as Polo taught it, but Li Po and Kubla Khan look to China for their religion.

Richardson, Henry Handel. *The Fortunes of Richard Mahony.* Norton.

Australia with its crude life proves too much for an English doctor. He seeks solace in spiritualism and mysticism.

SHORT STORIES

Blackwood, Algernon. "Running Wolf"; in *Wolves of God.* Dutton.

Beside a lake "fairly stiff with fish" a clerk from a Canadian city found an experience that he had never reckoned on. The white man's religion and Indian magic are convincingly woven into the experience.

France, Anatole. "Our Lady's Juggler"; in *Mother of Pearl Tales.* Dodd, Mead.

Who showed the greatest faith, who paid the finest sacrifice to Our Virgin?

For Further Information

Bogardus, E. S., and Lewis, R. H. *Social Life and Personality,* Unit 7. Silver, Burdett.

Frazer, James George. *The Golden Bough,* Chapter 4. Macmillan.

Link, Henry C. *The Return to Religion,* Chapter 1. Macmillan.

McLean, Donald. *Knowing Yourself and Others,* Chapter 42. Holt.

Feelings Play a Big Part in Personality

SO FAR WE HAVE CONSIDERED a number of master drives common to all of us. These drives are usually accompanied, or influenced, by feelings. Acts of self-preservation, for example, are often accompanied and influenced by fear, anger, and disgust; though, of course, other feelings may enter the picture. Similarly, acts of affection and gregariousness occur when some degree of affection is present. Efforts to excel and to be important are usually accompanied by elation or dejection, and behavior reflecting a desire to believe in something that endures, as we have discussed it, is usually accompanied by a feeling of wonder. The parallel between master drives and emotions is not exact, but as we come to see their relationships, our understanding of the whys of behavior deepens.

What is an emotion? Perhaps you can think of an occasion when you were very much afraid; most of us can without much trouble. You experienced the emotion fear. What was it that you experienced? Can you say just how you felt, or just what went on inside of you? Were you excited? Did something take place in your body? Did you really know you were afraid?

An emotion is sometimes defined as an excitement or disturbance accompanied by certain bodily changes. When a person experiences love, fear, anger, or any other emotion, he is disturbed, excited, or upset to some degree. Moreover, it has been found that certain actions in the body go with these feelings. Glands secrete fluids and pour them into the blood stream, and various bodily changes take place. When one is angry, for example, the adrenal glands, located near the kidneys, release a small drop of a powerful chemical called adrenin into the blood stream, and this fluid makes the heart pump faster so there will be a quick flow of blood to the muscles. (The muscles will need extra energy for fighting.) Scientists have not found out all about glandular secretions and bodily changes in connection with emotions, but they have found out a good deal, and there is no doubt that all emotions are accompanied by some changes in the body. Every emotion does something to you. Likewise, every emotion makes you do something.

We are going to study the emotions as we find them in ourselves and others rather than from the standpoint of their development beginning with childhood. For the present we shall say, "Everyone has emotions. What have they to do with personality, and how can knowing about them help us in our personal development?"

Feelings lead to action. A study of emotions will suggest ways of dealing with ourselves and others because emotions lead to actions. Fear may lead to running, anger to fighting, disgust to turning away, dejection to giving up all effort, and so on. Of course, most actions are not simple like those just mentioned. For instance, a person who is afraid may not run at all. He may stay right where he is, even though he has an impulse to run. When he meets a stranger, he may be full of fear and yet not run. But if he is afraid, some action will result from the fear. He may blush or stammer or clear his throat; he may suddenly do all the talking or giggle or remain absolutely still. He may do one or more of a number of things, but he will do something, though it may be something that you would not notice unless you were a keen observer and knew the person very well. In fact, in the case of one of those well-controlled individuals with a so-called poker face, there may be only an internal muscular movement which no one could observe. But action there will be; an emotion leads to action.

As our knowledge of this truth grows, we shall see that, if we wish to have someone do something, it will be important to help him feel accordingly. If we want another person to like us, we shall be careful not to do anything that will make him fear us. Our study of the emotions will help us to know more about ourselves and others.

WHO'S AFRAID?

Why is a man of fifty generally more afraid to drive seventy miles an hour than is a young man of eighteen or nineteen? Why are people afraid of strangers? Should a person be afraid of deep water when he cannot swim? Can you overcome fear by sheer force of will? What makes a coward a coward? Is courage or bravery always commendable? What is bravery, anyway?

Fear is often valuable. Do not think that fear is bad or something to be ashamed of. At the right time it is an extremely valuable emotion, leading to self-protective actions of escape or of fighting. It is natural to have fear in time of danger.

A boy who saw a lion crash out of his cage in the zoo stood for a dread moment in surprise while fear suddenly flooded through his entire body. When the lion made after him, the boy took to his heels faster than he had ever run in his life. He made for an open toolshed and slammed the door in the nick of time. The emotion of fear drove him to escape.

During the last month of the semester a certain student realized that he was probably going to fail in his algebra course. He had never failed in a subject before, and, as he thought of it, his heart sank. What to do? In desperation he began to carry his algebra book home and study every evening. He studied carefully for the examination, passed it, and also passed the course. His fear of failure had driven him on to a final spurt of effort. He tackled his problem and won.

Fear of failure may lead one to success. Fear of doing the

wrong thing may lead a person to study his behavior and improve it. Fear is a valuable emotion, especially when it comes at the right time. As we have seen, it is always followed by action. It is for us to make this the right kind of action.

Fear is harmful when not understood. A fear that is not understood is damaging because it is usually impossible to remove it unless we know why it is there. A young man who had always been afraid of dogs was never able to dispel the feeling until one day his father told him that he had been attacked by a mad dog when he was a baby. The incident that occurred in his infancy had so frightened him that he had always been afraid of dogs. Knowing the cause, he set about overcoming the fear. He began to read about dogs, bought a large dog for himself, and spent some time every day with it. At first the fear continued, but later it faded, and finally there seemed to be no trace of it left. Incidentally, he became very fond of the dog.

One way to overcome fear is to make a study of it — when it began, when it recurs, how long it continues, and what it makes you do.

Fear is harmful when it does not lead to worth-while action. A fear that does not lead to some form of worth-while action is damaging both physically and mentally. It is harmful physically because the emotion of fear is accompanied by glandular secretions harmful to the body if they are not used up in muscular activity. It is mentally harmful because fear often leads to disorganized behavior and thinking.

During the first World War there was a farmer lad, Bill M——, who, when he received notice to report for military service, was so seized with fear that he did not eat or work during the whole day or sleep that night. The following day he remained in bed, sick. If Bill had forced himself to work hard for a few hours, he might have succeeded in facing his problem like a man, for hard work is a good remedy for fear even when you do not know what to do about the fear itself. What happened was that army officers came to the house to get him, and now, years later, Bill still feels embarrassed because of the incident.

Any kind of hard work helps to dispel fears because work uses up some of the energy that would otherwise be used in the emotion of fear.

Fear is harmful when it lasts long. A fear that lasts long is harmful for at least two reasons:

(1) Because of glandular secretions that are harmful when continued for a long time.

(2) Because constant fear may establish the habit of fear.

Not infrequently an eighth-grade graduate from a small rural school will enter a high school in town and be frightened on the first day by the strangeness of everything — his program of studies, the building itself, and the multitude of strange faces. The fear may continue; he may do nothing to overcome it because he is afraid to speak to anyone. He may lose his appetite, dream over his books, and go on from day to day for a month without making any friends or acquaintances among students or teachers. Every such day is a failure in itself. Very likely his first report card will show very low marks. Then he may wish he could escape — quit school — work on the farm, where everything is familiar. If his parents insist that he continue at school, he may lose weight, become ill, and finally have to quit because of ill health and continued absence. In such a case constant fear over a long period of time not only forms a habit but also destroys physical health.

Whenever you have a fear from morning till night and day after day, you can help yourself by talking it over with someone, by writing about it in secret, or by doing some hard physical work every day.

You can overcome your fears. One of the best essays on the subject of fear is the chapter, "The Mastery of Fear," in J. J. B. Morgan's book, *Keeping a Sound Mind.* It is worth reading and re-reading, and though it is a little difficult for high-school students, every bit of time you spend studying it will be worth your while. Under the paragraph heading, "How to Overcome Fears," Professor Morgan gives many suggestions, some of which are used in a simplified form in what follows.

1. *Fear should be thought of as a help rather than a hindrance.* Fear is the signal that you are in danger. You may be in danger of losing your job, of failing in a subject, of losing an election for office, of being beaten physically or mentally, of being run over by an automobile; there are any number of dangers for which fear

is a signal, like a red light at a railroad crossing. A person who does not experience fear when danger comes is not normal in that respect, and he is at a disadvantage in comparison with a person who does experience fear. You should think of fear as a helpful sign. The next question is what to do about it.

2. *Fear should lead to activity.* When you experience fear, always do something about it. If you are afraid you will lose your job, you may be able to improve your services so that your employer will wish to keep you. If you are afraid you will fail in a subject, you may get down to work and master it. If you are afraid you will lose the election for class president, you may try to behave in such a way as to make people want to vote for you. If you are afraid that someone is going to give you a physical beating, you may choose to run (if that would be honorable under the circumstances), or you may fight all the harder and win or go down fighting. If you are afraid of being defeated mentally, as in college entrance examinations, or in a competition for a scholarship, or in a debate, you may try all the harder and know that you have won a victory within your own self by doing your best even if someone else should be superior to you. Fears should always lead to activity. As soon as you are afraid, do something about it.

3. *Study your fear.* Do not be afraid of fear. Do not shut your mind to it by trying to think of something else. Rather, face the facts, look at the fear, and try to learn all you can about what causes it. As soon as you begin to examine your own feeling, as a scientist would examine a small bug under a magnifying glass, you will find that the fear becomes less intense. It is hard to explain just why this takes place, but it does. Your fears cannot stand up under your own honest examination of them. Therefore, as soon as you realize that a fear disturbs your personality and you do not know what to do about it, make a careful study of it. In case you do not know how to study your fear, or in case your study does not seem to help, take someone into your confidence and talk it over with him or her. The other person sees you from the outside, not as you see yourself from the inside, and he may be able to help you understand the fear.

4. *Fight the cause of fear.* As soon as you have come to some

Symbol of faith is this church that helps to satisfy man's desire to believe in something Eternal. Likewise, the members of the family saying grace at mealtime (*below*) are expressing their belief in something greater than themselves.

Fear and anger are often valuable, for they may give us greater strength to resist superior forces, whether those forces are attacking us individually (*above*) or seeking to destroy our way of life (*below*).

understanding of the cause leading to your fear, you should fight that cause. The fear will die a natural death when you carry on your efforts against the thinking that causes it. It is a mistake to try to fight fear itself. For example, if you are afraid you will fail in a subject, it will not help to fight that fear itself and try to force yourself not to feel afraid. The cause is still there. What is the cause? Maybe it is lack of knowledge of the subject due simply to lack of study. When you know the cause and do something about it, the fear itself fades away. Strangely enough, we are inclined to fight fears rather than causes. We try to forget the fear without studying why it came or without doing anything about the cause of the fear. As a consequence, worry, nervousness, and other personality difficulties arise.

5. *Substitute some other emotion, if possible.* Laughter can often suddenly replace extreme fear. This has been illustrated many times in a panic. When a crowded building is bombed and people, seized with fright, almost destroy each other in their efforts to escape, the man who succeeds in making people laugh saves the day. Laughter is a good substitute for fear in certain situations. Another substitute, in other situations, is anger because it readily leads to fighting, and fighting, like laughter, will serve as an outlet for a sudden flood of emotion brought on by fear. The best substitute for fear in some situations is affection. The young man who learned to love dogs no longer feared them. Experience shows that if we can turn hatred of an enemy to liking, or, sometimes, to true understanding, we no longer fear him. In human relations this is often extremely difficult, but also often supremely worth while. "Love casteth out fear"; that sentence, which occurs in the Bible, is profoundly true.

There are, then, five suggestions to help you overcome your fears. They are, in summary:

(1) Fear should be thought of as a help.
(2) Fear should lead to activity.
(3) Fear should be studied.
(4) The cause of fear should be attacked.
(5) Some other emotion may be substituted for fear.

There are many wrong reactions to fear. There are many unhealthful ways to react to fear; a few of the most common will be discussed here. Perhaps you will be able to see in the illustrations some similarity to reactions you yourself have experienced — and how to change them to successful ways of meeting fear.

1. *Escape.* Most incorrect reactions to fear take the form of an escape. Although it is occasionally wise to run away from danger — sometimes very wise, as in the case of a great flood or an automobile charging past a red light — it is usually wiser to face most kinds of danger and struggle through them. Any number of illustrations of the wrong use of escape might be given here, for it seems to be the universal error in case of fear. Think of the high-school freshman who is afraid because everything is new; he prefers to stay at home instead of facing his problem and seeing it through. Think of the boy who is afraid to meet another boy who wants to fight with him; he prefers to walk around the block and thereby escape meeting with the enemy.

Some people escape from the problems of life so frequently that escaping becomes a habit. They escape from school work by making themselves too busy with something else, or by getting sick, or by any method that will help them avoid doing school work. They escape from an unpleasant job by quitting, or getting themselves discharged, or having an accident, or in some other way. They escape from their problems in meeting people by not attending group meetings, by not talking with people, by remaining silent most of the time, by having nothing to do with others, and so on. Problems like these, and many other problems of ordinary living, must be faced and solved. Everyone must work out his own best solution for his own problems.

Escaping does not solve anything; in fact, it creates more serious problems within the personality. Running away from a problem that can be met and tackled leads to a feeling of embarrassment. Deep down, a person knows that he is running away, and his own self-respect falls when he does not face his problems like a man. He is not living up to his ideal self. Gradually he loses self-confidence as he avoids his problems, and his attitude toward future problems becomes full of fear.

Every time you react to fear by escaping or running away, you make it easier to run away the next time. Fortunately, the opposite is also true: every time you react to fear by facing the danger, you make it easier to face danger the next time. Perhaps it is safe to say that escape is always wrong when it is not necessary.

2. *Fear of failure.* Many people who think they will fail in some undertaking are afraid to begin it. Thus, a person may decide to be a teacher instead of a lawyer, as was the case with Watson R——, who had always wanted to become a lawyer. He had a brilliant mind, but he did not know it because his poor study habits had given him low marks in grade school and high school. During his school years, he thought of himself as just an average student. When he entered college, he was afraid to take the pre-law course because he had heard a great deal about the difficulty of pursuing it and passing bar examinations. In college, however, he improved his study habits and began to do much better work. Gradually he rose from a D to a C to a B student, and during his senior year he had an average of A minus. He might have studied for the law and fulfilled his life's ambition; he did not, simply because he was afraid he would fail.

Fear of failure is illustrated hundreds of times by high-school students throughout the country when they postpone or eliminate difficult subjects in their courses. They are afraid they will fail. Students who have never had an introduction to biology, Latin, or bookkeeping will say, "I don't like biology," and so forth, though they know nothing about it. Advisers and principals know that the student is really saying, "I have heard that biology is a hard subject, and I am afraid that if I take it, I will either fail or will not do good work."

Some students have given in to their fear of certain subjects so many times that making out a program for the next semester is an ordeal for them. In time every subject frightens them. Perhaps it would be better to say, "I am afraid of biology because John Doe failed in it. I'll have to work pretty hard to succeed, but it's in my course, so I'll take it and get the most out of it. Besides, if I dodge a subject just because I am afraid of it, I may get the habit of dodging everything that I'm afraid of." The psychologist William James said, "If we often flinch from making an effort, before we know it the effort-making capacity is gone."

There is the case of John R——, which is not uncommon. When he was looking for a job, something told him that he did not want to apply in this or that office, and he felt timid and afraid. On second thought, he would enter the office anyway and apply for a job; the more nervous he felt, the more certain he would be to go in. Gradually he experienced less and less fear and his confidence grew. By forcing himself to perform a task that he really dreaded, he strengthened himself for tasks in general. Had this man given in to his fear and simply walked by each office where he dreaded to apply for a position, he would have found himself afraid more and more frequently, until finally he might not have been able to summon enough courage to apply for a position anywhere.

Students experience the same thing in school work. When they fail to do their Latin one night and then a second night, it is especially difficult to begin the third night because the task is harder and there is more chance of failure. If the book remains unopened the third night, a habit of dodging the work is fairly well established. We cannot afford to dodge a given task, not only because the work must be done, but also because in dodging we lose our effort-making ability, and we cannot afford to let our effort-making ability waste away.

One way to overcome a fear of failure is to begin each task with a will to succeed. Tell yourself you cannot fail and work at the job with that thought firmly in mind.

3. *Timidity.* In Unit I it was pointed out that the habit of withdrawing from people is usually established in childhood. When a child makes his first contacts with other people — his parents, brothers and sisters, or other boys and girls in the neighborhood — he learns to get enjoyment from these contacts or to withdraw from them. Embarrassing moments, as when an older person ridicules the child for something he says or does, may be responsible for these first withdrawals. Withdrawing may also be begun by moments of fright, as when someone shouts at the child or treats him brutally. If such experiences occur frequently, the child will not enjoy contacts with other people and may develop a fixed habit of keeping away from them.

Timidity may also develop in later life, especially in adolescence, between the ages of thirteen and nineteen, when a youth is growing fast physically and in general is somewhat more sensitive than at any other time in his life. At such a time moving from one city to another or changing schools, or even moving from one home to another, may be too much of a disturbance. The difficulties in connection with these changes are social, involving the need for making new friends or getting acquainted with an entirely new community of people. If the difference between the new place and the old one is very great, the boy or girl may be unable to get any pleasure from new associations and stop trying to get acquainted. He may withdraw from social contacts and develop a timidity that he never had before. It would be mentally healthier if, instead of doing this, he would get the help of teachers or older people, pick out one or two or a few possible acquaintances, and establish friendly relations with them gradually. A stranger is frequently thought of as an enemy just because he is a stranger. People are a little afraid of him, although they may not know it, because they are not sure whether he will be hostile or friendly. It takes time to acquire a circle of friends in a new environment.

Timidity is a symptom of fear. Whether the habit of withdrawing began in childhood, adolescence, or adulthood, it is well to remember that you have no one to fear but yourself. Why should you fear anyone? Is it that you have harmed someone and are afraid of revenge? Then make it right. Is it that someone is jealous of you and you are afraid that he will do something to your disadvantage? Then develop your affection for him; you can find a good reason to feel kindly toward even your worst personal enemy. Is it that you feel inferior to someone? Then compare yourself with him honestly, and if he is superior to you in some respect, give him his due. Ask yourself whether anyone should be afraid of you. No? Then neither should you be afraid of anyone.

In the degree that you are afraid of others, you weaken your own personality and upset your mental health, for there is nothing that destroys personality as fear does. Timidity may be overcome by constant effort. In time your timidity will fade away. Your entire personality will improve.

A timid person usually refrains from speaking first, and other people seem to him hard to get acquainted with or conceited.

Suppose everyone waited for the other fellow to speak first; the human race would soon be totally dumb. Two very simple recommendations might be made to people who are timid:

(a) Say "hello" first.
(b) Smile when you meet another person.

Thousands of people have overcome their timidity by training themselves to do these two simple things. If you are a timid person, you can do what thousands of others have done.

4. *Self-consciousness.* As the word implies, a person who is self-conscious thinks too much about himself. When he joins a group of people, he feels uneasy; he may be concerned about his appearance, about how the other members of the group will take him, and about many other minor selfish details. He should be concerned about the members of the group — what they are saying and doing and what their desires are. Deep down in the mind of a self-conscious person something like the following reasoning takes place: "I am afraid I shall do something that will give people a bad impression. I want others to think I am quite a top-notch individual — one who does not make mistakes, who can speak with ease, and who can be a real addition to the group. But I am afraid they will see some of my faults (I know that I have many), and, if they see my mistakes, they will not be seeing me as I should like to have them see me. I wish I could handle myself so that no one could find any fault with me, so that I would make a perfect impression on others."

What is wrong with such reasoning? In the first place, good will is established on the basis not only of your virtues but also of your weakness. If you are as full of virtues as a Christmas turkey is of stuffing, the other fellow's reasoning is going to be something like this: "Here comes John Jones. He dresses better than I do, expresses himself better, and handles himself much better in every way. I feel uneasy with him because in comparison with John I am a very inferior person. I'd rather be with Dick Doe, who is more like myself."

In the second place, good will is established on the basis of your interest in the other fellow. The more you think about your own success, or lack of it, the less you think about the success of others. It cannot be said just exactly how other people sense where our interests lie, but they sense it and sense it immediately. They can tell whether we are interested primarily in them or in ourselves. If they feel that our interest does not go out toward them, they will not feel friendly toward us. (The shoe may be on the other foot, of course. There are times when we want and need the other fellow's interest in our affairs. We are the more likely to get it if we have been generous with our interest in his.)

In the third place, the more time you spend thinking about yourself, the less time you have to think about the other fellow. The self-conscious person coming into a group would have little time to think about his appearance, the impression he was making, or his success, if he concentrated on what the group was saying and doing.

You undoubtedly know that some people are very well liked even though they make mistakes that everyone can notice (as all of us do at one time or another). If you study these people, you will find that they are not self-conscious.

Self-consciousness is like a red flag hanging over your head, notifying other people that you are an egotist, interested in yourself and not in them. They do not tell you this and very likely do not realize that they think it, but they do, and they will shun you.

All this applies equally well to classroom recitations, singing or playing in public, making speeches, and so on. Self-consciousness shows that you are more concerned with your own success than with your audience, and back of this is egotism. There are certain ways by which you can overcome self-consciousness in these situations.

(a) *Study your subject.* If you have to give a talk, fill your mind with so much information about the subject that you will know a great deal more than you will cover in your talk.

(b) *Practice a great deal.* Your ability in speaking, singing, or playing should far exceed the difficulty of the thing you are to do. Thus, if you are going to give a talk on Lincoln's Gettysburg Address, you should know much more than just the address. If you are going to play Beethoven's "Minuet in G," you should be able to play pieces much more difficult.

(c) *Concentrate on your subject.* Whatever it is you have to do, that job is more important than you are. It must be done and cannot be done unless you are in earnest about the job rather than about yourself.

(d) *Think of your audience.* Speak, play, or sing for the audience's enjoyment, not for your own. Try to shift your attention away from yourself to your message and to your audience.

The same suggestions can be applied to overcoming self-consciousness in all ordinary social situations. The wording is changed, but the main ideas are the same:

(a) *Study the technique of dealing with people.* You should know how to listen, do your share of the talking, agree and disagree, show approval, smile, laugh, and respond to others. You should know how to time your smiles and actions, for there is a right time for everything. You should know how to fit yourself to people with whom you associate. Knowing these things takes study, but you can acquire the necessary knowledge and skill gradually.

(b) *Practice a great deal.* Whenever you have a chance to be in a group, be there. At any rate, don't stay away for fear of making mistakes. Everyone makes mistakes. The more experience you get in being with people (and the more difficult the situations are, the better), the easier it will become for you.

(c) *Concentrate on others; forget about yourself.* If you want to overcome self-consciousness, you must become "other-conscious"; that is, be interested in the people around you. What do they want? (Never mind about what you want.) What is interesting about them? (Never mind about how interesting you are.) What have they got to say? (Never mind about what you want to say.) Concentrate on these things and forget about yourself.

(d) *Act to please the other person.* Try to say and do things for the enjoyment and happiness of those who are with you rather than for your own.

Even if you follow these guides to overcome self-consciousness, it will take time. Don't think that you can overcome a habit of self-consciousness in a day when it has been in your personality for a long while. The removal of a habit or personality trait requires constant, conscious application.

5. *Worry.* Another wrong reaction to fear is worry. Although it may be true that no one is completely free from worry, most people worry more than they should. Worry might be called a long-drawn-out fear. It should not be confused with concentration or serious concern about a matter of importance. Life presents many problems that must be solved, and thinking people spend a good deal of time trying to solve them. A high-school student, for example, may be seriously concerned about his history course, which he needs as a credit toward graduation. It is important that he succeed in it. Naturally, he is concerned about it, and he will plan to study regularly, meeting the difficulties of the course as they come during the semester. So long as he is concerned about this problem in a fear-free manner, his concern should not be thought of as worry. However, when the serious concern begins to control him so that from day to day he is uneasy and feels afraid, it does become worry.

Fear and worry interfere with clear thinking and effective action. A person may worry because he wants something, but the worrying itself makes it harder for him to get what he wants. Of course, it will never do to tell a person, "You worry too much," for that would be saying, "You have a fault, namely, worrying." The effect of such a remark would be to make him feel inferior and worry still more.

What can be done about worry? First, realize that your problems are not by any means unique; other people have had to meet the same problems. Second, work faithfully and trust that you have done your best. Third, remember that worry, because it is fear, actually keeps you from succeeding with your problem. In case these three guides do not help, it is always safe to find relief in hard physical labor, or in a frank discussion with someone about your problem.

Six points about fear. Our study of fear may be summarized for the sake of getting the chief points clearly in mind as follows:

(1) Fear is a natural and valuable emotion.

(2) Fear is harmful, (a) when it is not understood; (b) when it does not lead to some worth-while action; and (c) when it lasts a long time.

(3) Fears can be overcome by following certain techniques:

(a) Think of fear as a help rather than a hindrance; (b) make your fear lead to activity; (c) study your fear and do not be afraid of fear itself; (d) fight the cause of your fear; (e) substitute some other emotion, if possible.

(4) A few of the most common harmful reactions to fear are: (a) running away from danger; (b) being afraid you will fail even before you begin; (c) timidity, or withdrawing from people; (d) self-consciousness, or concentrating on yourself rather than on others; (e) worry, or permitting your fear to take the place of controlled concentration.

(5) There are at least four things you can do to overcome self-consciousness in front of an audience: (a) Study your subject; (b) practice a great deal; (c) think of your subject rather than yourself; and (d) think of your audience rather than yourself.

(6) Similarly, there are at least four things you can do to overcome self-consciousness in ordinary social situations: (a) Study the technique of dealing with people; (b) practice a great deal; (c) concentrate on others; forget about yourself; and (d) act to please the other person.

FOR CLASS DISCUSSION

1. Jack B—— was a very timid person. He was exceedingly quiet among his fellows in the private school he attended, and he definitely shunned girls. He never attended the mixed parties arranged by the headmaster for the boys. Dancing lessons were provided at school, but Jack always refused to join a class. He gave as his reason that he despised tea dances; they came at a time when a fellow ought to be studying. Though he had never danced, he said he loathed dancing.

Why did Jack refuse to learn to dance?

If he had learned to dance, with what problem would he have been faced?

What is his problem now?

2. Martha L—— was only six years old when, one day, she found some of her father's order books and made presents of them to her friends. Her friends were glad to get these books because they contained carbon paper and the carbon paper was good for duplicate writing. But Martha's father, a grocer, did not buy order books for

free distribution, and, when one of his customers told him what was going on, he had to do something about it. He called Martha to him one afternoon and quietly asked her if she had given any of his order books to her friends. Martha denied it. He asked, "Not any, Martha?" and she answered, "Not a one, Daddy." Her father then tried to persuade her to admit the truth, for he was sure of the facts, but Martha persisted. Then he spanked her. Still she persisted. He continued to spank her until she admitted that she had given away the books.

Why did Martha lie when her father asked his first question?

Why did she persist in lying?

Why did she finally admit the truth?

What was Martha's reason for giving away the books in the first place?

3. When you were small, did you like to listen to ghost stories at night? Do you like horror stories on the motion-picture screen? Why?

4. Do people ever enjoy the emotion of fear? Explain.

INDIVIDUAL ACTIVITIES

1. In case you are inclined to be timid, try to smile and say "Hello" to ten people all on the same day. Describe their responses to you.

2. If you are afraid to go into a dark room, use the methods suggested in this section and go into the room to get something.

3. Make a study of a person who gives you a feeling of fear or uneasiness (if anyone does). Try to see his virtues and to feel kindly toward him when you next meet him. Describe the results of your meeting.

4. If you are timid in a certain class, make up your mind to volunteer to recite at the first opportunity. Study the lesson and be prepared; if necessary, memorize what you are going to say.

5. Observe three of your teachers. Write a paragraph describing what you think is interesting about them, whether it be their method of teaching, tone of voice, gestures, appearance, and the like. It will probably be better not to mention their names, but to call them Mr. A., Miss B., and Miss C.

6. Think of someone who you know worries. Write a paragraph analyzing what you think is the reason and make a list of suggestions which you think might be helpful to him in overcoming his difficulty.

WHERE DO I STAND?

In the chart given below, place marks above the words "always," "often," and so on, according to your most careful opinion about yourself. Then connect these marks with a zigzag line from the first to the second, to the third, and so on to the tenth. Ideally, this line would be a straight one, connecting all the words in the first column at the left of each line; however, no one quite reaches that ideal. Filling out charts of this kind may help you to know more about yourself.

(NOTE. *Do not write in this book,* unless it is your own. Make a copy on a separate sheet of paper.)

1. I think of fear as a help rather than a hindrance.

| always | often | rarely | never | I don't know |

2. I follow fear with some worth-while activity.

| always | often | rarely | never | I don't know |

3. I study my fears.

| always | often | rarely | never | I don't know |

4. I try to remove the cause of my fear.

| always | often | rarely | never | I don't know |

5. I substitute some other emotion for fear.

| always | often | rarely | never | I don't know |

6. I run away or try to escape when I am afraid.

| never | rarely | often | always | I don't know |

7. I am afraid I'll fail even before I start.

| never | rarely | often | always | I don't know |

8. I am inclined to be timid.

| never | rarely | often | always | I don't know |

9. I am inclined to be self-conscious.

| never | rarely | often | always | I don't know |

10. I worry.

| never | rarely | often | always | I don't know |

READINGS

In Literature

ESSAY

Broun, Heywood. "The 51st Dragon"; in *Modern Essays for Schools.* Harcourt, Brace.

> A satire. Are the brave brave?

SHORT STORIES

Blackwood, Algernon. "The Valley of the Beasts"; in *Wolves of God.* Dutton.

> Fear of the primitive and the animal.

De Maupassant, Guy. "A Coward"; in any collection of De Maupassant's stories.

> In the morning he would fight his first duel. In spite of his skill with the sword and the pistol, the night was one of anxiety until . . .

Hemingway, Ernest. "The Killer"; in *Men Without Women.* Scribner.

> How does a man feel when a "mob" is looking for him?

Morrow, W. C. "The Permanent Stiletto"; in *The Ape, The Idiot, and Other People.* Lippincott.

> Can fear kill a person?

For Further Information

McLean, Donald. *Knowing Yourself and Others,* Chapter 43, pp. 240-244. Holt.

Morgan, John J. B. *Keeping a Sound Mind,* Chapter 3. Macmillan.

Wright, Milton. *Getting Along with People,* Chapter 2. McGraw-Hill.

HE FLEW OFF THE HANDLE

Have you ever known fear to lead to anger? Which of these two feelings can be more harmful to you? Can anger be helpful? Why do you become angry when someone calls you a name? Do you ever become angry when you don't get what you want? Do you ever become angry for any other reason? If so, what reason? Do you know the relation between jealousy, fear, and anger?

What is anger? Everyone has experienced anger as a feeling of keen displeasure and antagonism. Like the feeling of fear, anger begins in babyhood. If an infant wants to play with a rattle and you take it away from him, he cries. You have interfered with what he wanted to do. If you hold his hand in an uncomfortable position at his side, he will soon show keen displeasure. In general, anything that interferes with a baby's natural movements — or his freedom of movement — will lead to the emotion of anger.

Anger in an older person has the same cause, though the cause can be much more complex. Whenever a person experiences this emotion, his movements or desires have been thwarted. The wants of an infant are simple and largely physical, but an older person has a wide range of mental desires also. We have already studied five major wants common to all men — the desire to live, to love, to be with people, to excel, and to believe in something lasting. It is natural for a person to have these desires, and when any one of them is disturbed or interfered with, he will react with anger. He will have a feeling of antagonism toward whatever it is that interferes with his efforts to satisfy the desire. He may control this feeling, but he has it.

To illustrate: The boy who comes home with a big appetite after a long afternoon of exercise and finds that dinner is not ready, and that he has to go to the grocery store, may become angry because his natural desire to eat is interfered with. The girl who does not receive a bid to the Junior Prom and spends a week quarreling with all the members of her family may be angry because several desires are thwarted: she may want to show her new dress and be important, to be with all the others at the party, and to see someone for whom she cares a great deal. The stenographer who quarrels with a typist promoted in preference to her may become angry because her desire to excel is interfered with. People worshiping in a church are annoyed by those who cause a commotion because their desire to worship is disturbed.

A study of the nature of anger contains a suggestion that, as far as possible, we should refrain from disturbing, thwarting, or interfering with the proper actions of others.

Anger is sometimes of great value. All emotions are essentially good and serve purposes necessary to life. It is the uncontrolled and extreme forms of emotion that lead to wrong behavior and poor mental balance. Anger should be thought of as a useful emotion rather than as one that should be completely erased from the personality. There are occasions when anger is very helpful, as, for example, in self-defense. A person may be confronted with the prospect of great physical harm, which may excite his fear, and in turn his anger. Immediately his body fluids work to help him protect himself especially well by fighting. When crises force a person to defend himself against a hateful person, anger will help him to put up a good fight.

Frequently a person suddenly tackles his job much better when he becomes angry over its difficulties; the anger helps him with renewed determination and effort. Again, anger in the form of righteous indignation is useful; we become angry when we see a stronger person abuse a weaker one, or when we see an injustice done or a good thing destroyed, and the emotion may lead us to give a great deal of help and thus sometimes prevent a wrong.

Anger sometimes leads to mistakes. Nevertheless, many kinds of faulty behavior result from anger, and these we should learn to control or eliminate. They may be grouped under four headings: fits of temper, peevishness and irritability, jealousy, and revenge.

1. *Fits of temper.* Uncontrolled anger of any kind is not only harmful to you but is disapproved of by everyone around you. Children and, even more, adults are criticized for temper tantrums. The remark, "He threw a fit because he couldn't get his own way," is not made in kindness. People who are given to outbursts of temper show that they are "spoiled"; that is, they have had their own way too much and have not learned to give up their desires at the times when they should. Life presents every human being with many thwartings; on many occasions his natural movements are interfered with or his wants cannot be satisfied. A person who has good mental health has learned to accept these disappointments without anger.

2. *Peevishness and irritability.* You may also show an undesirable form of anger in irritableness and peevishness when your wishes are not satisfied. This state of mind may last a whole day or a whole week, or it may even become a habit, a regular part of one's personality. For instance, you have been refused a date by a girl or failed to secure a certain job. Instead of continuing your efforts to get what you want or accepting the inevitable, you may show a constant resentment over dozens of little things that come up in daily life and are apparently not related to the original desire at all. Without good reason you may be quarrelsome, sarcastic, and unpleasant. Such behavior would show that you have been thwarted in some way. The person who makes this reaction a habit is rarely happy, not only because his own irritability directly interferes with happiness, but also because other people keep away from him much as they would from poison ivy. Don't be a poison ivy vine.

3. *Jealousy.* Anger shown in jealous behavior is also unpopular. Jealousy is a peculiar feeling of unhappiness made up of two emotions, fear and anger. When a person is jealous, he is afraid someone else will take his place of importance and angry because that same someone else is interfering with his natural desire to be important. For example, in the case of jealousy over someone else's attentions to a girl friend, the reasoning, deep down in the

mind, is somewhat as follows: "I'm afraid Jack will make a good impression on my girl, and then I shan't be secure with her. I'm angry because, when he pays attention to her, he takes her attention away from me and disturbs my relations with her."

Similarly, one student may be jealous of another, and the reasoning will be something like this: "Jane received another A in history, and I'm afraid she will take my place as the best student in the class. I am angry with her because her success is keeping me from the success I want." Or one stenographer may be jealous of another, reasoning unconsciously: "I'm afraid because Miss Jones is making a hit with the boss, and that will leave me second in line. I'm angry with her because she is interfering with my ambition to be the head stenographer here."

People who are jealous are not consciously aware of the mixture of fear and anger in their emotional state. Careful study, however, will show that these two emotions are present, and the continual shifting from fear to anger and from anger to fear makes a jealous person feel miserable.

Jealousy is a powerful force. It has been responsible for murders, and whole novels and dramas have been written about it. In love, some people think jealousy is a sign of strength, but it is not; always and everywhere it is a sign of weakness, to be overcome by our own inner strength. In everyday situations, you can overcome jealousy by becoming what is called "a good sport." If you can develop the attitude expressed in the saying, "May the best man win," you will not be jealous of someone who is superior to you in one respect or another. Any two people, on comparison, will be found to be superior to each other in some respects and the reverse in others; no one person is superior in every respect to another. The suggestions made previously for overcoming fear can be applied to jealousy because jealousy contains the element of fear.

4. *Revenge.* There is no lasting value in revenge. A wrong done against you is never made right by a wrong of yours done in return. The backwoods mountaineers who used to kill one another off in long feuds got nowhere in the end except in jail; even the cause of the feud was sometimes forgotten, so that revenge was the height of futility. If a person snubs you, his — or

her — error is not made right by your snubbing him. "No," you say, "but at least we're even." What value is there in "evening accounts" in this way? When you snub him, you are using your anger in just as wrong a way as he did, even from your own standpoint; for if you did nothing at all, he would be the only one to suffer. The more he snubbed you, the smaller he would become, whereas the more you avenged yourself, the more you would be like him. The best reaction to someone who snubs you is to ignore him or to feel sorry for him. In fact, you can go still further; if possible, anger should be replaced by affection, not by a desire for revenge. This is the best way to control anger. Before you can do it, you have to understand why the other person wronged you, and then you have to be big enough to forgive him. After that you may be able to feel sorry for him, see his good qualities, and feel kindly toward him.

How to win a quarrel. Quarreling is perhaps the commonest example of what we have just been talking about — two people trying to get even with each other. For instance, suppose a brother calls his sister a liar, and the sister says, "You're another." (Such things do happen even in peaceful families.) As soon as she does this, she lowers herself to his level and helps him to feel that he is no worse than she. As the quarreling continues, both try hard to avenge themselves at every come-back. What has been gained? Only some bad feelings. Suppose, on the other hand, that the sister says nothing when her brother calls her a liar. That would probably end the argument, and the brother would be left in the weaker position because he had behaved badly. If he continued his abuse, he would weaken himself still more. If the sister is a liar (just as an assumption), she will only make matters worse by not owning up. If she is not a liar (which we hope is the case), she has no need for revenge, but can honestly feel sorry for her brother for abusing her, and maybe, by being reasonable, she can make him ashamed of himself, so he will act differently, next time.

Criticism that rouses anger is likely to be partly true. When you try to avenge yourself on someone else, you are really admitting that the other person is able to damage you, and therefore that you are the weaker, not the stronger. Most of the harm that anyone can do to you is not real; it is the result of your own thinking. As a matter of fact, whenever you are criticized and react with anger, it is likely that there is some truth in the criticism. Perhaps your critic has expressed a fault that you had wished to keep hidden. There was a girl named Rosemary, for example, who did not usually take good care of her hair, so that she rarely presented a fresh, well-groomed appearance. One evening, as she entered the school building to attend a club meeting, another girl remarked innocently, "Hi, Rosemary. You've got your hair all fixed up tonight." With anyone else this would have brought a pleasant reply, but Rosemary snapped in a flash of anger, "Meaning it isn't fixed up any other time, I suppose!"

To return to the point: while the critic is talking, you realize that your effort to hide your fault has been thwarted. Somebody knows about it. You realize that you are seen in a truer light than before, and one less complimentary to yourself. You resent this, and, instead of recognizing the weakness and deciding to improve, you follow your resentment with revenge. Hence you do not improve and actually are damaged by your critic. On the other hand, suppose you silently admit that the criticism has some truth in it and resolve that you will try to correct the error in the future (as our friend Rosemary should have done). Then, no matter how abusive the critic has been, he has actually helped you. His action may be evil, but its effect upon you is good.

You can control your anger. It has already been pointed out that anger is basically an emotion that comes when freedom of action is disturbed, interfered with, or thwarted, and that no life is without its thwartings and disappointments. Normally we learn in time to meet these disturbances and interferences without anger. The spoiled individual, however, who did not have to face as many obstacles as others, perhaps because his parents gave him his way too much, finds it increasingly difficult to meet the obstacles of life when he grows older and spends more time outside the home. We say of such a person, "He will have to take a lot of hard knocks." No doubt the hardest knock, or handicap, of all is the obstacle of his own personality — the inability to forego any of his own wishes. Many of the difficulties that normal people learn to meet in childhood, a spoiled individual must learn to meet in later life, when it is much more difficult.

Life is a long series of obstacles. It is impossible to live without being thwarted in many ways. You might like to have a new fountain pen — or even a new car — but are thwarted because you cannot get enough money; or to get a certain job — but you do not qualify for it; or to go to a show Friday night — but you have to help at home after supper. A normal person will not react with anger every time he meets an obstacle. An infant will, but not a normal grown-up.

Five ways to control your anger. It is unquestionably true that most people feel angry too much of the time. Certain ways of overcoming and controlling this emotion are suggested here.

(1) Relief from anger can be obtained in hard physical labor, preferably such work as will help one to perspire freely. Work in the garden, shovel snow, carry in wood, or do any work that will make you physically tired.

(2) If there is no opportunity to work — as there is not in a city apartment, for instance — any other exercise, such as a fast walk, or a game, or competitive sports, will serve as an excellent outlet for emotions. You not only get the exercise, but take your mind off yourself and your grievances.

(3) If you feel like hitting someone, it will help if you take out your feelings on a punching bag or a pillow or an overstuffed chair.

(4) It usually helps to talk things over with someone who has a sympathetic feeling toward you. Maybe he can give you a better understanding of the situation because he is not excited as you are. Maybe he can tell you what to do about it. In any case, your own anger will be less intense after you have told someone about it.

(5) If you can make yourself feel kindly, or, if possible, affectionate, toward those who inspire anger in you, you will have achieved the highest form of control and the best possible technique.

FOR CLASS DISCUSSION

1. When Elaine received her Latin test paper, she saw that it had a very low mark and many corrections. As the class left the room, she

walked up to the wastebasket near the teacher's desk and tore the paper with plenty of flourish so that the teacher could not help but notice it. Then she threw the scraps into the basket and was about to leave, when her teacher said, "What do you think I mark your papers for, young lady? So you can tear them up in a fit of temper?"

Why did Elaine become angry?

Why did her teacher become angry?

What would have been a better procedure for Elaine? For the teacher?

2. Arthur had a date for the evening and was waiting to ask his father for the car. As soon as his father returned from work, Arthur made the request. But his father refused without a good reason. A quarrel ensued before supper. After supper his father changed his mind and offered to let Arthur take the car, but Arthur answered, "No, thanks. I don't want it any more."

Why did the father refuse Arthur at first?

Why did he later change his mind?

Why did Arthur refuse to accept?

Is it wise to make plans, as Arthur did, without knowing whether he could use the car?

3. Betty Lou prided herself on being one of the best-dressed girls in school. One Monday morning she came to school with a new dress that made her look stunning. But Lola, one of her friends, said, "Oh! Betty Lou, your dress is so pretty. Did you know that Wilma's wearing one just like it this morning?" Betty Lou's face fell, and she made it a point to have a look at Wilma as soon as she could find her. Sure enough, they had bought identical dresses in different towns over the week-end. Betty Lou was disappointed and annoyed, but she tried not to show her feelings at school when girls remarked about her dress. At noon, for no good reason, she quarreled with her mother. She wore a different dress to school that afternoon.

What desire of Betty Lou's was thwarted when she learned that Wilma was wearing an identical dress?

Why did she quarrel with her mother?

Why did she prefer to control her feelings among classmates?

How could the situation that arose be avoided or corrected?

Why did Lola call attention to the fact that Wilma's dress was identical?

4. Is it true that people are inclined to say "yes" when they feel good and "no" when they are tired or cross? Why?

INDIVIDUAL ACTIVITIES

1. The next time someone tries to start a quarrel with you by saying something mean or doing something that would ordinarily provoke your anger, refrain from answering him or showing anger. If possible, do just the opposite — agree with him, laugh, or smile. How does this action influence him? How does it make you feel?

2. Sometime when you feel keenly angry about something, instead of venting your feelings on somebody, put in an hour of hard work. Describe results.

3. On another occasion, follow your anger with an hour of hard play. When you are through playing, do you still feel as angry? What has happened to your feelings?

4. Sometimes it is better to take it out on a pillow or something that has no feelings to be hurt. You might try it. Punch, sock, abuse, or kick a pillow or punching bag when you are angry.

5. Try sometime to change a feeling of anger toward someone into a feeling of kindliness based on understanding. This is an individual activity that takes a lot of practice and thought.

6. Keep a check on yourself for three or four days to see how many times you become angry. Make two columns on a card or sheet of paper, one for minor feelings of anger and annoyance, and one for serious and intense feelings. You will find that you have a tendency to decrease the number of instances from day to day. Perhaps this is because you are checking on yourself, looking inside, so to speak, a procedure which usually helps to remove the problem.

READINGS

In Literature

SHORT STORIES

Hudson, W. H.   "The History of the Piebald Horse"; in *Tales of the Pampas.* Knopf.
    He flew off the handle when it meant his happiness.
London, Jack.   "The White Silence"; in *Son of the Wolf.* Grosset.
    He flew off the handle and it cost his life.

For Further Information

McLean, Donald. *Knowing Yourself and Others,* Chapter 43, pp. 245-249. Holt.

Morgan, John J. B. *Keeping a Sound Mind,* Chapter 10, pp. 319-327. Macmillan.

Webb, Ewing T., and Morgan, John J. B. *Strategy in Handling People,* Chapter 27. Garden City.

Wright, Milton. *Getting Along with People,* Chapter 2. McGraw-Hill.

WHERE DO I STAND?

On the lines provided below, place marks above the words "always," "often," and so on, according to your most careful opinion about yourself. Then connect these marks with a zigzag line from the first to the second to the third, and so on to the last. If you are not satisfied with the resulting diagram, plan how you can improve it during the next few months.

(NOTE. *Do not write in this book,* unless it is your own. Make a copy on a separate sheet of paper.)

1. I control my anger.

| always | often | rarely | never | I don't know |

2. When I am angry, I work it off.

| always | often | rarely | never | I don't know |

3. When I am angry, I exercise or play hard to remove the anger.

| always | often | rarely | never | I don't know |

4. I substitute some other emotion for anger.

| always | often | rarely | never | I don't know |

5. I listen to criticism, whether given kindly or unkindly.

| always | often | rarely | never | I don't know |

6. I take revenge.

| never | rarely | often | always | I don't know |

7. I am jealous.

| never | rarely | often | always | I don't know |

8. I am peevish and irritable.

| never | rarely | often | always | I don't know |

9. I have fits of temper.

| never | rarely | often | always | I don't know |

10. I quarrel.

| never | rarely | often | always | I don't know |

11. When someone is angry with me, I am angry with him.

| never | rarely | often | always | I don't know |

I LOATHE THE SIGHT OF IT

Is the feeling of disgust like anger or like fear? What makes you feel disgusted? How do you feel when someone around you says, "And how!" every few minutes? Is the feeling of disgust ever helpful to a person? Can you learn anything about a person by knowing what disgusts him or her? How is disgust related to making and keeping friends?

AVERSION OR DISGUST should not be confused with anger. The word *disgust* is often misused in the sense of annoyance or angry disappointment, but in this book it is used in the sense of loathing, which leads one to turn away.

Training and familiarity make a difference. A certain clerk is rather sensitive to unpleasant subjects of conversation at meal-times; he says they ruin his appetite and give him indigestion. Two years later, the same clerk is in the army, at the front in a great battle. When the chow comes around, he eats heartily in the midst of scenes that he could not have stood in his old life.

A man in a "quick-and-dirty" restaurant along the waterfront gobbles his food gluttonously, eating much of it with his knife. No one pays any attention to him or apparently thinks that his actions are unusual. The same manners, in a high-class hotel dining room, would make all the other patrons disgusted.

Why does one person feel disgusted in a given situation while another person does not? The answer lies in the differences in training or upbringing which the individuals have received. If you know what disgusts a man, you know a good deal about the man himself.

Some people learn to "get over" their disgust at certain things, such as unpleasant sights or odors, and become accustomed to them. On the other hand, as a person grows older, he may become more sensitive to certain other things of which his social group does not approve and experience an even more intense disgust than he did when he was younger. Individuals differ greatly in what causes them to feel disgust, and these differences, as well as the changes within individuals themselves over a period of time, are due to training.

For example, a chemist will not turn away in disgust from carbon disulphide, but a student entering a chemistry laboratory in which CS_2 fumes are in the air may at first experience a keen feeling of disgust, loathing, or aversion — perhaps nausea. A trained nurse does not object to ether fumes, but many people avoid paying visits to hospitals because of the sickening feeling brought on by the smell of ether. A celery farmer does not object to weeding celery in wet muck, but others not accustomed to such work will hesitate to put their hands in the soil because the touch of the dirt leads to the feeling of disgust.

Disgust comes through sensations and ideas. A person who is sensitive to order, beauty, and cleanliness will feel disgust when he meets with ugliness, disorder, and filth. The emotion is not confined to sensations, such as come from smelling, tasting, and touching, but also includes *ideas,* such as ugliness, disorder, and cruelty. Disgust inspired by sensations comes earlier in life than disgust inspired by ideas. A high-school boy who wears his heart on his sleeve, and in sight of everyone shows his affection for a girl, is said to behave in a disgusting manner. His behavior makes others turn away. As a rule, children are not sensitive to such behavior and experience no disgust in its presence. Although a small child might not feel any aversion when a dirty story is told, an older person who is sensitive to proper conduct will experience keen disgust. Loathing is an emotion having a great deal to do with human relations, for any action that inspires disgust has a tendency to make people turn away from the person who behaves in such fashion.

Some behavior is disgusting. People should avoid actions that cause the onlooker to turn away with loathing. As we have seen, all actions do not affect all people in the same way. Whether a person will or will not respond with disgust to any given act depends to a large extent upon what he is used to. There are certain actions, however, that almost universally inspire disgust. For example, almost everyone responds with disgust to sudden changes in the subject being discussed, to impolite and unseemly stories at mealtimes, to extreme styles and clashing colors, to undue, uncontrolled show of emotions, and to monotonous repetitions.

Behavior should, if possible, be suited to the group. If this rule is followed, the emotion of disgust is avoided.

1. *Changing the subject.* When a serious discussion is going on, it is disgusting to have a member of the group suddenly change the attention to a ridiculous subject. This is especially the case if the discussion is near a climax. If you want to fit in with your group, try to avoid such action. The other members may laugh, but their laughter is only a way for them to drive away their feeling of disgust. After the serious discussion has continued a long time, however, the same ridiculous remark might be considered quite welcome. Timing the change of subject is important here.

2. *Unseemly tales at mealtime.* Many people object to tales of blood, filth, or sickness at mealtime. Some people become nauseated and leave the table. Even a mild feeling of aversion is unwelcome at mealtime. If you want other people to enjoy your company at the table, you should be careful to bring up for discussion only such subjects as lend an air of interest and happiness to the occasion.

3. *Clashing colors.* Many people are so sensitive to clashing colors that they react unfavorably to the sight of a person dressed in extremely clashing colors. People who wear such clothes may do so to attract attention, but they rarely win friends through such behavior, for many respond to them with aversion. All show of bad taste, especially when it is extreme, inspires disgust in many who notice it. It may be acceptable to be a little different from the group, but it is usually disgusting to be extremely different.

4. *Uncontrolled show of emotions.* Many people respond with

disgust to young couples who, wearing their hearts on their sleeves, make love in plain sight of others. High-school students generally feel disgust at seeing the same two sweethearts mooning in the same corridors at the same times every day. Similarly, making too much show of one's grief soon inspires disgust in others. Continued irritableness and lack of temper control are also disgusting to others. Most people respond with the feeling of disgust when they are faced with too much show of feeling.

5. *Monotonous repetitions.* A saying or statement that is meaningful and effective, when used once or sparingly, may inspire disgust when often repeated or used continuously. A person may say, "And how!" to show that he heartily agrees; but when he uses this expression again and again, it is not effective; it becomes monotonous and disgusting. Likewise, a word of praise is encouraging to most people and inspires a feeling of elation; but when praise is given insincerely in an attempt to flatter, or when it is repeated over and over again, it becomes monotonous and disgusting.

What can you do about feelings of disgust? It cannot be denied that we do meet disgusting experiences that cannot be avoided. Frequently it is possible to get used to the unpleasant taste, odor, sight, sound, or thought. There are many unpleasant, dirty jobs that have to be done in the world and we should train ourselves to take them in our stride. Thus, a chemist or trained nurse rarely feels disgust in response to an odor, or a doctor in response to the sight of blood. Turning away from all suffering and ugliness, simply because of the disgust inspired, may, in many instances, indicate a serious lack of courage and willingness to face necessary life problems. We can take a scientific attitude and questioningly study, for example, just what the qualities of the odor are. Or we can reason that, scientifically, one odor is as good as another. Laughter also helps to relieve our feeling. If we are confronted with a disgusting scene or incident and cannot avoid being there, it is wise to try to get used to it, to study it, or to laugh it off.

FOR CLASS DISCUSSION

1. When Ned Jackson was five years old, his parents sent him to his uncle's farm because they wanted him to get fresh air and sunshine during the summer vacation. He enjoyed his stay in the country very much. At first he was very fond of fresh milk, but one morning he drank too much milk and became ill. Since that time milk has been disgusting to him.

Some time after his return home, Ned became underweight and generally in poor health. His parents wanted him to drink a glass of milk twice a day, but the very sight of milk at his plate spoiled his appetite, and he refused it.

Would it be a good thing for Ned to learn to like milk again?

How could he go about this?

If Ned solved this problem, would it be any easier for him to solve other food problems that might arise?

2. Do younger people or older people more often feel disgust? Why?

3. Are there any experiences in school life that do inspire disgust o which one ought to be accustomed? If so, what are they?

4. Why does the scientific approach — that is, the studying approach — have a tendency to remove the feeling of disgust?

INDIVIDUAL ACTIVITIES

1. Make a list of the actions, sights, sensations, etc., that inspire you with disgust. Which of these are reasonable; which are not? Could you become accustomed to all of them? Should you want to become accustomed to all of them?

2. The next time you get a keen feeling of disgust, try to laugh about something. How does this affect the feeling of disgust?

3. Can you get used to the sight of a dissected frog or night crawler? How long does it take you to accustom yourself to it? If you want to study to become a doctor, nurse, laboratory technician, or dental assistant, should you accustom yourself to such sights?

READINGS

In Literature

NOVELS

Hugo, Victor. *The Hunchback of Notre Dame.* Dutton.
> The Hunchback is a figure of loathing in a story of romance, intrigue, and horror.

Wells, H. G. *The Island of Dr. Moreau.* Duffield, Green.
> The narrator visits this extraordinary island and lives to describe one of the strangest experiments conducted by man.

SHORT STORIES

Ferber, Edna. "Afternoon of a Faun"; in *Gigolo.* Doubleday, Doran.
> "Oh, Nick, some dame on the phone."

Gilman, Charlotte. "The Yellow Wall-Paper"; in *Book of the Short Story,* edited by E. A. Cross. American Book.
> Can wallpaper drive one insane? Why are some people moved so strongly by feelings of disgust?

For Further Information

Black, Kathleen. *Manners for Moderns,* Chapter 3, pp. 49-55, and Chapter 6, pp. 99-100. Allyn and Bacon.

Boykin, Eleanor. *This Way, Please,* Chapter 3, p. 37. Macmillan.

Goodrich, Laurence B. *Living with Others,* Chapter 3, pp. 57-63. American Book.

Wright, Milton. *Getting Along with People,* Chapter 2, McGraw-Hill.

WHAT IS LOVE?

Are you likely to feel affectionate toward someone who makes you feel disgusted? Is it possible to be angry with someone and at the same time love him? Why do people usually find it difficult to feel affectionate toward strangers? Why is love sometimes referred to as the greatest of all emotions?

PREVIOUSLY we have considered love as one of the master drives in personality. We shall now study this emotion, which underlies so much of our conduct, in greater detail, in order to understand more fully what love is, what kinds of behavior it inspires, how it is to be distinguished from jealousy, how it may be developed and controlled, and how we can tell when a person is in need of affection.

Making the other person's wants your own. Love is the strongest of all emotions and can cause hatred, jealousy, disgust, and all the other human feelings to become unimportant, fade, or die out entirely. Webster's Dictionary defines *love* somewhat as follows (the wording has been changed a little): "Love is a feeling of strong personal attachment brought on by that which is pleasing or that which commands admiration; it is a sympathy that comes from understanding or kinship." In all forms of love there is to some extent a blending of two or more personalities into one. The person loved becomes a part of the one who loves. A person who loves another, no matter how little or how much, desires the desires of the other in preference to his own. The other person's wants become his. This was called the common denominator of love in our previous discussion.

Love is not always returned. Affection is not always mutual; that is, the love felt by one person for another is not always returned. This fact has been the theme of tens of thousands of poems, plays, short stories, novels, and motion pictures. It also occurs when the two sexes are not involved; one brother might have a strong affection for another and yet not be loved in return. In such a case one person makes the desires of another his own, but the other does not reciprocate. They have no desires in common; therefore, their affection is not mutually felt. Mutual affection depends upon both people wanting, wishing, sharing, and doing the same things together — not necessarily all the same things, but some things that are important to both.

Having desires in common. Mutual affection, as it exists in friendship, love affairs, and family life, and even among the people in larger groups, such as clubs, lodges, states, and nations, is based upon desires commonly held and satisfied together. Two students who have hardly known each other during three years in high school may, in their fourth year, be thrown together in some school activity like laboratory work or dramatics. They both want to promote the same activity and they work together. As they work together on the same project, having similar desires, they may become close friends. It is only when people share in certain wants and activities that they develop a mutual affection for each other. The same process often takes place among whole groups of people. Clubs, for example, that have been traditionally rivals, may become very friendly toward each other when they cooperate in some work that satisfies desires common to both groups. In all such cases, of course, there must be a true sharing. People can seem to be working for the same ends, yet be bitter enemies, because each is really working for some more or less selfish advantage.

Keeping desires in common. Continuation of mutual affection depends upon continuation of mutual desires. Often two people almost forget each other after years of separation. When they are far apart, they hardly know what each other's wants and interests are, and the distance between them prevents a sharing of common desires. Boys and girls who were bosom friends in grade school sometimes drift apart during high-school years because the desires and activities they once shared are not being continued. Their affection for each other may not quite die, but it fades for lack of cultivation. Each may have found other friends with whom he has more desires in common.

Affection needs care. Affection, like a plant, needs cultivation for life and growth. If you want to keep alive the affection that exists between yourself and someone else, bear in mind that it can be done as long as you both have things in common. Some of your wants, feelings, and activities must always be mutually shared. If you want to develop affection between yourself and someone else, you must study that person and discover or create desires and interests common to both. And you have to plan to share in these desires and interests, either by talking about them or, better, by working them out together.

Childhood friendships are based on emotion. It is difficult for high-school students to realize that the friends of childhood are frequently the ones that remain longest in the memory, no matter what happens in after years. Older people can understand this because they have experienced it. The older you are, the more critical and cautious you become toward the people with whom you associate. In childhood and youth it is possible to extend one's affection to others without a great deal of criticism and caution; the friendships made in this period are emotional friendships that may last through years and troubles. It is normal for everyone to have friends with whom he or she may share ideas, experiences, and loyalties, and every young person should develop more than one such friendship. If you do not have any true friends, perhaps you are a little selfish, more interested in yourself than in your associates. Surely, among your many acquaintances there is someone good enough to be an intimate friend, someone toward whom you can feel the emotion of love and from whom you can accept a similar feeling in return.

Love begins in home life. Although there may be a good deal of bickering and hostility among the members of a family, this does not mean that there is no love. It is impossible for anyone to hold the emotion of love constantly without any change whatever. It is even natural occasionally to feel hateful toward one we love. Those we love the most can hurt us the most. Parents,

Obstacles were no barrier to Helen Keller, who could neither see nor hear, nor to Thomas A. Edison, who was born in poverty.   They kept on trying and achieved success.   In contrast, the down-and-outers (*below*) have surrendered to discouragement and dejection.

Wonder is a strong driving force, for curiosity drives the scientist to explore the unknown with microscope and camera, and wonder inspired by true beauty drives us to find new meaning in life.

for example, tend to call forth more responses of anger from children than do other people. Psychologists call this ambivalence. They say that there are times when a person feels both hateful and affectionate toward another.

Occasional fights, then, do not mean that two people do not love each other. There are ups and downs in the best of families. But the downs are kept at a minimum; there is a constant effort to cultivate the affection that underlies the family relationships, and in this every member must play his part. Many families are torn by rivalries between brothers and sisters, and no adequate effort is made to heal the wounds or cultivate the simple courtesy, kindness, and unselfishness needed for the enrichment of home life.

Love shows itself in kindness. Unselfish acts are usually acts of kindness and spring from affection. Our own happiness depends largely, if not entirely, on our ability to be kind to others. You are a lucky person if you were brought up in a home where kindness prevails, where you learned to be courteous and considerate of others' wants. Kindness means that you are concerned about the welfare of the other fellow. His welfare may depend upon your sympathy and understanding, your willingness to see his point of view, your sharing of thoughts, material things, or duties.

Through a little effort we can train ourselves to be kind. Say the pleasant word at the right time. Lend a hand in household tasks. Go out of your way to take someone home. Be a good listener. Share some things the other fellow would enjoy. Smile. Turn away anger with silence or kindness. Take the sting out of criticism by admitting that it is partly or wholly true. Think well of the other fellow. The more you practice kindness the more happiness life holds for you. Practice will do it. You can begin any time. Kindness leads to good mental health because it gives us a chance to extend our interests beyond ourselves.

Going to extremes. Like all other emotions, love needs to be balanced. When it is not, it can play havoc with the personality; and this is especially true of love between the sexes. When a person's love for another forces him to give up all work and useful activity, it causes his personality to become extremely one-sided. A person so seized with love gives himself up to it at the cost of

being a useful member of society. Surrender such as this sometimes leads to foolish, embarrassing conduct.

As an example, take the case of Walter C——, a high-school
senior. During his first three years in high school Walter had
maintained a good record, both scholastically and in extra-curricular activities. At the close of his junior year he had been
elected president of the Hi-Y Club and treasurer of the senior
class. At the beginning of the senior year, however, something
happened that changed his whole attitude — in a physics class he
became acquainted with Lucille. From that time Walter was all
gone. He walked hand in hand with her to and from classes. He
sat with her in the library and either whispered throughout the
study period or wrote tender notes. He never noticed that others
noticed him.

When he was not walking with Lucille, he could be seen holding his head high, a smile on his face, his eyes staring happily off
into the distance. He neglected his duties as Hi-Y Club president. He failed to attend meetings of either the senior class or
the club. He neglected his studies; most of his spare time at
home was taken up with thoughts of Lucille, and instead of
studying he would compose love-letters and poems to her. Later
that year, a more serious problem arose when he began to want to
buy things for Lucille. He did not have enough money to get
all the gifts he wanted for her, and, since he lost the part-time job
he had held, money was more scarce than ever. He borrowed
from his parents, from an older brother, and from his grandmother when she visited the family. Finally he borrowed from
the senior class treasury, and only by the most careful handling of
matters by the sponsor was he saved from disgrace.

During all this time Walter was a joke among his fellows. His
actions disgusted them, and they found it hard to imagine that a
young man who had been such a regular fellow the year before
could go to such extremes in his love affair. They had no objection to his being in love, but they wanted him to show more restraint and self-control.

One of the interesting points to think about in this case is
whether Walter or Lucille was the more to blame for his going to
pieces as he did.

Jealousy should not be confused with love. We have already seen that jealousy is composed of the emotions of fear and anger — fear that one's place of superiority will be taken by someone else and anger because one's freedom of action in the position of superiority is disturbed. Where true affection exists, personalities come together in a new unity, each desiring the desires of the other and denying himself in favor of the other. The bond that develops between a man and a woman who are in love is extremely close as affection grows; yet the nature of the bond is such that each is willing to have the other accept someone else instead of himself or herself, provided the loved one's happiness is thus fulfilled. Perhaps love rarely exists in so pure and ideal a state that it leads to this complete unselfishness, but when it does, the sacrifice is possible because each desires the desires of the other rather than his own.

One reason why "love does not run smooth" is that, though two people have important wants in common, they also have strong wants that are not common to both and that may actually pull them in opposite directions at times. For example, a man may consider that his desire for a hunting trip is more important than his wife's desire to save money; a boy and a girl in high school may be very fond of each other, but one may refuse to learn to dance even though the other has a strong desire to do so. Jealousy is not involved in these examples, but it leads to similar situations. A boy may choose a certain girl because she is popular and he wants to excel by having a girl who is well liked. His interest in her is then more the result of his own desire to be important than of his affection for her, and as soon as he feels that some other boy is endangering his place of security with her, he is likely to become jealous.

Where jealousy exists, the master drive for power is more in evidence than the master drive for affection. The jealous lover reasons somewhat as follows: "Here comes Mary butting in again, just for a chance to talk with Jim. She annoys me because I can't have him to myself while she is taking his time. And I'm afraid because Mary may take him away from me." If she were truly in love with Jim, her reasoning might be as follows: "If Jim should prefer Mary to me, I shall be terribly unhappy, but, after all, I love him so much that I want him to have the girl he wants most." Probably, however, most people experience jealousy in this relationship because love is so often mixed with the desire to excel, the desire to be with people, and the desire to believe in something.

You can develop your ability to feel affectionate toward people. Life and desire go together. Everyone has many wants and wishes. Unfortunately, most of us are busy too much of the time satisfying our own wants; we are, as it were, in love with ourselves. The personality does not grow if we are too self-centered; it grows as our interests extend outside ourselves toward others. To the degree that you develop your ability to understand what other people want and then help them get it, you are developing your ability to feel affectionate toward people. It is as simple as that, and this holds true in every sphere of life.

You can improve your control. On the basis of what we have thus far learned, it can be understood that a careful study of emotions will indicate some ways to control them. It may show whether or not love is justified in a given case, whether or not the behavior resulting from it is acceptable, and whether or not the feeling is really love or the result of a wish for importance.

If your affection for someone is so overpowering that you are extremely unhappy or do not know at times what to do with yourself, why not go skating or swimming or play tennis or work hard physically for two or three hours? The exercise will do you good and will at least temporarily relieve your emotional tension. If you should decide that you are devoting yourself too much to one person, divide your attention; spend some time with other friends. These are simple recipes, but they are based on sound reasoning, and they work.

Some actions reflect a need for love. Children who do not receive enough affection show their need for it by various awkward actions. The same might be said of adults. In fact, all people who are not loved betray their need for affection by conduct that is not approved of by the group. A study of such behavior shows a peculiar cycle. For example, a boy who is not loved by his brother may be mean to him. When he is mean, he gives the brother cause to reject him again. When his brother rejects him again, he is mean to him again, and so on. A similar "vicious circle," causing and perpetuating the incorrect behavior, exists in practically all cases of rejection or lack of affection.

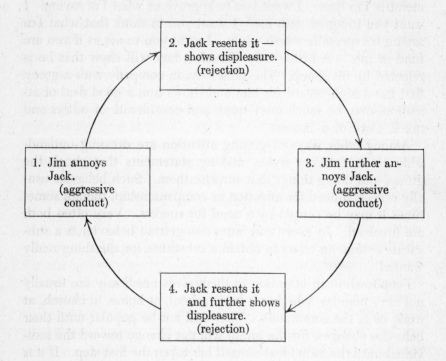

The cycle illustrated here may be expressed as follows: Rejection leads to aggressive conduct, which leads to rejection, which leads to aggressive conduct, which leads to rejection, and so on.

There are perhaps only two ways to break the circle: (1) The rejected person must stop doing the things that make other people dislike him, or (2) the people who dislike him must forgive him and find things to like about him. It is better, of course, if both changes take place at the same time.

Calling attention to oneself. Attention-getting behavior may sometimes be thought of as affection-getting behavior, for in receiving affection one receives attention. Attention may become a substitute for affection, and a person who calls attention to himself may be trying to get such a substitute. Examples of this are very common. The boy in the group who shouts and laughs the loudest and makes the most noise may really be saying: "Listen to me. Pay attention to me. Look at me. Think of me. Remember I'm here. I want you to approve of what I'm saying. I want you to agree with me. I want you to think that what I'm saying is especially worth while. I want you to act as if you are fond of me." A little study of such a boy will show that he is rejected by his group. The same boy, in company with a group that has a high regard for him and shows him a good deal of attention, may be much more quiet and considerate of others and much more of a listener.

Among other ways of getting attention are dressing outlandishly or in extreme styles, making statements that shock the group, and doing things that surprise them. Such behavior usually reflects a need for affection or companionship, though sometimes it may be caused by a need for success. Very often both are involved. In every case attention-getting behavior is a substitute action, an effort to obtain a substitute for the thing really wanted.

People who call attention to themselves needlessly are usually not very popular, whether it be in school, at home, in church, at work, or in the community. They will not be popular until their behavior changes, for the group will not change toward the individual until the individual himself has taken the first step. If it is possible for a rejected person to do so, he should become interested in other people, pay attention to them, find something to like about them. Then, after a while, they will just naturally become interested in him, pay attention to him, and develop affection for him.

Going out every night. Some young people who are starved for affection — and many older ones also — live a hectic night life. Among these are many of the "playboys" you read about. They take in every show in town, go to every party they can crash, escort a different girl every evening or even more than one during the same night. On careful study such people are frequently found to come from unhappy or very strict homes, or homes where there is not much affection. By rushing madly from one amusement to another, they are making their bid for a happiness that did not come to them by the natural way of true friendships and parental affection. Although this explanation will not hold in every instance, it frequently does.

Talking incessantly. Some people carry on the conversation all alone, even though there are five or ten in the group. They find it embarrassing to remain silent even as long as a few seconds. As a matter of fact, everyone should learn that breaking an awkward silence in a group is everybody's responsibility, not only his own; consequently, he need not feel more uneasy than the others. The rejected person thinks of himself so much of the time that when such a period of silence occurs he feels that everyone is waiting for him to break it. It would be better for him to wait occasionally and let someone else do the talking. Besides, congeniality in a group does not require a constant, uninterrupted flow of conversation. When a certain person has carried the conversation for a long time and when he is the one to end every period of silence, the group automatically expects him to be the first one to talk. Whether they approve or disapprove of him, they instinctively wait for him to begin to say something. It would be better if he tried to do only his share of the talking and let all the others do their share.

Stealing. Perhaps it is true that every boy and girl has stolen something sometime during his or her childhood. A human being is not born with a sense of respect for property and ownership; this trait is gradually developed in the home, the school, the church, and the community in general; it is a result of group living. Many children who occasionally take something that belongs to someone else will eventually get over it as their sense of social morality develops. This universal experience is not the one under discussion here, however. The point here is that occasionally children who are rejected have a tendency to steal for quite a different reason — as a way of getting something in place of the love they have missed. In these cases, stealing, like attention-getting, is a substitute satisfaction. When parents and teachers of a child who steals for this reason learn the true cause of his behavior, they are often able to help him to stop it completely and suddenly by giving him affection, tenderness, and attention.

Only a few symptoms of the need for affection have been mentioned here. There are a great many, varying with individual cases. All the symptoms, however, have one common characteristic. Each is an effort to get something — attention, success, material things — in place of the affection really desired.

FOR CLASS DISCUSSION

1. Mr. M—— had two sons, one of whom was a bright young man who got himself into many a scrape. The other son was not bright, but he was faithful, diligent, and a good citizen. Mr. M—— was so much devoted to the son who had to be bailed out of jail four or five times a year that he paid little or no attention to the other son who gave the family no trouble.

What was wrong with Mr. M——'s attitude toward his sons?

Why didn't he pay more attention to the son who kept out of trouble?

What could be done to improve the situation?

2. Mary C—— was a member of a good family that decided to take a certain orphan girl into their home. This lonely girl had no friends, and it was the intention of the family to give her a home and the affection she needed. During the six months that followed, Mary devoted herself entirely to her adopted sister and was so busy showering attention and kindness upon her that she had no time left for old friends who had been close to her from childhood days. These girls did not approve of Mary's action. They resented it and criticized her for it.

What was the main fault in Mary's affection for the girl?

Were her girl friends justified in their resentment?

How could the situation be improved?

3. Natalie was the older of two sisters. Inez was about two years her junior. During their childhood and youth they often quarreled because Natalie did not want Inez to take up knitting, crocheting, cooking, etc. Their mother praised Natalie for this and said that Natalie wanted to protect Inez from housework. She thought it was unselfish of Natalie to discourage the younger sister from taking up various household activities. But Inez did not feel right about it. She wanted to do these things because she thought it was pleasant. She did not know how to express herself, but she resented Natalie's attiude.

Did Natalie show her love for Inez by discouraging her? Give reasons.

Was Inez right in sensing that Natalie's intentions were not noble? What would you do in this case if you were the mother?

4. If a girl is admiring the sunset and her boy friend tells her that he does not think much of it, is his action likely to lead to greater friendship between them? Explain.

INDIVIDUAL ACTIVITIES

1. Help one of the members of your family to get what he wants and see whether your actions influence the affection that exists between you.

2. It is usually difficult to understand the wants and wishes of a person you do not like. Try to make a list of the wants of a schoolmate whom you do not like. Working out this problem carefully should help you to feel more kindly toward him. See whether it does.

3. Help someone whom you do not like to get something he wants. How does your action affect the relationship?

READINGS

In Literature

SHORT STORIES

Brand, Anna. "Entry of Ramon"; in *Prose and Poetry of Today*. Singer.

Old Mexico, the Southwest, and a child opposed to the Border Patrol bring out the meaning of affection for one's benefactor.

Galsworthy, John. "The Apple Tree"; in *Five Tales*. Scribner.

This story of a young man's first love has the ring of true experience.

For Further Information

Fedder, Ruth. *A Girl Grows Up*, Chapter 4. McGraw-Hill.

McLean, Donald. *Knowing Yourself and Others*, Chapter 8. Holt.

Morgan, John J. B. *Keeping a Sound Mind*, Chapter 6, pp. 183-189. Macmillan.

Wright, Milton. *Getting Along with People*, Chapter 2. McGraw-Hill.

WHERE DO I STAND?

The check list given below is one that will prove most helpful to you if you talk it over with some older person in whom you have confidence.

On the lines provided below, place marks above the words "often," "rarely," "always," and so on, according to your most careful opinion about yourself. Then connect these marks with a zigzag line from the first to the second to the third, and so on to the last. If you are not satisfied with the resulting diagram, make a plan for changing those parts that can be changed in the future.

(NOTE. *Do not write in this book,* unless it is your own. Make a copy on a separate sheet of paper.)

1. I study others' wants and help them to satisfy their wants.

often	rarely	always	never	I don't know

2. I deny my own wants in favor of others'.

often	rarely	always	never	I don't know

3. In my childhood I had close friends.

many	few	one	none	I don't know

4. At present I have close friends.

many	few	one	none	I don't know

5. Life at home is friendly and affectionate.

always	often	rarely	never	I don't know

6. I am kind to people.

always	often	rarely	never	I don't know

7. I am jealous.

never	rarely	often	always	I don't know

8. I train myself to like people.

always	often	rarely	never	I don't know

9. I call attention to myself.

never	rarely	often	always	I don't know

10. I am a good listener.

always	often	rarely	never	I don't know

UP AGAIN, DOWN AGAIN

Can a person maintain the same keen feeling of affection toward another indefinitely? How would you describe the feeling you have when you have been successful in something? Why is it that when you feel sad you do not want to play or work or do anything? Why do emotional ups and downs occur more frequently in youth than in adulthood?

THE FEELINGS of joy and sadness — or elation and dejection as the psychologist prefers to call them — occur so frequently by turns and are so much like opposites that they may be understood best when studied together. These two emotions are closely related to certain problems of personality, and some of the suggestions contained in this section may be of special value to you.

When you're feeling "just swell!" The feeling of joy or pleasure brought on by success or the hope of success is called elation. It is the feeling you get when, for instance, you improve your marks, solve a difficult mathematical problem, complete an article of furniture, make the basketball team, or get something you want, such as a five-dollar bill, praise for something well done, a job, a friend, or — not the least important — a new understanding of something you did not understand before.

Happiness must be learned. People who have not experienced much happiness do not know how to be happy. You cannot suddenly begin to be happy. Being a happy person, being able to get joy out of life, is to some extent a matter of habit. Some people habitually see the bright side of life while others habitually see the dark side. With some it is a habit to respond with elation; others have a habit of responding with dejection. That is why some people are called optimists and some pessimists. A child who has experienced very little elation is not happy, is usually self-conscious, and is timid about making the next move. Normal personality growth through the years of childhood and youth requires a good deal of success, satisfaction for the self, and elation. In adolescence, however, especially during high-school years, a person arrives at an age when he can begin to enjoy the happiness of others and shift his interest in personal welfare and success to the welfare and success of others.

Older people, especially people who are socially mature and have good mental health, feel elated when they have succeeded in making someone else happy, in excelling in service, in constructing something for someone else, in solving a problem that is of value to others, or in getting something that will be used for the benefit of others. This kind of elation is, of course, a higher type than that experienced in youth.

Success breeds energy. At every success, elation gives you an extra supply of energy. A renewed feeling of confidence fills you and you are in condition to go forward toward another success. If you are wise, you will take advantage of each new spurt of energy for a new effort. Many people make the mistake of wasting their energy in gloating over success. Elation is bad for you if it makes you talk about your success to a number of people, take it easy for a while, or strut around with an air of importance. It will damage your personality because it does not lead you on to greater effort, but rather to laziness.

Every time you experience the pleasure of elation, you should get to work, preferably at the very thing in which you succeeded. If this is not possible, it would be better to use the extra energy for reading, writing, studying, bringing in wood, exercising, carrying on any useful activity. By so doing you will establish a habit of using your successes constructively. Success breeds energy, and the energy should be used, not wasted, if you are to put into practice the best that is in you.

Get the success habit. Tackle such tasks as give you a fair chance of success. Avoid undertaking things in which you are certain to fail (but make sure you are right about it; sometimes people underestimate their abilities and give up too easily). If you cannot honorably avoid an undertaking foredoomed to failure, then devote yourself to it with all there is in you, and at the end you will at least have the satisfaction of knowing that you did your best. There is, of course, no disgrace in failure of this kind. As a rule, however, one should choose activities somewhat suited to his ability, somewhat difficult for him, yes, yet within the realm of probable success.

Start each job with a will to succeed in it. The more you succeed, the more you will succeed. Each successful experience develops a feeling of confidence for the next thing you have to do. Begin in a small way; develop yourself gradually; get the success habit.

Modesty wears well. If you study the behavior of your fellows who are successful and well liked, you will see that when they are praised they are modest. Although they may feel that they have accomplished something, they realize that they could have done more, and they hope to do more in the future. They do not brag about their achievements, tell their friends about their successes, or extol their own abilities. They are modest. When you have succeeded in doing something or in getting something, it will be well for you to remain silent about it and let others do your advertising for you. Remember that the one who is most frequently successful is the least excited about his own success because he is accustomed to elation, whereas the person who is rarely successful is inclined to make a show of his few achievements.

When you're feeling "blue." Dejection is somewhat like anger in its origin, but is very different in its effects. Anger, the emotion experienced when our natural movements or desires are disturbed, leads us to fight or to desire to fight. Dejection, which is also brought on by interference with our movements or desires, is not accompanied by a desire to fight, but rather to stop fighting, to give up. This distinction, of course, is extremely important.

It is possible to divide the causes of dejection into three main classes:

(1) *Failure to achieve something hoped for,* as when a student works hard during the entire marking period to achieve a better mark and then finds that he has not succeeded.

(2) *Realizing a state of insufficiency*, as when a student is keenly aware of his poverty and consequent inability to dress as well as his fellows, go to parties, and buy the things that others can buy.

(3) *Losing something of value* – a loved one, a friend, or perhaps some material thing such as money or a new fountain pen.

When any of these things occurs, it is natural to feel cast down, to experience sadness or a falling of the spirit.

Elation and dejection. Dejection may be thought of as the opposite of elation; it is natural to feel elated when we have succeeded, dejected when we have failed. This is not the whole story, however, for a study of people indicates that everyone has his ups and downs. No one can feel either continuously elated or continuously dejected without interruption. Life does not continue in a straight horizontal line, thus

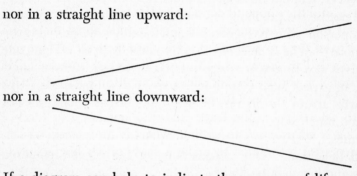

nor in a straight line upward:

nor in a straight line downward:

If a diagram can help to indicate the progress of life, perhaps a rising wavy line would serve that purpose for the average successful young man or woman:

Such a line, however, does not describe the progress of a person who is on his way down. Even such a person will not experience an uninterrupted fall such as might be indicated by a straight downward line; he will have ups on the way down, and his progress might be depicted by a falling wavy line, thus:

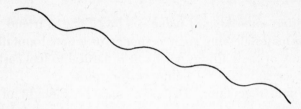

Most of the climbing, rising, or improving in life comes during youth; hence the normal progress in youth would be described by a rising wavy line.

Whether it is caused by successes and failures, or by an emotional rhythm of the body, or by both, most people do have an up-and-down pattern of elation and dejection. The normal person, however, will not be dejected more than he is elated. Dejection will not be the predominant emotion of his life. On the contrary, a person who has good mental health will probably be elated more than he is dejected. As has already been said, no one ever arrives at a time when he is constantly happy without interruption; to expect such a time is to expect the impossible. Ups and downs are in the nature of life, but normal people do not attach too much importance to a period of dejection.

Extremes. No two people experience the same intensity of elation and dejection. One person may be fairly even-tempered whereas another may be flighty. A line describing an even-tempered person might be somewhat as follows

whereas one describing a person who experiences extreme heights of elation and depths of dejection might be as follows:

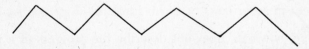

Young people react intensely. This line perhaps describes the emotional rhythm of youth more than it does that of older people, for as we grow older we become more accustomed to successes and failures and react to them with less intensity. There are, of course, people who are exceptions to the rule, but many regard such exceptions among older people as childish individuals, persons who have not learned to control their emotions, but who still react with youthful intensity to every success or failure that comes their way. The normal trend of life is toward serenity; that is, even-temperedness. No one could achieve perfect serenity, even though he were to improve through eighty years of effort, for a certain amount of rhythm is in the nature of life. Serenity can be developed to a considerable degree, however, and when it is, we are no longer unduly excited by dejection or elation, or by any other emotion.

Dejection may give you a new sense of values. Dejection has two important effects on the personality. The first is good, in that dejection gives us a new sense of the value and importance of what we have not achieved, what we do not possess, or what we have lost.

When a student fails to make the varsity team in debating, basketball, football, badminton, soccer, or whatever it may be, the dejection that follows shows him how much this achievement would have meant to him. If he reacts in the right way, he will continue his efforts in order to be ready to fill a vacancy on the team when one occurs. When he becomes keenly aware of some insufficiency, such as poorness in penmanship or spelling, or financial poverty, again the dejection that follows shows him the value of the quality or the thing he does not have. In these instances also he should try harder than ever to achieve the sufficiency he lacks.

When a young person loses a member of the family, perhaps his mother, through death, the dejection and grief that follow strongly impress on his mind the value of the one who has been lost to him. If he reacts the right way, he will alter his life to some extent in accordance with his ideal of the person for whom he grieves.

It is a peculiar fact that we hardly realize the value of a thing while we have it and only come to a full realization of its value when it is about to be taken away or is actually taken away. Dejection is the emotion we feel when the value of something taken away is more fully realized. Probably it is a good thing that life gives us many opportunities to get a better understanding, through dejection, of what is valuable and worth striving for, even though at the time the experience seems hard to bear.

Dejection may lead to inactivity. The other effect of dejection is bad in that dejection is always accompanied by inactivity. When we feel dejected, we are inclined to say, "Oh, what's the use?" We want to give up fighting, we do not know which way to turn, or we just sit and brood in our grief. For the sake of our health we ought to shorten these periods of inactivity, brooding, or giving up. Giving up for a long time makes it harder to begin again, and the more we give in to despair, the easier it becomes to continue a habit of hopeless inactivity.

Failure, insufficiency, and loss are common to all. If you are one who has failed, for example, to make the school team after much hard work in athletics, remember that you are not the only one who has had this experience; many others have failed in exactly the same way. Similarly with other experiences; you are not the only one who has come to a realization of your own insufficiency — your poverty, perhaps, or your ill health, or your lack of a brilliant mind; everyone has to realize some insufficiency. Again, you are not the only one who has lost a friend, a sister, a mother, or a father through death. Death comes to all, and everyone sooner or later will know the dejection that follows such a loss. Think of such experiences as universal to mankind, not as peculiar to you, and above all, not as some special punishment of Fate measured out to you alone. Your sadness, your grief, your castdown spirit, your dejection, can be of great value to you if it helps you to see the real worth of that which you desired, and if, soon after, you continue your striving with new courage. Dejection should not end in dejection. It should end in determination and renewed activity.

Do you enjoy dejection? Some people enjoy dejection, especially the emotion that follows the loss of a loved one. It is hard to understand that this could be the case, yet it seems to be true.

Not infrequently a man or woman who loses a sweetheart or wife or husband through death or separation will refuse to return to normal life, even after weeks, months, or years. At every possible opportunity such a person lapses into the old grief as though it were welcome, sinking into long periods of indecision, inactivity, and brooding, and thus failing to make the most of life. The individual seems to enjoy the fact that tragedy has entered his or her life. He does not wish to give it up because the tragedy means to him that his love was greater than life and greater than the loves of other people. Perhaps he reasons as follows: "Other people have no conception of the tremendous love that existed between us. Other people could not love as deeply as we did. My tragedy shows a greatness of soul that others do not have." Meanwhile, he wastes his life and fails to make efforts that would lead to worth-while achievement. Instead of developing himself by continuing a struggle that is essentially noble, he gives up the fight for the sake of what is essentially a selfish pleasure.

Your friends do not want you to make them feel blue. If you want to make a new friend — with emphasis on the word *new;* this may not always hold true in the case of an old friend — you should not make him feel dejected. You should not, for example, call his attention to his failures or to some sad experience he has had. When you make a person feel dejected, you can expect him to enter a period of inactivity, listlessness, or indecision. He may not tell you, but he will think, if not consciously then subconsciously, that you are a person who does not make him feel elated, happy, or proud of himself.

If you want to make a new friend, you should not let him know that you think he is too short or too tall, that his hat makes him look "goofy" or his suit is too small for him, or that what he is saying is of no interest to you. These things will make him feel more or less dejected — unless he responds with anger and tells you a few unpleasant things too — and it is natural for him to shun the person who makes him feel that way. You should let him know by your actions or your words that you think well of him. Teasing and sarcasm also tend to arouse the emotion of dejection, however well a person may hide all evidence of this feeling. Avoid it if you want to make or keep friends. Friendships are developed and maintained among people who give one another a feeling of well-being and happiness, not among those who give one another a feeling of dejection.

FOR CLASS DISCUSSION

1. John H—— was a junior in high school. He was a good violinist and was to have taken the first desk in the orchestra in September. But he broke his right wrist during the first week of school. This accident kept him from playing for at least five weeks and left him with a stiff wrist. It was two months before John limbered his wrist and regained his previous technique, and by that time his position in the orchestra had been secured by another player. Naturally, he felt dejected.

Classify the cause of John's dejection under one of the three causes listed on pages 101 and 102.

What would be the best way for John to solve this problem?

2. Jeanne T—— had just received a bid for the annual Christmas dance, but she refused because she did not have a formal dress or the means of getting one. She loved to dance and did attend all the informal school dances, but had to forego the Christmas dance. That night she cried herself to sleep. The next day, however, she felt much better and had a good time at school.

Classify the cause of Jeanne's dejection under one of the three causes listed on pages 101 and 102.

How do you account for the change in her feelings overnight?

3. Helen N—— was a commercial student who worked part-time as a typist in an office. She was able to take dictation and transcribe almost as rapidly and as accurately as a good stenographer. One day her employer complimented her and said, "Helen, you're doing fine work here. I wouldn't be surprised if we can use you full time this summer." Helen was overjoyed. When she arrived home that evening, she spent much time talking about her possibilities as Mr. Jones's secretary. Meanwhile, her school work was left untouched. The following day in Stenography II class, when her teacher made a comment on her lack of preparation, she tartly replied, "Oh, I guess I'm not so bad if I'm going to be Mr. Jones's secretary in another month."

Criticize Helen's conduct and recommend a better procedure.

4. Why does dejection sometimes interfere with solving the problems of life?

5. Why does elation frequently lead to a waste of time and energy?

6. Is it ever possible to make a friend by causing him to feel blue?

INDIVIDUAL ACTIVITIES

1. The next time you feel dejected, get to work. Does the activity help you to overcome the feeling of dejection?

2. For one week keep a record of your own moods of elation and dejection and their causes. What do you recommend for yourself?

3. The next time you feel especially pleased because of some success, such as receiving a good mark, baking a good pie, or receiving a word or merited praise from someone, use your energy immediately in some worth-while activity, such as study, work, or helping someone, without spending even a moment gloating. Make a record of the incident.

4. No matter how much you wish to tell someone about a success of yours, say absolutely nothing about it until someone mentions it to you. This is practicing restraint, which gives you inner strength.

READINGS

In Literature

NON-FICTION

Brande, Dorothy. *Wake Up and Live.* Simon and Schuster.
Jackson, J. A., and Salisbury, H. M. *Outwitting Our Nerves.* Century.
Pitkin, Walter. *Life Begins at Forty.* McGraw-Hill.
   Good books in the field of making the most of your personality. Much detail about moods of depression and elation and how to use them.

For Further Information

Morgan, John J. B. *Keeping a Sound Mind,* Chapter 11. Macmillan.
Overstreet, H. A. *Influencing Human Behavior,* Chapter 15. Norton.
Webb, Ewing T., and Morgan, John J. B. *Strategy in Handling People,* Chapter 22. Garden City.
Wright, Milton. *Getting Along with People,* pp. 26, 30, 112, 194. McGraw-Hill.

WHERE DO I STAND?

On the lines provided below, place marks above the words "always," "often," and so on, according to your most careful opinion about yourself. Then connect these marks with a zigzag line from the first to the second to the third, and so on to the last. If you are not satisfied with the resulting diagram, plan how you can improve it during the next few months.

(NOTE. *Do not write in this book,* unless it is your own. Make a copy on a separate sheet of paper.)

1. I try to overcome my dejection by work, play, or exercise of some kind.

always	often	rarely	never	I don't know

2. I am moody for days at a time.

never	rarely	often	always	I don't know

3. I go to extremes in elation and dejection.

never	rarely	often	always	I don't know

4. When I feel elated because of some success, I get to work.

always	often	rarely	never	I don't know

5. I begin each task with a will to succeed.

always	often	rarely	never	I don't know

6. I tell many others about my successes.

never	rarely	often	always	I don't know

7. I am a happy person.

always	often	rarely	never	I don't know

8. I am an unhappy person.

never	rarely	often	always	I don't know

I WONDER ABOUT THAT

Have you ever wondered about the workings of a clock, vacuum cleaner, or refrigerator? Why is a fly able to walk on the ceiling? Why is a fly so formed that he can walk on the ceiling? Why do some people study astronomy? Are wonder and curiosity more keen in youth than in middle age?

WONDER IS A FEELING of surprise and admiration that comes when one is faced with something new, not fully understood. One is amazed, then curious. If no one in an isolated village had ever seen a glider, and one suddenly sailed into view, the people there would stand staring at it. After it had skidded to a stop in an open field near by, they would probably gather around it, gazing at it, examining it, trying to find out more about its design and its controls. They would have a feeling of wonder and the impulse of curiosity.

Wonder is a strong driving force. The curiosity to which wonder leads has been one of the most potent forces in the modern world, since we can say that it is back of most scientific developments. Wonder and curiosity have driven men on long voyages of exploration into unknown lands, during which they faced great hardships willingly. The same urges or impulses led Galileo to discover that the world is round instead of flat, as everyone believed in his time. Wonder and curiosity led the Dutch linendraper, Leeuwenhoek, to make the first crude microscope and with it squint at every kind of hitherto invisible little creature he could find; and this, too, opened up a whole new world not before suspected to exist. Wonder and curiosity led Benjamin Franklin

to try to find out what caused the lightning; they led the Wright
brothers to study the flight of sea gulls and thereby discover
some of the laws of flight; they led young Henry Ford to tinker
with engines; they led Einstein to work out new conceptions in
physics.

Wonder inspires the artist, scientist, and philosopher. Wonder
and curiosity, then, are impulses to be cherished, cultivated, and
used. If we do not let them stop with mere idle wonder and idle
curiosity, but harness them with our brains, discipline them, and
express them in action, they can lead us on and on to extraordinary achievements; and always, beyond, there are still broader
horizons for wonder and curiosity. This is the case with every
really creative scientist. It is also the case with every great
artist. Wonder led Michelangelo to try to picture the beginning
of the universe in vast paintings, Dante to write his long poem
on the after life, Beethoven to express his feelings about life in
magnificent music, and Socrates to question himself and his pupils
about the final nature of everything. Other motives were involved in these activities, of course, but in science and art and
philosophy, wonder and curiosity play a large part.

Wonder and curiosity were among the motives that made you
elect this course and read this book. You wanted to know more
about yourself and other people — what makes us think and feel
and act as we do. After you have finished this course, perhaps
wonder will lead you still further into psychology. You may even
make some new discoveries in this field. There is plenty to be
discovered.

Youth wonders at things; age wonders at ideas. In youth the
feeling of wonder is usually associated with the mechanics of
things, rather than with the mechanics of ideas. The reason for
this is that young people are still unfamiliar with many things
around them. Older people, who have for a half-century satisfied their curiosity about the mechanics of things, become more
curious about ideas, because ideas inspire them with wonder.
For example, the idea that by denying oneself one really saves
oneself may fill an adult with a feeling of wonder and a desire to
understand it more fully. A child, however, may feel no surprise
or admiration toward such an idea, though he would be com-

pletely arrested by the sight of an electric train in operation on
the living-room floor at Christmas time. As one grows older, one
tends to become more and more curious about principles, ideas,
and the reasons behind things; wonder leads one deeper into the
meaning of life and the ever-interesting world roundabout.

Have you had your first view of the Grand Canyon? The feeling of wonder is usually pleasant. People travel to Niagara Falls or
to the Grand Canyon or to the ocean beach again and again, because they enjoy the awe inspired by the sight. They stand wondering at the sight of nature, and as they grow older, try to understand how these awe-inspiring sights fit into the scheme of all
knowledge. They try to see meaning in all these things. At
each repeated visit they stand in awe again and come away with
deeper understanding.

An art-lover will spend a whole morning in study of the *Night
Watch* by Rembrandt, or the *Mona Lisa* by da Vinci, because he
enjoys the feeling of wonder that comes to him in the presence of
a thing of beauty, and he remains to study and satisfy his curiosity. A scientist may keep a lifelong curiosity about things —
birds, trees, new inventions, and what not — but, with the passing
of years he wonders more about the value and the meaning of
things that interest him on first glance. The laws of nature and
how these operate fascinate him more than they did when he
was younger and did not recognize them. A philosopher may
spend hours — and continue throughout life to do so — thinking
about the nature of Change, for him that idea contains the
riddle of the universe. He is filled with wonder in thought about
it, and he is curious to understand how Change affects his life, the
life of others, and the whole world in which he lives.

Wonder may lead to faith. The shift of interest from things to
ideas makes the emotion of wonder different in childhood from
the same emotion as adults experience it. A child's interests are
mostly in things, whereas an adult's interests go deeper, delving
into the reasons behind the things. Because of this difference,
the emotion of wonder leads to religion more especially in adulthood than in childhood. The beginning of reverence, humility,
and altruism may sometimes, however, be seen in youth.

Some young people are more curious about the reasons behind

things than others are. As their understanding of causes grows, they feel a reverence for the broad laws of life and nature. Because of education, home, and church, they learn more and more about an underlying plan for all things, and they have a feeling of reverence toward it. This plan is usually thought of as God or as the work of God.

Wonder may lead to humility. As a person's understanding of the universe and of the Great Plan behind it grows, his feeling of self-importance declines. He becomes humble, for he realizes that he is only one in two thousand million now living on the earth; that he is less than a speck of dust on a scale; that he does not amount to so much; that the whole world cannot turn around him; and that none of his troubles is very different from the troubles of his two thousand million fellows. Through the emotion of wonder his curiosity has been aroused, and gradually, as his understanding increases, he is led to some form of religion that helps to explain his place in the universe.

Wonder may lead to altruism. Altruism, or regard for the other fellow, comes with humility. In the degree that one understands his own place in the universe, he will understand the importance of his fellow men and will come to consider them first in everything he does. Thus, the emotion of wonder finally blossoms out in the Golden Rule, "Do unto others as you would have them do unto you."

FOR CLASS DISCUSSION

1. In 1934 Admiral Richard E. Byrd spent five months in a cabin at the South Pole. He was in the coldest and darkest spot on the earth, and he was alone. During this time his arm went lame, his pressure lamp dimmed, and his lungs became poisoned by carbon monoxide fumes from an engine. He became seriously ill and almost died. During these days of danger and loneliness he thought about the unknown.

Admiral Byrd had alway been a scientist, curious about the things he could feel, touch, see, and hear. In the Antarctic he had been studying weather conditions and had been gathering scientific information for the United States Government. But when he was left alone, and it became a question whether he would ever get away alive, Byrd became curious about the things he could not touch — ideas — and his thoughts ran over the reasons behind the universe, the plan behind the world, the idea of God.

How can you account for the fact that Byrd wondered about God, the hereafter, and similar ideas when he was alone?

How did his emotion of wonder lead to actions during his stay at the South Pole which were different from his actions before that time?

What bearing did his aloneness and his illness have upon the object of his curiosity?

Would thoughts of this nature be likely to help Byrd meet his personal problems at that time?

2. Do you remember Uriah Heep in *David Copperfield*? His part in the movie was taken by Roland Young. He was a very humble person, or he made out that he was. When Mr. Heep first met David, he said, "I am well aware that I am the 'umblest person going, let the other be where *he* may. My mother is likewise a very 'umble person. We live in a 'umble abode, Master Copperfield, but have much to be thankful for. My father's former calling was 'umble; he was a sexton." Uriah always emphasized his humility to others, but meanwhile lived like a sneak.

Why did he make-believe that he was humble?

Did his humility spring from a deep understanding of his place in the world?

What basic desire led him to his show of humility?

3. Discuss the saying, "Pride goeth before a fall."

4. Is it possible to be too humble? How?

READINGS

In Literature

NOVELS

Davis, Clyde. *The Anointed.* Farrar, Rinehart.

> Men are strange, but seamen are stranger than other men. Hunger and thirst at sea tests them. And their wives cannot understand.

Dickens, Charles. *David Copperfield*, Chapter XVI.

SHORT STORY

Henry, O. "Roads of Destiny"; in *Roads of Destiny.* Doubleday, Doran.

"If we could only relive our lives," we often think. O. Henry offers a surprising answer to our plea.

NON-FICTION

Byrd, Richard E. *Alone.* Putnam.

Fabre, J. Henri. *Life of the Caterpillar.* Dodd, Mead.

It is possible to look at science through the eyes of the poet.

Maeterlinck, Maurice. *Life of the Bee.* Dodd, Mead.

We take it for granted that the life of animals is simple and governed by a few immutable instincts. Maeterlinck shows that this is a mistaken notion. Bees think.

For Further Information

Bogardus, E. S., and Lewis, R. H. *Social Life and Personality,* Unit 7. Silver, Burdett.

Law, Frederick Houk. *He Got the Job,* Chapter 10, pp. 170-172. Scribner.

McLean, Donald. *Knowing Yourself and Others,* Chapter 42. Holt.

Wright, Milton. *Getting Along with People,* Chapter 2. McGraw-Hill.

❧ UNIT III ❧

What Are Your Abilities?

WHAT ARE YOUR ABILITIES?

You can, of course, read, write, add, subtract. Maybe you are better at reading than at writing, or at adding than at multiplying. Undoubtedly you have some special ability, though perhaps you have not discovered it. Are you good in dramatics? In mechanical work? At cooking or sewing? Perhaps you have special ability in some branch of cooking, such as making pies, or in some branch of mechanical work, such as rewinding motors.

Your abilities vary in strength. Everyone has thousands of skills; for instance, the same person can run, walk, skate, dance, talk, read, use a knife and fork, apply lipstick, and so on. If all the abilities of any one person were lined up in order from worst to best, as indicated in the accompanying diagram, he would be found to be very poor in a few, average in a large number, and highly superior in a few.

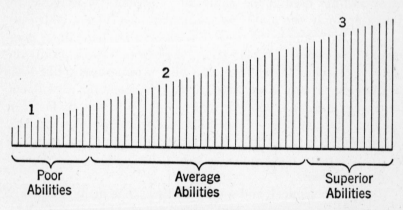

The figures 1, 2, and 3 may be thought of as marking any three abilities, for example the ability to read, to hear, and to memorize, respectively. As the chart indicates, a given person may be poor in reading, average in hearing, and superior in memorizing.

The abilities of no two persons are alike. Bill Jones may be a good pitcher, but a poor penman, while Jim Brown may be the reverse. We constantly see these differences between individuals. It is important for everyone to know a good deal about his own abilities, so that he may plan his life accordingly. A student with a very poor scholarship rating may have certain abilities far above average, which, if developed, would enable him to be a superior worker.

Do not think that just because a fellow student gets better marks than you do, he is superior to you in every respect. There is no doubt that you have certain abilities in which he would be inferior to you. You may not know at present what these aptitudes are, but you should not feel inferior when you notice that someone else does some things better than you do. Try to find out what your strongest abilities are and make the most of them. This is so important for your whole future life that it is worth a great deal of thought.

Abilities are complex. It is frequently said that someone is an excellent typist or an excellent driver, as if typing and driving an automobile were two special abilities. Actually, however, typing and driving like most of the things we do with the greatest of ease and without even a second thought, are really made up of many abilities used at the same time. Typing, for example, requires not only the ability to manipulate the fingers with ease, but also, for example, to read, to spell, and to space lines, paragraphs, and pages. Driving an automobile requires not only the ability to manage the controls, but also to remember traffic rules and to judge at any given time whether to speed up, slow down, proceed at the same pace, or stop. One typist may be faster or more accurate or able to type more difficult copy than another. One automobile driver may have better eyesight than another or be able to react more quickly or to drive under more difficult traffic conditions.

Mental, mechanical, and social abilities. The many abilities of human beings are sometimes grouped for convenience under three broad headings — mental, mechanical, and social abilities. Mental abilities are used in activities that are essentially of a reasoning nature. Mechanical abilities are used in activities carried on largely with the help of the muscles in handling tools and materials. Social abilities are used in dealing with people; that is, in human relations.

Abilities are not separate. There is, of course, a great deal of overlapping among these three groups. It would be difficult to think of a mechanical ability that does not bring into play certain mental and social aptitudes, or to think of a mental ability that does not involve certain social and physical aptitudes, or of a social ability that does not include certain mental and mechanical aptitudes.

A tennis player, for example, uses predominantly mechanical abilities. Sometimes star tennis players are by no means star scholars, yet tennis players learn the rules of the game, the method of scoring, and so on, and this calls on mental abilities. They also learn the many courtesies of the court, which requires social abilities. Illustrations of this type could be multiplied to show that most of the activities of life, even though they may be predominantly mental, mechanical, or social, nevertheless call into play aptitudes from all three groups.

The present unit is planned to give you some information about abilities in general, under the three divisions suggested. Mental abilities will be considered first.

MENTAL ABILITIES

Would you recommend trigonometry for all students? What do you mean when you say that So-and-So has brains? Is it possible to have too much intelligence? Do you think great mental ability insures success in life? How can you tell whether you have average or above-average mental ability?

What is mental ability? Mental ability is the ability we draw on in reasoning, in understanding, and in using ideas, not only in such fields as mathematics and science, but in all kinds of everyday affairs. Obviously, mental abilities are used in school studies, and they are of first importance in various professions, such as engineering, law, medicine, bookkeeping, accounting, and many others.

What is intelligence? Though in daily life we talk about intelligence as if we know what the word means, psychologists have been deeply puzzled by this word for more than a generation. Intelligence — mental or intellectual ability — may be defined as an individual's general ability to meet new problems and conditions in life wisely. It remains more or less the same in relation to age throughout life (this point is discussed later), and varies greatly among individuals. Special or specific abilities, such as memorizing, are learned rather than inherited, may be improved by practice, and do not remain constant throughout life.

Use the brains you have. It has been said that most of the time the average human being uses only about one per cent of his mental ability. If this is true, or if it is only a half or a quarter true, we may conclude that a person who does not have a great deal of intelligence, but who makes more than average use of what he has, will find himself on a par with or superior to his fellows. George Washington may have been such a person, for he has been described as a man of average ability who through constant diligence achieved superiority. No doubt we can all call to mind one or more friends of average intelligence who succeed very well at school. These individuals do not have superior intelligence, but they are using what they have in a superior way by diligence and hard work.

The intelligence quotient. During the past generation many efforts have been made to measure intelligence. The measures now commonly used in the schools are called intelligence quotients, or I.Q.'s, and are secured by dividing one's mental age (indicated by the test) by his life age and then multiplying by 100. Thus, a fifteen-year-old who successfully completes a test for a person his age is said to have an I.Q. of 100; a fifteen-year-old who successfully completes a test for a person fourteen years old is said to have an I.Q. of 93 (14 ÷ 15 = .93 × 100 = 93); and a fifteen-year-old who successfully completes a test for a person sixteen years old is said to have an I.Q. of 107 (16 ÷ 15 = 1.066 × 100 = 106.6).

There is a great deal of variation in I.Q.'s among individuals, and it has been possible to classify them in such a way as to give them more meaning. A person with an I.Q. above 140, for instance, is "gifted," and one with a very low I.Q. is feeble-minded. A young person with an I.Q. of 50, for example, cannot learn much from an ordinary school, and usually is too stupid ever to earn his own living.

Why tests are used. It has already been said that a person's intelligence in relation to his age remains about the same throughout his life. This is a very difficult idea to grasp. It does not mean that a person's *knowledge* is the same at five years of age as at fifteen, but that at five years you can predict in a general way what his *mental ability* will be at fifteen — in relation, of course, to the problems of that age. An accurate I.Q., then, can be a great help to teachers in guiding a student through proper courses in school. A careful study of any given test may also show that a student is deficient in reading, say, or arithmetic, and

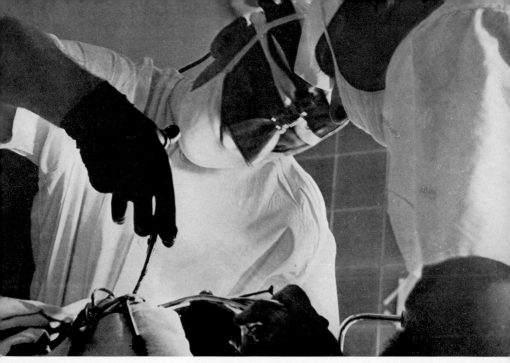

Intellectual and mechanical ability of a high order enable the great surgeon (*above*) to save a life. Repairing a car (*below*) requires the same kinds of abilities but is a job within the reach of more young men.

Social ability is not so necessary for draftsmanship as for salesmanship. The draftsman (*above*) works alone much of the time, but the saleswoman (*below*) must continually deal with people and must please them. Customers avoid sales people they do not like.

with such information a teacher can give him special help. Many special tests have been devised to measure a student's ability in reading, writing, computing, retaining historical information, and the like, and the most valuable use that can be made of such tests is for improving upon particular inabilities.

I.Q. is sometimes misunderstood. There is no proof that the so-called intelligence tests now used are absolutely reliable measures of a person's intellectual ability. A person may have a large number of abilities not covered in the test. Furthermore, the rating on the test depends to some extent on how the person feels when he takes it; if he is not feeling well, the rating may be to some extent incorrect. Most intelligence tests now commonly used in high schools require reading ability, because the tests have to be read in order to be filled out. Thus, students who have superior intelligence but poor reading ability might receive a low I.Q.

Other reasons might be cited, but these are sufficient to suggest a few important cautions: (1) An average I.Q. should be thought of as anywhere between 90 and 110, because the test is imperfect; (2) the I.Q. may change somewhat (in spite of what has been said above), depending upon special abilities, such as reading and computing; (3) a below-average I.Q. may be compensated for by special abilities, such as the ability to get along with people, unusual diligence, or some special mechanical ability; (4) having a below-average I.Q. certainly does not mean that a person is doomed to a life below average in success or happiness; (5) and, on the other hand, a high I.Q. is no guarantee of success.

Other measures of mental ability. There are other measures of mental ability that are more important and more meaningful to a high-school student than test scores and I.Q.'s. These measures are the marks you get on your report card in such subjects as languages, natural sciences, mathematics, and social science. Your success in these subjects means more than I.Q. because it indicates what you are actually doing with your mental ability, and this in turn points the way toward the studies and the vocation you should take up in the future. Your progress or lack of progress in each subject is one of the things that indicate whether you have the mental ability and the study habits needed for this or that field of endeavor. The ability to get to work promptly and to stick to a given task is as important as high mental ability itself. Many brilliant people literally waste their lives because they do not have the drive to get to work and stick to it, while many others, not blessed with a brilliant mentality, have fortunately developed habits of diligence that make them successful throughout life.

Abilities and planning for the future. Young men and women of high-school age are seriously interested in planning their future, and particularly in selecting the vocation in which they will have the best chance of success. There are many aids that may be called upon in making this selection, among them the help of older persons, such as vocational counselors, the high-school principal, and teachers. These people and your parents, one or all, may be able to help you to understand more fully both your special abilities and the abilities required in certain vocations. This is so important a question that it is worth while to get much more information about it than this brief discussion can give. A number of excellent books on vocational guidance are available. Take your time, study them, and make sure that your plans for the future do not conflict with your abilities.

FOR CLASS DISCUSSION

1. Mary T—— was a junior in high school when she learned that her I.Q. was 132. Her older sister had given her an intelligence test at home and had told her the result. She had explained that the test indicated a very superior intelligence and had also said that she was not surprised, because the sister even in babyhood had shown superior mental abilities: she talked at an exceptionally early age and had learned to read some words in the funny paper before she entered kindergarten.

This bright girl, however, had never learned to study. In grade school her marks were very poor and the same record continued through high school. She was a restless girl, unable to stick to anything and having difficulty beginning and finishing her work. Unlike many people of superior intelligence, she showed no special ability and had no hobby to which she devoted hours of concentrated effort.

When she really tried to learn something, she could learn it in less time than most of her girl friends; but she rarely tried.

On hearing that her I.Q. was 132, she felt puffed up and told one of her friends, "Oh! I can get all that stuff all right, if I'd only crack a book. I've got an I.Q. of 132." Maybe it was true that she could get her school work as easily as that, but she did not "crack a book."

What is this girl's problem?

What are her chances for the future?

Will she be likely to get down to business when she is fully grown up, say, at the age of twenty-two?

2. Arthur L—— also was a junior in high school, but his case was almost the reverse of the one just described. Arthur learned that his I.Q. was 95. He thought, "I knew I'd have about that. I always have to work hard for what I get." That was, indeed, true. All through the grades he had had to study a little longer than others in order to succeed. He also found it slow going to learn other things, like the operation of a bicycle sprocket, building a bird house, and so on.

But Arthur had a habit of sticking to a thing until it was finished. He never felt right about killing time before his work was done. He found school work difficult, but he made a pretty fair record as a rule. Sometimes he had D's, but at the end of the semester his average came around C plus. He had worked up a small newspaper business for which he hired three boys to peddle papers with him. Checking the papers and the money in and out went slowly for Arthur. Still, he did it with very few mistakes.

What are Arthur's chances for success in the future?

What is the quality that pulls him through?

3. Which is more promising, to have high intelligence and poor work habits, or to have low intelligence and good work habits? This question need not be thought of as referring to school work alone.

INDIVIDUAL ACTIVITIES

1. Rank yourself as to what you think your mental ability is as compared with the other members of your class. Write their names from best to worst, placing your own where you think it belongs. Check your list with the teacher's opinion of your rank in the class.

2. Similarly, rank yourself according to work habits and see how your opinion agrees with the teacher's.

3. Make a list of rules for yourself in order to insure the best use of your mental ability at the present time.

4. Measure your powers of concentration. Go to work with a watch or clock at hand. Check the time you really start to concentrate, and check when you find your mind wandering. Studies of this kind have been made, and they show that many people can concentrate only a very short time. After they have practiced, however, they are able to lengthen their periods of concentration.

READINGS

In Literature

NOVELS

Mitchell, Margaret. *Gone With the Wind*. Macmillan.

> An admirable picture of the end to which intelligence, unguided by love for others, can lead a woman. Scarlet O'Hara could gain money and material things, but in the long run she could not gain affection, respect, or happiness.

Walpole, Hugh. *Jeremy at Crale*. Macmillan.

> Intelligence and ability to learn from books do not always lead to respect from others and to positions of trust. Jeremy's school life shows how a boy who is slow finds a place of leadership in school life as well as in football.

SHORT STORY

Wilde, Oscar. "The Happy Prince"; in *The Happy Prince and Other Fairy Tales*. Doubleday, Doran.

> What is happiness? How do we gain it? There is no better answer than the way of the happy prince.

For Further Information

Bliss, Walton B. *Personality and School*, Chapter 24. Allyn and Bacon.

Law, Frederick Houk. *He Got the Job*, Chapter 1. Scribner.

McLean, Donald. *Knowing Yourself and Others*, Chapter 33. Holt.

MECHANICAL ABILITIES

Would you say that a person does not need brains to be clever with tools? Does a person need to be able to get along with people in order to be a good mechanic? Which came first in the history of the human race, tools or language? Why? Why is it good for everyone to do things with his hands?

Can you handle tools? Do you find yourself most content when you are working with tools and materials? Do you like to use hammer, saw, and plane? Do you like to work with chisels on a wood-turning lathe? Do you like to make the many adjustments on a machine lathe and master the shaping of hard metals? Do you like to build model airplanes? Do you find it satisfying and easy to become skillful with certain tools? If you do, you are probably mechanically inclined.

Or — to put these questions for one of the feminine sex — do you like to operate office machinery — the typewriter, the duplicator, the mimeograph, the adding machine, and the calculator? Do you like to try new recipes in the kitchen and make use of all the latest mechanical devices? Do you like to sew by hand? Do you like to use the sewing machine and its many attachments for various kinds of hems? Is it easy for you to rig up the machine to work for you as you want it to? Do you like to handle things, arrange them, finish and polish them, or demonstrate them? Do you find it satisfying and easy to become skillful with certain tools? If you do, you, too, are probably mechanically inclined.

What are mechanical abilities? As certain abilities are essentially mental, so others are essentially mechanical. Mechanical abilities have to do with handling things, including tools and materials, whereas mental abilities have to do with handling ideas. It should be repeated, however, that we do not have mechanical abilities to the exclusion of mental or social abilities. No human being is a robot with ability to do only one thing in life. Every personality is a complex mixture of abilities.

Examples of people who deal with ideas would include the civil engineer, who may spend most of his time with very difficult equations, formulas, and mathematical problems, and the historian, who may spend years carefully reading old newspapers, magazines, and books in order to find out what the historical trends were during a certain period. On the other hand, the cabinetmaker, who must be expert in working with tools, woods, metals, and finishes, and the dressmaker who must be adept with the needle, thread, scissors, and sewing machine, are examples of people who deal with things rather than ideas.

Most of us are mechanically inclined. Most people are by nature suited to tasks requiring mechanical abilities. Fortunately, there is a great need for mechanical ability in the modern world; in fact, it would seem that everyone not especially gifted socially or mentally can feel confident of developing some mechanical ability that can be used as a foundation for his life's work. Lincoln said that the Lord must have loved the common man since He made so many of them. The same might be said of those who are mechanically inclined, for there are more people who find their life's vocation in mechanical pursuits of one kind or another than in pursuits requiring predominantly mental or social abilities.

Make use of your special abilities. Jack R ——, a big, nineteen-year-old fellow in the twelfth grade, had been a great problem to his teachers in mathematics, English, science, and history. Even during his tenth semester in high school, he seriously doubted that he would graduate. If it had not been for the vocational subjects, he would never have remained to finish his high-school education. Whereas he received very low or failing marks in other subjects, he consistently had high marks in machine shop and auto mechanics. Of course, superior mechanical ability does not necessarily go with low intelligence (in fact, it generally goes with high intelligence), but this happened to be the case, more or less, with Jack.

On one occasion the principal, who had always looked forward to having Jack graduate from high school, called him in and asked him to do some repair work on his car. Jack stood and listened and said nothing. The principal continued to explain what was wrong with the car, and finally said, "Did you get that all right, Jack?" A look of vague puzzlement crept over Jack's face, and the principal began to explain all over again. The young man evidently had not understood much of what was said the first time.

As the principal repeated his explanation, Jack suddenly interrupted him and blurted out, "Just let me get my hands on it, Mr. Jones." The principal looked surprised, but handed him the keys. Half an hour later, having located the trouble and repaired it, Jack returned the keys. He had made use of his special abilities.

This same young man is now head mechanic in a garage, interested in his work, and drawing good wages. Of course, he still has trouble every time he has to fill out a report on repair jobs, and he will never go much farther until he develops more skill in the use of English and mathematics; but he did make the most of his abilities and found a useful place for himself. If he could only get his hands onto a motor, he would quickly know what to do with it and how to use the tools available. Fortunately for him, his interests and abilities came together in his vocation.

Your interests and abilities should go together. It is just as important to know what your mechanical abilities are as it is to know what your mental abilities are. Once a person has discovered his own superior abilities, whether they are mental, mechanical, or social, he can plan his future accordingly. In trying to find out more about your abilities, one important question to ask is, What am I especially interested in? As a rule, we develop ability in the work that interests us most. It is also true that we develop interest in the work that we can do well. Usually, both the interest and the ability go hand in hand, and when this is the case there is the best chance of happiness.

If your work, present or future, satisfies your main interest and calls into play your highest abilities, it is the right work for you. To know whether it does, or will, these three questions must be considered: (1) What are my strongest abilities? (2) What are

my greatest interests? (3) Do my interests and abilities go together? These questions will be studied further in Unit XI, Section 36.

You can become interested in the thing you do well. After a
careful study you may find that you have been interested in one
kind of work while your abilities indicate that you have a better
chance of success in another kind This was the case with Marian
T——, who was interested in typing, but found it very difficult to
hold a stenographic position. She liked to meet the people who
called at the office, but she did not enjoy taking dictation and
transcribing. Many of her letters had to be retyped because of
errors in punctuation and spelling, and frequently she had trouble
reading her own shorthand notes. Finally she decided that stenography was too difficult for her and she changed to a selling
position in a department store. Here she could use her ability to
meet people. She had more satisfying experiences and became
an excellent dress saleswoman, keenly interested in her work. As
Marian herself expressed it: "I wish I had gone into selling dresses
right away, but I had my heart set on stenography. I know now
I was wrong because I wasn't fast enough or accurate enough for
that. I'm much happier where I am." She had adjusted her interests to her abilities.

Some high-school students know definitely what their specific
interests and abilities are, and they are planning their education
and life accordingly. Others remain uncertain. There are a
number of reliable tests of ability and aptitude on the market.
Undoubtedly your school has some of these. You may be able
to arrange with your teacher to take one or more of these tests and
then discuss the results with him. If you want more information
about yourself, you should find out especially about your interests
and abilities. It will help you to plan your future on a safer
foundation.

FOR CLASS DISCUSSION

1. A master mason was once heard making the following statement:
"After all, it's the workers who make the world what it is. Brains

don't go far. Everything that really counts in the world today was made by fellows like me who know how to handle tools and do a neat job."

How far wrong, and how far right, was this master mason?

2. Some people say Henry Ford was a mechanical genius. Some say he was a mental giant. What do you think?

3. What do you think of the following argument: The first abilities shown by a child are mechanical abilities. As soon as he gets out of the cradle he does things with his hands. He plays with blocks and toys. A little later his parents buy him little tools — a shovel, a rake, a pail — the use of all of which requires mechanical ability. As an adult, no matter how superior he may be in mental or social pursuits, he must always spend some time regularly in mechanical work or play in order to be a well-balanced and happy person.

4. What would be more promising, to have mechanical ability, a plan for future work, and interest in it, or to have mental ability and no plan for the future?

READINGS
In Literature

NOVELS

Eliot, George. *Adam Bede.* Houghton Mifflin.

Adam, who is neither handsome nor brilliant, makes others happy, but his brother, who is both, brings unhappiness to others.

Other stories of especial interest to high-school students, and illustrating the importance of mechanical ability, among other things, are the following:

Gollomb, Joseph. *That Year at Lincoln High.* Macmillan.

Grey, Zane. *The Young Pitcher.* Harper.

Johnson, Owen. *The Tennessee Shad.* Little, Brown.
  The Varmint. Little, Brown.

Perry, Lawrence. *The Fullback.* Scribner.

PLAY

Shaw, George Bernard. *Pygmalion.* Dodd, Mead.

A hothouse experiment in character building that all will enjoy.

SHORT STORIES

A number of interesting stories describing mechanical abilities have been written by Ralph H. Barbour and William Heyliger. Your librarian may be able to help you to select suitable titles.

For Further Information

Fedder, Ruth. *A Girl Grows Up,* pp. 190-192. McGraw-Hill.
Law, Frederick Houk. *He Got the Job,* Chapter 1. Scribner.

SOCIAL ABILITIES

How far do you think a good mechanic or typist could go in his work if he were not able to get along with people? In what way is being sensitive valuable? Does a hermit need social ability? Why? Does a doctor?

THERE IS A VERY DEFINITE cause and effect relationship that runs through all human behavior. A person who has great social ability both understands it and knows how to use his understanding in dealing with people. Everything we do, from the most important step we take to the simplest unnoticed action, is an effect which has a cause or a group of causes. Thus, a human being eats because he is hungry, but he can also eat because he is lonely or nervous or has a stomach ulcer, or simply because he is in the habit of eating at a certain time. In every case there are one or more causes for the behavior called eating. Yet how little we know about the causes of human actions! Civilization has gone ahead much faster in other sciences than it has in the science of human behavior.

A good many things we do might be understood readily were it not for the fact that we have not been trained to understand them as we have from childhood been trained in reasoning, say, or in arithmetic.

What is social ability? We have already seen that mental ability is the ability to reason and use ideas and that mechanical ability is the ability to manipulate tools. What is social ability? It includes the ability (1) to sense the feelings and desires of others; (2) to react toward them with due regard for their feelings and desires; and (3) to feel friendly toward them — to like them.

1. *The ability to sense the wants of others.* Even without consciously realizing it, you reason from effect to cause in a thousand little actions. You use your knowledge of the logic of human behavior to interpret the actions of others. If a certain person is restless and turns his glance away while you are talking to him, you sense that he is not interested, that he feels bored and wants something else. If he is timid and self-conscious, you sense that some feeling of inferiority causes him to be afraid to speak freely. A person who has a good deal of social ability must be keenly sensitive to the feelings and desires of others. But sensitiveness alone is not social ability.

2. *The ability to react in relation to others' wants.* Many people are able to understand others, but are unable to react to them in their favor. For instance, a man may sense that the person he is talking to is not interested in what he has to say, but instead of cutting the story short or changing the subject, he may try all the harder to arouse interest by sheer force — speaking more loudly, using stronger words, making emphatic gestures, or taking hold of the other person's arm. He is not able to react to the other person in terms of that person's desires and feelings. If you have a good deal of social ability, you can talk to people who want to listen and listen to people who want to talk. You can be formal among those who like formality and rough and ready among those who like a more carefree manner. In other words, you are able to suit your actions and manners to the desires and feelings of others.

3. *The ability to like people.* Before you can put yourself in the other fellow's place and sense what his feelings are, you have to identify yourself with him — more or less — to feel as if his feelings are your own. And this is a matter of having had somewhat the same feelings yourself on some occasion, so that you can sympathize with him. Before you can react to him in such a way that you take his feelings and wants into account, you have to respect him as a human being — all human beings are entitled to some respect — and if possible, actually like him.

If you are telling your favorite story while the gang is eager to get started on a trip, you have to understand and respect them as individuals in order to sense their impatience and stop your story to please them instead of yourself. You have to like people in general — not necessarily every individual you meet — in order to feel their feelings, be willing to concede to their wants, and act accordingly. If you like people in general, you are willing to meet almost anyone at least halfway.

Everyone needs social ability. Life forces us to deal with people — the grocer, the butcher, teachers, fellow students, fellow workers, and so on — whether we like to or not. A person may have good reason to believe that his strongest abilities are mechanical or mental rather than social, but he cannot escape some contacts with people, and these contacts require social ability. A person who is sensitive to the wants of others, able to respond accordingly, and friendly in his attitude and manner, manages most of these contacts smoothly. One with little or no social ability has difficulty and unhappiness in the everyday social relations of life. Developing your social ability, therefore, is a necessary part of growing up.

You can develop social ability. In childhood, before you were aware of it, you were developing social habits. They became part of your personality, growing up with you like all the rest of yourself. You did not know it, but you were learning by imitating your parents, brothers, sisters, and friends, and now, at high-school age, it is second nature to you to like or dislike your fellows, to understand them and react toward them in certain ways. As time goes on, you can replace poor habits with good ones and further develop the good habits you already have. By trying day after day, year after year, many people replace old habits of fear, suspicion, and fault-finding, with those of trust, friendliness, and understanding. By constant conscious effort you can develop your ability to like people, to sense what their actions mean, and to react favorably in relation to their wants.

Reacting favorably shows acceptance. Everything we do in dealing with others reflects either that we accept them or reject them. If we show friendliness, make others feel at ease, feel confident in their presence, and respect them, we are showing that we accept them, or at least are not hostile. In some cases, where an individual's faults are particularly glaring, it might seem that

"*Don't be surprised if there are big things in store for you, dear. I told your boss all about how you think the business is so stupidly managed.*"

HINTS FOR DISCUSSING THE CARTOON

What could have been this young lady's reason for telling her husband's employer about the mismanagement of the business? Do you think her social ability will be a help to her husband? Why? Would you say she is a good listener? How will the incident pictured here be likely to influence the husband's "shop talk" hereafter?

we should reject him. On closer study, however, we know that everyone has virtues as well as faults and that both are caused by circumstances which the individual may not have been able to change. Once you fully understand the reasons behind someone's actions, you have the reasons to forgive, overlook his mistakes, and accept him. Oftentimes we wonder why a person has not more shortcomings when we understand the unfavorable circumstances at the root of those he has.

People who are effective in their social relations are able to accept as they are those with whom they associate, without faultfinding. They understand why their associates behave the way they do, and with this understanding they can help them to do their best.

Reacting favorably inspires others with self-confidence. Everyone has a strong desire for self-preservation. We want to feel safe, whether we are in an airplane, in a ship on the ocean, or in a social group in the living room at home. We want to feel secure, and anything or anybody that threatens us with danger is fought off or shunned. In human relations danger threatens when someone laughs at you instead of with you, or looks inquiringly at your clothes, or slights, scorns, ignores, criticizes, or disagrees with you, or makes you feel that he does not like you — in general, when someone makes you feel uncomfortable or unsafe.

People want to feel safe with you; they want to feel confident that no harm, even the slightest, will come to them through you. When you laugh with them, look approvingly at their clothes, pay attention to them, agree with them, seem to consider their opinions interesting, and in fact appear to like them, they get a feeling of self-confidence and safety when they are with you. Then you are in a position to give them cooperation and obtain it from them, and your social relations with them will be effective.

Some people can inspire just such confidence. This ability is needed in all successful careers that depend upon contact with many people, and it can be developed by constant, conscious effort. It depends upon adjusting your own desires to the other fellow's in all your dealings with people.

Reacting favorably is often face-saving for the other fellow. Miss Jones, a Latin teacher, showed a good deal of social ability in handling the case of Art B——'s cheating. Art was a well-liked sophomore in high school, but during a monthly test he was copying the conjugations of *amo* from a slip of paper kept up his sleeve. When Miss Jones saw what he was doing, she wrote a note and, unnoticed by the class as a whole, quietly placed it on his desk. It read, "Draw a line across your paper and I'll give you full credit for the rest of the examination." Art read the note and after a few minutes of thought drew a line across his paper and resumed his writing. Miss Jones had saved his face; she had saved his reputation in that classroom by handling the incident quietly. Furthermore, she trusted him to go on with the examination honestly. All was not lost.

Later that day, in a private conference, she told the boy: "I know you didn't do that because you're dishonest. Everybody does the wrong thing occasionally, but that doesn't mean that everybody is all wrong at heart. You're not the only one in this school, Art, that gets behind in his work and then has to try something in order to get by. It's really easier in the long run to get through by studying regularly."

When Art left the room, he did not feel that he was the meanest boy in school and had made a mistake no one else had made. Miss Jones had saved his opinion of himself, and instead of feeling that his case was hopeless, he felt that he could correct what was wrong. Miss Jones never paid especial attention to him after this incident, but she knew from his daily work thereafter that he did not have to cheat during tests.

To be able to react to others in such a way as to give them a chance to save their faces when a mistake is made, as Miss Jones did in this case, is a social ability of great importance.

You should react in terms of the other fellow. Some people are keenly sensitive to the feelings and desires of others, but they do not have much social ability because they tend to react constantly in terms of their own feelings and desires. A person may sense, for example, from the slightest indication, that his presence is not wanted in a certain group. His understanding may be correct. But he may react in terms of himself and remain or try to force himself upon the group. People who are sensitive and easily hurt may understand the feelings of others, but they are not able to satisfy others' wants in preference to their own. It is natural that the desires of individuals should frequently conflict. The socially able person can fit his own wants to those of the group or of another individual.

People are sometimes criticized for being too sensitive. It is not harmful to be sensitive, provided our reactions are unselfish. The socially able person is extremely sensitive, but he is not irritated, annoyed, or hurt when another's wants run counter to his own.

FOR CLASS DISCUSSION

1. Marilyn M—— had just arrived in Centerville, where her father had secured employment. She was a complete stranger in town. Soon after arriving, however, she became acquainted with Alma, who lived next door and who was a well-known member of the senior class in high school. During her first visit with Alma, Marilyn let her know that she was a good violinist and had frequently played in public; that she loved dancing; that she had a large number of friends, and boy friends, too, back in Big Town; that she had two other sweaters as good as or better than the one she was wearing at present; and gave a lot of other similar details about herself.

Why did Marilyn tell these things about herself?

Supposing Alma has a good deal of social ability, how did she react to Marilyn's remarks?

Suppose Marilyn acquires a number of friends, how will her behavior be likely to change?

2. Who could go farther in developing his social ability, a sensitive and irritable person or a congenial and stupid one? Why?

3. If the persons referred to in (2) are both sixteen years old, which of them has more social ability? Which if they both are sixty years old?

INDIVIDUAL ACTIVITIES

1. For one day keep a record of the instances when your wishes differed from those of the people you were with. Then check the list to see whose wishes were followed, yours or theirs.

2. On the following day make an effort to study the wishes of others and satisfy them before your own, if possible. Activities like this one,

---

if carried on day after day, will have a remarkably favorable effect upon your social ability.

3. Study the people with whom you come in contact, whether you like them or not, to see what reasons there might be for you to feel friendly toward them. Once you feel friendly toward a person, it is easier for you to understand his feelings and act accordingly.

READINGS

In Literature

ESSAYS

Baker, Ray S. *Adventures of David Grayson.* Doubleday, Doran.
Would you like to be a man with many friends? These essays describe how David Grayson became such a man.

SHORT STORIES

Canfield, Dorothy. "The Heyday of the Blood"; in *Hillsboro People.* Holt.
Grandpa shows a young man how to enjoy life.

For Further Information

Morgan, John J. B. *Keeping a Sound Mind,* pp. 394-412. Macmillan.

Trilling, Mabel B., and Nicholas, Florence W. *The Girl and Her Home,* Problem 1. Houghton Mifflin.

Webb, Ewing T., and Morgan, John B. *Strategy in Handling People,* Chapter 3. Garden City.

Wright, Milton. *Getting Along with People,* Chapter 6. McGraw-Hill.

❧ UNIT IV ❧

Kidding Ourselves Along

EARLIER IN THIS BOOK we saw that the master drives — the desire to live, to love, to excel, to be with people, to believe in something — all lead to problems, each of which requires a struggle of some kind, slight or great. Failure to solve these problems causes persistent dissatisfaction and unhappiness. There are right and wrong ways to go about their solution. Looking at the problems of life with an open mind and struggling to solve them in a forthright, direct way usually brings success and happiness. Going at them in a roundabout, indirect way is likely to bring failure and unhappiness.

Either of these two approaches can become a habit. A habit is an often repeated way of meeting a frequently recurring problem. To give a simple illustration: Most adults, while dressing, always put on the same shoe first; they have met the problem of putting on their shoes so often that they have become habituated to solving it in the same way every time. This occurs with complex problems as well as with simple ones. Such habits are called mechanisms. In this unit we shall learn more about the habits, or mechanisms, that people use to meet problems that come up in everyday living. Many of these mechanisms, we shall see, are roundabout ways of meeting problems; they are self-deceptive. Much of the time we just kid ourselves along.

FACING INFERIORITY

Can you think of someone who feels inferior because he cannot get along with people? Does everyone feel inferior about something? Is it helpful or harmful to know what your inferiority is? What can you do to overcome an inferiority?

SOME PSYCHOLOGISTS maintain that all behavior should be studied in the light of a feeling of inferiority and the desire for power that follows. They argue that everyone feels inferior about something — shortness of stature, poor health, lack of a brilliant mind, color of hair, shape of teeth, and so on; and, in order to make up or compensate for his inferiority, he tries to excel in something. The will to power springs from a feeling of inferiority, according to this theory, and if behavior is to be fully understood, it should be studied in relation to the inferiority at the root of it.

Actions may reflect inferiority feelings. People may not know what they feel inferior about, and they may not even admit that they have a feeling of inferiority; but their actions reveal it. The story is frequently told of three children who were taken to the zoo for the first time. They had never seen a lion before, and as they approached the cage, they heard it growl and saw it snarl. One of the children buried his head in his mother's skirts and cried; another trembled all over and said, "I'm not afraid of you." The third child glared at the lion, stamped his foot, and said, "Mother, shall I spit at it?" Naturally, all three children felt inferior to the lion, but they reflected their feelings in different ways. The first child admitted it to himself as well as to others. The second tried to deny it by using words that meant just the opposite, and the third covered up his inferiority with actions supposed to make him look superior to the lion. Whether the story is true or not, it illustrates three typical ways of meeting a sense of inferiority.

The sense of inferiority begins in childhood. It is said that a child has feelings of inferiority long before he is consciously aware of the fact. As a newborn infant, everything is done for him, and he does very little striving to gratify his own desires. Soon, however, he begins to want things and occasionally his wants are not fulfilled; or he wants to do things and finds that he is not able to do them. As he grows up, he is confronted with many disappointments that arise from his own inability. Later, comparing himself with others, he frequently finds that he is inferior to them in various ways. This experience is common to everyone, and normally we learn to make the best of our abilities, thus overcoming the feelings of inferiority that would otherwise persist. Not all feelings of inferiority begin in childhood, of course. For example, a long series of failures at any time in life may lead to such a feeling.

What is an inferiority "complex"? A person who continually has a feeling of fear and timidity about everything he undertakes, and who does not feel up to the tasks of life, is sometimes said to have a general inferiority complex. He is afraid to begin anything for fear he will fail in it. In his development there may have been a time when he failed in one very important task or in a number of tasks, and, consequently, he became afraid to tackle new tasks for fear that he would fail in them also.

In a more correct use of the term, however, the inferiority complex governs only a particular kind of activity. In this sense an inferiority complex indicates that a person is afraid to tackle a certain activity. He is convinced that he is unable to manage it and has given up trying to do so.

Case One. This was the case with Mary B——, a very bright girl who received high marks in everything but Latin when she started high school. In Latin she passed with a D, which was as bad as a failing mark to her, and she decided never to take Latin again. Despite the advice of the dean of girls, she would not elect it in her junior year. She did take it in her senior year, however, because she knew she needed two years of Latin to enter college. Mary entered the class with a keen feeling of inadequacy. She was almost sure she could not carry the subject successfully, but, thanks to the help of her parents and the Latin teacher, she was encouraged from day to day for every minor success in translating, vocabulary work, and pronunciation. She received a C at the end of the first marking period, a B the next time, A's the rest of the year; and at the end of the year she smilingly told the principal that she had had an inferiority complex about Latin. For two years at least she had been convinced that Latin presented problems she could not meet successfully. She had been kidding herself along.

Case Two. Dick R—— had an inferiority complex about dancing. As a junior in high school he refused to go to any of the school dances, speaking of boys who danced as "dance-hall spoonies." He called dancing a "sissy sport." Dick was popular except for the fact that he never entered into any mixed social affairs. The thought of seeing a girl home frightened him. During his senior year he developed a warm friendship with Mr. B——, his adviser. Two weeks before the Senior Prom, Mr. B—— casually asked, "Aren't you going to the Prom, Dick?" Then Dick made his usual sarcastic remarks about dances. Mr. B—— managed to draw him out, and during the next half-hour Dick told his adviser what he had never discussed with anyone before.

During the summer vacation of his sophomore year he had been out of town and had taken a few dancing lessons. Soon after, in company with one or two people, he had attended a dance. That evening he had asked five different girls for a dance and had been refused by each one. Every one of these five experiences was to him not only a keen humiliation but a serious defeat, and he decided then and there that he would never go to another dance. His first experience had been so unsatisfactory that it had left him with an inferiority complex about dancing.

Dick hardly realized at the time how valuable this discussion was for himself, but it so happened that he attended a small private party shortly before the Prom, and, when the rug was rolled back and the radio turned on, instead of sitting out all dances as he had previously done, he once more asked a girl for a dance. This time he was not refused. Dick was by no means a graceful dancer, for it takes practice to become one, but he danced several times that evening and went home with a different feeling about his ability to dance. The following week he was at the Senior Prom. He had overcome his inferiority complex by once more tackling his problem and trying to solve it honestly. When he tackled the problem, he stopped kidding himself about dancing.

The hidden ones are the damaging ones. Inferiority feelings that are not understood, that cannot be traced back to their beginnings, are the most difficult to contend with. People who have an inferiority of this kind are usually timid, not only in their social activities, but also in all the things they do. They are afraid to go ahead and take a chance at failure. Even a simple task seems difficult, for they are afraid they will meet another defeat.

Fortunately, such cases of inferiority are rare, for the most timid people do some things very well. A person may have had unsatisfactory experiences socially, but may develop some other ability or succeed in some work, such as bookkeeping, that does not require a great deal of social contact. Of course, it would be better to overcome the inferiority if possible, because it interferes with behavior that might be successful. There is no reason to believe, for instance, that a person who is timid about meeting people cannot develop the ability to meet them, or that one who feels inferior about his selling ability cannot become a good salesman. If there is no physical or mental defect, success can be achieved by constant, conscious effort.

What to do about inferiority feelings. From the foregoing discussion a few suggestions may be summarized:

1. *Face the facts.* You need not be afraid to admit that you have an inferiority in one respect or another. Everyone has inferiorities. You cannot begin to do something about your weakness until you have studied it and have removed your fear regarding it.

2. *Work hard and try again.* You may be able to overcome your inferiority by hard work and constant effort. If you have a keen desire to excel in some activity in which your inferiority

might be a hindrance, first make sure that the inferiority is not so severe as to spell certain failure. Then set yourself with will and diligence to the task of making a strength out of a weakness.

3. *Do not blame yourself.* More than likely, you have been entirely helpless so far as the origin of your inferiority is concerned, and you should feel no sense of blame about it.

4. *Devote yourself to some other activity.* If your weakness really stands in the way of your success, do not hesitate to try for success in another field. For example, if you are sure that your mental ability is not keen enough for you to succeed in professional work, take up some other work in which you will have a fair chance of success.

What is compensation? The effort to get a substitute for an inferiority is called compensation.

Case One. Alice B—— was well aware that she had a very large nose and would never be beautiful, but from childhood she made up for this inferiority by friendliness and neatness. As a result, she came to be one of the most popular girls in high school. She excelled in social affairs, where she had a fair chance of success; but, of course, she would never enter a beauty contest, where she was bound to fail.

Case Two. Arthur C—— studied as faithfully as most students, but he was not able to get more than a C in his school work, so he took up athletics and became one of the most valuable players in both football and basketball. He excelled in athletics, where he had a fair chance of success; but with only an average mental ability it was impossible for him to excel in scholarship.

Case Three. Harlan L—— was one of the shortest boys in his class, well built for his size, but too small for varsity athletics. He enjoyed athletics very much, however, and wished to excel in something. When his gymnasium teacher organized a tumbling team, Harlan quickly realized that he could excel all others in this sport because his size was an advantage. He actually did become the star tumbler on the team.

Case Four. James N—— was truly a physical weakling, thin, pale, and unable to stand much exercise. He attended gym classes, but never did well in any athletic sport. He was blessed with a good mind, however, and at an early age developed good study habits. School work came easy to him, and he ranked as one of the ablest students in his class.

There are, of course, innumerable ways of compensating, some good and some bad. The illustrations given are all good compensations. In each case a conscious effort was made to develop an ability in which there was fair chance of success.

Glen Cunningham. In rare instances it is possible, by exercise and special attention, to correct a serious inferiority. A famous case of such compensation is that of Glen Cunningham, the great track star, who in childhood had infantile paralysis, yet through careful attention and a great deal of practice became one of the country's greatest milers. He excelled in an activity where his inferiority would have been a serious handicap if he had not been able to compensate for it.

Demosthenes, the Lisper. Another illustration frequently given is that of Demosthenes, who as a child lisped and stuttered, yet had an overpowering desire to become an orator. As the story goes, Demosthenes would go to the seashore, put two or three pebbles in his mouth, and practice pronouncing words and then saying lines, sentences, and finally paragraphs with only the rolling waves for an audience. His theory is said to have been that by practicing with increased handicaps and overcoming them he would be the more able to speak effectively before an audience when the pebbles were not in his mouth to interfere with his pronunciation. Eventually he became one of the greatest orators of his day.

These illustrations are two of the few exceptions recorded in history in which major handicaps were directly overcome. Only with the will and diligence of a genius can such serious physical handicaps as these men had be overcome directly. So far as the rest of us are concerned, we should strive for our compensations in fields more promising of success.

Compensate in your special talent. Illustrations of good compensation for a real weakness could be multiplied. They will show conscious rather than unconscious effort, and a great deal of it. In most instances a successful compensation involves turning to an activity in which the inferiority would not be a hindrance. This was the case with the four students mentioned. Glen Cun-

ningham and Demosthenes had to remove their inferiority before
they made a successful compensation. As a rule, in cases where
there is a real inferiority, it is unwise to try for excellence if the
inferiority would be a hindrance.

Such a mistake was made by Margaret L——, who, because of
infantile paralysis, was not able to control the heel of her left
foot. Margaret became so intensely aware of her inferiority that
she spent a good deal of time reading about ballet and toe
dancers and attended as many dance revues as came to her city
or neighboring cities. She soon wished to become a toe dancer
herself and began to take lessons, even though, as the instructor
informed her parents, Margaret hadn't a chance in the world to
become a toe dancer. Although the hours of practice actually
helped her control of the handicapped foot, she was finally forced
to admit to herself that toe dancing offered her no chance of success and that her efforts had led to failure. As soon as she admitted the facts, she was ready to stop kidding herself along. It
took Margaret a long time to recover from the defeat, but finally
she did so by making a good compensation. She took up the
violin and became an excellent player.

What is a superiority complex? The expression *superiority
complex* is an incorrect one, even though it is frequently used to
describe persons who seem conceited. In reality, a person who
has a so-called superiority complex has an inferiority complex
which he is hiding from himself and others. He, too, is kidding
himself along, trying to compensate for his feeling of inferiority.
In his mind there is a conflict going on which might be described
in a particular case as follows: "I know that I am inferior, especially in mental ability, for my school work has always been very
poor, but I want to cover it up, even from myself. I am very
confident of myself in everything I do. I am afraid of nothing
and no one, and I can walk around with my chin up. I really
am a little better than everyone around me." Of course, the individual would not be aware of this conflict, for he is unconsciously
making up for an inferiority. One of his purposes is to keep himself guessing. We are generally annoyed by such people, but we
should feel sorry for them because their behavior is symptomatic
of a feeling of weakness which they are trying to hide or forget.

A conceited person does not know he is conceited. It is a peculiar fact about people who seem conceited that if someone tells them so they are surprised if not angry. They usually do not know that they give that impression. In all seriousness they may ask "What do I do that makes people think I'm conceited?"

How does conceit show itself? Although they are not aware of it, conceited people frequently have a swagger to their gait, talk with an air of overconfidence and certainty, do most of the talking and least of the listening, are first in line, gossip or speak sarcastically of their fellows, especially those who are their betters, ignore people who are superior to them in some respect, and make a big show of the few things they do accomplish. The attitude of conceit or superiority is, of course, an incorrect form of compensation for a basic feeling of inferiority.

Unfair competition. Feelings of inferiority may lead to extreme forms of competition for superiority. A girl may have such a keen feeling of inferiority about her appearance that she has an equally keen desire to win in a race for graduation honors. She may be unkind, impolite, discourteous, and even dishonest with her competitors. She is not making a good compensation for the inferiority feeling that hurts. She has not studied her problem, faced the facts, nor done anything about the inferiority itself. If she does win the honors for which she is fighting so hard and so unfairly, her inferiority is still there. She will still have to face it or find another indirect way of compensating for it.

Rivalry. Feelings of inferiority may lead to the extreme competition known as rivalry, which is often damaging to the personality. Rivalry between students is common throughout the high-school years, and it is also very common between young people in the same family. Perhaps one reason for this is that an older child has a superiority over a younger one because he is bigger, stronger, and better able to get around. Again, one child may get more of his parents' attention than another child. In either case the difference may lead to an inferiority feeling and rivalry as a means of compensation.

Jealousy. Jealousy is usually associated with a feeling of inferiority, whether it occurs in childhood, youth, or adulthood. It frequently leads to unconscious compensations. One high-school student may be jealous of another who has been selected for the cast of the senior play or who has received higher marks. Jealousies may occur over a bid to the Prom, a date for a party, a school honor, a girl friend, a boy friend, or any number of things. At the root of all jealousy you can easily find some feeling of inferiority and an effort to compensate for it. If a person were to face the facts, admit his inferiority, and try for something else in which he could succeed, it would be easier for him to accept his loss and avoid being jealous.

Compensation is sometimes very unpopular. Occasionally inferiority feelings lead people to compensations of an extremely unsocial nature. Rejected at home and at school by parents, teachers, and fellow students, they compensate by calling attention to themselves. They will be the bad boys or the bad girls of the school. It is as if they reason thus: "Nobody loves me; therefore I am very inferior and do not excel in normal behavior, but I certainly can make up for it in other ways. I can call attention to myself and show everybody that they have to take notice of me. I'll raise enough Cain to make everybody know I'm here. They don't want to show me any attention, but I'll show them they have to." Such persons have not tackled their problem face to face and are really kidding themselves along. The consequences can be serious if they continue the habit into adulthood and become real social problems.

Don't call attention to others' inferiorities. If you want to make a good impression on someone, you will study his superiorities and not only regard him highly for the best that is in him, but also avoid making any statements that will cause him to feel inferior. Everyone has a strong desire to be superior. Help him to feel that he is on his way.

FOR CLASS DISCUSSION

1. Helen is fond of her girl friend, Jane, but she often speaks slightingly about Jane's dates. She never approves of Jane's boy friends. Helen rarely has a date herself, but she says that is because she does not care about boys.

In what way is Helen kidding herself along?

Why does she disapprove of Jane's boy friends?

What could Helen do that would change her actions toward Jane?

2. Lillian, a junior in high school, is 5 feet 1 inch tall and weighs 170 pounds. She dresses carelessly, has few friends, and spends hours after school sitting at soda fountains or in restaurants in an attitude of nonchalance, munching peanuts and smoking cigarettes.

What is Lillian's problem?

What suggestions would you make to her if she sincerely asked your help?

What could you do if she said, as her attitude shows, that she doesn't need any help?

3. Ruth lives in a village ten miles from a large city. She rides the bus to and from school with students from her own community and is well liked by them. She is a good scholar and is vice-president of her class. Yet she often complains that city girls snub her, that they have their own cliques and are not friendly to rural students. She maintains, moreover, that rural students often take most of the scholastic honors. When her mother tells her to be friendly to her city classmates, she says, "What's the use? They don't want to be friendly anyway."

What is Ruth's problem?

What can she do about it?

INDIVIDUAL ACTIVITIES

1. Make a list of the things that make you feel inferior and check this list with your teacher in order to get his help in understanding yourself more fully.

2. Decide on some plan to compensate for an inferiority and follow the plan until you really have made up for the inferiority.

WHERE DO I STAND?

On the lines provided below, place marks above the words "none," "one," "few," and so on, according to your most careful opinion about yourself. Then connect these marks with a zigzag line from the first to the second to the third, and so on to the last. If you are not satisfied with the resulting diagram, make a plan for changing the characteristics you do not like in yourself, during the next few months.

(NOTE. *Do not write in this book,* unless it is your own. Make a copy on a separate sheet of paper.)

1. I do have feelings of inferiority.	none	one	few	many	I don't know
2. I know why I feel inferior.	always	often	rarely	never	I don't know
3. I know how these feelings began.	always	often	rarely	never	I don't know
4. I study them and face the facts.	always	often	rarely	never	I don't know
5. I have plans for removing or compensating inferiorities.	always	often	rarely	never	I don't know
6. In case of failure I work hard and try again.	always	often	rarely	never	I don't know
7. In case the inferiority cannot be changed, I try to succeed otherwise.	always	often	rarely	never	I don't know
8. I feel ashamed about my inferiorities.	never	rarely	often	always	I don't know
9. I am conceited.	never	rarely	often	always	I don't know
10. I am rivalrous.	never	rarely	often	always	I don't know
11. I make other people feel inferior.	never	rarely	often	always	I don't know

READINGS

In Literature

NOVEL

Eliot, George. *Mill on the Floss.* Houghton Mifflin.
There were four men in Maggy's life.

ONE-ACT PLAYS

Barrie, James. "What Every Woman Knows"; in *The Plays of J. M. Barrie.* Scribner.
Would you marry a woman who was ugly in appearance but fine in disposition?
Gregory, Lady. "Spreading the News"; in *Seven Short Plays.* Putnam.
Gossip could lead to murder.

SHORT STORY

Steele, Wilbur Daniel. "Footfalls"; in *Tower of Sand.* Harper.
Blind, and murder going on in the house!

TRUE EXPERIENCES

Seabrook, William. *Asylum.* Harcourt, Brace.
A drunkard who wishes to overcome his habit of drinking enters an insane asylum voluntarily. It is an interesting book.

For Further Information

Link, Henry C. *The Return to Religion,* pp. 130-131. Macmillan.
McLean, Donald. *Knowing Yourself and Others,* pp. 250-256. Holt.
Morgan, John J. B. *Keeping a Sound Mind,* Chapter 8. Macmillan.
Wright, Milton. *Getting Along with People,* Chapter 17. McGraw-Hill.

BEATING AROUND THE BUSH

Why are your day-dreams usually pleasant? How could inferiority lead to dishonesty? Would an honest person be dishonest with himself? Have you ever been mean to someone without a good reason? Do you think it is possible to forget anything you really want to remember? Does everyone like to grow up?

IT IS NOT ALWAYS WRONG to beat around the bush. In hunting birds, for instance, it is necessary to do so. Unless a hunter has a trained dog for this purpose, he must do it himself, or the birds will not rise and he cannot get a shot. A hunter's problem is to flush the game so that he may have a fair shot at it. He solves the problem by beating around the bush where game takes cover.

In daily life, however, we usually disapprove of this method of solving problems. When a person has something to say, we want him to come to the point; we do not like to have him talk all around the subject and miss the point or leave his main idea confused in our minds. We do not like to have him beat around the bush.

People often try to solve their personal problems by beating around the bush instead of going right to the point. They often dodge the truth by refusing to take a look at it. You may recall the case of Dick R——, referred to in the previous section. The mechanism Dick used to meet his problem of inferiority is called rationalization, and it will be explained later in this section. He felt inferior about dancing, and, instead of admitting that he had not made a success of his first try at it, he made believe that he

*"But, Mom, if I scoop a path clear out to the garage,
it will only spoil the beauty of it all!"*

despised dancing. He also forced himself to forget the embarrassing incident. Later, with the understanding help of an older person, he called it to mind, faced the fact, studied it honestly, and gave dancing another try. Then he solved his problem, not before.

What is self-deception? When we try to solve our personal problems by beating around the bush, we are kidding ourselves along. We are practicing self-deception. Usually we do not know that we are doing it, but it goes on deep under the surface of our conscious life. Dick R——, for instance, did not at first know that he was deceiving himself. And yet beneath the surface of his consciousness he must have had an argument with himself that ran something like this: "I feel extremely embarrassed because I failed at dancing. I hate to think of it because, instead of becoming a good dancer and getting all the dances I want, I turned out to be clumsy on my feet and unable to get a partner. Dancing makes me feel much less important than I'd like to be. I certainly don't want the other fellows to know how I failed and how I feel, and I don't want to think about it myself, either. Let me cover it up by saying that dancing is a sissy sport. If I can concentrate on this I don't have to admit to myself or to them that I failed, because anybody who despises something just naturally wouldn't be expected to take it up."

We deceive ourselves when we let ourselves believe something that is not true in order to avoid an unpleasant truth. We kid ourselves along by dodging the issue, by avoiding a full-face view of our problem, by beating around the bush.

Six of the most common ways of beating around the bush are explained in the following pages. All of us occasionally use these ways of solving our problems, so there is nothing to be ashamed of in them. Only when we understand them fully can we begin to eliminate them and get the habit of facing problems squarely and solving them directly. Even so, probably no human being ever completely gets over beating around the bush in one way or another at one time or another.

1. BUILDING CASTLES IN THE AIR

Escaping in a day-dream. Some people meet the difficulties of life by not meeting them — by running away from them, by escaping them. Day-dreaming is a common form of escape from the realities of life, though not all day-dreaming is necessarily an escape. As a matter of fact, many people permit their minds to wander off into dreams about future actions and then follow these dreams with work. Day-dreaming that is not followed by purposeful action is of little value at best, and if it is a way of escaping from the problems of life, it is an unhealthful mechanism.

Arthur N—— was a high-school student of average mentality who found it fairly difficult to do good work in school. He did not enjoy studying, nor was he able to buckle down to it for the sake of a successful vocation in the future. He was interested in sports; they came easy to him and he had a good physique. But he did not solve this problem any more directly than he did that of his school work; his coach found him somewhat lazy, sometimes late, sometimes absent, and generally uninterested in steady routine periods of practice. The fact is that Arthur preferred to become an imaginary athlete rather than a real one. He could spend hours day-dreaming, picturing himself as the hero of the day, leading all others in competition, bowing and smiling to the spectators and receiving applause. Of course he was simply escaping from reality.

Day-dreaming, as a form of thinking, is largely uncontrolled. You can day-dream about the past or the future, about possible things or impossible things; you can day-dream usefully or uselessly. You day-dream about things you want to day-dream about.

Day-dreams may keep you on your course. If you are having a hard time of it now, but your present work is a necessary preparation for the future, occasional day-dreams about that future may give you heart to carry on today.

Day-dreams may lead to new ideas. Edison conceived of inventions while he allowed his mind to follow its own bent in day-dreams. In a day-dream the mind is less controlled than in conscious thought. You never know what idea may come into your mind when it is free to follow an uncontrolled course.

Useful day-dreams have to do with possibilities. It is of little use to dream that someone gives you a million dollars and you are spending it for all the things you want. Such a dream really means that life is too full of refusals and failures for you to meet it and work for what you want. You turn away from the real world of hard work to the unreal world of dreams in which you have only to wish for something and the wish is fulfilled.

Useful day-dreams have to do with the future. It is also of little use to dream of the past. You may have had an easier life some time ago and you find it pleasant to dream about those good old days. This dream also means that you find the present too difficult and unpleasant and want to get away from it rather than make the most of it by hard work and renewed effort.

Day-dreams should not keep you from duty. The boy who whiles his study hours away dreaming about last night's date is not doing the work that must be done. Day-dreams are common in most people's lives, but duty comes first. People learn to control their wandering minds and "snap out of it" when their dreaming interferes with real life.

Even if your day-dreams are full of good plans and closely related to life, you cannot afford to let yourself dream too much. In time people lapse into day-dreaming as a habit unless they exercise conscious control. They should forcibly pay attention to the present and engage in active work when they find that day-dreaming keeps them from meeting their responsibilities.

Follow your day-dreams with work. It is a good plan to carry into practice as soon as possible any new thought that has come to you in a day-dream. By doing this you are emphasizing the importance of reality. It is as if you were saying, "Day-dreaming has value only if it works in real life."

Hard work after a day-dream also tends to cancel the desire to escape from life. If you do not do anything to curb the wandering of your mind, it may become easier to live in a dream world than in the real world.

READINGS

In Literature

NOVEL

Wells, H. G. *The History of Mr. Polly.* Dodd, Mead.

>He thought arson and suicide would be a good escape from his financial and home troubles. Strangely enough, this is not a gruesome story, but one full of delightful humor.

PLAY

Barrie, James. "Alice-Sit-by-the-Fire"; in *The Plays of J. M. Barrie.* Scribner.

>A mother teaches her day-dreaming daughter the realities of love.

SHORT STORY

Knight, Eric. "Flying Yorkshireman"; in *Flying Yorkshireman; Novellas by E. Knight and Others*. Harper.

A man's strange escape mechanism becomes a sensation of the year.

For Further Information

Eastburn, L. A., Kelley, V. H., and Falk, C. J. *Planning Your Life for School and Society*, pp. 50-51. Scribner.

McLean, Donald. *Knowing Yourself and Others*, pp. 207-210. Holt.

Morgan, John J. B. *Keeping a Sound Mind*, pp. 119-133. Macmillan.

2. RETURNING TO CHILDHOOD

Some people meet the problems of life by using the same methods that brought results in childhood. This was the case with Stella N——, a young typist whose employer was at times very brusque to his employees and had a habit of indulging in sarcasm when anything went wrong. All the girls knew this and had become accustomed to it. Some of them were frightened, and said nothing; some "sassed him back"; but Stella cried. As the tears fell on her typewriter, word went around the building that Mr. K—— had been mean again. Her problem, of course, was to correct what was incorrect and learn to pay no further attention to her sarcastic boss. Instead she did what she used to do when she was a child and her mother scolded her: she cried.

This mechanism is called *regression*. When a small child does not get what he wants, or when his natural movements are interfered with, he may become angry, sulk, cry, or go into a temper tantrum. Too frequently he gets what he wants by such a mechanism. The normal child, however, outgrows these methods of solving his problem and adopts others — cooperation perhaps, study, work, persuasion, or resignation.

When a grown-up person — or a person of high-school age, for that matter — meets a difficult problem by the mechanism of sulking, "flying off the handle," turning away in anger, or crying, he is going back to his childish methods and is employing a regression mechanism. He is not meeting the difficulty face to face, but is escaping from it in an emotional excitement of one kind or another.

Regression is sometimes seen in school. A student who, upon receiving a failing mark on a test, immediately tears the paper into shreds and throws it into the wastebasket, is not facing his problem, which is to master a body of knowledge. His approach to that problem should be faithful study. Instead, he shows a temper, as he did in infancy.

A girl or boy of high-school age who has considerable difficulty in making friends at school among fellow students and teachers and who goes home to his mother for affection, tenderness, and sympathy is also using a regression mechanism. He is escaping from the problem of adjusting himself to his world at school by seeking the consolation of infancy in his mother's caresses.

How can one overcome regression mechanism? Fits of anger and crying are typically childish ways of reacting to difficulties. As one becomes older, he outgrows the childish approach to life and learns more and more to face facts and make the best of them. He learns to cooperate with people, to study the causes of difficulties, to work hard, to use persuasion instead of force or teasing, and to accept those things that cannot be changed.

READINGS

In Literature

PLAY

Moody, William Vaughn. *The Great Divide*. Houghton Mifflin.
> A girl of Puritan stock on a lonely ranch finds herself faced by three bandits. The scene is a tense one and the development of the plot and the climax will stir your emotions.

SHORT STORY

Cather, Willa. "Paul's Case"; in *Youth and the Bright Medusa*. Knopf.
> A motherless boy in a strict and colorless home lives for the stage he knows as an usher. He escapes into a land of dreams of his childhood. But circumstances force the issue; his teachers and father cut him off from the theater and he is put to work. Then comes the daring act.

For Further Information

Fedder, Ruth. *A Girl Grows Up*, pp. 53-57, 74-78. McGraw-Hill.

McLean, Donald. *Knowing Yourself and Others*, p. 211. Holt.

Morgan, John J. B. *Keeping a Sound Mind*, pp. 195-198. Macmillan.

3. IMITATING THE HERO

When a child adopts certain mannerisms from grown-ups or friends or people whom he admires, he is said to be using the mechanism of identification. A great deal of behavior is imitative; in fact, it has been said that about ninety-five per cent of all behavior is the result of imitation. Children watch others to see how they manage their lives, and if they admire another person they are inclined to adopt certain of his methods. There is no doubt that growth of character and personality as a whole is influenced to a large degree by the mechanism of imitation or identification. Perhaps it is safe to say that most identification mechanisms are useful to growth.

People who identify themselves with Abraham Lincoln, for example, and imitate his great quality of honesty have undoubtedly adopted a mechanism which is useful to the growth of their personality. In so far as we imitate the virtues of our heroes and sincerely try to develop these qualities in ourselves, we are using the identification mechanism to advantage.

Imitation is sometimes self-deception. Not all imitation or identification is useful to growth, however. A girl who adopts the jauntiness and the hairdress of her favorite movie star may be covering up her own feeling of social inferiority. Instead of studying why she does not get along well with others, she tries to assume the appearance of a person who is nationally popular. The reasoning is simple: "Jane Cinema is popular. I walk and look like Jane. Therefore I am popular."

Likewise, a boy who adopts the semi-snarl and the swagger of the high-school coach may be covering up a feeling of inferiority about something. He does not face the fact of his own weakness. In order to help himself forget his inferiority, he tries to put on a front in imitation of the person he admires.

Both of these individuals are trying to solve a problem in a roundabout way.

Smoking is sometimes imitation. Smoking among high-school students and younger children is in most cases a mechanism of imitation. The boy wants to grow up. He sees grown-ups smoke, and he reasons somewhat as follows: "I don't want to be a child. I want to be a man. Men smoke; therefore, if I smoke, I am a man." In such a case smoking is a roundabout way of trying to solve the problem of growing up. So is wearing a mustache. So is drinking.

Imitation or identification are poor short-cuts to success. The person who identifies himself with someone else usually flatters himself by imagining that he has the same qualities as the person he admires and he proves it by adopting one or more of that person's mannerisms. If he wants the same success achieved by the other person and if he takes all the difficult steps that person took — hard work, patience, and the like — then he is tackling his problem in a direct way; he is building his character and may eventually get the success he wants. All of us, however, are likely to be impatient, lazy, or fearful at times, and it is then that we resort to roundabout methods of satisfying our wants. The mechanism of identification in such cases provides a quicker, but unreal, satisfaction for a strong desire — an earlier, but unreal, solution of an important problem.

Why does imitation seem peculiar? People are usually not aware that they are using the identification mechanism. They do not realize it when they adopt the mannerisms of a favorite hero or heroine and imagine themselves as good, strong, learned, beautiful, successful, or what not, as the hero or heroine is. Others can see the oddness of their behavior, but they themselves are usually blind to it. The adopted mannerisms in such a case appear strange because they do not fit the rest of the personality, because they have not grown into the personality in a direct struggle with life.

READINGS

In Literature

NOVELS

Caine, Hall. *The Christian.* Appleton-Century.

Hall Caine shows that one who follows in the footsteps of Christ lives a full and a stirring life.

Roberts, Kenneth. *Northwest Passage.* Doubleday, Doran.

The hero and narrator of the story lives in the shadow of Colonel Rogers whom he admires and imitates for his military genius.

SHORT STORY

Edmonds, Walter D. "Judge"; in *Prose and Poetry of Today.* Singer.

The son of a ne'er-do-well finds in the judge a true friend and grows to be like the man he thought too big and important for him even to speak to.

For Further Information

Eastburn, L. A., Kelley, V. H., and Falk, C. J. *Planning Your Life for School and Society,* pp. 55-56. Scribner.

McLean, Donald. *Knowing Yourself and Others,* p. 206. Holt.

Scharmer, Fay Mack. *Boy's Guide to Living,* pp. 4-5. Allyn and Bacon.

4. THE FOX SAID, "THE GRAPES ARE SOUR"

A classical example of a "poor excuse" is Aesop's fable about the fox who, going through the woods, spied some grapes on a vine several feet off the ground. The fox jumped again and again, but was unable to reach the grapes. When he was tired out and saw no way of getting them, he said, "Those grapes are sour anyway."

You can give your "alibi." We ought to have good reasons for what we do; then our actions are at least justifiable if not actually good. But all of us do some things that cannot be justified. The tendency to justify every act remains, however, and as a result we search for excellent reasons to back up our most serious mistakes. If we could not find good reasons for wrong actions, we should have to admit that to some extent we were falling short of the ideal self, which each of us constantly tries to uphold.

The process of finding good reasons for bad actions is called rationalization. This mechanism may be called a defense mechanism, for when we employ it, we are defending ourselves against admitting our own weaknesses.

Illustrations of rationalization. A girl does not want to admit that the college preparatory course is too difficult for her, so she says she is not interested in it. A boy does not wish to admit that his school work is too difficult for him, so he says the only thing he is interested in is athletics. Some students will continually explain that they fail in school because of excessive work at home. Some will explain their withdrawal from extra-curricular activities by saying that real education comes from studying, when, as a matter of fact, they withdraw because they have not been able to get along with their fellow students.

Among young people there are always a few so-called woman-haters and man-haters. Such persons are probably very much interested in the opposite sex, but they do not want to admit the real reason why they do not have dates. Hence they let it be known that they "hate women" or "despise men."

A girl whose parents cannot afford a party dress may tell her friends that she is not going to the party because it is being run by a clique. She offers a good reason, but it is not the real one.

A person may say he became angry with someone because it was a help to the other fellow; it "put him wise." This sounds virtuous, but the truth is that he became angry because he was annoyed and wanted to punish the other person, not help him.

Illustrations of the mechanism of rationalization could be multiplied. Under this heading come all forms of giving good reasons for bad actions. The "Alibi Ike" is one who frequently rationalizes his mistakes and failures with such flimsy excuses that everyone can see through them. Of course, the person who makes excuses and explains his mistakes to his own advantage does not realize that he is not facing the facts, that he is using an argument which at best has very little bearing on the question. When his attention is called to the truth of the matter, he usually becomes angry because the weakness he has been trying to hide even from himself has been thrown into the open. He has tried to defend himself against admitting this very weakness. But when someone explains the truth to him, he is suddenly forced to face it. Then his desire to hide the weakness is thwarted, and he automatically responds with anger.

READINGS

In Literature

SHORT STORIES

Bierce, Ambrose. "A Horseman in the Sky"; in *In the Midst of Life.* Modern Library.

> Families were divided in the Civil War — brother against brother, father against son. Now, if such a father stood on the top of a hill in full view of his sharpshooting son, what should the son do?

Bierce, Ambrose. "The Occurrence at Owl Creek Bridge"; in *In the Midst of Life.* Modern Library.

> What thoughts would go through your mind if you stood with a rope about your neck? Would you plan how to escape the rifle fire and even the cannon fire of the soldiers who had held you?

For Further Information

McLean, Donald. *Knowing Yourself and Others,* p. 212. Holt.

Scharmer, Fay Mack. *Boy's Guide to Living,* p. 8. Allyn and Bacon.

5. "TAKING IT OUT ON THE DOG"

The man who "takes it out on the dog" may be transferring to the dog the emotion of anger aroused by the office manager, who may have annoyed him. He may not, or dare not, express himself to his boss; but he feels safe in expressing his feelings to the dog. He may kick the dog (he would like to kick the office manager). The dog will lick his hand afterward; the boss would have fired him.

In the mechanism of transference, one shifts attitudes from the original cause to another person, thing, or idea — or to an animal, frequently — that is not the cause. Thus, a boy in school may adopt the same attitude toward a teacher that he adopts toward his father, not because of anything the teacher has done, but because the teacher either looks like his father or stands in a place of authority as his father does.

Transference may be positive or negative. The transference mechanism is sometimes spoken of as positive or negative. A positive transference might be illustrated by the case of the girl whose older brother, for whom she had a strong attachment, left for college. When she re-entered school, she happened to elect a course taught by a new teacher who resembled her older brother. She immediately found herself kindly disposed toward the teacher and soon developed as strong an attachment for him as she had had for her brother. She had transferred the attitude of friendliness and affection to the new teacher.

A negative transference might be illustrated by the case of Norman D——, who, without apparent reason, disliked a new fellow student in school. This new student had certain mannerisms that reminded Norman of a boy who had mercilessly teased him through grade-school years. Norman had transferred his attitude of dislike from the enemy of bygone days to this new student, who, in certain minor respects, was similar to the boy he had disliked.

Similar traits do not make identical personalities. A great many illustrations of transference might be given, all of them showing the same error, namely, reasoning from a similarity to identity. A person who has wavy hair like your brother's is not necessarily like your brother in other ways. Because a person reminds you of your enemy, that does not say that he is really like your enemy. Your girl friend may have a smile like your mother's, yet be a totally different kind of person. And it is no proof, because your boy friend reminds you of your father, that the two are at all alike. Mannerisms may indicate something about a person's character, but they are not the character itself. The chances are, for example, that the person toward whom you transfer an attitude of hatefulness does not merit that attitude and has many excellent qualities.

Transference and projection. There is a similarity between transference and the mechanism called projection. In the former case we transfer an attitude from one person or thing to another on the basis of some apparent likeness between the two. In projection we transfer a fault of our own to someone or something else. We blame someone else for a fault we do not consciously recognize in ourselves. This was the case with John K——, who was a freshman in high school. He had a great deal of difficulty with a project in shopwork, the making of a tie rack. He found it difficult to use the square, the plane, the hammer, the screw driver, and the mitre saw. His mechanical abilities were very inferior and he knew it, but he could be heard from day to day talking to his tools with abusive language, laying the blame on them. Finally, when he had assembled the parts and held the awkward piece of furniture in his hands, he broke out in another torrent of rage. "You blankety-blank, good-for-nothing tie rack!" he said, and crashed it to the concrete floor.

Helen H—— was a senior in high school who had for some time kept steady company with Roger D——. Although they had sworn faithfulness to each other, Helen occasionally found herself interested in other boys — as sometimes happens. Soon she began to imagine that Roger was showing attention to other girls in the senior class, and she accused him of being interested in them and of not keeping his word to her.

Both John K—— and Helen H—— were projecting their own faults into something or somebody else. We have a tendency to hide or forget thoughts that put us in a bad light, and sometimes we blame other people for things we do ourselves, or accuse other people of our own faults. A person may constantly criticize others for gossiping, while he himself is the one who gossips; he may accuse others of jealousy, when it is he who has these faults. He may accuse others of being unfriendly, cold, and hostile, although he himself is unfriendly, cold, and hostile toward others. John K—— did not say, "You good-for-nothing" to himself; he projected his faults into the tie rack. Helen H—— did not accuse herself of fickleness; she accused her boy friend. Projection, like the other mechanisms studied thus far in this unit, is a way of avoiding reality and refusing to face facts.

What do you dislike most in the other fellow? It is a peculiar characteristic of human nature that we hate most in others the very faults we ourselves are trying most to hide. Whenever we

feel intensely critical about a certain fault in someone else, it is
a good idea to bring ourselves up short and ask, "Why do I feel
so intensely about that? Am I trying to hide a similar fault in
myself?"

READINGS

In Literature

SHORT STORY

Cather, Willa. "Paul's Case"; in *Youth and the Bright Medusa*.
Knopf.
Excellent case of transference.

For Further Information

McLean, Donald. *Knowing Yourself and Others*, pp. 213-214. Holt.
Morgan, John J. B. *Keeping a Sound Mind*, p. 117. Macmillan.

6. FORCING YOURSELF TO FORGET

It is sometimes said that we forget what we want to forget.
Perhaps this was the case with Norma D——, who, in one school
year, lost parts of her gym clothes twelve times. She had tried
her best to get the principal to excuse her from physical education, but, since she was the picture of health and had no doctor's
statement, he could not excuse her. She was constantly in difficulties with her physical education teacher and frequently
claimed illness during gym class or stayed home on the days her
program called for a gym class. In addition to the absences
caused by these devices, she had to be absent twelve times because her gym clothes were missing. Is it possible that Norma
wanted to forget where she had left her things?

You can try to forget. One way of not facing the problems of
life is to refuse to think them through or to think about them at
all — in other words, to repress them. There are many unpleasant
facts, such as embarrassment, wrong desires, and memories of
defeat, that people try to forget. The mechanism of trying to
forget is called repression. Some psychologists say that nothing
is ever forgotten, that the conscious mind is only a small part of

the mind, and the subconscious mind contains all the information that has been repressed and apparently forgotten. Perhaps they are correct when they say that the ideas forgotten by the mechanism of repressing them do not remain dead and inactive, but exert a great deal of influence on the conscious mind and on behavior.

The case of the young man who was afraid of dogs, discussed earlier in this book, is an instance of repression. He had repressed, or pushed down into his subconscious mind, the memory of the fright a dog had given him when he was a child; but it continued to influence his behavior in the form of an abnormal fear of all dogs. You will remember that this young man solved his problem by calling to his conscious mind the details of that early incident and thereafter carrying out a program of dealing with dogs realistically instead of under the influence of his fear of them.

Facing unpleasant facts will strengthen you. It is usually better to face unpleasantnesses, think them through, and do what you can about them, than forcibly to forget them and, in effect, try to run away from them. A certain young man in college had never learned to swim. When his chum, who enjoyed swimming above all sports, urgently invited him to spend a week at a certain lake, he finally agreed, but said he would not care to go swimming. He rationalized his dislike of swimming by saying that the water was not very clean, since a large number of bathers swam in it every day, and also that he took cold easily and was afraid of getting chilled. Later, it was learned that this young man had been extremely embarrassed as a child when a group of boys took him against his will to an old swimming hole, and, after having frightened him by taking off his clothes and throwing him into the creek, had sent him away without his pants. This experience had proved to be so tense emotionally that the boy tried to forget it and ever after avoided bathing places and never learned to swim. It would have been far better for him to have faced the facts and conquered that early embarrassment; for one thing, he would have avoided many uncomfortable situations, and for another, he would have enjoyed a healthy sport.

The case of Dick R——, given on page 142, also illustrates a repression mechanism. Dick had had an unsatisfactory experience at his first dance and he refused to call it to mind again except in the one instance when he felt safe to confide in his good friend, the adviser. When he did, he was able to meet the problem squarely.

Repression does not remove the problem. The damaging effect of repression comes from the fact that, although an idea or an experience is willfully forgotten, it is by no means removed from one's life, but remains in the subconscious mind as a secret force leading to behavior not accepted by the group. A person who has good mental health will avoid repression before he has faced the facts, studied the problem, and done something about it. Usually the fear and embarrassment connected with such a problem will leave when the problem is carefully studied and corrective action is taken. When the fear or the emotional quality of the unhappy problem is removed, we no longer feel a need to repress it.

READINGS

In Literature

SHORT STORY

Mansfield, Katherine. "Life of Ma Parker"; in *The Garden Party*. Knopf.
>   She surely keeps her chin up. What a fine woman she is!

For Further Information

Fedder, Ruth. *A Girl Grows Up*, pp. 68-69. McGraw-Hill.
McLean, Donald. *Knowing Yourself and Others*, pp. 212-213. Holt.
Morgan, John J. B. *Keeping a Sound Mind*, pp. 276-277. Macmillan.
Wright, Milton. *Getting Along with People*, pp. 249-250. McGraw-Hill.

FOR CLASS DISCUSSION

1. Ned W—— lived in an impoverished home. Both his parents were in poor health, and there was no one else in the family old enough to earn money. Many of the things that other boys had, Ned had to do without. He felt very unhappy about this. In the seventh and eighth grades he became quite a dreamer, and instead of studying,

he would often sit with his head on his hand, looking off into space. By the time he was of high-school age, day-dreaming had become such a habit with him that when he got a part-time job he was discharged because he did not pay attention to business. His boss said that he was a dreamer. His high-school grades were poor; he failed in some subjects; and teachers complained that even when they tried to wake him out of his dreams, he would go back into them as soon as their backs were turned.

What did Ned probably day-dream about?

Why did he day-dream?

What would he have to do to get over the habit?

2. Janet L—— was a member of the Pep Club, which traditionally planned an outing for the last week of May. At a special meeting called to discuss plans for this outing, Janet enthusiastically presented her plan — to have the girls spend a week-end at her father's cottage forty-five miles away. Certain members of the club, however, were not able to make arrangements for a week-end party, and, after full discussion, Janet's plan was not accepted. Toward the end of the discussion, when she could see that her plan was not going through, she became sarcastic and sulky. Later, when the girls decided on an outing nearer by and taking up only one day, she blurted out, "Well, if you won't come over to our cottage, I'm not going."

Why did Janet sulk and become angry?

What was her reason for being generous in the first place?

What recommendations can you make for Janet?

3. Tim T—— had about fifteen pictures of Johnny Weismuller in his room. He went to every Tarzan picture that came to town, and when there was time, he sat through two showings. Tim was a small boy for his age and not at all like the athlete, Johnny Weismuller; but he liked to drape himself with the tiger-skin rug that belonged in front of the fireplace. He would place a butcher knife between his teeth and climb an apple tree in the back yard. Then he would swing down from a limb and try to perform the agile feats that were the daily life of Tarzan. But Tim never took part in athletics and always tried to get out of taking gym class.

Explain Tim's actions.

What was his problem?

Could he do anything to solve it? What?

4. One of Mary Jane's friends came to school one day with an attractive, wine-colored sport coat. Mary Jane wanted one like it for herself, so she begged her mother to get her one. Her mother

priced them and decided she would have to get a less expensive coat for her daughter.   Mary Jane was extremely unhappy about it.   The next day, however, she told several girls at school very emphatically that she disliked wine color and wouldn't care to have a wine-colored sport coat for herself.   When she came home from school that day, lo and behold, her mother had a beautiful wine-colored coat for her! Her mother had thought it over and purchased one because of Mary Jane's disappointment.   The girl, of course, was very happy, but when the other girls saw her wearing the coat, she blushed and did not know how to explain her previous remarks.

Why did she say she disliked the color?

What would you have done if you had been she?

What do you call the mechanism Mary Jane used to meet her problem?

5. Jim did not get along with his older brother, Bill.   One morning, just before leaving for school, he had a fight with Bill and, of course, got the worst of it.   When he neared the school building, he met Bill C——, who was more his own size and always reminded him of his brother because both had the same first name.

Bill C—— said, "Hi," as he joined Jim: but Jim answered gruffly, "Hi, yourself."

Bill said, "What's the matter, you sore?"

"What's it to you, anyway?"

A few more words between them and they were fighting.   This time Jim got the better of it and Bill C—— felt hurt in more ways than one.   But Jim made up with him immediately and apologized, and the two walked to school together.   Jim would fight anybody who made any slighting remark about Bill C——'s getting licked.

Why did Jim pick a fight with Bill?

Why did he make up with him?

After the trouble was over, did Jim understand his behavior?

6. Girard B—— had a very embarrassing experience in Civic Hall. One day, when he was listening to a speaker there, he answered a rhetorical question.   The speaker was driving a point home by asking dramatically, "Would anyone do such a thing?"   The audience was deathly still except for Girard, who answered clearly, "No!"   Then suddenly everyone looked around at him and there he sat, blushing to his ears.   Soon afterward he forgot all about it, but he never returned to the same auditorium.   Whenever a concert or entertainment was scheduled there, Girard did not go.   Four years later, one of his friends said to him, "I think I know why you never go to anything in

Civic Hall. You probably still feel embarrassed about that time when Senator Blank talked." And then the incident came back to Girard. Fortunately, he was able to think it through again and see that it was not such a bad error after all.

Why did Girard forget his mistake?

Why did he become embarrassed because of his mistake?

Do you think he would continue to avoid Civic Hall after having remembered?

7. Why do some girls say they do not want fur coats because fur coats make them look fleshy? What is the mechanism?

8. A certain musician habitually finds fault with other musicians even though they are superior to him. What mechanism is involved here?

9. A certain person who is known for his habit of gossiping says that of all human weaknesses he despises gossiping most. What mechanism is used in this instance?

10. Suppose you have an older sister who dominates you. Recently you have acquired a new friend. You think a lot of your friend and are eager to know what your sister thinks of him. After she has met him, she tells you, "I like him all right. He's a fine young man." Then she adds, "But I detest his mustache. I think it's the silliest-looking thing. I despise his mustache."

How does she feel about your newly acquired friend?

What is the mechanism she employs?

WHERE DO I STAND?

Since people as a rule do not recognize the mechanisms they themselves use in meeting the problems of life, you may find it necessary to get some other person to help you to fill out this check list.

On the lines provided below, place marks above the words "never," "rarely," "often," and so on, according to your most careful opinion about yourself. Then connect these marks with a zigzag line from the first to the second to the third, and so on to the last.

(NOTE. *Do not write in this book,* unless it is your own. Make a copy on a separate sheet of paper.)

1. To get away from monotony and unpleasantness I day-dream.

never   rarely often   always I don't know

2. I day-dream about plans for the future.

always   often   rarely   never   I don't know

3. My day-dreams interfere with my work.

never   rarely often   always I don't know

4. I follow my day-dreams with work. always   often   rarely   never   I don't know

5. I use childish methods to get what I want.

never   rarely often   always I don't know

6. I cry when I don't get my way.   never   rarely often   always I don't know

7. I sulk when I don't get my way.   never   rarely often   always I don't know

8. I have a fit of anger when I don't get my way.

never   rarely often   always I don't know

9. I imitate the mannerisms, make-up, etc., of others.

never   rarely often   always I don't know

10. I give good reasons for bad actions. never   rarely often   always I don't know

11. I make alibis.   never   rarely often   always I don't know

12. When I am angry, I take it out on someone.

never   rarely often   always I don't know

13. I become angry at physical objects when they interfere with my desires.

never   rarely often   always I don't know

14. I force myself to forget unpleasant facts.

never   rarely often   always I don't know

15. I frankly study unpleasant facts. always   often   rarely   never   I don't know

◦ℑ UNIT V ℑ◦

Becoming an Adult

ADULTHOOD, in the broad meaning of the word, is not determined by the legal age of twenty-one, nor is it reached when we are full-grown in size and strength. Rather, it is a time when our appearance and behavior consistently show control over our emotional life and a strong, perhaps predominant interest in the welfare of others. An adult is *emotionally* mature, which means that he has control over his feelings, and he is also *socially* mature, which means he is interested in other people fully as much as in himself and is capable of forgetting himself in the service of others. Both of these ways of reacting have become habits with him because he has spent so much time and effort learning them.

But if learning goes on as long as we live, when have we learned enough to be called true adults? Do we ever complete our learning and arrive at a stage of complete adulthood when no more learning is necessary? The answer is obvious; we do not. Adulthood is really an ideal of personal adjustment toward which we are all striving. We are always on the way, but we never quite arrive. We may be called adults, but we know there are times when our actions are those of children. We know we still learn long after twenty-one or thirty-one or forty-one.

We learn as we go, as long as we go. But how does this learning take place and what is it that is learned? Are there any techniques that may improve our learning?

TO LIVE IS TO LEARN

How do some people manage to remember names? When you muff a ball, are you learning to catch it or to muff it? Can you learn to do the wrong thing? Do you think that skill in roller-skating would help you to learn ice-skating?

WHEN A TYPIST begins work in a new job, she changes noticeably during the first few days. She not only learns many details about her work; she also learns where things are in the office, who her fellow workers are, and so on. She may be somewhat tense and bewildered the first day, but she will be more composed the next. She is changing; the new things she is learning are becoming a part of her. She gradually becomes more efficient, learning to eliminate false motions, to work more quickly, to get along with her employer and fellow workers, and to see the value of her work in the whole organization. As learning takes place, she is changing. Moreover, this learning, or changing, continues.

Learning goes on all the time. We learn as long as we live. In fact, living is learning. We can't escape it. Part of the time we are learning worth-while things and part of the time harmful things, but we are learning all the time. *Learning* is simply the word used to describe our changing way of meeting events in life. Learning that is worth while helps us to grow up and become adults. Much of what we learn becomes a matter of habit without our conscious knowledge that habits are being formed; we learn gradually without any sudden or noticeable change.

Not all learning is improving. As the previous paragraph

*"I'll be glad when I'm through school and never have
to think again — like grown-ups."*

points out, some learning is harmful. For example, Bill Jones,
a senior in college, felt very despondent when he flunked a mid-
semester test in economics. To escape from this feeling of de-
spondency, he joined two of his friends and spent the night
drinking. Early the next morning he was taken home. Three
days later, he failed in another mid-semester test and telephoned
his friends to arrange for another party. He was learning to
meet the unhappiness of failing in school work with the escape
mechanism of drinking. During the next two months of the
semester, his school work did not improve and he resorted more

and more frequently to this way of meeting his problem.   It became a habit.   At the end of the semester, he failed in his examinations and did not graduate with his class.   Fortunately, with the help and understanding of a certain teacher and his parents, Bill came to realize his mistake and planned a more worth-while program for the coming semester.   With some difficulty, he substituted a good habit for a poor one and learned to face his problem instead of trying to escape from it.   By hard work and occasional tutoring he was able to graduate in the middle of the next year.

Learning follows certain definite rules.   Careful study has shown that learning takes place in certain definite ways and this has led to the discovery of certain laws of learning.   Three of these laws have been called the Law of Association, the Law of Exercise, and the Law of Effect.

We learn by associating one part of our knowledge with another.   This Law of Association is employed by some people in remembering names, for example.   When they are introduced to someone, they notice some particular thing about his appearance or his personality, such as his teeth, his eyes, his hair, his clothes, his manner of smiling, or the tone of his voice, and they consciously relate this knowledge to the person's name.   Then, in trying to recall his name, any one or more of these bits of knowledge will help because they are associated in the mind with the person's name.   Furthermore, in recalling a name under such conditions, there is much more than just a name that can be remembered.   The various bits of knowledge associated with a name help us to learn the name in the first place.   A good deal of what we know is learned through association.

We learn by exercise, or repeating thoughts and actions.   In general, it may be said that a thought or action is better learned on repetition than without it, and in fact is forgotten without repetition.   This is not always the case, but for our present purposes it will help to think of the Law of Exercise in these terms. This law also may be employed in learning to remember names. As soon as one is introduced, he can repeat the name by saying, "How do you do, Mr. Warren," instead of merely, "How do you do."   Somewhat later in the conversation he may ask a question, using the name — "Have you been in Centerville a long time, Mr. Warren?" or, "How do you like the weather we are having in Centerville today, Mr. Warren?" or, "What do you think of our school, Mr. Warren?" By repeatedly using knowledge in a real situation we are learning through exercise.

We learn most readily and most easily those things that we enjoy. Conversely, we find it difficult to learn and to recall those things that we do not enjoy. If the effect produced by the thing we do or say is pleasant, we are inclined to repeat it and to learn it with less effort. This law also operates in learning to remember names. If we enjoy being introduced to a certain person, the effect upon us is favorable, and we are more inclined to remember that person's name than if the introduction were an embarrassing, uncomfortable, or unhappy moment. As a matter of fact, people are inclined to forget the names of those whom they do not like.

The Law of Effect is perhaps the most important of these three laws because it plays such an important part in all learning. It should be remembered that we learn the things we like to learn, the things that we accept and that please us. For instance, a student who collects stamps may learn an amazing amount about them, often becoming an expert simply because he likes stamps. The learning process in this case is practically effortless and certainly is not painful. The same student may find it extremely difficult to learn elementary algebra. The subject is no more difficult than philately, but he does not enjoy it.

It is easier to understand people we like. This is the fundamental reason why we learn to understand people we like and fail to understand those whom we dislike. We learn to fit in with those we like and find it difficult or impossible to behave correctly toward those we dislike.

But notice that, in either case, learning is involved. We learn to remember a person's name, or we learn not to remember it. We learn to accept our fellows, or we learn not to accept them. We learn to study diligently, or we learn not to study diligently. Whatever we learn, we learn to the degree that we enter into the activity with pleasure, willingness, and wholeheartedness. We can learn very thoroughly not to study, for example, if we get sufficient pleasure out of not studying.

Learning by imitation. Much of our learning may be influenced by imitation. This would apply to the great many little actions with which we reflect our personality. Manners, for example, are to a large extent learned by imitating others. We little realize how much we imitate others. Whistling, applauding, yawning, laughing, and smoking are, in most instances, imitative. It is probably through imitation that all the members of one family sometimes have the same gait or the same laugh. It is probably through imitation that all girls of a high-school group wear similar style hairdress, or that all the boys on a football squad have brush cuts. A great deal of what we learn is imitated, most of it unthinkingly, very little of it consciously.

Learning by observation. Imitation is always based on observation, however, because we must observe, through sight, touch, smell, or any of the senses, before we can imitate. But learning through observation is not all imitative. In a biology course one may study the anatomy of the frog by careful observation and learn to classify its bones, muscles, and veins. Imitation has nothing to do with learning in this case. The typist referred to earlier in this unit was learning a good deal about her employer and fellow workers through careful observation, which is necessary on such occasions to speed up learning. Life is made up of an endless series of new situations, to which we want to adjust ourselves as quickly as possible; therefore, we keep our eyes open for hints as to the best way to react.

Learning without knowing that we learn. A great deal of our learning is done incidentally while we are trying to learn something else. In a history class, for example, students learn more than the facts, dates, and ideas discussed in the classroom or contained in the textbook. Without knowing it, they are learning such things as promptness in getting to class, how to get along with fellow students, and how to use the English language in writing and speaking. Other more subtle things may also be learned without conscious effort or knowledge; in this same class one might learn about the curvature of a picture molding, the effect of rainy weather on the teacher's disposition, the pleasing or tiring influence of the interior decoration of the room, or the way a sparrow alights on the window sill or a fly crawls up the wall. Learning at any given moment is not confined to the particular thing we are studying, and the incidental learning is sometimes the most important. Learning the habit of punctuality, for instance, might be more important for someone throughout his life than the knowledge he was consciously trying to get in attending a history class.

Efficiency in learning. It is often said that we learn by trial and error, but many psychologists maintain that we learn by success rather than by error. As a matter of fact, we learn whatever we do, both success and error. If we are making mistakes, we learn to make mistakes. If we are doing the right thing, we learn to do the right thing. By careful planning, harmful learning may be avoided and worth-while learning may be increased. Becoming an adult requires efficient learning habits.

Here are three rules that some people find effective in learning:

1. *Have a purpose.* If you want to learn a new habit, such as friendliness (assuming that you have never learned how to be friendly with people), be sure you know why you want to develop that habit — in this case, why friendliness is extremely worth while. In other words, have a strong motive for breaking the old habit and learning the new one. This rule makes use of the law of effect, just as in the case of the boy who enjoyed collecting stamps.

2. *Work hard at it.* Make a strong beginning and try to put your whole self into the effort to learn. This rule also makes use of the Law of Effect.

3. *Don't miss a chance.* Whenever you have a chance to practice what you are learning to do, practice it. Don't miss a chance. The more often you practice friendliness, for example, the better you learn to be friendly. Soon it will become a habit. This rule makes use of the Law of Exercise.

Efficiency in study. All these rules apply, of course, to any kind of learning, not only the learning of new habits. One of the most important aspects of the learning process for students is that connected with school work — learning from books, classroom lectures and discussions, laboratory work. Here are a few rules that help students to learn more efficiently:

1. *Have a purpose.* You should know why you are studying a

given subject. Is it because you need a high-school diploma? Is the subject a necessary part of your program? Will it serve as part of the foundation on which you are going to build your future? Whatever the purpose, if it is a strong one, you can study with more determination. If you believe strongly in what you are doing, you will not readily be distracted from your work.

2. *Plan your study hours* so that they do not conflict with other activities, and eliminate outside influences that might distract you during those hours — for instance, visits with members of the family or friends, listening to the radio, watching the dog.

3. *Do the most difficult work first.* The rest will be easy, once the hardest problem is out of the way.

4. *Make yourself enjoy what you are studying.* There is such a thing as beginning your study with a will to enjoy it — with an attitude of acceptance toward it — then, by working hard and mastering it, you get the additional satisfaction of accomplishment both in the work and in your own self-control.

5. *Read thoughtfully and restate the main idea* of each paragraph after you finish it. Writing out this thought in your own words serves as a repetition that aids learning. This suggestion is based upon the Law of Exercise, which says that we learn by using knowledge.

6. *Look up from the page and think.* Try to relate the information to other things you know. This suggestion is based upon the Law of Association, which says that we learn by associating one part of our knowledge with another.

7. *Finish the assignment* before you leave it. If it is too long to finish at one sitting, divide it into parts and finish each part before you interrupt your study.

8. *Write an outline* as soon as you have completed an assignment, and fill it in with the main thoughts of the paragraphs. This suggestion is based upon the Laws of Exercise and Association.

9. *Review* makes further use of the Law of Exercise. Review what you have read thoroughly at once, and review it again after twenty-four hours have passed. All of us forget a great deal of what we have learned a day or so after we have learned it.

Acquiring efficient learning habits is a gradual process. A person does not suddenly adopt all the rules given here for efficiency in learning. Gradually, as he matures, he learns to reduce false motions to a minimum and confines himself to habits that work most efficiently. Undoubtedly you already use some of the suggestions given in this section. When you try to observe the others, you may find yourself, after a short time, falling back into some of your previous, less efficient habits. But then, if you keep at it again and again, you will find yourself gradually adopting these newer habits which at first seemed unnatural or awkward. The improved results, of course, will be pleasing and will encourage you to carry on. Gradually you come to tackle your work as a grown-up person should.

The adult learns to reason his way through problems. It is characteristic of an adult to give preference to reason over emotion in meeting life's problems. He has learned that his feelings, however important and inescapable, are very changeable. If today, for example, a student of pathology should feel that it is simply an annoying waste of time to spend four hours in the laboratory, why, tomorrow he may feel that it is interesting, revealing, and stimulating. But he knows — and here he is thinking — that laboratory work is absolutely necessary in his profession today, tomorrow, and as long as he is a pathologist. Therefore, acting on reason instead of feeling, he goes right ahead with his work.

Becoming an adult is, in a way, becoming a thinking, reasoning person. All this is a learning process in which we are now — and shall continue to be — engaged.

FOR CLASS DISCUSSION

1. Stubb Downie spends most of his time with the River Gang. He is only fourteen years old, but has been a truant since the age of eleven. During the past year he and his pals were implicated in five petty crimes and Stubb is now on probation. Still he is frequently absent from school and pals around with the same old gang.

What is he learning?

What would he have to do to change?

2. Marjorie D—— is a rather timid girl who has decided to replace

her habit of withdrawing from people with a habit of friendliness. How should she go about it?

3. What law of learning is employed by those who develop some skill, like singing, playing an instrument, or handling tools?

4. Jim A—— has the success habit. Whenever he begins something, he first makes up his mind that he cannot fail. He is fully determined to succeed when he begins. Which of the laws of learning does he employ?

5. Mrs. Jones never has trouble about getting dishes washed. While the children are busy at them, she often praises them for being helpful and keeps up a chatter of fun that has them laughing much of the time.

Why don't her children object to washing dishes?

Which of the laws of learning does she employ?

6. Would it help you to enjoy what you are doing if you imagined yourself to be the ideal you are striving to attain? For example, if you want to be a doctor, would it help you to imagine yourself one when you are dissecting a frog? Why?

INDIVIDUAL ACTIVITIES

1. Using the suggestions for efficiency in study (on pages 179 f.) as a check list, check yourself this evening and see how many of the suggestions you followed in your study habits during the day.

2. Make a "curve of forgetting" for yourself. Select from one of your subjects a list of items you have to remember. First, memorize them so that you can give them fluently. An hour later, recite as many as you can remember. Without reviewing, do it a second, third, fourth, and fifth time at each successive hour. Plot a curve showing the number of items recalled at each hour. This experiment becomes almost shocking if you carry it out by twenty-four-hour intervals.

3. You can get good evidence on the value of reviewing if you perform an experiment somewhat similar to that described in (2). Vary the procedure in only one respect — after each recitation, review the whole list of items.

WHERE DO I STAND?

On the lines provided below, place marks above the words "always," "often," and so on, according to your most careful opinion about yourself. Then connect these marks with a zigzag line from the first to the second to the third, and so on to the last. If you are not satisfied with the resulting diagram, plan how you can improve it during the next few months.

(NOTE. *Do not write in this book,* unless it is your own. Make a copy on a separate sheet of paper.)

1. I have a purpose clearly in mind when I begin to study.

always   often   rarely   never   I don't know

2. I plan my study hours to avoid conflicts and interruptions.

always   often   rarely   never   I don't know

3. I refuse to be called away unnecessarily.

always   often   rarely   never   I don't know

4. I do the hardest work first.

always   often   rarely   never   I don't know

5. I do the easiest work first.

never   rarely   often   always   I don't know

6. I begin my studying with a will to like it.

always   often   rarely   never   I don't know

7. I restate the main ideas in my own words.

always   often   rarely   never   I don't know

8. If possible I finish an assignment before leaving it.

always   often   rarely   never   I don't know

9. I review by restudy, writing an outline, or by some other method.

always   often   rarely   never   I don't know

READINGS

In Literature

NOVELS

Dickens, Charles. *Oliver Twist.*

Oliver has lots to learn, from not asking for a second helping at the orphanage to how to pick pockets in old Fagin's "school."

London, Jack. *Smoke Bellew*. Appleton-Century.

> A rich tenderfoot learns how to face the hard facts of life in the Yukon gold rush. Exciting trips through rapids, portaging around falls, etc.

Waterloo, Stanley. *The Story of Ab*. Doubleday, Doran.

> Life was exciting and mind-stretching in the days of the cavemen.

Wister, Owen. *Philosophy IV*. Macmillan.

> How the bookworm was beaten at his favorite game of having perfect lessons makes an interesting story.

SHORT STORIES

Anderson, Sherwood. "I'm a Fool"; in *Horses and Men*. Viking.

> "And he learned about women from her."

Russell, John. "The Price of the Head"; in *31 Stories by 31 Authors,* edited by Ernest Rhys and C. A. Danson. Appleton-Century.

> How a drunkard, a man actually stewed in liquor, is kidnaped by a Pacific islander and learns the way of being a man.

For Further Information

Bliss, Walton B. *Personality and School,* Chapters 19-23, 27. Allyn and Bacon.

Eastburn, L. A., Kelley, V. H., and Falk, C. J. *Planning Your Life for School and Society,* Chapter 8. Scribner.

McLean, Donald. *Knowing Yourself and Others,* Chapter 35. Holt.

Morgan, John J. B. *Keeping a Sound Mind,* Chapter 12. Macmillan.

SECTION 19

ARE YOU EMOTIONALLY GROWN UP?

Can a high-school student be an adult? At about what age is a person able to control his emotions? When is a person physically mature? When is he emotionally mature? Would a grown-up ever shed tears? Are there any persons over twenty-five who laugh, cry, sulk, and fly off the handle like a child? Are they grown-up in any sense of the word?

IT HAS ALREADY been made clear that becoming an adult is a learning process; we change as we grow through childhood and youth to adulthood. But it is perhaps less clear what adulthood really is. What are its characteristics? How does an adult act in various circumstances in comparison with one who is not an adult? How can a person tell whether he himself is acting like an adult?

Adult behavior is too large a subject to tackle all at once; hence we shall consider it from two standpoints, emotional development and social development. First, let us compare a grown-up and a child from the standpoint of emotional development.

What are the marks of childishness? If you studied very small children long enough, you would find that there are three outstanding characteristics of their behavior:

(1) They cannot put up with things.
(2) They want immediate attention.
(3) They do not control their reactions.

A small child naturally makes a fuss when he is uncomfortable, cold, wet, or hungry. He does not wait until his mother is ready to take care of him, but immediately cries and makes himself

heard in no uncertain manner. And he seems to make no effort
to control himself. These characteristics of a child's behavior are
perfectly normal at that time of life. But when an older person
behaves in this way, his behavior is called immature or childish.

What are the marks of adulthood? "When I was a child,"
wrote Saint Paul, "I spake as a child, I felt as a child, I thought
as a child: now that I am become a man, I have put away childish
things" (I Corinthians 13:11). There are three important characteristics of the behavior of a grown-up which are exactly the
opposite of those just given:

(1) He is inclined to accept things as they are when they cannot be changed.
(2) He can wait and work toward future satisfactions.
(3) He controls his reactions.

There are not many people who achieve such heights of adulthood at all times. Probably no one does. Yet as our personality
grows, we achieve more and more of the adulthood described by
these three ideals.

Childishness may be shown in many ways. Lena L—— is a
married woman whose behavior shows emotional immaturity in
various ways. She cries easily and frequently. She "flies off the
handle" when things do not go just right or when she does not get
her way. Her disgust at certain odors — frying onions, for example — keeps her from preparing a number of dishes especially
liked by her husband. In a group she laughs more and louder
than the others. She frequently makes shocking statements, tells
impolite jokes, and calls attention to herself. She fails to see the
humor of a joke on herself and will either blush or become angry
when one is told. She pays little attention to her four children
and shows no mother-love for them, and from time to time develops "crushes" on other men. She invites flattery and seems to
have no suspicion of the baldest compliments. She craves excitement, is constantly restless, is moved to extreme heights of
elation, and is frequently in depths of despair, ready to give up.

Peter F——, thirty years of age, was a good-hearted person, big,
well-built, healthy, and strong, whose social difficulties were
closely related to his emotional underdevelopment. There were

*"Isn't that her car? I've a notion to smack her fender
for what she did to me on that five-no-trump bid!"*

HINTS FOR DISCUSSING THE CARTOON

Is there anything childish about this woman's
reaction to losing? Explain your opinion of her
sportsmanship. Does she play bridge to lose, to
win, or just for the enjoyment of it? Do you
think she is the sort of person who would bid
as high as Five No Trump if she thought she
could make it? Why? What mechanism (see
Section 17) is she employing here?

three ways in which Peter F—— was immature. As was the case
with Lena L——, he laughed a great deal more often and longer
and louder than others in a group. Frequently other people in-
voluntarily watched him and felt uneasy about this too easy,
rather childlike laughter, which tended to keep some people from
seeking his friendship. He was also immature in that he showed
a constant need for recognition. He was always "fishing for compliments"; that is, turning the conversation around so that the
person with whom he talked would have to compliment him on
his work or his ideas. He seemed to have a childish need for the
experience of elation in connection with any success he might
achieve. Other people responded to this overeagerness for compliments and recognition by withholding their encouragement
and even by finding excessive fault with him.

A third immaturity of Peter's was his inability to know when to
stop doing something he enjoyed very much. For instance, if he
began to work on a piece of furniture for his home, he would stick
at it until three or four o'clock in the morning and then crawl into
bed completely worn out — with the result that he was not very
efficient at the office the following day. On other occasions he
might read a book all night or until he fell asleep over it in his
chair. Several times a year Peter F—— was on the verge of losing
his job because his inability to be moderate in such things, which
were of course not harmful in themselves, impaired his value as a
bookkeeper.

Additional illustrations of childishness. Several illustrations of
emotional immaturity are given here, all showing the three characteristics mentioned: (1) inability to put up with things; (2)
impatience for immediate relief; and (3) lack of control.

1. People who want to stop playing a game, quit a job, or withdraw from any group activity because they are not getting their
own way, because their particular idea is not being carried out,
or because they are not getting enough recognition for their idea.
These people are angry because their own desires are interfered
with. They are not able to put up with things for the sake of the
group as a whole. They wish immediate relief from the emotion
of dejection and show an immature need for elation.

2. People who like to tell a joke on others, but become annoyed

when the joke is on themselves. **They** are immature in being too easily dejected.

3. People who are too impatient to wait for something they want to have, perhaps a new dress, a new car, or some success looming in the future. They are not able to put up with the delay necessary for the working out of events that will lead to what they want, but are impatient to experience the emotion of elation immediately.

4. People who "fly off the handle" when they cannot have what they want. Their natural movements and desires are interfered with, and they respond with anger as a child does.

5. Adults who weep when they cannot have what they want. Their desires are thwarted, and they regress to a childish way of trying to get what they want.

6. People who make "wise-cracks" or exaggerated statements in order to get attention in a group. These people show need for the emotion of affection. They feel that they are not loved, and, when the group's attention is not centered upon them, they suffer from dejection, from which they wish immediate relief.

7. People who show a need for flattery. Everyone likes to be commended, but these people are not satisfied with the usual amount of elation that comes to one in the ordinary course of events.

8. People who hang on to their grief for an abnormally long time. They show an abnormal desire for the emotion of dejection. Because they enjoy this emotion, they do not make an effort to substitute a more healthful one — love, for example — which builds instead of destroying the personality.

9. People who cannot remain true to a friend for a long period of time but jump from one friendship to another. They are emotionally immature in that they prefer elation to loyalty. Their own happiness is more important than that of their friends.

Can you give up a pleasant activity? One characteristic of an emotionally mature person is that he is able to shift his attention from one activity to another when it is necessary or advisable to do so. For example, a girl who likes to do handwork, like knitting or crocheting, may enjoy the mild feeling of elation that comes from completing every line or section; but there are dishes in the kitchen that her mother has asked her to wash. In order to develop emotional maturity, she should lay aside the handwork for a short time until the dishes have been done. In this way she develops or strengthens the habit of self-control and guides her activities by thought rather than feeling.

Some people willfully continue a mood or an emotion. An emotionally mature person practices self-control in emotions as well as activities. Certain emotions, such as fear, anger, and dejection, break down rather than build the personality. We should not allow ourselves to hold these emotions so long that they upset a well-planned life.

On first thought it may seem that no one enjoys the emotions of fear and anger or the moods of despair and bitterness; but upon closer study it becomes evident that they are enjoyed and that many people foolishly indulge in such emotions for long periods. In 1925, the great screen lover Rudolph Valentino died, and his body could be viewed in a funeral parlor in New York City. Newspapers told of one middle-aged woman, in no way related to the famous movie star, who stood in line for hours on six different occasions. She did this to repeat and prolong the emotion of sadness.

Prolonging an emotion does not reflect self-control. Illustrations could also be given of persons who have carried grudges against each other for years, thus continuing the emotion of anger. Other instances of the same sort are such habits as restating the closing of a letter in three or four ways, and repeating and prolonging farewells. In these instances, in which the individual hesitates to shift his attention to another activity, he is prolonging the emotion merely to satisfy himself and is no longer reacting normally to a given situation. An emotionally mature person is willing to deny himself such satisfactions and is willing to change to a more healthful emotion or shift his attention to another activity when it is normal to do so.

Can you make and follow a planned routine? The ability to plan a day's activities in advance and then follow the plan is characteristic of adulthood because any day's program requires frequent shifts from one activity to another and from one emotion to another. Children find it difficult to plan and follow the plan, but adults have learned to do this. There are, of course, a great many so-called adults who do not like to plan a routine and carry it out from step to step, but they are not truly adults. They have never learned to control their emotions well enough to fill the day efficiently with the various tasks that must be done.

Control the activities and you control the emotions. People who wish to improve their emotional control are willing to train themselves accordingly. They plan ahead for days, weeks, months, and years, and they try to adhere to the plan. Routine becomes acceptable and natural to them. In fact, an important step in the development of emotional maturity is to follow routine or planned activity, for every activity has emotional quality, and, in so far as one can control his activities, he also controls his emotions.

When is a person emotionally mature? In the section entitled "Up Again, Down Again," page 102, some references were made to the difficulty of maintaining complete serenity. It was pointed out that no one can hold the emotion of elation or the emotion of dejection without interruption. This statement could be enlarged to include all emotions; in fact, all the experiences of life. There is a constant rhythm of feeling and action in normal people. As a youth becomes more and more adult, the rhythm of life is more within his control; he gradually becomes the master of his mind, his moods, his actions. He is always becoming the master, however; he never achieves complete mastery. Neither a youth nor a grown-up ever attains such perfect emotional control that there is no room for improvement. No matter how strong a personality one may have, one can always profitably continue the study of oneself and one's fellows for the purpose of retaining and improving emotional and social control.

As a youth grows into his ideal self, he develops greater acceptance of life, greater patience and ability to wait for future satisfactions, and greater self-control.

FOR CLASS DISCUSSION

1. If you are emotionally mature, will you worry about a test while you are dancing? Explain.

2. Should you think about a boy friend when you are studying? What emotion is not controlled when you do?

3. Suppose you are eager to have a new dress or new suit, but must wait because there is not enough money to buy it. Should you become sad, angry, or afraid? What will you do if you are emotionally mature?

4. What childish characteristic is shown by the person who frequently interrupts conversation, says good-bye six or seven times, finishes the other person's sentences, sulks about the weather, begins many activities, but drops them before they are finished?

READINGS

In Literature

AUTOBIOGRAPHY

Day, Clarence. *Life with Father.* Knopf.

    Clarence Day's father certainly was interesting because he was emotionally immature. You can have all the fun of reading about him without having to live with him.

NOVEL

Forester, C. S. *To the Indies.* Little, Brown.

    The storms at sea, shipwrecks, and mutinies of the usual Spanish Main story are here; but Forester brings a reality to them that makes his books appeal to the more mature student as well as the one who merely likes adventure. Columbus in the background is excellently portrayed and offers a case study in emotional immaturity.

ONE-ACT PLAY

Schmitt, Gladys. "Miracle in Louisiana"; in *Prose and Poetry of Today.* Singer.

    Even an immature child can influence adults to positive action. This is a radio play that can be enacted in class.

For Further Information

Eastburn, L. A., Kelley, V. H., and Falk, C. J. *Planning Your Life for School and Society,* pp. 49-52. Scribner.

Fedder, Ruth. *A Girl Grows Up,* pp. 10-13. McGraw-Hill.

McKown, H. C., and Le Bron, Marion. *A Boy Grows Up,* Chapters 3 and 4. McGraw-Hill.

McLean, Donald. *Knowing Yourself and Others,* Chapter 41. Holt.

Trilling, Mabel B. *The Girl and Her Home,* pp. 207-211. Houghton.

ARE YOU SOCIALLY MATURE?

How does an adult take criticism? Who would feel slighted more often, a child or a grown-up? Why? Who would do more teasing, a child or a grown-up? Why? What is a happy medium in sociability?

PRACTICALLY ALL the ways by which a person shows that he is socially mature can be grouped under two main characteristics: he is cooperative instead of competitive, and his interest has shifted from himself to others. Since we mature gradually rather than all at once, the individual shows those characteristics in varying degrees at different ages. A person can be socially mature *for his age* when he is in kindergarten, or when he is in the eighth grade, or when he is in senior high school. Neither as a child nor as a youth, of course, would he be expected to have the social maturity of an adult.

For further light on this question of social maturity, suppose we consider again the cases of Lena L—— and Peter F——, given in the previous section.

Lena L——. Some of the indications of emotional immaturity in Lena L——'s behavior — for example, her insistence on having her own way and calling attention to herself — are also naturally indications of social immaturity. In other ways her social immaturity is distinct from emotional immaturity. She has a tendency to become bored at parties that she herself planned, and sometimes she even leaves her guests to shift for themselves while she goes off to be alone for an hour or more. She rarely takes part in a game or activity that she did not suggest or in which she is not personally interested, and seldom cooperates in a group led by someone else. At bridge, when her hand is being played by her partner, she leaves the table or shifts her attention from the game and busies herself with other things. She hardly ever accepts suggestions, and is likely to blush, become angry, or walk away when anything is said that might be interpreted as containing the slightest criticism of her.

Lena's social standing reflects her failings, for she has no friends who have remained constant over a period of years. She frequently rushes some new arrival in town or suddenly picks up with a person previously outside her circle of acquaintances. Her husband is very well liked and has many friends, but he has difficulty in keeping some of these friendships because the men as well as the women are annoyed by Lena's childish behavior.

Peter F——. It was characteristic of Peter not to be sensitive to the responses of the group toward his suggestions. He would press his ideas even in the face of evident opposition or dislike on the part of others, and it was a common occurrence at the end of a group meeting to have the members get together and talk about Peter's mistakes. He also had little sense of propriety in his manner of dress and was as likely as not to be formally dressed on an informal occasion or vice versa. People thought of him as peculiar and were disinclined to seek his friendship.

How do you show your ability to cooperate? The two cases discussed are examples of immaturity. Now let us consider some of the positive characteristics of maturity. Here are a few of the traits you find in a true adult that show cooperation rather than competition:

1. *He is tactful.* The true adult is careful to express his opinions in such a way as to make them acceptable to others and see that his actions are such as to result in a minimum of damage and maximum of advantage to others.

2. *He knows how to play.* Whether the game be physical or intellectual, he enjoys the contest for its own sake, not to show his superiority or someone else's inferiority. Although he is interested in winning, he is modest when he wins and pleasant when he loses.

3. *He is a good conversationalist;* that is, he does not monopolize a conversation, and he listens attentively to the other person

without, for instance, letting his eyes wander restlessly elsewhere. He enjoys humorous as well as serious talk and can take part in both.

4. *He enjoys team work* and can get real satisfaction from taking a small part in a big enterprise; that is, he does not have to be the leader in everything he does. You can depend on him to do his particular job along with others.

How do you show your interest in the other fellow? Here are a few of the traits you find in a true adult that show interest in others rather than in the self:

1. *He studies people's wants.* The true adult not only has some understanding of other people's wants, but he is constantly trying to understand more deeply the reasons behind other people's actions.

2. *He is altruistic;* that is, he has regard for the other fellow and tries to practice the Golden Rule: Do unto others as you would have them do unto you.

3. *He is willing to receive criticism,* whether it is given kindly or unkindly, for criticism gives him a chance to improve himself and it shows how other people see him.

4. *He is friendly,* trying to see the best in everyone around him and to feel kindly toward human beings in general. He is self-denying, and he tries to be helpful and generous in his thoughts, words, and actions.

5. *He is sympathetic.* Because he understands human nature better than young people do, it is easier for him to put himself in the other fellow's place. He lives other people's emotions, sharing their happiness and grief.

Evidences of adulthood showing both cooperation and altruism. Many traits you find in a true adult spring from both cooperativeness and interest in others. Here are three examples:

1. *He is willing and able to adjust himself to circumstances.* When circumstances are unfavorable, he tries to do what he can to improve them; but if he sees that this is impossible, he accepts what must be and adjusts himself in such a way as to find happiness in spite of difficulties.

2. *He lives according to a plan.* It is characteristic of a true adult to have a broad plan for his life extending over a number of

"Can't you hurry a bit?   I have to catch a train!"

HINTS FOR DISCUSSING THE CARTOON

Just what is it in this lady's point of view that makes the situation amusing? If she really has less time to make the train than those ahead of her, will her excitement help matters or hinder? How?   In what respect does her behavior reflect a lack of social maturity?   What could be done to improve it?

years, as well as to plan day by day and week by week. Living according to a plan does not mean making a detailed blueprint of all our activities and then trying to carry it out, because that would be impossible, at least in our rapidly changing world. It does mean that today's activities have a recognized meaning for the future; they fit into a general pattern and are not haphazard. Good planning of this sort means budgeting time and money for health, security, and service.

3. *He is a leader in some things and can be a leader in others when called upon.* He is able to trust people to carry out their share of a given task and gives them freedom to do it. He considers that leadership, if it is entrusted to him, is a matter of service rather than domination; it enables him to serve more people and get more accomplished than he could otherwise, because it involves cooperation.

Have you a sense of humor? It is frequently said of a socially mature person that he does not take life too seriously. Perhaps this means that he is able to see things in their true light by standing apart from himself and looking at them as a scientist would; or perhaps it means that he can see an element of error in everything and that this element is the funny side of life. A great deal might be said about a sense of humor. It does not consist simply in laughing at jokes or telling funny stories. It must be a philosophy of life that helps one to understand life in such a way as to take off the bitterness when errors begin to damage the personality or destroy happiness. A person who takes life too seriously looks at these errors only in relation to himself in the immediate present, whereas a person who has a sense of humor looks at them in relation to his whole life and in relation to everything he knows.

Perhaps it is true that there is no good without evil, and perhaps it is also true that there is much more good than evil in the world. A person who takes life too seriously pays more attention to the evil than the good, or magnifies the evil; whereas the adult with a sense of humor never loses sight of the good, even though he is well aware of the evil.

It is difficult to define a sense of humor, but whatever it is, it is a part of mental health. It grows as the personality grows and achieves greater unity.

Do you ever feel slighted?   One of the marks of adulthood is
the way we take slights or give them.   A slight is an act or the
omission of an act planned to arouse the feeling of inferiority.
We speak of having been slighted when we are ignored, snubbed,
cut, or belittled by someone else.   No one likes to be made little
of, but the immature personality shows a supersensitiveness to
slights and suffers a good deal of unhappiness because of such incidents.   Perhaps nine-tenths of the time that people consider
themselves slighted, they are mistaken, only imagining things.
There is a tendency, especially among people who are not yet
fully grown up, to be unduly sensitive about their own importance, and the merest hint or indication of something that
seems to reflect on them in a belittling way may immediately be
taken as an intended slight or insult.

Why do people insult and slight one another?   Nevertheless,
slights do occur.   Everyone is slighted occasionally, though there
is a distinction between being slighted and feeling slighted.   It
is important not to feel hurt over a slight.

Why does one person slight another?   Because he or she (1) is
ignorant and impolite, or (2) has a mean disposition, or (3) wants
revenge for some previous wrong or fancied wrong, or (4) is
jealous.   In every case a slight or insult is intended to give pain
by calling the attention of a person to his inferiority.   The person slighted feels hurt because he does not wish to feel inferior.

Despite the fact that there is no good reason for one person to
slight another, the truth is that the inferiority to which the slight
calls attention may actually exist.

What can be done about it?   Should we then deny the fact of
the inferiority in such a case?   What attitude should we take toward the slight?   It is not healthful to suffer intense mental an-
guish or become emotionally unbalanced every time we are
slighted.   It is not necessary and it is not grown-up.   Think of
the reasons that make people slight each other — ignorance, mean-
ness, revenge, and jealousy — not one a good motive.   If it is
true that we do have some inferiority, let us face it honestly and
refuse to be "broken up" as a victim of another's evil intentions.
Ignore the insult or feel sorry for the person who is so immature
as to try to slight you.

Why do people tease? So many people indulge in teasing that it is almost necessary to be able to "take it," even if one is not clever enough to give as much in return. Why do people tease each other? There are many reasons; here are a few of the most common:

1. Many people tease others because other people tease them. If there is some person who frequently teases you and gets the better of it, you can be pretty sure that someone else teases him and gets the better of it with him. He teases you because he wants to make up for his defeat.

2. Many people tease others because they feel inferior about something. When they can make others squirm, they themselves feel superior.

3. Teasing is a safe way to punish someone, for it is always possible to say, "I was only teasing and didn't mean anything," after the damage is done and the other fellow has been hurt.

4. With some people, teasing is a habit, learned at home or among friends and adopted as a form of conversation.

5. Teasing is sometimes used as a defense mechanism, as when a boy shifts the attention of a group away from himself toward another person whom he ridicules.

6. It is also sometimes a way of showing affection. It is a peculiarity of boys and men that they often hesitate to come right out and show their tenderest feelings, so they use an indirect method.

What to do about teasing. There are not many well-adjusted adults who do a great deal of teasing. They don't want to take the chance of hurting someone's feelings, so they get out of the habit. Well-adjusted people also know what to do about teasing when they themselves are being teased. Here are a few suggestions:

1. Pay no attention to the person who is teasing you or to what he says. If you can remove all emotional reaction, you will really make it unpleasant for the teaser.

2. Cooperate with the teaser and do not argue with him. If possible, get a "kick" out of what he is saying at your expense. When he sees he is not hurting you, he will either stop or the teasing will continue as a friendly conversation.

3. Make an equally clever remark to silence the other fellow. He will know when he has the worst of it and will not come back for more very often.

4. If you do not like to be teased, never tease *anyone* yourself.

Can you avoid extremes? The course of life from childhood on is largely a struggle for the happy medium. Each of us has an individual problem in satisfying our deepest needs in order to achieve happiness, and at times the struggle goes to extremes; we try too hard today and then perhaps tomorrow give up trying altogether. Adulthood is in sight when youth has learned certain habits that reduce the extremes and add balance to an otherwise unbalanced personality.

For example, a high-school student who does nothing but study for good grades and who has few or no friends, attends no school affairs, and is timid and seclusive, may well make a conscious effort to smile and say hello to fellow students, attend school dances or school parties occasionally, take part in extra-curricular activities, and spend some time with other people. By so doing he adds balance to his life and helps to make himself socially mature. He avoids the extreme of living too much away from people.

There is a happy medium for each individual. It cannot be denied that everyone lives in a world of many people, all of whom are more or less dependent upon each other and should cooperate and if possible get along with each other enjoyably. This applies to each of us, whether or not our natural tendencies make it easy for us to deal with other people. Everyone is forced to have at least some social relationships, in his home, school, church, community, or job, or in all of them together. The well-balanced adult should be able to enter into these social relations with comfort both for himself and for others. In whatever way he gets his greatest satisfaction, he will always think of the other fellow. Young men and women of high-school age are on their way toward the happy medium in social relations.

Sociability can be carried to extremes. A person who is socially mature is not necessarily a social lion or extremely popular, nor does he get all of his pleasure in life from social contacts. We should not confuse extreme sociability with true adulthood.

Florence D—— was an extremely sociable person. She was

called Flossie in high school by her great many friends. She was hail-fellow-well-met and could be seen sailing through the corridors, smiling, waving, and saying, "Hi, Jo," "Hi, Bess," "Hi, Kid," right and left. She belonged to four or five high-school organizations, took part in several extra-curricular activities, was often heard to make suggestions which were frequently of little value, but created good will and provoked laughter on the part of the group. She preferred parties to movies, did not have the patience to listen to the radio, and spent few evenings at home. She frequently had "crushes" on boys and readily "flew off the handle," but was quickly on good terms again.

Florence's friends did not expect her to take a stand and hold it if the majority disagreed with her, and when something came up that involved a matter of principle, they did not force her to support it, for they felt she would fall in line when the majority had accepted the idea. Florence devoted little time to her school work and graduated "by the skin of her teeth," but she did not care. Her friends knew that she was not easily offended, that she was glad to have them help her in her school work, and that she was at times careless about her belongings and her personal appearance. They dealt with her accordingly. After high school Florence enjoyed her work as a saleswoman in a department store, and, although she frequently made mistakes in giving change, she thought she was good and did not hesitate to ask her employer for raises. In many respects Florence was still a child.

Tips for the sociable type. A person who is socially inclined should avoid extremes. His natural tendency to be with people may lead to a lack of self-reliance and to many interruptions in his work. He may jump from one thing to another and from one friend to another, becoming superficial both in what he does and in his friendships. He may sacrifice his principles just because he wants to do what the other fellow wishes.

He should make a conscious effort to restrain his impulsiveness and deliberately stick to a task that he has begun until it is finished; he should try to become self-reliant; he should strive for loyalty in friendships; he should take time to think long and deeply through a problem rather than skim it and pass to another; and he should try to be willing to sacrifice his popularity for the right when there is an important principle at stake.

FOR CLASS DISCUSSION

1. Frequently when Jeanne L—— was called upon to serve in an important position, like being chairman of a meeting or pouring at a tea, she became ill at the last minute, although she was a normally healthy person, and someone else had to take her place.

Why did she become ill?

Why did she accept the responsibility in the first place?

She must have had certain sociable qualities to be asked to serve. What might these have been?

Would people be likely to continue to give her responsible social assignments? Give reasons.

2. Raymond M—— is a talented and sensitive person. He is an accurate draftsman and has a wide knowledge gathered from reading and study. Whenever he looks at a structure, whether it is a house, a bridge, or only a chair, he is critical of the mistakes that were made in its design or construction, and he usually spends more time discussing its faults than its virtues. "This is how I'd have done it," he says.

What is wrong with his point of view?

Which emotion does he arouse in others by continually finding fault?

What could he do to become more grown-up?

3. Which of the two main characteristics of social maturity is illustrated in each of the following activities:

Getting assignments and books for a student who is confined at home.

Asking the class president if you can help with anything.

Telling a boy that the girl he wants to date is in a certain place where he can speak to her.

Finishing the clean-up work when everyone has left.

4. Classify each of the following expressions under the headings, "Social Maturity" and "Social Immaturity." If any do not lend themselves to exact classification, explain why.

Watch me.	I know better.
You can't tell me.	What do you think?
Do it again.	That sounds swell.
Take my advice.	Listen to me.
Good for you!	Let me go first.
Show me how.	I'll show you how it's done.
Get out of the way.	I'm right with you.
Tell me about it.	You don't know what you're
I'll follow you.	talking about.

READINGS
In Literature

NOVEL

Maugham, William Somerset. *The Moon and Sixpence.* Doubleday, Doran.

Strickland was not exactly lacking in social maturity; he just had no social feelings whatever. The novel is an interesting study of a man who strews human wreckage in his wake and is without compunctions for the feelings and needs of others.

SHORT STORIES

Lardner, Ring. "Champion"; in *Round Up.* Scribner.

What is a prize fighter — a champion — like? Compare this interpretation with that of Wallace Beery in "The Champ."

Suckow, Ruth. "Midwestern Primitive"; in *Children and Older People.* Knopf.

What are famous people like when they take off their masks? It took Grandma to get the masks off, though.

For Further Information

Fedder, Ruth. *A Girl Grows Up*, Chapter 2. McGraw-Hill.

McKown, H. C., and Le Bron, Marion. *A Boy Grows Up*, pp. 88-99, 131-148. McGraw-Hill.

McLean, Donald. *Knowing Yourself and Others*, Chapter 17. Holt.

Scharmer, Fay Mack. *Boy's Guide to Living*, Chapter 3. Allyn and Bacon.

Wright, Milton. *Getting Along with People*, Chapter 5. McGraw-Hill.

WHERE DO I STAND?

On the lines provided below, place marks above the words "always," "often," "rarely," and so on, according to your most careful opinion about yourself. Then connect these marks with a zigzag line from the first to the second to the third, and so on to the last.

(NOTE. *Do not write in this book,* unless it is your own. Make a copy on a separate sheet of paper.)

1. I am tactful in dealing with people.	always	often	rarely	never	I don't know
2. I know how to play and enjoy it.	always	often	rarely	never	I don't know
3. I can either listen or talk with ease.	always	often	rarely	never	I don't know
4. I enjoy taking part in team work or team play.	always	often	rarely	never	I don't know
5. I study why people do what they do, especially when they seem to offend.	always	often	rarely	never	I don't know
6. I practice the Golden Rule.	always	often	rarely	never	I don't know
7. I am willing and able to receive criticism even if it hurts.	always	often	rarely	never	I don't know
8. I have a friendly feeling toward people.	always	often	rarely	never	I don't know
9. I sympathize with others.	always	often	rarely	never	I don't know
10. I readily adjust myself to circumstances that cannot be changed at the time.	always	often	rarely	never	I don't know
11. I live according to a plan.	always	often	rarely	never	I don't know
12. When called upon, I am willing to lead or to follow.	always	often	rarely	never	I don't know
13. I see the funny side of life.	always	often	rarely	never	I don't know
14. People slight me and hurt my feelings.	never	rarely	often	always	I don't know
15. I slight others.	never	rarely	often	always	I don't know
16. People tease me.	never	rarely	often	always	I don't know
17. I tease others.	never	rarely	often	always	I don't know
18. I am self-reliant.	always	often	rarely	never	I don't know

If You Want to Know More

You have been studying psychology and mental hygiene, fields of science that can give you a great deal of information if you want to know more. Psychologists and mental hygienists have written excellent books containing the results of much study, experience, and experimentation. The ideas discussed in Part One are only a beginning, a mere introduction, to the sciences from which the ideas are drawn.

If you want to know more about the master drives of personality, and if you want to try your hand at books that go deeper than this one, read:

Adler, A. *Understanding Human Nature*, Chapter 5. Garden City.

Dashiell, J. F. *Fundamentals of General Psychology*, Chapter 6. Houghton Mifflin.

Shaffer, L. F. *The Psychology of Adjustment*, Chapter 4. Houghton Mifflin.

Starch, D., Stanton, H. M., and Koerth, W. *Controlling Human Behavior*, Chapter 2. Macmillan.

If you want to know more about human feelings, especially the feelings of young people, read:

Adler. *Understanding Human Nature*, Chapters 2-5.

Burnham, William H. *The Normal Mind*, Chapter 15. Appleton-Century.

Dashiell. *Fundamentals of General Psychology*, Chapter 7.

Dorsey, J. M. *The Foundations of Human Nature*, Chapter 7, Sections 2-4. Longmans, Green.

Starch, Stanton, Koerth. *Controlling Human Behavior*, Chapter 11.

Zachry, C. B. *Emotion and Conduct in Adolescence*, Chapters 2-6. Appleton-Century.

If you want to know more about the abilities of people, read:

Dashiell. *Fundamentals of General Psychology*, pp. 303-311 and Chapter 13. See also additional references in the index.

Encyclopedia of Educational Research. Walter S. Monroe, Editor. See Section 12 under "Child Development."

Starch, Stanton, Koerth. *Controlling Human Behavior*, Chapters 4-8.

If you want to know more about the mechanisms people use to get what they want, read:

Adler. *Understanding Human Nature,* Chapters 2 and 3.

Freud, S. *A General Introduction to Psychoanalysis.* Garden City.

Jastrow, Joseph. *The Subconscious,* Part I. Houghton Mifflin.

Morgan, John J. B. *Keeping a Sound Mind,* Chapters 6 and 8. Macmillan.

Shaffer. *The Psychology of Adjustment,* All of Part II.

Most of the books listed just above deal with information about how the true adult does not behave. They are based upon the idea that, if we fully understand the motivation of behavior, we will be better able to avoid the wrong reactions and use the right ones. Inasmuch as the true adult has good mental hygiene, the study of books in the field of mental hygiene will increase your understanding of the true adult. Here are a few good titles:

Burnham. *The Normal Mind.*

Dixon, W. M. *The Human Situation.* Longmans, Green.

Groves, E. R. *Personality and Social Adjustment.* Longmans, Green.

Hollingworth, Leta S. *The Psychology of the Adolescent.* Appleton-Century.

Jastrow, Joseph. *Keeping Mentally Fit.* Greenberg.

Jastrow, Joseph. *Piloting Your Life.* Greenberg.

PART 2

GETTING ALONG
WITH OTHERS

◄ UNIT VI ►

Doing the Right Thing at the Right Time

GETTING ALONG WITH OTHERS comes easy after you know about yourself and put what you know into practice. Part One, therefore, was planned to give you a better knowledge of yourself. We have been asking, "What are the reasons behind our actions and how can we control these actions?" After you understand yourself, you can better understand others and, using your knowledge, deal with them effectively. This is the foundation upon which Part Two is laid. It will deal with the problems of living with others in formal groups, in family life, in boy and girl relationships, and in married life.

The first unit of Part Two, "Doing the Right Thing at the Right Time," takes up specific problems that we usually meet in more or less formal groups of people. It is not intended to serve as a handbook of morals or manners but to give guiding principles and answer a number of questions frequently asked by high-school students who are puzzled about why a certain thing is right or wrong and want to know how to do the right thing at the right time.

If you want to get along with people, you should know their manners and customs and act accordingly. The sections in this unit should be helpful for your immediate interests; and in case you wish to know more about the subject, a number of interesting books, some of which may be had in your school library, have been listed at the end of the sections.

SECTION 21

WHY DO THE RIGHT THING?

What is a white lie? Is it ever right to tell one? Is it possible to have good manners and yet not be sincerely courteous? Is there any good reason why a man should tip his hat to a woman? Why is it right to speak well of people?

EVERYONE HAS BEEN PUZZLED at some time — and most of us many times — as to the right thing to do under certain circumstances. Frequently we are not only puzzled but embarrassed. Is there any guiding principle that underlies right actions?

Right conduct defined. All of us would agree that it would be right to take good care of our own property and wrong to harm someone else's unnecessarily. It would be right for a junior to cooperate with his class in preparing for the Junior Prom, and, except under unusual circumstances, it would be wrong to refuse. It would be right to guard one's reputation with care and wrong to harm another's needlessly. It would be right to do that which takes into account the wants, wishes, and rights of others and wrong to do the opposite. Right conduct, then, is based upon one solid foundation stone, namely, consideration for others; and this is the foundation, not only of right conduct in morals, but also right conduct in manners. It includes justice and obedience to law, which are based fundamentally upon consideration for others.

The right thing to do is moral. Most of the world's unhappiness comes from unwillingness or inability to give due consideration to the other fellow. This may not seem obvious; think about it, and you will agree. We are all more or less at fault in this, and

so far as we are at fault, we are immoral; for lack of consideration for others is the basis of immorality. Normally, each of us
should, as we grow older, improve in our consideration for others.
But even so, no one reaches perfection, and much unhappiness is
caused in everyone's life by his own immoral acts and those of
others.

Everyone has a share in the world's wrongs. In a very real
sense, then, everyone shares in the responsibility for the world's
mistakes, for everyone is to some extent immoral, or, as we have
expressed it, inconsiderate of the other fellow. Knowledge of
human nature tells us that if our dealings with another person
take his wants into account, that person will be more inclined
to deal with others in a similar manner; but if our dealings with
him are without due consideration for his wants and wishes, his
conduct toward others will tend to be inconsiderate. We are inclined to treat others as we are treated. We are inclined to do
the right thing toward others when others do the right thing
toward us.

The right prevails. It is possible to think of the world as
having an accumulation of small and large immoral acts, which
serve as obstacles to justice. But it is also possible to think —
and believe — that each of these obstacles, in itself, is temporary,
and that in the end (though the end may be a long way off)
justice always triumphs.

Though on the one hand we have a keen feeling for the right,
we frequently see that wrong is done and right does not prevail.
The line,

> Truth crushed to earth will rise again,

is hopeful in its meaning, but it also implies that truth sometimes
is crushed to earth.

This often happens in a quarrel when the stronger person
silences the weaker. Oftentimes the one who is less able to
express himself, or less confident of himself, or smaller in size,
loses the argument even though he is in the right. He goes down
to defeat and the thing he fought for loses out — temporarily.

Yet in the long run, we believe, the right must prevail.

Ideally, one should always be just, always do the right thing, even though he knows that not everyone will be just and right in return. You cannot expect others always to be just to you, but you can expect yourself to try to be just to others.

Young people find it especially difficult to stand by and wait for truth to rise again. It is usually older people who have more patience and get consolation from the thought that "the mills of God grind slowly, yet they grind exceeding small." It is usually older people who have seen truth rise again, because they have lived longer.

Consideration for others is also basic to manners. Consideration for others governs manners and customs as well as morals. In many cases, good manners are clearly habitual acts of courtesy and need little explanation to show that they spring from consideration for others. Why, for instance, does a man follow the woman in going upstairs, but precede her in going downstairs? Because in the latter case he can help her if she slips, stumbles, or falls. Why, at the theater, does a man enter the row first in case it is necessary to pass people before reaching the seats? Because he can then beg pardon for both himself and his companion and to some extent clear the passage for her.

There are other manners and customs that at first glance seem trivial and unimportant, but upon further study are found to have a reason for existence. All are based on the idea of consideration of others. It is customary, for example, for a girl to be given the inside of the sidewalk and for her escort to take the curb side. Is there any sense to this? There was in the remote days when the custom originated. In those days the inside was the dry and clean side of the walk, and less subject to splashing from horses, wagons, and coaches passing by. There was a clear and unmistakable courtesy in giving the girl the inside edge of the path. Now, however, the custom remains purely as a tradition, though in most places the reason for it no longer exists.

There are many customs of this kind. Notable among them is tipping one's hat. This had its origin hundreds of years ago when a knight in armor raised his visor in order that his face might be seen. This custom, too, remains as a tradition, the hat taking the place of the visor.

"I can't say much for their manners. You'd think anyone who hung around as late as we did would be invited to stay for dinner."

Many customs like these are now simply small acts of courtesy and politeness which no longer have any other reason than a sincere desire to do as others like to have us do. And where this is true, it is a good enough reason. Apparently trivial and even senseless matters of etiquette can have their roots in courtesy and consideration for others. By observing them, we show other people that we have consideration for them.

Many things may be done habitually in the same way. One important thing about the manners, customs, and etiquette of any group is that they are more or less uniform for the entire group; that is, they are the same for all members of the group. All men in our society are expected to take off their hats to women; it is the right thing to do. Similarly, everyone is expected to say, "I beg your pardon," or words to that effect, when passing in front of someone, and at a formal party everyone is expected to wear formal clothes.

High-school students often ask such questions as, "Is a boy introduced to a girl, or a girl to a boy?" "When do you write bread-and-butter letters?" "If there is no usher, does the boy precede the girl down the theater aisle?" "Should you put crackers in your soup?" "When there are three forks at your plate, which one is used first?" People who ask these questions and many similar ones show that they know there is a uniform or "right" way to do these things. They want to know what this way is, so that once having learned it they may act with confidence wherever they go.

Uniformity makes things easier. It is this characteristic of uniformity that makes it advantageous to know the right thing to do. A person who has made good manners a habit does not have to be puzzled at every turn about knowing how to act. When a woman enters the room, for instance, he will rise without thinking about it or interrupting the conversation. If he is interviewing someone for a job, he will know how to act courteously and can give his whole attention to the main point — answering questions adequately.

Etiquette in human relations is like lubricating oil in a machine. It makes things run much more smoothly, eliminates confusion, and enables the individual to concentrate on more important problems or objectives — as well as to enjoy himself more.

Knowing how is a duty. As a member of society every person will find it convenient for his own sake to know the accepted ways of doing things, because this makes it unnecessary to learn new ways to meet every situation that arises in ordinary social affairs. There is, however, another side to the matter. Every member of society has a responsibility to the other fellow, as well as to himself, to know the accepted ways of doing things. Out of a sincere feeling of consideration for others, he will make himself familiar with these ways of behaving, so that others will not be confused in their relations with him. A hostess, for example, might find it convenient to set her dinner table according to a pattern followed everywhere; but even if she did not find it convenient, it would still be her duty to do so out of consideration for others, in order that behavior during the dinner might be simplified for her guests.

Not knowing how is embarrassing. Young men and women of high-school age realize very well that ignorance in social affairs leads to self-consciousness, embarrassment, and a feeling of not belonging. If you know how to do the right thing at the right time, and do it with a sincere feeling of consideration for others, you get a feeling of confidence. You know you are doing what is being done, what other people do. You get a feeling that you belong, that you fit in, that you are one of the group.

What if you don't know? Few persons know and practice all the rules of etiquette, and this is certainly the case with those of high-school age. Moreover, in everyone's life situations often arise for which there is no set form of behavior. At such a time ask yourself, "What would be the courteous thing for me to do? What would show the greatest consideration for the other fellow?" You will not be far wrong if you are sincere; you will do the right thing and have the confidence that comes from knowing that your behavior springs from genuine politeness.

FOR CLASS DISCUSSION

1. Jack played end on his high-school football team. Occasionally he broke training and word of it came back to the coach. The coach talked with Jack and gave him to understand that he would be kept on the bench if it happened again. Jack promised the coach that it would not happen again. He made up his mind to abide by all training rules from that day forward.

Being one of the four best men on the team, Jack had his competitors and enemies. Several boys would have been glad to have had his place. One of them managed to have word brought back to the coach that Jack had broken training again even after the reprimand. When the coach heard this, he called Jack in and talked with him. During the conversation Jack did not convince the coach of his innocence, and the coach told him that he would be warming the bench during the next game. Jack became furious, said things he should not have said, and turned in his suit.

Was justice done to Jack?

Did Jack do the right thing?

What should he have done?

2. Jacqueline M—— had a pair of knitted mittens exactly like those of Mary J——. One day Mary told the dean of girls that she had lost her mittens, but she knew who had them — Jacqueline M——. The dean of girls called Jacqueline in and found sufficient evidence to prove that Jacqueline had not stolen Mary's mittens. But Mary insisted that the mittens were hers. When the case was dismissed, Mary told her friends that Jacqueline had stolen her mittens and that the dean of girls was afraid to make Jacqueline give them back.

Was justice done to Jacqueline? To the dean of girls?

Could Jacqueline have given her own mittens to Mary without harm to herself? Why?

Could Jacqueline bring about justice for herself? If so, how? If not, what could she do about the rumors being spread by Mary?

3. Is it right to drive past a red light when there is no traffic in sight and no officer near by? Why?

4. Is it right to speak evil of someone, even though what you say is absolutely true? Why?

READINGS

In Literature

NOVELS

Farnol, Jeffrey. *The Amateur Gentleman.* Little, Brown.

> What is a gentleman? The son of an ex-prize fighter and an innkeeper discovers what the standards are.

Wharton, Edith. *Ethan Frome.* Scribner.

> Not following the standards of society is dangerous, as Ethan Frome learned.

PLAY

Barrie, James. "The Admirable Crichton"; in *Plays of J. M. Barrie.* Scribner.

> When Crichton and his master and family were wrecked on a desert island, Crichton knew what to do and how to do it. There he was prince and Lady Mary loved him. But after they were rescued . . .

SHORT STORIES

Glaspell, Susan. "Jury of Her Peers"; in *Best Short Stories of 1917,* edited by Edward J. O'Brien. Small, Maynard.

> The only clue was the dead canary. Who committed the murder? Why? How much of life depends upon living by the rules!

Henry, O. "A Retrieved Reformation"; in *Roads of Destiny.* Doubleday, Doran.

> Jimmy Valentine, skilled safe-cracker, meets a girl and a crisis.

Wunsch, Robert, and Albers, Edna. *Thicker Than Water.* Appleton-Century.

> A collection of stories that interest high-school students.

For Further Information

Allen, Betty, and Briggs, Mitchell Pirie. *Behave Yourself,* Introduction. Lippincott.

Barbour, Ralph Henry. *Good Manners for Boys,* Chapter 1. Appleton-Century.

Black, Kathleen. *Manners for Moderns,* Chapter 1. Allyn and Bacon.

Boykin, Eleanor. *This Way Please,* Chapter 1. Macmillan.

LOOK THE PART

Which of the master drives is expressed in the desire to be well-groomed? Does consideration for others dictate what you wear? Is it right or wrong to be clean? Can a person be too well-dressed?

> All the world's a stage, Bassanio,
> In which each man plays his part.
>   SHAKESPEARE.

IN THE DRAMA OF LIFE you, too, play a part. Do you look the part you play?

In a certain girls' college in the East it is customary during the week to dress in serviceable, practical skirt and sweater get-ups. The girls look almost dowdy; they know it and like it. It's the thing that's done during the week on that campus. They are comfortable; they can sit or lounge wherever they like without being fussy about soiling their clothes. On the other hand, on week-end parties these same girls dress to kill. Again they look the part — immaculate, flowery, well-groomed, smooth.

Cleanliness comes first. Good grooming is first of all a matter of just plain cleanliness. Soap and water, and plenty of it, can make anyone look in the pink of condition. Add a good night's rest and you are fresh for the day's work and fun. Vigorous washing not only brings color to the skin; the feeling of cleanliness that results actually makes a difference in the personality.

Perhaps it is not necessary — or is it? — to remind people of high-school age that their eyes, ears, and teeth should be clean, that the fingernails should be clean and well-shaped, that the scalp should be clean and the hair glossy, and that the body should be bathed often enough to remove offensive odors. Those who do not fulfill these minimum requirements of good grooming are still children who have not yet learned the habits of grown-ups. There are, of course, plenty of adults who have not learned them. The statement still holds; these adults are to that extent immature.

If you are well-groomed, you will not look out of place. Fitness as well as cleanliness is involved in good grooming. A girl who came to class in yellow pajamas or a kitchen apron, a plumber who went to work in a tuxedo and to a formal dance in overalls, would be stared at, to say the least. Such things can be done in a stage farce, but not in real life. There is a certain elementary fitness about dressing for the occasion which has nothing to do with fussiness over clothes. You are not well-groomed when your appearance and dress make you look out of place.

Standards of appearance at work. The appearance a person makes has a great deal to do with his success in getting along with his fellow men. Every group has certain standards of appearance for its members, and if any member ignores these standards the group will disapprove even if he is otherwise a fine fellow. This is the case among groups of workers. Stenographers and clerks are expected to wear serviceable rather than flashy clothes while at work. Garage mechanics are expected to wear coveralls and nurses plain white uniforms. The list could be much enlarged. If a worker does not look the part, he or she is regarded as queer, not fitting in, odd; he is sometimes criticized by his employer and may even be discharged if he does not live up to the standards of appearance accepted by the working group.

Grooming as a courtesy to others. The same principle holds in social groups away from the job. Every group has certain standards from which its members may not greatly vary. Most people like to be well-groomed and want to present an appearance acceptable to the group. They like to look the part. It is not necessary to give them a reason for being well-groomed. Nevertheless, there is a good reason, the same reason given for doing the right thing in matters of etiquette — consideration for others. Think of a person — and there are quite a number of

them — who does not care about being well-groomed and has
no personal desire for cleanliness or neatness and no sense of the
suitability of clothing. In spite of his own indifference, such a
person is still bound by common courtesy to maintain an appearance acceptable to his group. He would have to argue the point
as follows: "I think it's nonsense to be constantly washing and
bathing, and a nuisance to keep my clothes neat; but if I don't do
these things there are bound to be some members of my group
who disapprove of my appearance and even feel embarrassed or
offended because I don't live up to their standards. I don't want
to antagonize them, so I will have to play the game."

Clothes should be neat. As for school clothes, it is of course
not necessary to spend a great deal of money or to have the best
that money can buy. On the contrary, the average student expects his friends to be neat but not gaudy. It is even possible to
take a certain pride, as Thoreau did, in the economy represented
by patched clothes, provided they are kept patched and clean
and pressed. Worn shoes look better polished than unpolished.
Carelessness and slovenliness are the things people dislike, unless
they happen to be snobs who put the emphasis on expensiveness.
The army is a good case in point. A soldier is expected to keep
his uniform and equipment clean, neat, and in good order at all
times. That is one of the most elementary rules of good morale
and group pride.

Grooming can be overdone. Although good grooming is one
of the essentials for successful relations with other people, it can
be overdone. This reflects some personality problem, as was the
case with Bernard M—— and Imogene A——.

Case One. Bernard M—— was nicknamed Dandy by the other
boys in school. He had great difficulty with his school work
and was not very bright; though he rarely failed in a subject, his
grades were always on the borderline. Perhaps it was to make
up for a sense of mental inferiority that he developed an excessive
neatness. His shoes were polished like mirrors, his trousers
pressed to a knife edge; he changed his shirt and tie every day,
and his hair was always slicked and shiny. He never played
baseball, football, or any other game involving physical exercise,
though he was well built and in good health. Some suspected
that he did not want to get dirty.

Occasionally Bernard would get into a fight with some fellow student who did not handle one of his books with the greatest of care or who soiled or misused his clothes in some slight way. The first thing he did after the fight was to dust himself off, straighten out his clothes, comb his hair, and wash his hands. The other boys naturally thought of him as queer. Unfortunately, his form of compensation — if that is what it was — led to a good deal of unhappiness for him because he did not practice a reasonable amount of restraint. He was too well-groomed.

Case Two. Another illustration of excessive grooming is that of Imogene A——, who felt rejected because she had no friends. Girls said of her that she used too much make-up — not only too much lipstick, but an eyebrow pencil and even mascara. They did not like the way her clothes emphasized her figure, or her habit of being the first to come out with every new fad. This overgrooming, which may have been Imogene's way of compensating for lack of friends, did not solve her problem, but rather made it more difficult for her to make friends. Many of the boys thought her appearance meant that she was "fast" and some kept away from her because of it.

Grooming is not for show. Good grooming should not be used as an opportunity to show off, but simply to present a clean and neat appearance in the group. It is not considerate of the others if you always dress noticeably better than they do. On the contrary, you call attention to yourself, jealousies begin, and what you gain in satisfying your desire to excel you lose in good will. Your fellows will like you better if they do not feel inferior to you because you wear better clothes than they. Your clothes should help you at all times to look the part, whether you are at work or at play; but people should be more impressed by your personality than by your clothes.

FOR CLASS DISCUSSION

1. Muriel E—— was not an offensive girl in any way except in her appearance, which often embarrassed others. Her teeth were visibly decayed; hence smiling and laughing were unbecoming to her. She did not take care of her hair, and her make-up was usually smudged on in a childish fashion. Her clothes were expensive but unsuitable

for school wear, and she always looked "different." Muriel's greatest unhappiness, she told one of her teachers, was the fact that she had neither boy friends nor girl friends.

Why did fellow students keep away from her?

If you had been the teacher, what would you have told Muriel?

2. Benson B—— was always coming to school in his coveralls. He was interested in mechanics and his hobby — which amounted almost to a passion — was to work on old motors. He did not like to bother to change his clothes for school or for dinner. His fingernails were lined with grease, and sometimes his hair and face showed smudges that had not been washed off. In his senior year Benson became interested in dancing, but when he attended an after-school dance dressed in his overalls, one of the teachers asked him to leave.

Did the teacher do the right thing?

Did Benson?

What would his fellow students be likely to think of Benson's habits of dress and cleanliness?

3. Suppose Benson were a promising mechanical genius. Should he still try to "look the part" of a student when he was in school? Why?

4. What do you consider improper grooming at one of your informal school dances?

INDIVIDUAL ACTIVITIES

1. Describe in detail the dress and appearance while at work of a person in your favorite occupation. If you have no favorite occupation, tell how one of the following manages to "look the part": garage mechanic, beauty operator, barber, nurse, carpenter, cabinetmaker, stenographer, saleslady, plumber, receptionist, druggist, shipping clerk, or telephone lineman.

2. Describe in detail the dress and appearance of a student in your school who "looks the part."

3. Ask a person whose opinion you value whether you are well-groomed.

READINGS

In Literature

NOVEL

Prokosch, Frederic. *The Asiatics.* Harper.

    From Beirut to China, the hero meets hundreds of people — strange people, kindly people, likable people. There is no book like it, quite. But one thing the young man always finds is that clean clothes and a well-shaven face are necessary to a hitchhiker.

SHORT STORY

Henry, O. "Lost on Dress Parade"; in *Four Million.* Doubleday, Doran.

    Life plays an ironical joke on Mr. Towers Chandler.

For Further Information

Allen, Betty, and Briggs, Mitchell Pirie. *Behave Yourself,* Chapter 2. Lippincott.

Barbour, Ralph Henry. *Good Manners for Boys,* Chapter 2. Appleton-Century.

Boykin, Eleanor. *This Way, Please,* Chapter 3. Macmillan.

Burnham, Helen A., Jones, Evelyn G., and Redford, Helen D. *The Boy and His Daily Living.* Lippincott.

Byers, Margaretta. *Designing Women.* Simon and Schuster.

Hillis, Marjorie. *Orchids on Your Budget.* Bobbs-Merrill.

Law, Frederick Houk. *He Got the Job,* Chapter 2. Scribner.

Scharmer, Fay Mack. *Boys' Guide to Living,* Part II. Allyn and Bacon.

THIS IS HOW IT IS DONE

How should a girl introduce one of her friends to another? What should a boy say when he is trying to date a girl? What should the girl say? When is it polite for a girl to refuse a dance? Who goes down the theater aisle first, the boy or the girl? At dinner who begins to eat first? What is your share of a conversation in a group?

IN THIS SECTION you will find answers to some of the questions most commonly asked by high-school students about the right thing to do in making introductions, in arranging dates, in dancing, in attending the theater, in dining, and in conversation. You will undoubtedly have questions not answered here; in that case, consult one or more of the books on manners listed at the end of each section. You will find that no single book on manners and etiquette contains all the answers; nor, perhaps, do all of them together, since some situations arise that do not get into the books.

It has already been pointed out that courtesy and consideration for others underlie all matters of etiquette. The basic idea should be your guide in deciding how to act when you are not sure there is a particular way to act. Do the considerate thing out of courtesy for others.

1. HOW DO YOU DO?

The order and form of introductions are puzzling to many people. Some never do learn how to help others get acquainted quickly and with ease. But it is not at all difficult if you follow three rules:

1. *Present the less important to the more important person regardless of age or sex.* For example, you would present your mother to the governor of a state, even though your mother is a woman and might be older than the governor. "Your Excellency, may I present my mother, Mrs. John Brown? Mother, His Excellency, Governor Robinson."

2. *Present the younger to the older person regardless of sex in case there is considerable difference in age.* For example, at high-school age, you would present your girl friend to your father. "Dad, may I present Helen Joy? Helen, this is my father."

3. *When there is no significant difference in age or rank, present the man to the woman, the boy to the girl.* For example, you would present your high-school coach to the new home economics teacher. "Miss Cook, may I present Mr. Broadchest? Mr. Broadchest, Miss Cook." Or, in introducing one student to another you would say, "Helen, this is Art Robinson. Art, Helen Jones."

The intention in each case is to introduce a person to the one whom you wish to honor.

How about the complicated introduction? The following question presents an interesting problem in introductions for people of high-school age: If a boy is coming to call for a girl on his first date and the room is filled with friends and relatives, how should the introductions be made? The following persons are in the group: mother, father, grandmother, and grandfather; sister, twenty-four; brother, seventeen; aunt, middle-aged; and a neighbor, a man, also middle-aged.

Here clearly is a situation that can become strained if not embarrassing. In order to avoid awkwardness, the girl may present the boy to her mother first, then to her father, then go around the other members of the group, presenting them in turn to the boy.

The conversation ensuing would be somewhat as follows: "Mother, may I present John Jones? John, my mother. Father, may I present John Jones? John, my father. And the others here, John, are" — naming them in order as they are standing or seated around the room — "my grandmother, Mrs. Robinson; my grandfather, Mr. Robinson; my sister, Helen; my brother, Bob; my aunt, Mrs. Robinson; and Mr. Neighbor, who lives next door."

What shall you say? The most common form of recognizing an introduction is, of course, "How do you do?" Other permissible expressions are, "I am glad to make your acquaintance," "I'm very happy to meet you," and "I'm glad to know you." Saying, "Pleased t' meet you" is not considered good form any more, probably because it has been used too much. Whatever you say, say it clearly; don't mumble or seem to be repeating a formula.

The most important thing to remember in saying "How do you do?" or whatever you say when you are introduced to someone is that you should feel the part and show it in your face and bearing. Are you indeed happy to make a new acquaintance? If so, you may be further interested in him and will want to carry on a conversation with him if it is convenient at that time. Look at the person; let your face open up with a smile; let him see that you are interested in him and glad to meet him, as you say you are.

Shall you extend your hand? Boys usually shake hands when introduced to boys; men do as a rule when the circumstances permit. Girls rarely do when introduced to girls; women may, but don't as a rule. It is considered a gesture of friendliness for girls and women to extend their hands, but it is not required form. An older woman usually extends her hand to a younger.

In case of mixed introductions, a girl does not extend her hand to the boy; however, if she does, he takes it as if it is the right thing to do. A woman does not extend her hand to a man, though she may if she wants to. A man always waits and watches to see whether the woman extends her hand and then responds accordingly.

Follow the custom of the group. Customs governing such manners as extending one's hand may vary from group to group. What is the custom in your community? Take your cue in details such as this from the particular group in which you find yourself, and from the individual to whom you are being introduced.

Introductions are important. Introductions are society's way of getting people acquainted quickly and easily. Be sure to pronounce each person's name clearly and in such a way that the other person gets it. Take your time; there should be no hurry.

READINGS

For Further Information

Allen, Betty, and Briggs, Mitchell Pirie. *Behave Yourself*, Chapter 5. Lippincott.

Black, Kathleen. *Manners for Moderns*, Chapter 3. Allyn and Bacon.

Boykin, Eleanor. *This Way, Please*, Chapter 5. Macmillan.

Scharmer, Fay Mack. *Boys' Guide to Living*, pp. 37-47. Allyn and Bacon.

2. DATING

Dick W—— was one of the boys who had a good many friends among both the boys and the girls in school. He was not the sort who tried to "go steady," but, like the other fellows, he did want a date once in a while. Dick had no trouble getting dates, though there was nothing special about his way of arranging for them. Here is how he dated Susan for the Junior Prom that year when three other boys were dating her.

Three weeks before the Prom, he happened to meet her as she arrived at school. Noticing that no one was talking with Susan while she placed her wraps in a locker, he walked up and said, smiling:

"Hello, Susan."

"Hello, Dick."

"How is the lab. manual coming?"

"It's about half finished, I guess. Gee, I'll have to spend all of my spring vacation working on it."

"All except the Prom, I hope. Say, Susan, that's what I wanted to ask you about, to see if you'd let me take you this time."

"Oh . . . That's still three weeks off, Dick."

"I know it is. I wanted to get my bid in first, see."

"Well . . . I'll tell you after lunch . . . Thanks."

That morning Susan was, of course, thinking about whether she could get a new dress and all the trimmings. She would have to talk that over with mother, and she did it at luncheon.

After luncheon Dick did not stand guard at Susan's locker, but he was within range, so that when she came it would be easy for her to see that he was interested. As she stood at her locker, he came by, as he had done that morning.

"Hi, Susan, what's the word?"

"O.K., I guess."

"Gee, that's swell. See you later."

Now, there was nothing mysterious or puzzling or complicated about this conversation between Dick and Susan; it was simply a courteous, straightforward discussion about a fair question. Susan was glad to be asked to the Prom, and Dick had a right to ask her. He did not have to get down on his knees. He asked his question the best way he could, and he knew that it was her privilege to accept or refuse. Dick would not have felt that the bottom had fallen out of everything if he had been refused; he might even have asked the same girl again.

Dating by telephone. During Dick's senior year the Varsity Club planned a mixed skating party. He knew that all the boys would be getting their dates as soon as possible, but he had been busier than usual and had not had a good chance to ask Mildred, the girl he hoped to take to the party. He rarely telephoned a girl for a date, but, rather than wait, he decided to phone Mildred. Mildred's mother answered the phone. He politely gave his name and asked if he might talk with Mildred. When Mildred came to the phone, he said:

"Hello, Mildred. This is Dick W——."

"Hello, Dick."

"I tried to get to see you at school today, but I didn't have a good chance. You know the Varsity Club is planning a skating party, and I wanted to ask if I could take you. I thought if I waited until Monday and asked you at school, I might be too late, so I thought I'd call. You don't mind, do you, Mildred?"

"No, that's all right."

"I think it will be a nice party, Mildred. You've heard about it, haven't you?"

"Oh, yes, there's lots of talk around school about it."

"It's next Friday, and I'd sure like to have you come."

"How late will it be, do you think?"

"We plan to start around eight or eight-thirty. Maybe it'll last until twelve or so."

"Wait a minute, I'll ask mother."

Mildred briefly told her mother what she knew about the party, and when her mother did not object to the hours, she returned to the phone.

"Hello. Yes, I can go."

"Thanks. That's swell. I'll see you Monday."

"All right, Dick."

"Sorry I had to phone you. I just didn't want to take a chance. Thanks again, Mildred."

"You're welcome. I'll be glad to go. G'bye."

A boy should not try to arrange a date with a girl by telephone if he is afraid to face her personally. On the other hand, a girl would rather get a date by telephone than go without. If possible, talk to the girl personally. This is a safe rule to follow during high-school days and in adult life as well.

Refusing the boy. Dick W—— was not always as successful in getting his dates as he was with Mildred and Susan on these two occasions. He had been refused. Somehow he did not let a refusal floor him, but accepted it along with all the other give-and-take of life. When he asked a girl for the privilege of taking her to a dance, a party, or a show, he understood that she had the right to refuse him, and if she did, he took it sportingly. It was the same Mildred who accepted his invitation over the telephone to the skating party who also refused an invitation of his to the Football Swing-Out.

It was an annual event in that high school to plan a school dance on the first Friday following the last football game. Dick had been thinking of asking Mildred, but had seen Bill B—— talking with her a long time one day, and he thought that he might be too late. Nevertheless, he asked her at the first opportunity. It was after school on Monday, when they both happened to be in the library checking out books for outside reading in American Literature. He noticed a book she was taking, as the librarian stamped the date on Mildred's card, and said to her:

"Hm. *The Oregon Trail.* Is that good?"

"Yes, quite. I have to finish it pretty soon, because I'm using it for a paper in history."

"I thought that book was on the American Lit. list."

"It is," she answered laughingly, "but I'm going to use it for both. Killing two birds with one stone. Get it?"

"Well, what is it about?"

By this time they were leaving the library together.

"It's one of those historical books about the West. Has a lot of American history in it."

"Say, Mildred, Friday's the Swing-Out, you know. May I take you?"

Mildred turned toward him. "Why, thanks, Dick," she said simply, "but I've been asked."

"I was afraid of that, but I wanted to make sure, anyway. I'm sorry."

"So am I, Dick, and thanks awfully for asking."

She left in Dick's mind a feeling that she would like to go with him, but that circumstances prevented it. Later that year, when Dick asked her to go to the skating party, she did not refuse.

There was nothing mysterious, puzzling, or complicated about this refusal. Mildred refused Dick politely and gave him an excellent reason. That was all there was to it. The moral, of course, is that a girl should refuse kindly and courteously, and, if possible, give a reason, so that the boy who asks for the date does not feel that there is something personal about the refusal.

READINGS

For Further Information

Black, Kathleen. *Manners for Moderns,* Chapter 4. Allyn and Bacon.

Boykin, Eleanor. *This Way, Please,* Chapter 17. Macmillan.

Law, Frederick Houk. *He Got the Job,* Chapter 5. Scribner.

3. *MAY I HAVE THIS DANCE?*

At an informal school dance in the afternoon or evening, it usually takes the average high-school boy about twenty minutes to get up enough courage to ask a girl for a dance. Still, it is a very simple matter. All he has to do is to walk up to the girl, give her time to end her conversation with someone, and ask, "May I have this dance, Jane?" If Jane wishes to dance with him, she will smile and say yes, and they will walk on to the floor, the boy making a way through the crowd for her, or, if there is no crowd, the girl preceding the boy. At the end of the dance, the boy thanks her in some such words as, "Thanks for the dance, Jane. I hope I may have another after a while," or, "You're a good dancer, Jane — I enjoyed it a lot." Jane can answer, "I enjoyed the dance, too, thank you," or any response to that effect. She takes his arm, and he walks with her where she wants to go and leaves her, perhaps thanking her again.

Refusing a dance. A girl may not with courtesy refuse a dance unless she has a good reason. In case she feels that she must refuse, she should do so kindly, with some such remark as, "I'd rather not dance this one. I'm tired," or, "Thanks, Jack, but I have this dance." If she feels that she has had too many dances with the same boy and he asks her again, she may say, "Thanks, Bill, but I'd rather sit out one or two dances." Then, if he sits with her and she does not wish to be seen with him, she may leave after a few minutes, perhaps saying, "Will you excuse me, Bill? I want to fix up a bit."

Grooming for the dance. At an informal after-school dance boys and girls are not expected to be dressed up, but they should be quite clean. In most parts of the country, and especially when the weather is cool, it is not considered permissible even at an informal after-school dance for boys to appear in shirt and trousers. If they wish to dance, they should wear a suit coat, or at least a sweater or jacket of some sort over their shirt.

At an informal evening school dance girls may or may not wear long dresses, but this depends upon the custom prevailing in the school. Boys will come in full suits, or coats and trousers of contrasting shades, but not in tuxedos or tails.

At a formal school dance girls will wear long dresses. Boys will wear tuxedos if they have them, or full suits, preferably dark, or coats and trousers of contrasting shades. Customs prevailing in the subtropics — in southern Florida, say, or southern California — are somewhat different because of extreme temperatures part of the year.

Dancing posture. During the past few years the posture of high-school students on the dance floor has improved a great deal in most schools (jitterbugging excepted!). Apparently bad dancing posture is going out of style. A few years ago one could see some couples dancing like two barrel staves balanced against each other at the top, other couples dancing as if the girl were bound to fall forward over the boy any minute, others as if they were trying to see how far the girl could bend backward before breaking her back. Still others could be seen wrapped around each other and forgetful of everyone else on the floor, hardly moving, hardly dancing, only swaying in one small two-by-four corner of the floor. These styles have gone out of vogue, it is good to say.

Exchanging dances at a formal dance. At a formal school dance there is no stag line, and couples who are not acquainted with each other must be introduced before dances may be exchanged. After introductions have been completed, or if introductions are unnecessary, one of the young men will say to the other, "Shall we exchange a dance, John?" John will look at his program and say, "Sure, which one do you say?" They will then compare programs and find a dance not yet signed for and in the space write each other's names. The couples will plan to meet at the beginning of that dance, and after the dance the young men will thank their partners for the dance and each other for making the exchange.

Refusing to exchange dances. It is not considered polite for the man to refuse to exchange dances or to avoid exchanging when there are opportunities to do so. He is entitled to the first dance upon his arrival and to the last before leaving with the girl he is escorting. Half of the intervening dances should be shared with other couples if requested. If before the dance begins, the young man writes his program full with his partner's name, she may say, with a laugh: "I'm glad I rate so well with you, Jack, but I won't rate so well with Mary and Dosey and two or three others if they don't have a dance with you. How about putting me down for the first and the last and half of the others? That way they won't be so jealous of me."

Coming by automobile. Couples usually come to a formal dance by automobile,[1] two couples in a car, and one of the young men will drive, even if the car happens to belong to the father of one of the girls. Upon arrival the young man in the back seat immediately steps out and helps the girls, watching carefully that no part of her long dress becomes soiled at the curb. In case there is a parking problem, he will also help the other young lady out and leave her escort free to take care of the car. Weather permitting, the three will wait there or at the entrance of the building until the other young man comes up. In case of bad weather the three will go inside the building and wait until the driver joins them.

Seating arrangements in automobiles. In case it is necessary to plan three couples in a five-passenger car, two girls and one boy will take the rear seat, the boy sitting on either side, so that he need not cross in front of one of the girls in order to open the door for them. Two boys will sit in the front seat, the third girl between them. In most cars there is a little more space in the back seat; hence two girls, rather than two boys, are seated there.

You don't have to "put on dog." In some communities, it is the custom for high-school students to hire a taxi if their parents do not have a car; in some, it is necessary for the escort to provide a corsage for the girl he is escorting; in some, the tendency is to make formal parties as expensive and exclusive as possible. All these customs are fast going out of vogue, and today the general tendency is to avoid the use of taxis, corsages, and restaurant dates after the dance, and to cut down the expense of parties so that a boy is not broke or in debt for a month on account of one formal affair.

This tendency, strangely enough, has received its strongest ap-

[1] During wartime taxis and privately owned automobiles cannot be used as freely as peacetime permits, because of restrictions on fuel, rubber, and automobile production. All sorts of substitute arrangements are then resorted to, and people are quite willing to go by bus, subway, streetcar — for a lark, by hack — or on foot.

proval from the majority of girls, many of whom would like to attend formal parties, but do not get invitations because few boys can afford the expense.   As one girl put it, "I'd rather go without a corsage than go without the Prom and stay at home all night, thinking about what a swell time I could have had if it wasn't so darned expensive."   Formal high-school parties have become more democratic and many more students are able to attend them.

READINGS

For Further Information

Barbour, Ralph Henry.   *Good Manners for Boys,* Chapter 11.   Appleton-Century.

Black, Kathleen.   *Manners for Moderns,* Chapter 5.   Allyn and Bacon.

Boykin, Eleanor.   *This Way, Please,* Chapter 11.   Macmillan.

4. DO YOU GO TO THE MOVIES?

On entering a movie, play, or concert with an escort, a girl will not rashly lead the way toward the orchestra section, but will observe carefully whether her escort plans to take her there or elsewhere.   If his tickets are for the less expensive seats, she will be as pleasant as if he had secured the best in the house.   No doubt he spent what he could afford, and if he appears slightly embarrassed or is apologetic, she will put him at ease by saying, "I'm so happy I'm here, Bob," or, "I love to sit up here," or, if she knows him well, "I'm so glad you didn't get orchestra seats, Bob.   They're just too expensive."

Going down the aisle.   Stubs will be handed to the usher, who will precede the couple down the aisle, the girl following him, and her escort following her.   In case it is necessary to pass people in the row in order to get to the seats, the usher will ask the people to rise, and the girl will enter the row first.   The boy will follow and adjust her seat as she reaches it.   After she is seated, he will take his seat and help her remove her wrap, if she so desires.

If there is no usher, the boy will go down the aisle first, and

"Pardon me, Sir!   I can give you seats together now."

arriving at the row, he will enter it first if it is necessary to pass people on the way to vacant seats.

Conduct during the entertainment. During the movie, play, or concert, young people are not expected to sit in each other's laps, or with their arms around each other.   If they carry on any conversation, they should make it as brief and quiet as possible. Others in attendance object to disturbances of any kind, and it is in deference to them that one should remain quiet.   It is also out of consideration for others that the girl should remove her hat soon after taking her seat so that those in the row behind may more easily see and enjoy the entertainment.   Very tall men are sometimes thoughtful enough to sit low in their seats to give people behind them a better view.

Laughter and applause inspired by the entertainment will, of course, sweep over the audience, for responses of this kind are catching and imitative. It is not good form, even for children, to break out with laughter or applause when no one else does. Whistling, cat-calling, screaming, horse-laughing, and other boorish conduct at an entertainment in public or in school is, naturally, bad. People who behave in such ways are calling attention to themselves for one reason or another. They have some personality problem. Understanding is what they need. If they are asked to leave the building, they have succeeded in calling a great deal of attention to themselves and will probably behave in a similar manner again.

Leaving the building. Before leaving the theater, a boy will help the girl with her wraps, and on leaving he will precede her out of the row if it is necessary to pass more than one person before reaching the aisle. He will do this even if he has to pass the girl before passing the others. In the latter event he will say, "Excuse me, Betty," and then to the other people, as he passes by them, "I beg your pardon," or, "I'm sorry." He will also fold back all vacant seats if the rows are too close together for a reasonably easy passage. If the boy and the girl are sitting near the aisle and there is only one person between the girl and the aisle, the boy will indicate to the girl that they are leaving by that aisle, and, on passing that person, he will say, "I beg your pardon," even though she has done so before him.

As they leave the aisle, he will follow close behind her, perhaps half a step, until they reach the level floor of the foyer, where he can walk abreast of her. If they have to descend steps, he will precede the girl by one step, or, if they have to climb steps, he will follow her by one step. As explained elsewhere, this procedure serves as a protection for the girl in case of slipping, falling, or stumbling.

Walking together. In most communities it is not customary for a girl of high-school age to take a boy's arm while walking on the street. When they are walking together from the theater to the restaurant or to the girl's home, she does not take his arm except when they are crossing the street. Occasions may arise at any moment, however, when the boy finds it necessary as an escort and a protector to take the girl's arm and shield her from some unpleasantness, such as a mud puddle, or a group of rowdies, or an accident suddenly taking place before them. With the exception of such instances as these, the boy does not take the girl's arm while they are walking together.

Three is a crowd. Occasionally people go to the theater in parties of three, two boys and a girl. In this case, one of the boys will precede the girl down the aisle and one will follow her. If there is an usher, the first boy will follow the usher, the girl will follow him, and the other boy will follow her. They will enter the row in the same order and take seats in that order. They will also leave the row in the same order — or the reverse order, if they leave at the other end — but as they go up the aisle, both boys will follow the girl. As they walk on the street, the girl will be in the middle.

If the party is made up of two girls and a boy, the girls will follow the usher down the aisle, or follow the boy if there is no usher. The boy will not sit between the girls, nor will he walk between them on the street. He takes the curb side. He will avoid showing a preference for either of the girls and they will make it a point to thank him for having taken them both. "Three is a crowd." It takes a gentleman to handle that crowd gracefully.

READINGS

For Further Information

Barbour, Ralph Henry. *Good Manners for Boys*, Chapter II. Appleton-Century.

Boykin, Eleanor. *This Way, Please*, Chapter 15. Macmillan.

Goodrich, Laurence B. *Living with Others*, Chapter 8. American Book.

5. *LET'S EAT*

In a restaurant the girl precedes the boy and selects the table and her chair. The waiter or waitress or her escort will place the chair for her.   The boy will sit opposite her.   If the restaurant is crowded, however, the boy should precede the girl.   In case the party is made up of two couples, each boy will take the seat opposite the girl whom he is escorting.

How much shall a girl order?   If the girl is doubtful about her escort's financial condition, she will hesitate before she places an expensive order.   She may say, while looking over the menu, "I'm not very hungry."   Then the boy will make suggestions that will give some indication as to what he can afford.   If he strongly urges an expensive meal, she has the right to believe he is sincere and may accept his suggestions if they appeal to her.   Any member of the party who does not wish to eat should nevertheless order something, out of courtesy to the others.

In more or less swanky restaurants orders are given by the men of the party.   The women express their wishes to their escorts, who, in turn, give instructions to the waiter.   In ordinary restaurants girls and boys separately give their orders, girls first.

When visitors come to your table.   In case another person comes up to the table, the boys will rise.   Unless this person tells them to remain seated, they will remain standing until he leaves. However, if he continues in conversation for a long time, the boys have a right to excuse themselves and sit down again.

Sandwiches.   Sandwiches that can easily be handled with one hand may be taken up in the left hand, and other sandwiches should be eaten with a fork.

Napkins.   Napkins are used for blotting, not for scrubbing or washing.   They are not folded when replaced on the table at the end of the meal, but neither are they to be rolled up in a ball.

The dinner party.   At a dinner or dinner party the table appointments and seating arrangements are all arranged according to a plan that will provide the greatest amount of attractiveness and style.   The books listed at the end of this section will give you complete information about table etiquette.   The paragraphs that follow answer some of the questions most frequently asked by high-school students.

A dinner party for young people of high-school age will probably include the following courses in order: fruit or fish cocktail or soup; main course, consisting of meat or fish, vegetables, and salad; dessert and beverage. In case there is soup, and crackers are provided, they are eaten with the soup, not crushed and dropped into the soup. In case sweet corn is served, ears may be broken and held in one hand while the corn is eaten from the cob. In case the dessert is a fruit dish containing pits, if you are unable to separate the pits from the fruit by means of a spoon, use the spoon to return the pits from your mouth to the dish.

Silverware is placed according to a definite pattern — forks on the left, knife and spoons on the right. A butter spreader — if one is used — will be placed on the bread-and-butter plate, which is to the left of and above the dinner plate. If three forks are provided, they are placed in the order in which they are to be used, the outside one first. The outside one might be for the main course, for example, the middle one for the salad, and the one next to the plate for pie or other dessert. In case more than one spoon is provided, the same rule applies; the outside one — which might be a fruit cocktail or a soup spoon — should be used first. In case a beverage is served with the main course, a teaspoon will be placed next to the dinner knife.

It is no crime to be ignorant about matters such as these, but it makes things go more smoothly and comfortably if you know how it's done. Watch your hostess (but do not stare at her).

A more formal dinner might include the following courses, in order: soup or cocktail; fish; main course, or entrée; salad; dessert; coffee or demi-tasse. Dinners of this type are fairly complicated affairs. Very few public high-school students ever have occasion to attend them, and those who do would probably not be in need of suggestions.

At the table. Members of a dinner party do not eat until the hostess has begun or has urged them not to wait.

If you have no appetite, at least make a pretense of eating.

If you don't like a certain food, take a very small helping and do not show your dislike.

In case of an accident, such as spilling foods or dropping a fork or a dish, express your regret, but make as little fuss as possible. The hostess will try to put you at ease, and you should let the matter be forgotten quickly. Let the conversation turn on something else immediately and make no further reference to the error. Just remember that every other person at that table has had an accident at some time or other.

When in doubt about how or when to eat certain foods, watch the hostess.

Let your behavior at the table correspond to that of the others. For example, if everyone else folds his napkin before replacing it beside his plate, you should do so, too, even though it happens to be the first time you ever did it.

The hostess will make every effort to help the guests feel at ease. She wants them to have a good time, and she will not call attention to any mistakes they may make. She is not there to criticize, but to entertain.

The hostess is happy to see you enjoy your food, and second helpings may be accepted with a word of praise. A compliment about the table decorations or anything else that particularly pleases you is welcomed by any hostess.

Table topics. Conversation at a dinner is in some ways different from conversations elsewhere. Arguments on any subject should be avoided. Quarrels or unpleasant remarks of any kind are out of place, of course. Topics having to do with disease, death, dirt, or any unseemly subject bring on a feeling of disgust in some people which destroys their appetite. At mealtime, if ever, the conversation should be pleasant, optimistic, on the bright side of life, and full of good will and good wit.

READINGS

For Further Information

Allen, Betty, and Briggs, Mitchell Pirie. *Behave Yourself*, Chapter 3, 7, and 8. Lippincott.

Black, Kathleen. *Manners for Moderns*, Chapter 2. Allyn and Bacon.

Boykin, Eleanor. *This Way, Please*, Chapters 9, 10, and 15. Macmillan.

Law, Frederick Houk. *He Got the Job*, Chapter 4. Scribner.

6. LET'S TALK

Like painting or writing, conversation is truly an art for which a long apprenticeship is served. A person's conversation so closely reflects his real self that it changes as he changes, revealing his moods, his state of health, his successes and failures.   As a general rule we know our friends mainly by their conversation.

Conversation reflects the inner self. Since the art of talking with people is so closely related to one's inner nature, there is little use in giving a list of do's and don'ts for conversation. If a person's conversation is to improve, he himself must improve, and this improvement does not take place through learning a few hints, bright sayings, or epigrams, or looking up topics in advance. It is necessary to go deeper than that, discover the reasons for one's conversational faults, and eliminate the causes.

Conversational faults may reflect personal problems. From previous study in this book we have learned that a person who habitually talks a great deal about himself is likely to be doing so in order to convince himself and others who are listening to him that he really is somebody. He is not very confident of himself, even though he may try to give the impression of great self-confidence. A person who argues wherever he goes has an overpowering desire to succeed in argument, to best the person with whom he is arguing. He, too, is struggling for superiority, perhaps because of a serious inferiority which he does not recognize or understand.

Practice and understanding help. Inasmuch as personality problems may be solved by gaining insight into their causes and then making constant effort to improve, conversational faults, since they reflect the inner self, may be removed by the same method. Improvement in conversation is, after all, a matter of practice and experience. Here are a few hints, which by constant conscious effort and understanding may help you to improve in the art of conversation:

1. *Listening is a good half of the art of conversation.* It is considerate to listen with interest. People instinctively feel complimented if you listen to what they have to say.

2. *Strained silences are everybody's responsibility.* Conversation ends when all members of the group stop speaking. It would seem reasonable for one who has done very little of the talking to break the silence rather than one who has been talking more than his share of the time.

"Susan could be very popular. I tell her all sorts of cute things to say to the boys but she won't even try to remember them."

3. *Do your share of the talking, not much more and not less.* Maybe it is worse to do much more than much less.

4. *Avoid talking about yourself.* If the group thinks you are the best subject of conversation, they will talk about you and your successes.

5. *Agree if possible; disagree if necessary; argue in private.* There is always some truth to what the other fellow says if you are only big enough to see it. If you disagree, make a qualified rather than an absolute response. Say, "Yes, there is some truth

to what you say, but isn't there this side of the question?" or, "Yes, I can see how you would look at it that way; still, I wonder if it isn't possible to look at it this way too." As for arguing controversial matters, such as capitalism versus socialism, keep such arguments for bull sessions with your close friends who like to argue with you.

6. *Use a soft tone of voice.* Nasal, harsh, and rasping voice tones are not pleasant to listen to no matter how interesting the words that are spoken. Young people are very seldom aware of the subtle but important effect produced by unpleasant voice tones.

It is worth while to cultivate a low tone of voice and a slow tempo in speaking. Oftentimes people do not know what it is that makes a certain person so interesting and attractive, and later they realize that it is his tone of voice as much as what he says.

7. *Look up, not down.* The habit of looking down betrays lack of self-confidence, timidity, and sometimes dishonesty or guilt. When a person is looking at you, look at him. If he fixes his glance on you too long, shift your gaze to someone or something else at the level of your eyes or at a higher level. Avoid habitually looking at your hands or at the floor when you do not feel comfortable about looking at the other person. Look up.

8. *Avoid staring at people while you talk.* When you are in conversation, let your glance move about rather than remain fixed on another person's eyes. People do not feel comfortable when you look at them too long at one stretch while you talk to them.

READINGS

For Further Information

Allen, Betty, and Briggs, Mitchell Pirie. *Behave Yourself*, Chapter 12. Lippincott.

Black, Kathleen. *Manners for Moderns*, Chapter 3. Allyn and Bacon.

Boykin, Eleanor. *This Way, Please*, Chapter 6. Macmillan.

Goodrich, Laurence B. *Living with Others*, Chapters 2 and 3. American Book.

Law, Frederick Houk. *He Got the Job*, Chapter 3. Scribner.

FOR CLASS DISCUSSION

1. At a formal dance one evening, Jim B—— said to his friend: "Emily, I want a dance with Marlene. Come along, and I'll introduce you to her and Bill." Then he ushered her through the crowd, and, confronting the other couple, said, "Hi, Marlene and Bill, this is Emily Johnson. Let's exchange a dance, what d'you say?"

After the dance was over, Emily scolded Jim. She told him he ought to have better manners than to present her to his friends. He ought to know enough to present them to her, etc., etc.

Just what was wrong with Jim's behavior?

What was wrong with Emily's?

Could she do anything to help Jim have better manners? What, if anything?

2. Charles bragged about his dates. He told the fellows how easy it was for him to get dates, how beautiful the girls were, and how much they enjoyed his company. He didn't date the girls at Central, of course, because they were too kiddish. The reason why fellows never saw him with girls was that he didn't bother with anything so juvenile as high-school parties. He was at the night spots, while they were at a school dance. And so on.

Do you think Charles had many dates? Why?

Do you think the fellows enjoyed listening to him? Why not?

What would the girls at school think of Charles?

Suppose he were telling the truth, do you approve? Explain.

3. Ronny was rather small for his age, and somewhat bashful and awkward, but he was learning to dance. He did not express himself without self-consciousness when he asked for a dance or thanked a girl at the end of the dance. During the dance Ronny would concentrate on the time of the music and the steps he had to take. When his partner talked, he would answer briefly — "Yes," "No," "Maybe," "I think so" — until she stopped talking.

One night he felt his garter slide down the calf of his leg while he was dancing. He was seized with embarrassment. Before long the garter was flapping around his shoe at every step he took. He thought everyone saw it. He blushed, got out of step, tripped over his partner's pretty shoes, and all the while thought about his garter flapping around his foot. His embarrassment was so intense that he led his partner to a seat and left her without a word of explanation. She wondered whether she had done something wrong.

What was Ronny's problem? How did he handle it?

What should he have done about the garter?

Why did Ronny feel so sensitive about his garter's coming down?

4. Bill N—— was very happy about taking Zelma to the movie. She was the girl he had wanted to date ever since he started high school. Luckily, he had his father's car for the evening, and he felt excited as he drove up to Zelma's house and sounded the horn. After he had exercised the horn for some time, she finally came out, and then, taking corners on two wheels, he drove to the theater.

While they were standing in line for tickets, he said, "Let's sit down-stairs, eh? It costs more, but you can see better." Having purchased the tickets, he preceded Zelma past the ticket collector and followed the usher down the aisle. As soon as they were seated, he swung his arm around her and rested his knees against the seat in front. From time to time he laughed loud enough for everyone to hear and made comments about the picture. People sitting near by became restless and looked at him, but Bill thought they didn't know how to enjoy a good picture. After the show Zelma seemed to be rather quiet.

The following week he asked her for another date. She refused. He tried several times after that, but never was successful. Bill wondered why she did not date him again. He had had such a good time that first night.

Why did Zelma refuse?

What could Bill do about it?

5. Clinton had taken Elaine to the movie and was now sitting in a restaurant, waiting to order refreshments. Elaine looked up from the menu card and suggested a lamb chop dinner. Clinton saw it was listed at ninety cents. He swallowed, but gave the order. For himself he ordered a soft drink, though he had enough cash to order a dinner. Elaine felt uneasy when she noticed his order. They spent an uncomfortable hour, trying to make conversation, but not quite succeeding.

What was Elaine's mistake?

What was Clinton's?

What should they have done?

6. When Jennie goes to Arlene's house, she has the best time of her life. Everyone there is nice to her. They ask her about school, about her boy friends, about her clothes; they are interested in everything she tells them. They never find fault with her and they do not interrupt her while she is talking. At Arlene's house Jennie is the life of the party.

Does Jennie know the art of conversation? Explain.

Do Arlene's people? Why?

Is it good for Jennie to have Arlene for a friend?

7. Here is a quotation from an old deportment book: "If a person wishes to be served with more tea or coffee, he should place his spoon in his saucer. If he has had sufficient, let it remain in the cup." Would that be considered good manners today? Why?

GROUP ACTIVITIES

1. Make arrangements with the home economics department for a complete dinner. From your own class select the host and hostess. Select also committees for meal planning, table decorations, and seating arrangements. At this dinner it might be interesting to serve artichokes, lobster, or some food with which many in the group are not familiar.

If it is not practicable to arrange a full course dinner, prepare a table in the classroom completely arranged with china, glass, and silver for a full course dinner. A table can be secured in school. Various members of the class can be delegated to bring tablecloths, napkins, china, etc., for the table.

2. Assign to groups of two, four, and eight the exercise of making introductions in the classroom. In order to provide practice for every possible type of introduction, it may help to give fictitious names to various members of the groups. Thus, Johnny Jones could have a paper label pinned on his coat lapel, with the name, Governor Robinson. Mary Jones could be labeled Mrs. Jones, and so on, accounting for all conditions of age, sex, and importance that rule the form of introductions. Give each group enough time to make three or four introductions; that will help them to fix the method in their memories.

3. Plan to meet in the gym, during your regular class period, for an hour of dancing and dance instruction. An activity of this kind would provide opportunities to ask for dances, accept, and refuse them. Introductions might be made between prearranged couples, and dances might be exchanged or not, according to a prearranged plan.

INDIVIDUAL ACTIVITIES

1. Go to a movie earlier than usual, take a seat to the rear, and study the manners of people going down the aisle and entering the rows. After the show, remain to observe their manners on leaving. Does the lack of good manners lead to any complications? Describe one of the more interesting cases of ignorance in manners at the theater.

2. When you are in conversation with a teacher or an adult, make a definite point of keeping your gaze at the level of your eyes. Whenever you catch yourself looking down at the floor or at your hands, deliberately raise your eyes until you are looking at the person talking to you or at something from three to five feet above the floor.

3. Dig up an old book on manners and bring to class illustrations of how manners have changed since then. Can you explain the reasons for the changes?

4. Begin a conversation with someone or with a group of fellow students and try to do your share (but not more than your share) of the talking. Try at this time to listen intently when you yourself are not talking.

READINGS

In Literature

ESSAY

Herbert, A. P. "The Perils of Politeness"; in *Essays by Present-Day Authors.* Macmillan.

It is funny what complications can arise from coming late to a party.

NOVELS

Tarkington, Booth. *Seventeen.* Harper.

Boy meets girl — but how do parents and little sister feel about it?

White, Stewart Edward. *The Riverman.* Doubleday, Doran.

When a lumberjack enters society he has a great deal to learn.

Life at Home

YOUR HOME is the proving ground for your human relations. It is there that you first learn to smile or frown, to be kind or unkind and loyal or disloyal, to cooperate or not to cooperate, to save or to spend, to help or to hinder. There you make your first try at getting along with others. Many of your present habits in dealing with people were learned at home before you knew you were learning them. Now, however, you are growing up and beginning to know more about yourself. You are old enough to know what your habits are, whether they are good or bad, and whether you want to develop them or to change them.

At your present time of life your home is the best place to try experiments in human relations. If you want to put into practice the ideas you get in this book, your home is a safe place to try many of them. You are at an age when the happiness of your family rests upon your shoulders as well as upon the shoulders of your father, mother, and older sisters and brothers.

Needless to say, life at home should be happy (though there are likely to be occasional periods of unhappiness in any home) because members of a family have so much in common, including their desires and drives. Much of the time they love one another without especially realizing it. They all want success for one another. They share grief and joy. They spend a good deal of time together, using the same rooms, seeing the same furnishings, eating the same food, and talking the same language. If affection is based on common desires and the sharing of experiences, family life provides much opportunity for it.

But however these things ought to be, getting along with parents, brothers, and sisters is not always easy. What are some of the problems in family relations and how can they be solved?

Good manners mean doing the right thing at the right time, and are marked by courtesy and kindliness, as at the well-appointed dinner table (*above*), and by helpfulness and a spirit of fun, as at the picnic (*below*)

Getting along with others includes not only knowing what to do and say at formal social occasions, such as the dance (*above*), but also in informal situations of daily life (*below*).

GETTING ALONG WITH DAD AND MOTHER

Should you be more careful about doing the right thing when you are at home or when you are away from home? Do you think it is true that "Those who love you most can hurt you most"? Why do parents provide the leadership in most homes? What does the loss of a father or mother do to family life?

IN A DEMOCRACY each citizen has both duties and privileges; everyone shares in the planning that is necessary for efficient operation; each individual has a right to develop his own abilities so long as he does not interfere with the rights of others; leadership is provided by those who have the greatest experience and understanding; and the whole group is held together by group loyalty and respect for the individual. Substitute the word *family* for *democracy* in this sentence, and you have a picture of what family life should be.

There are other parallels between a family and a democracy. Like a democracy, a family changes according to circumstances and times, and it improves as its members improve. No democracy is perfect, but it always aims to move in the direction of improvement; and the same thing is true of a family. There is no perfect family; yours is not perfect, nor is your next door neighbor's. Fortunately, it does not take a perfect family to produce good citizens.

Leadership and parents. Normally, the parents are the leaders of the family; hence it is their job to guide and direct the others.

This creates difficulties, because the children, who are younger and less experienced, do not fully understand the reasons behind their parents' behavior. To a child parental leadership seems at times to be nothing more than a host of do's and don'ts, a series of refusals, and an undue use of authority. It must be admitted — at least the children will admit it — that parents do sometimes make mistakes in their leadership. They may "fly off the handle" occasionally; at times they may be unreasonable; frequently they are too busy to listen when children want to talk things over with them. But parents are human beings, after all, and every human being has shortcomings, faults, and imperfections.

Moreover, children are too close to their own parents to get the perspective that is necessary for full understanding of them. You may think that Mary Jones's mother is kinder to you than your own mother is; but remember that you and Mary Jones's mother see one another only once in a while, whereas you see your own mother, not only at her best, but also at her worst — and she sees you under the same circumstances. Perhaps most of the time you permit the difficulties that arise between you and your father and mother to mean more than all the rest of your life with them. At home the good is taken for granted; hence it loses its importance. The bad looms big and becomes more important than it really is.

Understanding leads to accepting. Besides, the people you love most can hurt you most, so that in family life the hurts are especially keen. There is a French saying, "Tout savoir est tout pardonner" — to understand all is to forgive all. If you use what you know about human nature — about why people do what they do — it will be easier for you to understand and forgive your parents when they are wrong and to appreciate them more fully when they are right. Ask yourself, "Why was Dad cross when he came home from work this evening?" (provided, of course, that he was cross). Try to answer that question and see if, in discovering the reasons, you don't feel more kindly toward him. There will be some things about your parents, naturally, that you will not fully understand, and perhaps some that will seem hard to accept, forgive, or forget. But they are your parents, the only ones you have; they are human beings, not gods, and in their way they do the best they can, just as you, in your way, do the best you can.

Your mother is a person. Do you think of your mother as a person apart from her relationship to you? Do you realize that she does not have an easy time of it? Day in and day out she has the same routine — planning meals, cooking, cleaning, dusting, mending, washing, ironing, pressing. Do you have chores, like helping with the dishes, and get tired of them? Most mothers have much the same grind all day long, week after week and year after year.

Housework should be recognized as important. "Man may work from sun to sun. But woman's work is never done." A woman's work — that is, housework and homemaking — does not receive the respect that it should receive. In the democracy of the home the care of house and family falls largely upon the mother's shoulders and is every bit as important as the money provided by the father. Does she get enough credit for it? Does she get the recognition that every personality craves? Suppose your mother is not always perfectly sweet about it, who would blame her? Besides, she is a woman, probably a little more emotional than a man, probably more given to ups and downs than he is. She has certain problems of her own. Do you try to understand them and her?

Your father is a person. The rôle your father fulfills is equally difficult, but in most cases quite different. (There are, of course, a good many women nowadays — at least in the United States — who work outside the home. It may be that your mother is one of them.) He goes to work every day; he has to be at his best in dealing with his fellow workers and is constantly working under pressure. The pressure is this: that he must bring home the bacon. He is the bread-winner, earning the money for the family. He must hold his job. He provides security for the family. If he happens to be upset or unhappy when he leaves the house in the morning, he must nevertheless be sure to keep amiable on the job. If he is tired or half sick, he must hide his feelings. If his fellow workers insult him, deal unfairly with him, or irritate him, he always knows that he can go only so far in fighting back, because he is under pressure; he has to hold his

job for the family's sake. He must be on his toes all day, trying
to handle every situation as well as he possibly can. He must
try to keep even-tempered, understanding, and kindly in his relations with others.

When the day's work is done, he naturally needs a change and
relaxation. He probably wants to let down. When he comes
home, he may be too tired to handle you with gloves on.
He may want to take it easy, read the paper, do something different from what he has been doing all day. Do you ever stop
to think that it is his wage or pay check that keeps bodies and
souls together in your house? Have you ever let him know that
you are grateful to him for working as he does? Letting your
parents know that you appreciate what they do is not flattery,
because they have it coming to them. Everybody responds to
appreciation, as you know from your own experience.

The quarreling of parents is overrated by children. Mistakes
will happen in the best-regulated families, and occasional quarrels are the rule rather than the exception. Still, even children
of very happy families are oversensitive about the occasional
quarreling — or what looks like quarreling — that goes on in the
home, and they worry about the possibility of their parents'
separating.

In a survey of 640 senior high-school students the author
found that more than half of them had at one time or another
worried about this matter. The chances were that, as their
parents had more or less successfully met the problems of married
life for fifteen years or more, they would continue to work
them out. But children and young people usually do not realize
that discussions and apparent quarrels between father and mother
are actually efforts toward adjustment and the solution of problems. When children see their parents arguing, they feel much
more intensely about it than the parents themselves do; for, while
the parents may have no thought of solving their problem by
running away from each other, children will sometimes secretly
fear that just such a solution is liable to take place.

It was an encouraging revelation to students in the survey just
mentioned to see from fourteen to eighteen hands in each class
rise in answer to the question, "How many of you have at one

time or another been afraid that your parents would not stay to-gether?" In every group questioned, more than half the mem-bers raised their hands, and a look of surprise and relief came over some students' faces when they saw that their fear was not an uncommon one, but was shared by many other people of their own age.

Children have a stake in family happiness. Occasional quar-reling is, of course, much to be preferred to dead silence, bitter-ness, and divorce. Young people of high-school age frequently contribute a great deal toward the solution of family difficulties. They are old enough to understand some of these difficulties, and they can take an active part in contributing toward a happy fam-ily life. It is their responsibility, for they are past the age of childhood, when life is largely receiving instead of giving. They are old enough to realize that they go up or down as their family goes up or down.

Youth strains against authority. Part of the growing-up pro-cess consists in getting used to laws and customs — especially what are called social taboos, or things that are forbidden. A small child is not born with a sense of property. It is natural for him to take what he wants. But little by little he learns that some things are his and some are the property of others. He learns to respect another person's ownership. This takes place before maturity. Everyone has to learn the laws of the home and of society as he learns the rules of a game. When a player breaks the rules of a game, he is penalized; after a while he learns to play according to the rules, and he is much happier because of it.

The rules of society are not all easy to learn, because many of them run counter to individual wishes. For instance, a boy wants to get to the football field faster than society thinks he should. He exceeds the speed limit and society punishes him. Many illustrations might be cited to show how young people have a tendency to kick against the rules of the world in which they live. They have a tendency to break with authority in school, in public, and in the home. It is hard for them to see that their own wants and wishes have to be subordinated to the greatest good for the majority. An adult is better able to think of other people first, abide by the law, and get his happiness within the law. However, adults sometimes forget that they were once young themselves and had that same urge to break with authority and do what they pleased rather than what was best for the group as a whole.

Parents are legally in authority. Parents stand in the place of authority in the home, and since they do, they plan the family life. They have always had the problem of helping their children to accept authority instead of breaking with it. In time, of course, the young ones become adults, but there is a strong tendency in youth to fight the rules and satisfy personal wishes before considering the wants of the group.

Training parents. This tendency on the part of children has much to do with unhappy relations between them and their parents. The more a child says, "No. I won't do it," the more the parent is inclined to say, "You must." The more a child says, "I'll do it anyway," the more the parent is inclined to say, "I'll see that you don't." Without knowing it, some children have trained their parents to say "No," to refuse them every wish, even without a second thought.

Home gives you a start in life. Your parents have provided a home. Perhaps you take it for granted, but if something happened to leave you homeless, you would suddenly realize its value, as millions of homeless people must be doing today in Europe. What does home mean to you? Home is a place for you to come back to, where you can rest and feel secure, where you can satisfy the first needs of life — food, shelter, and clothing. But it is much more. It is a place where you can find happiness — affection, companionship, understanding, and an opportunity to be of service. Your home gives you a start in life, and if it is a happy home, it gives you a send-off that will help you as long as you live to get along with others. As you pass the childhood years, you begin to realize the importance of family life and to take your part at home as one of the grown-ups. Then begins your chance to give instead of receive. It is your personal effort, as well as that of the others, that makes your home a happy one. Little by little, as you make this effort, you gain more of the confidence and admiration of your parents.

"May we use the car a while, Dad? Billy has been driving a tank and wants to demonstrate some maneuvers."

HINTS FOR DISCUSSING THE CARTOON

Why does Dad look doubtful? Can you detect any lack of confidence in his daughter or her uniformed boy-friend? How do you account for the difference in attitude between the father and the young couple? Do you think the young man will make a good soldier? Why?

Earning your parents' confidence. Young people earn their parents' confidence by acting grown-up. Perhaps the chief point is that a grown-up shares in the duties of his group. Do you share in the duties of your home? Do you help around the house? Do you make beds, wash dishes, iron, and mend your clothes? Do you take care of the furnace, clean the basement, and keep the lawn cut? Do you hang up your clothes and put away your toilet articles? Do you take care of the baby, bathe and dress him, and entertain him with games or stories? Do you varnish, paint, or repair furniture? Tasks like these must be done by someone in your home. Do you do your share? If you do, you will earn the confidence of your parents, for you are doing the things that a thoughtful, dependable, and responsible adult is expected to do. You are helping to make your home a happy home.

It is necessary to get your parents' confidence. Do some things that show them you are growing up. Agree with them whenever you can. Watch your hours. Spend your money for sensible things rather than fads. Save some money. These are all things that adults do. By acting as a grown-up person you show your parents that you are becoming dependable. They will feel safer about your decisions in general.

Spending time with the family. In one of his better poems, Edgar Guest says, "It takes a heap o' living to make a house a home." If you are one of those who spend every evening away from home, did you ever stop to think what it means? It means that there are other places where you would rather be every evening than at home, that you are not interested in visiting with your own parents, that they do not satisfy you in your leisure time, and that you have failed to be a source of enjoyment to them. What would you think of an American citizen who spent nine-tenths of his time abroad and came back once a year to check up on his property and see that he was financially safe? There are some citizens who have done this. Similarly, there are some children who spend most of their time away from the family and come home only to eat and sleep. If it is unpatriotic for a citizen to spend all of his leisure time in foreign countries, it is disloyal for a child to spend all of his leisure time away from the family.

*"Mom, while you're up to get Billy a glass of water,
will you run upstairs to get me my manicure set?"*

Obeying. As it is a mark of good sportsmanship to play a
game according to the rules, and a mark of adulthood to abide
by the law, so it is a mark of character in youth to obey their
parents. Parents may be wrong, but they stand in a position of
authority and they decide to give or refuse permission according
to their best lights. Of course, it is hard to see their reasoning
when the decision is unfavorable.

High-school students are frequently disturbed about disobedi-
ence. They know this boy and that girl disobey their parents;
why shouldn't they themselves? But on the few occasions when

they themselves disobey or deceive their parents, they do not feel right about it. They have a feeling of guilt. The question is whether it is better to disobey and do something you want to do, but have your conscience bother you, or to obey and have your conscience at rest. If it is necessary to choose between the two, choose the latter; it is better to feel thwarted momentarily than to have a feeling of guilt that lasts a long time. If possible, accept the decision of your parents and obey with willingness.

Do you allow your parents to sacrifice too much for you? Do your parents work so hard for their children that they look old before their time? Do they spend so much money for your fun and clothes that they cannot keep up their own appearance? It is worth a great deal to you to have your parents "keep up with the Joneses," that you may be proud to present your friends to them. They should have enough balance of fun in their lives to know how to be happy with the parents of your friends. If you let them sacrifice too much for you, the time may come when you feel embarrassed about them. The family, like a democracy, must improve together; then all the members will sustain each other.

FOR CLASS DISCUSSION

1. Bill J— had been a spoiled boy. Both of his parents had given in to his every wish. Though there were frequent quarrels because he wanted something he should not have, in the end Bill won out. As Bill grew older, his parents did not trust him because he stole money at home, got into many scrapes, and frequently lied to them. He never did anything around the house.

At the age of fourteen he took his new .22 revolver and held up a gas station. Since this was one of a long series of difficulties, he was sent away to a vocational training school. Six months later he was returned to his parents. One of the conditions of his parole was that he would regularly do certain jobs around the house. He was to take care of the furnace, the lawn, and the walks.

Bill's parents were surprised with his help, and at first doubted that it would last. After a few days they began to compliment him. Soon they let him take the car and run errands. He did not loiter on these errands. One Saturday he offered to help his father build a coal bin. With the dollar which was given to him when the job was finished,

Bill bought a tie and banked fifty cents. Occasionally he talked with his parents about his friends and tried to get their advice. Life at home became happier than it used to be. Bill thought his parents had changed. His parents thought Bill had.

Explain what Bill did to improve relations with his father and mother.

How did his father show that he had confidence in Bill?

What mistake had his parents made during Bill's childhood?

2. One day Linda's parents quarreled. Her mother got the worse of the argument and was still seething when Linda came to her with a request. Linda had always wanted a one-piece bathing suit, but, because of her father's objection, her mother would not let her buy one. Now Linda again asked her mother for permission to buy the bathing suit. Her mother consented.

Why did Linda ask at this time?

Why did her mother consent?

How will this incident affect Linda's relations with her father? Will it improve her relations with her mother? Why?

3. Who does more for a happy family, the father or the mother? Explain.

4. Is it possible for parents to treat all their children alike? Is it wise to do so? Explain.

INDIVIDUAL ACTIVITIES

1. Make a list of the things you could do in your family to get the confidence of your parents.

2. Select some daily task, like making beds or removing ashes from the furnace, and do it voluntarily for one week.

3. If you spend most of your evenings away from home, spend an extra evening at home and use the time in helping and visiting with your parents.

4. Discuss one of your personal problems with your parents. Ask their advice, weigh it, and follow it if you think you can.

READINGS

In Literature

AUTOBIOGRAPHY

Garland, Hamlin. *Son of the Middle Border*. Macmillan.

> The relations of son to father and mother are well described in the early chapters of the book. A hard life made tough personalities.

NOVELS

Tarkington, Booth. *The Turmoil*. Harper.

> This is a good story of how a young man struggles against the domination of his father and wins out.

Tarkington, Booth. *The Magnificent Ambersons*. Doubleday, Doran.

> This story shows the life of a spoiled child.

SHORT STORY

Dobie, Charles Caldwell. "The Hands of the Enemy"; in *Arrested Moment*. John Day.

> Did the boy murder his father? You'll like this boy and wish him well.

For Further Information

Allen, Betty, and Briggs, M. P. *Behave Yourself*, Chapter 1. Lippincott.

McKown, H. C., and Le Bron, Marion. *A Boy Grows Up*, Chapters 5 and 6. McGraw-Hill.

McLean, Donald. *Knowing Yourself and Others*, pp. 103-109. Holt.

Scharmer, F. M. *Boys' Guide to Living*, pp. 115-136. Allyn and Bacon.

Trilling, Mabel B., and Nicholas, F. W. *The Girl and Her Home*, pp. 21-41. Houghton Mifflin.

GETTING ALONG WITH BILL AND MARY

*Why do parents like to have their children get along
well with each other? Why do brothers and sisters
as a rule have more affection for each other than for
people outside the family? If a person gets along
well at home, is he likely to get along well outside
the home? Why? How does the misfortune or success of any one member of a family influence others
in the family?*

IT IS GENERALLY EASIER to get along smoothly with people outside
our family than with our own brothers or sisters, because the
latter are closer to us. Brothers and sisters are too well aware
of one another's faults and forgetful of one another's virtues. If
they used the same common decency with each other that they
use with their fellows, there would be little trouble between
them. For some reason we do not make the same effort toward
friendship in the case of a brother or sister that we make in the
case of strangers. The members of the family take each other
for granted.

Why do brothers and sisters quarrel? Brothers and sisters who
never have misunderstandings would be hard to find, but the
number that do have them is legion. Why do they quarrel?
There are many reasons; a few of the most common ones will be
given here.

Sometimes it is play that goes too far. Have you ever watched
a couple of dogs playing in the yard? First they make believe,
nip at each other, and miss. Then they take little nips at each
other's paws and throat, still playing. Then one of them for-

"See, Mom, that's how Sis acts when I talk through my nose. Her new boy friend does it all the time and she thinks it's cute."

gets the make-believe and really bites the other dog. Snarls pierce the air, and the game breaks up or a death fight ensues. The same thing sometimes takes place with brothers and sisters. Brother will give sister a light tap; sister will return with another, slightly harder; brother comes back with a slap; sister gets a little serious and really lets him have one; then brother finishes with a blow, the girl crying and probably calling to mama. The quarrel began in play, but went too far. Quarrels with words are worse, but they often begin with harmless teasing and end with sarcastic remarks that may be remembered a lifetime. Children have not yet learned where to draw the line between fun and fight; they lose control of themselves and go too far. The truly grown-up person controls himself and keeps the make-believe in the fun.

Sometimes it is rivalry for importance in the family. Rivalry between brothers and sisters is very common. One reason for this is that there is a difference in age; the older is superior to the younger because he is bigger, stronger, and better able to get around. The older one is also farther advanced in school, associates with older people, probably takes a more active part in family decisions, and in many ways has a life that appeals to the younger, for all children want to grow up as soon as possible. These differences may lead to a feeling of inferiority on the part of the younger child, which in turn leads to a desire for compensation and to competition with the older one for superiority. As a result there may be many quarrels, apparently without cause.

Sometimes it is rivalry for the love of parents. Brothers and sisters may vie with each other for first place in their mother's or father's affections. This struggle, hidden or obvious, may be at the root of many misunderstandings. The less favored child who does not gain so much of his parents' attention and affection may be jealous. He is thwarted in his desire to be superior. This leads to anger. He is also afraid, because he does not feel assured of his parents' affection. These two emotions make up his jealousy.

Accepting and rejecting. The relations between a brother and sister may also be hostile or friendly depending on whether they accept or reject one another. A brother shows that he accepts his sister by such actions as agreeing with her, listening to her, playing with her, helping her get something she wants from father or mother, introducing her to his friends, and showing her various attentions. On the other hand, he shows that he rejects her by such actions as disagreeing with her, turning away from her when she wants to talk with him, refusing to play with her, thwarting her efforts to get what she wants from father and mother, refusing to introduce her to his friends, and ignoring her in any way. The same thing is true, of course, in the case of two brothers or two sisters.

Being considerate is a habit to be learned. Young people of high-school age could contribute a great deal to family happiness if they made a constant effort to do so. Whereas they have a tendency always to want things for themselves, they might improve matters a great deal by trying to do something for their parents or brothers and sisters. Such conduct can become a matter of habit. Some children have the habit of being considerate of other members of the family. Others who do not have this habit can acquire it; they can begin by making a conscious effort to be helpful in some way every day for one week. The following week they can increase their helpfulness. They will get so much pleasure from such behavior that they will soon develop the habit of being considerate, and home will become a pleasanter place, closer to the ideal of happy family life.

Members of the family are interdependent. As a democracy the family needs the mutual good will and help of all its members. They can make home the best spot on earth. Brothers and sisters as members of the family have a responsibility to try to understand the problems that arise between them and to improve in their relations with one another. The younger needs the older, the brother needs the sister, each one needs the good will of the others. Your family is like a chain in which each member is a link; and the chain as a whole is no stronger than the weakest link. If your sister or your brother happens to be the weakest link, you should try to help him or her improve, if for no other reason than that the whole family will then become stronger.

Affection among brothers and sisters. We have previously learned that in all forms of affection there is a common ground of desires. This is also the case among children in a family. If they have affection for each other, they will have desires in common and will help each other satisfy these desires.

Certain wants that brothers and sisters have in common lie deep behind a thousand actions. For example, they all want a happy home. They all want a prosperous home. They all want a good name for the family as a whole. They all want each other to succeed in life. If brothers and sisters are to get along happily, they must work together in a common effort to satisfy such wants as these.

Helping each other in the little things. There are other wants in family relations that seem to be less hidden. A girl, for instance, may want to wear her sister's dress. When a want of this kind can be satisfied without harm to anyone, satisfying it leads to better relations than if it were refused.

The same is true if a boy wants to use his brother's baseball glove. The latter may want to keep the glove all to himself, but at the same time he may want to satisfy his brother's desire. If he decides to give up his own wishes and let his brother use the glove, he is adding to the happiness between them. Affection leads us to prefer the other person's wants to our own.

In a well-regulated family all the children have certain tasks to perform. Each one wants to get his job done (even the one who dawdles at his job). If brothers and sisters occasionally help each other with such chores as making beds or raking the lawn, they are sharing in each other's desires and working together toward satisfactions. Cooperation and service of this kind leads to happy relations among them and also increases the happiness of the whole family.

Innumerable illustrations could be given. You can tell what your brother or sister is after. Help him in his struggle for it, provided the desire is good.

You are never entirely separate from your family. When all your brothers and sisters are happy and prosperous, you share in their success both at home and outside the home. When they rise, you rise. When they fall, you fall. A person could not completely separate himself from his family if he tried all the rest of his life. His personality has been permanently influenced by parents, brothers, and sisters, and he has permanently influenced their personalities. Robert Louis Stevenson may have had that in mind when he wrote, "I am a part of all that I have met."

The ideal relationship among brothers and sisters is one that is mutually helpful, with due regard for the family as a whole and for the best development of each individual. Brothers and sisters in the happy family make this ideal their goal.

FOR CLASS DISCUSSION

1. Bernice did not like to take care of her clothes. She rarely pressed a blouse or skirt and very rarely mended her stockings. Yet she was popular with boys and had many dates. She managed to look prim on all occasions by wearing alternately the clothes of one sister and then the other. Sometimes her sisters came home and saw that their clothes closet and bureau had been ransacked and left in disarray by Bernice.

How do you think Bernice's sisters reacted to her habit?

What could be done to help Bernice take care of her own clothes and have a better sense of property?

2. George did not get along very well with five of his brothers and sisters. He argued with them, was sarcastic, sometimes fought with them, and refused to help them with anything. But he had one brother, Bob, with whom he was on good terms. Bob and George would go hiking together once in a while. They talked about everything, but Bob did most of the listening. George would help clean the chicken coop and Bob would tell him that he was a good worker. George broke Bob's bicycle one day, but instead of becoming angry, Bob looked it over and said, "Well, I guess we'll have to fix it some way, George." And then George ran almost half a mile to get three spokes from a bicycle shop. When he returned, Bob said, "Gee, I didn't think you'd be back so soon. You didn't have to run yourself all out of breath." Together they put in the spokes and Bob asked George to ride it and see if the rim was true.

Why was George able to get along with Bob?

Of what value to the other brothers and sisters was the fact that Bob could get along with George?

What might happen to George if he had not one brother or sister as his friend?

3. Why does the oldest child in many families have fewer privileges than the youngest?

4. Should a person have the same affection for all of his brothers and sisters?

INDIVIDUAL ACTIVITIES

1. Plan to help your brother or sister with some job he has around the house. Try it several days in succession and, if you find that it is satisfying to you as well as to the other person, continue the habit.

2. Discuss something of personal concern to you with a brother or sister. Confide in him or her and sincerely listen to advice.

3. Spend some time, say, a half hour, with a brother or sister you rarely play with. Repeat this several days in succession to see whether you become better friends.

4. Help one of your brothers or sisters get something he or she wants from your parents.

READINGS

In Literature

NOVELS

Alcott, Louisa May. *Little Women.* Little, Brown.
       Little Men. Little, Brown.
  Old favorites of millions of young people. Heart-warming stories of families growing up.
Tarkington, Booth. *Penrod.* Doubleday, Doran.
  Big sister didn't always appreciate Penrod, but then there was the time that an unwelcome suitor came and Penrod persisted in being a third party to every move.

SHORT STORIES

Cable, George W. "Jean-ah-Poquelin"; in *Old Creole Days.* Scribner.
  The people around town thought that Jean had murdered his brother. You'll be surprised when Jean's secret becomes known.
Steele, Wilbur Daniel. "Blue Murder"; in *Twentieth Century Short Stories.* Houghton Mifflin.

For Further Information

McKown, H. C., and Le Bron, Marion. *A Boy Grows Up,* pp. 70-76. McGraw-Hill.
McLean, Donald. *Knowing Yourself and Others,* pp. 110-115. Holt.
Trilling, Mabel B., and Nicholas, F. W. *The Girl and Her Home,* pp. 21-41. Houghton Mifflin.

✺ UNIT VIII ✺

The Opposite Sex

AT HIGH-SCHOOL AGE your interest in adulthood is heightened because you are so nearly mature in a physical sense. You naturally make many serious efforts to be and become grown-up. You show it in your plans for future education or work, in your increased knowledge, in your friendships, and in your relations with the opposite sex. A large majority of high-school students have almost attained physical maturity, and are in the transitional stage between childhood and adulthood. It is especially during the last two years of high school that young people take their biggest strides toward social maturity.

Association with members of the opposite sex and thoughts of marriage are usual rather than unusual in the life of young men and women in senior high school. The changes that occur during high-school years bring you new problems, many of a personal nature, that you want to face and think through. These problems should not be forgotten or repressed. Some of them have already been discussed, and the present unit will add to the information you have gained indirectly elsewhere in this book. In this unit we shall consider a number of questions that come up in social relations between members of the opposite sexes.

BOY MEETS GIRL

Did people have dates at the age of sixteen or seventeen fifty years ago? Prove your answer. If you are socially mature, should you be able to get along well with persons of the opposite sex? Why? Are boys and girls really different kinds of people or are they essentially the same?

WHETHER OR NOT it was normal fifty or a hundred years ago for boys and girls of the present high-school age to go out together, it is normal today. It is the rule and not the exception for a girl of high-school age to be escorted to school parties and theaters by boy friends. This is so common that boys and girls who do not have such social relations come to think of themselves as not fitting in, as bashful, or as rejected by the opposite sex.

If the question had to be asked (as indeed some parents do ask), "What is worse for John, never to go out with girls and feel 'out of it,' or to go out with girls occasionally, as the average high-school boy does?" then the answer should certainly be that it is worse never to go out with girls. Such a question should not have to be asked, however, for boys and girls in senior high school are young men and young women, and their age and physical development naturally lead them toward interest in the opposite sex. An important part of their personality development must be an increasing social ability in dealing with members of the opposite sex.

Dating brings new problems. A senior high-school student who is socially mature for his age shows an interest in becoming well poised and makes many efforts to this end. By taking a girl to a party, a boy is meeting certain important social problems which he must learn to handle with ease if he is ever to become a normal adult. Among the problems are those suggested by such questions as: How shall I conduct myself with a girl? How can I develop poise and self-confidence in the presence of girls? How much freedom can I have within the limits of self-control and the moral standards of the group? How can I judge a girl as to her possibilities for womanhood, wifehood, and motherhood? How can I draw the line between dating occasionally and "going steady"? How can I use my experience with girls as a help in becoming the kind of person I want to be?

A girl is meeting the same problems with such differences as are due to her sex: How shall I conduct myself with masculine friends? How can I develop poise and self-confidence in the presence of men? How much freedom should I allow and yet remain within the limits of self-control and morality? How can I judge a boy for his possibilities as a man, a husband, and a father? How can I draw the line between dating occasionally and "going steady"? How can I use my experiences with boys as a help in becoming the kind of person I want to be?

Boy and girl relationships have a leading-on value. Having social relations with members of the opposite sex is preparatory to marriage. This does not mean that every high-school senior should give serious thought to marrying the girl or boy with whom he or she spends an evening. Nor does dating the same girl a few times mean that the boy is in love with the girl. It might be better for him to take various girls to different school functions than to find himself thought of as a "steady" of a certain girl and consequently shunned by other girls. Boy and girl relationships, however, do provide young people with opportunities to study each other. A boy should study the girls in his company, and a girl, likewise, should study the boys; for it will not be long, maybe four or five years, when they will be thinking seriously of marriage.

What if parents say no. The struggle that sometimes takes place between parents and older children over the question of dating is of little value to either the children or the parents. Quarreling will neither help parents to see that their children have a need for social relations with the opposite sex, nor will it help children to cooperate and obey. After all, it is not absolutely necessary to have dates during high school, and if your parents cannot be persuaded to see the reasonableness of occasional dating, it is better to obey them. They are legally in authority over you, and, because of their age and experience and your loyalty to them, it is preferable to respect their opinions. You are left with a feeling of guilt if you fail in cooperating with your parents. Even though their demands do not always seem entirely justified, it is better to obey and await the time, not far off, when you will have more freedom.

How many dates a week? From a survey of student opinions, the author found that most seniors in high school considered it wise to be in by ten-thirty Sunday nights, in order to get enough sleep before school Monday mornings. They thought it was all right to be out until one o'clock Saturday nights, and some of them said one o'clock for both Friday and Saturday nights. They were mostly agreed that nine-thirty or ten was the right bedtime during week days.

If a survey had been made of parental opinions on the same subject, no doubt the results would have been somewhat different. Furthermore, if the survey had been made in various communities, the results might have differed from one community to another. Whatever the practice may be in a given community, we do know that physical health requires an average of nine hours of sleep for growing boys and girls. However important it may be for you to become gradually accustomed to dealing with members of the opposite sex, it is not more important than maintaining your physical health. Therefore, your plans should be made well within the limits of body hygiene. Staying out after twelve o'clock, except on special occasions, is probably unhealthful not only for young people but even for adults, because it puts a strain on body and mind. You may not notice it much while you are in high school, but reserve energy stored up during your youth will help you a great deal in later life.

That first "affair." Perhaps no love affair is more serious to a person than the first one in his life, and this frequently occurs during high-school years. It is this affair that is so mistakenly

272   GETTING ALONG WITH OTHERS

called "puppy love" by older people who do not understand that a love affair is serious whether it comes to a person at the age of fifteen or fifty.   Young people, it is true, are more idealistic than older ones, because the difficulties of life have not embittered them, whereas some older people have found that their loves do fade, if not die out entirely; and these disillusioned people sometimes sneer at others who are in love.   Their point of view, however, is not a sound one, for it is colored by their own unhappy experience and prejudice.   The true adult is mellowed rather than embittered by the difficulties of life, and his deep understanding of human nature helps him to see the importance of a "first affair" in youth.   Actually, there is no reason why a love affair begun in childhood should not continue until death.   Many childhood sweethearts have married later on in life and their affection has lasted as long as they lived.

However, there are love affairs and love affairs.   One that completely destroys a person's ability to work, play, or carry on something like a normal existence is extreme behavior.   We have already seen, in an earlier discussion, that it is usually regarded with disgust by others and may lead to failure in school, loss of friends, estrangement of family relations, and many other difficulties. Self-control should be exercised in love as in all other emotions.

Questions to consider when you feel "that way" about a certain person.   In general, high-school students do not disapprove of keeping steady company; but they do not mean by the term "steady" that the boy will absolutely never date another girl or the girl another boy.   They also expect a certain amount of dignity and self-control and do not approve of couples who are constantly seen mooning in the halls and making a public show of their affection for each other.

If a boy frequently dates the same girl, even though he realizes that marriage may be more or less remote, he should begin giving serious thought to such questions as: Is she the right kind of girl for me? Would she help me to realize the best that is in me? Does she come from a good home? Does she have character? Is she the kind of girl who will wear well through the years? Am I the right kind of young man for her? What have I to contribute, so that she may realize the best in life? Am I bringing a good family background to this relationship? Am I worthy of her in character and other personal qualities? Would I be loyal and faithful to that kind of girl through the years? Is it time for me to keep steady company? Will that interfere with her plans or my plans for the future? Has she had an opportunity to consider a number of other boys? Have I considered a number of other girls? If we should get married, what are our chances of a happy home life, successful motherhood and fatherhood?

The same questions — and others, such as, Would I want to be the mother of his children? — should be given serious consideration by a girl in these circumstances.

Beauty is only skin deep. You may have noticed that the previous paragraphs did not contain the question, "Is she beautiful?" Did you ever stop to think that a beautiful girl — using the term in the sense of obvious and striking beauty — may be handicapped because she is beautiful? This is true not only because other girls are somewhat jealous of her, but also because her good looks give her a head start with boys and make her more popular with them; hence she is not forced to develop her personality as less comely girls are. It is not always but frequently true that beautiful girls have little to give in the way of conversation, helpfulness, and inspiration. Girls who are exceptionally attractive physically should not neglect their personalities.

Breaking a date. A date is a date and it cannot be broken without good reasons. If a girl breaks a date without explaining, she is in effect telling the boy that she does not wish to be with him. And she is telling him in the most impolite way. She had the right to refuse the date in the first place. If she could not gracefully refuse, it is even less graceful to break the date later and leave the boy embarrassed. A girl needs courage at times to be honest; that will avoid a more serious difficulty later.

But it is generally considered a worse breach of manners for a boy to break a date, because girls are more subject to adverse comment when they are left in the lurch. Even if the boy has good reasons and makes them plain to the girl as soon as possible, she will be inclined to hesitate before she accepts another date with him. A more graceful way for a boy to break a date would be to try to postpone it to another definite time.

Breaking a date hurts the pride of the other person. At the least, it is a mistake in planning. On rare occasions conflicting circumstances force a person to break a date, and then every effort should be made to save the other person's pride. Consideration and common courtesy require the keeping of promises, and a date is a promise. If you break your promise to someone, you not only hurt his pride, but weaken your own ability to keep promises in the future.

Gifts. Greeting cards, boxes of candy, flowers, and minor gifts on special occasions between high-school beaus are not out of the ordinary. But it becomes somewhat embarrassing to accept too many or too expensive presents.

An interesting and somewhat puzzling law applies here. The more you give a person, the more that person belongs to you. If you give him ideas, the more you give, the more he owes you. If you give him money, clothes, books, and food (as parents do to children), the more he owes you. If you give him (or more likely, in this case, her) candy or flowers or other presents, the more she owes you, and the more hold you have over her.

This law also applies to the giving of gifts among boy friends and girl friends. A girl feels instinctively that she becomes indebted to the person who gives her something. If the gifts are too many and too expensive, she begins to feel too much obligated. That is why girls sometimes hesitate to accept gifts from boys; they do not wish to become obligated. And to put it in reverse, that is why boys sometimes buy expensive gifts for their girl friends; they want the girls to be obligated. Of course, the boys do not consciously plan it that way, but all the experience of giving and receiving inescapably contains the element of obligation, and boys use it as a device to secure girls to themselves.

In accepting gifts, ask yourself whether they are significant or not, whether they are important or not, whether they obligate you too much in the giver's mind or in your own. Do you want to be obligated to him? Do you gladly owe him all the thanks you would naturally feel for such a gift? You may wish to forestall expensive giving by references to it long in advance. Let him know, if you have the right occasion, that you do not believe in expensive gifts during high-school years and that you could

"Now look here, Peggy, I've spent $46.70 on our dates and I'd like to know where we stand."

not accept them if they were offered. He would hesitate to buy something if he thought he might have to return it to the store.

The horn-tooting caller. If you are one of the many girls who likes to have a boy call on you as a gentleman should, what would you do if he came and parked in front of your house, sounding the horn of his car? Some boys do this because other girls have let them get away with it, some because they are too lazy to go out after the girl, and some because they are too timid to enter the house and perhaps be faced with introductions and conversation.

The first time this happens to you, wait in the house until your caller comes to the door. If he does not come, but stays out there making a lot of noise, you may (1) finally go out to his car and cancel the date politely and firmly, or (2) put on your best disposition, keep the date, and if he ever wants another one with you, tell him then that you would prefer to have him call at the house without letting the neighbors know that someone is calling. The second method is much easier for the boy and may be much more satisfactory to both.

Saying good night. Many high-school girls, and older men and women, too, find it difficult to bring a good time to an end gracefully. They make their farewells too long, saying good-bye and good night so many times that the last one does not sound final. They have not learned to walk up to the house, open the door, and end the evening with, "Thanks for a swell time, Jim. I'll see you in Civics tomorrow. Good night."

Many a high-school girl feels uncertain about whether to let her escort kiss her good night, and whether to confine this intimacy to only one boy. Kissing is usually considered an intimacy that has some significance. At the least, it signifies more than casual acquaintance, for, surely, a girl would not allow a mere acquaintance that intimacy. A good-night kiss may have little meaning to either person, yet a girl would not permit the same privilege to every boy. She would not cheapen herself and her kisses by making them easy to get and free to all.

Count to ten. The old-fashioned notion that counting to ten is wiser than acting on sudden impulse may well be applied in boy and girl relationships, for occasions do arise when just a little deliberation prevents a mistake that would bring unhappiness to everyone concerned. There is often a strong temptation to give in to the desire of the moment; it is far wiser in such cases to restrain oneself. Impulsiveness — acting on the spur of the moment — has brought tragedy into many lives. Taking time to consider consequences will prevent hasty and ill-advised action, and is a sign of social maturity. High-school students, as a rule, use good judgment in controlling their impulses; most of them count to ten as a matter of habit, or use some other device that gives them time to think before they act.

FOR CLASS DISCUSSION

1. Bob S—— admired Sylvia L—— very much, but Sylvia did not feel the same way about Bob. Occasionally she dated him, but every time she did so she felt uncomfortable because he was "too serious" about her. On her birthday Bob bought an expensive box of chocolates and brought it to her house. Sylvia was not there, but when she came home and found the gift, she felt very unhappy about it. She never touched any of the candy. Her sisters and brothers ate it.

Why did she feel unhappy about it?

Why did Bob give her such an expensive box of candy?

Would Bob be likely to ask Sylvia for another date?

Should Sylvia accept the date?

2. Wanda had always admired Tom D——, and when he asked her for a date she was overjoyed. During the evening she was somewhat nervous, wondering whether he liked her. She kept up a steady flow of excited conversation and showed extreme interest in every subject. She made a great fuss about Tom's tie, and told him he was the best player on the basketball team and that he danced divinely, and so on. Every time Tom said anything, Wanda agreed with him and often restated in stronger terms what he had said. She lingered with him at her front door so long that Tom finally pecked a kiss on her cheek, said good night, ran to his car, and left. Wanda remained standing for some moments after Tom drove away, and then, in a trance, she slowly entered the house. The next day she told three girls that Tom D—— had kissed her. Wanda never had another date with Tom.

What mistakes did Wanda make?

How should she have behaved?

3. Is it true that "all boys go for is a pretty face"?

4. Are blind dates acceptable in your community? What have you to say for or against them?

GROUP ACTIVITIES

1. With your teacher's help make a survey of opinions in your class as to how often you should have dates and how late to stay out.

2. In the same way find out what are the opinions of your class members about "going dutch treat." How much money should a boy spend when he is on a date?

INDIVIDUAL ACTIVITIES

1. *For girls.* If you would like to have a date with a certain boy, find out what he is especially interested in and let him know you, too, are interested in that. For example, if he is on the basketball team, get one or two of your friends to go with you several times to watch basketball practice and attend all the games. At the first opportunity get him to tell you about his basketball trips, etc.

2. *For boys.* If you want a date with a certain girl and don't feel ready to approach her, find out what she is especially interested in, make yourself more or less familiar with her hobby, and ask her about it. If you can begin conversations with her on a subject in which she is interested, you will sooner or later feel more confident about asking her for a date.

3. It is sometimes said that everyone has to tell his secret to one person. If this is true, the one person has to tell another, and so on, till nothing remains secret. It is a good plan to keep many things that happen on your dates all to yourself. Even if you feel like telling someone, practice keeping it to yourself. You get a feeling of emotional security from being able to refrain from telling something that you really would like to tell.

READINGS

In Literature

NOVEL

Austen, Jane. *Pride and Prejudice.* Appleton-Century.

When they first met, she thought, "He's a Londoner and a snob." He thought, "She is beautiful. What could she see in me?" But Fate has a way with people.

PLAYS

Barrie, James. "Quality Street"; in *Plays of J. M. Barrie.* Scribner.

A street of good-mannered people and a girl with the innate qualities of a lady as well as the external ones. But she gets her man.

Rostand, Edmond. *Cyrano de Bergerac.* Macmillan.

A love story for the ages. No one ever made love more beautifully than Cyrano when he stood in the garden below her window.

SHORT STORIES

Bunner, Henry C. "Love Letters of Smith"; in *Short Sixes*. Keppler and Schwarzmann.

    Probably the queerest exchange of notes that ever lovers passed, brought these two together.

Henry, O. "The Third Ingredient"; in *Options*. Harper.

    Three ingredients were needed for the stew: meat, potatoes, and an onion. And the young man who brought the onion filled the bill.

For Further Information

Bogardus, E. S., and Lewis, R. H. *Social Life and Personality*, pp. 81-84. Silver Burdett.

McKown, H. C., and Le Bron, Marion. *A Boy Grows Up*, pp. 99-110. McGraw-Hill.

McLean, Donald. *Knowing Yourself and Others*, pp. 140-145. Holt.

Trilling, Mabel B., and Nicholas, F. W. *The Girl and Her Home*, p. 18. Houghton Mifflin.

MARRIAGE

Do you have to know how to get along with people in order to have a happy marriage? Why? How many members of the graduating class of two years ago in your school are married today? Why do some young people say they will never marry?

THE AVERAGE HIGH-SCHOOL SENIOR is within five years of marriage. The difficulties experienced by his parents are not essentially different from those he will experience when he is married. During recent years many young people of high-school age have been giving serious thought to this fact and have been coming to realize its meaning more fully. While successful marriage is one of the highest achievements in social relationships, it is folly to believe that success in marriage is a matter of chance and does not require the solution of many serious problems in human relationships. A man and woman marry because at the time they have certain interests in common and a strong identity of desires, but to remain together and maintain a firm marriage relationship over many years requires a great deal of adjustment. These adjustments have to do largely with ordinary habits of living.

Many people do not think beyond the honeymoon. Uninterrupted bliss is too much to expect from any relationship, least of all from marriage, in which two very different individuals are constantly exposed to each other's faults as well as virtues "until death do us part."

Marriage requires give and take. Successful marriage requires a constant willingness to give and take, a constant study of each

Lambert

Getting along with Dad will not be difficult for this young man (*above*). Together they have learned to share a common interest.

Boy meets girl for tennis (*below*). Here again a common interest forms a sound basis for a personal relationship.

Roberts

Marriage is a partnership requiring constant co-operation. The husband (*above*) is helping make a successful marriage by assisting his wife in the work of the home.

Children in the family shift parents' attention away from themselves. Notice that both parents (*below*) center their interest in their child.

other's virtues instead of faults, and a constant effort toward cooperation for future as well as present happiness. These requirements will be necessary, not for just a day, or just an hour — but always. They take into account a million little things that seem to have no bearing upon love or passion or romance.

Who is to take care of the furnace while the husband is at work? Shall breakfast be served while he is still in his shirtsleeves? Is the fingernail polish used by the wife pleasing to the husband? Why does one use a certain word too often to suit the other? Why is the coffee too hot or too cold? Shall the housework be done by the wife, the maid, the husband, or all of them? Thousands of questions like these, including many of even less importance, come up in marriage and lead to difficulties if they are not met correctly. These are things to think about before you decide that a marriage, like a movie, is going to be summed up in a fade-out clinch.

Keep one eye open. Young people who can enter marriage without complete romantic blindness have a distinct advantage over those who do, and, other things being equal, they have a better chance of continued success in married life.

Marriage should be thought of as a partnership leading to parenthood and a lifetime of cooperation. There is no reason why this cannot be achieved, provided young people consider the problem of selecting the right mate and make a constant conscious effort toward solving the difficulties that arise.

What is an ideal marriage? An ideal marriage is one in which, through cooperation, both husband and wife achieve a greater realization of themselves within the bondage of matrimony than they could have achieved separately in the greater freedom of single life.

Marriage adds limitations to living. Maybe you have not considered the bondage that marrying imposes. Here are a few illustrations: If you are married, you do not have freedom to keep company with persons of the opposite sex. You must make your plans fit in with the needs and wishes of your husband or wife; you are not free to come and go as you please, unless you want to disregard the interests of the person to whom you are married. You are not free to spend your money as you were when you were single, for there is someone else to consider. You must choose your friends to suit your husband or wife rather than yourself alone. To please your husband or wife, you may occasionally wear different clothes from those you would wear if you were single.

If you are married and interested in working out a genuine cooperation, you are willing to put up with a large number of minor unpleasantnesses which you are more free to shun if you are single. Yes, matrimony is distinctly a bondage; but a successful marriage is one in which husband and wife have found a new freedom within the bondage through cooperation. In such a marriage, what one gains far outweighs what he gives up.

What is an ideal husband or an ideal wife? The ideal marriage is not a partnership between an ideal husband and an ideal wife. There is no such thing as an ideal husband or wife, because happiness in marriage depends upon the relationship of two distinct individuals. A certain man may be an ideal husband for his wife and yet would be a failure if he were married to any other woman. Likewise, a certain woman may be an ideal wife for her husband, yet a failure married to anyone else.

Ideal qualities of wifehood or husbandhood are determined to a large extent by the cooperation developed between the two. Although there are certain qualities, such as sociability, generosity, unselfishness, physical health, and mental health, that would serve to recommend anyone for the marriage state, it is still necessary for every individual to develop himself ideally in relation to his mate. All personalities differ, and therefore all require different mates. The ideal relationship requires a never-ending adjustment of two personalities so both may continue to realize the best that is in them. The more socially and emotionally mature both are, the greater will be their achievement in married life, for marriage is the highest form of human relationship and offers the greatest satisfaction while also presenting the greatest problems.

FOR CLASS DISCUSSION

1. Mrs. John Doe says she has an ideal husband. Here are her reasons:

My husband never loses his temper.

He thinks I am the only woman for him and never looks at another woman.

He likes my family and is very nice to my mother.

He gives me plenty of money.

I have all I want for the house and a sizable savings account of my own.

He has made out his large insurance policies for my benefit.

He doesn't want me to work too hard. He always calls up and asks permission before he brings any friends home for lunch.

When it's hot, he calls up to tell me that we are to have dinner at some air-cooled restaurant.

What kind of woman is Mrs. John Doe herself?

Why does she think her husband is ideal?

2. Is it true that a woman is doing a man a favor in marrying him?

3. Who as a general rule gets the better deal out of marriage, the husband or the wife? Explain.

INDIVIDUAL ACTIVITIES

1. Study the young couples of your acquaintance to see whether they are well mated.

2. Make a list of the errors you personally want to avoid when you get married.

3. Whether you are seriously interested or not in the person with whom you have spent an evening, ask yourself the questions listed on pages 272 and 273.

READINGS

In Literature

NOVELS

Bennett, Arnold. *These Twain.* Doubleday, Doran.

So many stories end with the beginning of a happy (?) marriage; this one begins with the beginning of a happy marriage.

Edmonds, Walter D. *Erie Water.* Little, Brown.

His wife was an indentured servant. He bought her from the deck of a European boat just landed.

PLAYS

Barrie, James. "What Every Woman Knows"; in *Plays of J. M. Barrie*. Scribner.

Do men know "what every woman knows"?

Milne, A. A. "The Boy Comes Home"; in *One-Act Plays*, selected by Webster and Webster. Houghton Mifflin.

War changes a fellow, as one uncle who had dominated his family learned. The relation of Uncle James and Aunt Emily is delicately suggested.

SHORT STORIES

Bennett, Arnold. "From One Generation to Another"; in *Matador of the Five Towns*. Doubleday, Doran.

Delightful give and take between a young husband and wife, both of whom are used to having their own way.

Stevenson, Robert Louis. "The Bottle Imp"; in *Island Nights' Entertainments*. Scribner.

Don't you wish that you could have your every wish fulfilled? Perhaps you would change your mind, as Keawe did.

For Further Information

Bogardus, E. S., and Lewis, R. H. *Social Life and Personality*, pp. 75-81. Silver, Burdett.

Eastburn, L. A., Kelley, V. H., and Falk, C. J. *Planning Your Life for School and Society*, pp. 186-189. Scribner.

McLean, Donald. *Knowing Yourself and Others*, pp. 145-148. Holt.

THE RELATION OF MARRIAGE
TO THE HIGH-SCHOOL STUDENT

At what age is a girl legally permitted to marry in your community? What is the minimum legal age for a boy? Is there such a thing as love at first sight? Are there enough boys "to go around" in your community?

When will you marry?　Some time ago a questionnaire was sent to thirty-eight persons who had been members of a high-school class in personal problems.　At the time they received the questionnaire none of them had been out of high school more than two years, yet six of them were married.　No doubt, the majority of those former students were married before they were out of school five years.　At graduation students range between sixteen and twenty years of age; five years later they will range between twenty-one and twenty-five.　You can see how close to marriage an average high-school student is.　Serious thought, therefore, should be given to the selection of a mate and to your own preparation for wifehood or husbandhood.　High-school students should not forget their future responsibilities while they are enjoying school life.

It is not too early to ask yourself these questions: How can I bring to my marriage a healthy body and a healthy mind?　Am I developing myself in such a way that I shall become a worthy husband or wife and a good father or mother?

Dating is one of the preliminaries.　It is not only normal for boys and girls of high-school age to have dates; it is good for them and necessary to their development.　Boy and girl relationships, as has been pointed out earlier, have a leading-on value, providing young people with experimental opportunities to study themselves and each other in relation to the opposite sex.

It is not normal to be a woman-hater or a man-hater. There are some girls and boys who want themselves known as woman-haters or man-haters, but these attitudes are spurious in most cases. There is some reason behind this apparent desire. Perhaps the supposed woman-hater or man-hater is unable to get dates and, like the fox who called the grapes sour because he could not reach them, says he doesn't want any. Perhaps, as is frequently the case with boys, he does not have any money to spend on entertaining girls, and to cover up his unhappiness says he hates women. Perhaps the "hatred" of the other sex is merely a cover for timidity. Again, the attitude may be a technique to create interest. A girl may say she hates boys in order to throw out a challenge for boys to date her; a boy may say he hates girls in order to stimulate feminine interest in him. People who are genuinely not interested in members of the opposite sex do not advertise the fact. Even they, however, are not entirely normal in this respect.

Are you in love with love? As was pointed out earlier in this book, people are sometimes in love with love; that is, they so keenly desire to be in love that they fall in love at the first opportunity, without forethought or control. In so doing they are out of touch with realities and blind to many things that other people see very clearly. Love is a serious thing that requires thought; one should try not to be tricked into it by a temporary emotional state.

Several years ago a girl in senior high school told the author that she wished she could have a "crush" on somebody because life seemed boresome to her. In that state of mind this young lady was extremely susceptible to a sudden, uncontrolled romance. As a matter of fact, about ten days after the interview, she did get her "crush" and gave herself over to it so completely that she fell behind in her school work, lost her former girl friends, and finally, having eloped, was also estranged from her family. A year later she admitted that she had been in love with love, not with the young man, and had divorced him after three months of married life.

Do you need someone to love or someone to love you?   It is often true that the person who drifts into marriage is in love with love; that is, he has an overpowering desire to be loved.   This is readily understood when you consider that it is extremely gratifying to be loved devotedly; for one thing, it enhances the feeling of self-importance.   Nevertheless, it is, basically, a selfish motive for marriage, and, though many marriages occur in which one of the two surrenders himself or herself to the other without receiving the same surrender in return, these marriages are likely to "go on the rocks."   There must be mutual affection — both husband and wife must want to give as well as receive — for a sound beginning in marriage.

Are you looking for a mother-person or a father-person?   Many young people feel themselves drawn, without knowing why, to a person of the opposite sex who reminds them of their father or mother, as the case may be.   The resemblance may consist of something quite superficial, like a way of smiling or speaking, or the color of hair or the shape of the face.   What is the reason for the attraction in these instances?   Perhaps these people find it difficult to break with home ties; childhood relationships with their parents have been so binding that deep within them they wish to continue these relations into adulthood and find a substitute for father or mother.   The fact that you are looking for a mother-person or a father-person is not necessarily harmful, but it is mentioned here to help some who do not understand why they are interested in a certain person of the opposite sex.

Shall you drift into marriage?   The importance of planning for instead of drifting into marriage and the need of choosing wisely is emphasized by the facts about divorce available in detail from *The World Almanac.*   A few figures will illustrate the point.   In the year 1922-23 there were over 165,000 divorces in the United States.   Nine years later there were many more — seventeen divorces for every hundred marriages.   Unofficial reports for 1941-42 give the ratio of divorces to marriages as approximately one to six; that is, for every six marriages one divorce, a ratio which in wartime does not improve.   These figures are tragic and astonishing when you stop to think that there are only two simple reasons for almost all divorces: (1) People do not choose their mates carefully, and (2) they do not solve the problems that come up in the marriage relationship.

Marriage is so near at hand for high-school students, and it means so much happiness and success or so much tragedy and failure, that it should become a subject of thought and study as well as an opportunity for romance.

You can make your own secret observations of the way married couples get along or fail to get along. You do not have to talk these over with anyone. You can make your own secret observations of the persons with whom you have dates. Ask yourself whether this one or that one would help you to realize your best qualities and whether you are the right person to help him to realize his best qualities. Imagine yourself in every situation with him and see if you can visualize a happy, understanding relationship through favorable and unfavorable circumstances.

Marriage brings to both parties new responsibilities as well as opportunities for greater happiness. That many marriages do not lead to happiness is common knowledge. If you want to handle this problem successfully, it is worthy of careful planning and preparation.

FOR CLASS DISCUSSION

1. Should a girl's high-school education prepare her for marriage? In what ways? Should a boy's? How?

2. Should a high-school student make any plans for marriage? If not, why not? If so, what sort of plan?

GROUP ACTIVITIES

1. Make a survey of opinions in your class as to the age at which young men and young women should get married.

2. Make a survey of opinions in your class as to how many approve and disapprove of (a) dating during high school, (b) "going steady" during high school, and (c) getting married before completion of a high-school education.

INDIVIDUAL ACTIVITIES

1. Select four or five married couples from among your relatives and find out how old they were when they were married.

2. From your principal get the graduating class list of two years ago. With the help of one or two other people, check the number of those who are married now. Do the same for the class that was graduated three years ago.

If you were to carry this activity out for the five past graduating classes, you could construct a simple line graph showing the increase in number from year to year. However, you would have to get the help of city or county records. A graph illustrating the information you get in such a study would be of considerable value to your teachers.

READINGS

In Literature

SHORT STORIES

Hawkins, Anthony Hope. "Indifference of the Miller of Hofbau"; in *Heart of the Princess Osra*. American News.

The miller knew what qualities he wanted in a wife and the lady lost the bet.

Pain, Barry. "Lovers on an Island"; in *Golden Book* (July, 1931).

Will love hold out when tested by a "shipwreck" on a "desert island"?

Strindberg, August. "Love and Bread"; in *Married*. Liveright.

They married too young.

For Further Information

Bell, Howard M. *Youth Tell Their Story*, p. 43. American Council on Education.

Bogardus, E. S., and Lewis, R. H. *Social Life and Personality*, pp. 84-87. Silver Burdett.

Fedder, Ruth. *A Girl Grows Up*, Chapter 7. McGraw-Hill.

McKown, H. C., and Le Bron, Marion. *A Boy Grows Up*, pp. 295-296. McGraw-Hill.

A Home of Your Own

IT IS NATURAL to think about a home of your own before you really have one. You want your home to be an improvement over some you have seen. You want to avoid many of the mistakes others have made and yet be sure to do the worth-while things they have done. At present, when you think about a home of your own, you think of an ideal one; at least, it is still in the form of ideas. Suppose we follow some of those ideas and see where they lead.

We shall have to think about costs, because a home costs money; about the environment inside the home, because that has much to do with dispositions and moods; about keeping the relationship between husband and wife on a happy level; and finally, about children, because a home without children is not complete.

This home we are going to think about will be a good one.

WHAT IT COSTS

Is it true that "two can live cheaper than one"? Why should a good income help married couples to be happy? Can a person in love think straight? Can you expect him or her to be bothered about finances? Why?

OF COURSE, after marriage you cannot continue to "live in with the folks." This has often been done, almost always with the same unhappy results, so you would not plan your beginning that way. Even if your home is only a small apartment, it will be your own, and it will be full of interesting little touches that distinguish it as yours. You will be free to make your own mistakes, as your parents made theirs, without interference from well-intentioned in-laws.

A good home plans a budget. But it costs money to be on your own. Look at these budgets and see if they seem reasonable:

MINIMUM BUDGET FOR TWO		ALTERNATE BUDGET	
(if you have your furniture)		(no furniture, but larger income)	
	per month		per month
Rent	$25.00		$50.00
Food	20.00		40.00
Clothes	8.00		20.00
Entertainment	10.00		20.00
Utilities	10.00		20.00
Medical attention	2.00		4.00
	$75.00		$154.00

The minimum budget (which, by the way, does not provide a plan for saving or any kind of future security) requires about eighteen dollars a week — every week — or $936 a year. If you have no bank balance, what would happen if the bread-winner were laid off — for even two weeks? Where would you get the thirty-five dollars needed as a minimum to keep the wolf from the door? Suppose you have five hundred dollars in the bank. How far would that go in case of a lay-off, a serious illness, or some other misfortune?

Perhaps you would think twice before you took the step of setting up a home under these conditions.

Both budgets given violate the rule that rent per month should not be more than income per week.

The second budget is better than the first. It does not provide a plan for saving or future security, but it might be possible to cut down on certain items in order to buy furniture, and perhaps save a very little. The budget requires about thirty-five dollars a week — every week — or $1820 a year, which during normal times is a very good income for a young man at the average marrying age of twenty-two.

Living expenses would, of course, vary from place to place and from time to time, as would wages; but the budget plans give some idea of the expense young married couples have to meet. Are you planning for this? Will your pocketbook be ready when your heart is?

Standard budgets. Just to give you some idea about the distribution of expenditures in married life, a number of standard budgets are included on page 293. You can get budgets like these from your local banker or from the Department of the Interior, Washington, D.C. It would be necessary, of course, to fill out certain items, as "Health, Recreation, and Personal Advancement," according to the specific expenditures planned. Under this particular item might be listed expenditures for a hobby, such as stamp collecting; or for cultural advancement, as night school fees and books; or for entertainment, as fishing tackle, movies, and concerts. Married couples who plan according to a budget are adding order and discipline to the business part of family life. And this ordering, or disciplining, is helpful because it gives bal-

STANDARD BUDGETS*

Incomes per Month	For a Family of Two				For a Family of Three				For a Family of Four			
	$75	$100	$150	$200	$75	$100	$150	$200	$75	$100	$150	$200
Food........................	24	27	37	40	30	34	44	48	36	41	51	56
Clothing....................	10	13	20	22	11	14	20	25	12	15	21	28
Housekeeping expenses.......	7	10	11	18	5	9	12	20	5	8	12	20
Rent........................	12	16	20	25	12	16	20	25	12	16	22	27
Health, recreation and personal advancement.	7	10	12	14	6	8	12	14	4	6	10	13
Saving and insurance........	7	10	27	50	5	7	21	41	3	5	15	31
Charities...................	2	6	10	15	1	5	9	12	1	3	8	11
Miscellaneous...............	6	8	13	16	5	7	12	15	2	6	11	14
Totals..................	75	100	150	200	75	100	150	200	75	100	150	200

* Adapted from Nelson, Jacobs, and Burroughs, *Everyday Problems in Mathematics*, Houghton Mifflin.

ance to money problems.   We need balance in financial matters as well as in those pertaining directly to mental health.

Plans before the banns.   Such things as the family budget should be discussed before you reach the altar.   No matter if it is necessary to change these plans in some details — it is important to think through as far as possible whatever financial problems you have to meet.   By doing so you give yourself a chance to know before it is too late whether you will be able to manage your household affairs and enjoy managing them with the person who is becoming your husband or wife.   You should have tentative plans for insurance, for saving, for home buying, and for children.   Before marriage takes place you should be satisfied that both of you are interested in planning and managing a home and able to do it.

Why borrow?   It is not always foolish to borrow, though it is wise to avoid it.   Borrowing should give you an assured advantage which you could not have without the money.   For instance, many people borrow in order to buy a home, if they figure that making payments on a mortgage and meeting the other expenses connected with home ownership is cheaper or better in the long run than paying rent.   Before they go into debt, however, they should make sure that going into debt is better than not doing so.

Many people borrow in order to expand their business and increase their income.   Nowadays people do not borrow to expand in anticipation of more business, but wait until increased business requires expansion.   They are then more certain of a financial advantage, even though they must pay for the use of borrowed money.

Suits, fur coats, diamonds, wrist watches, paintings, or luxuries that could be postponed (and in wartime are considered unpatriotic), should not be purchased with borrowed money or on the dollar-down-and-dollar-a-week plan, because these things rarely pay in service for what it costs to borrow the money.   In particular, it is not good business to go in debt for things you do not need or use.   Besides, incurring debts for luxuries — and sometimes even for necessities — often leads to worry and may keep you dodging bill collectors, who do not help young couples to maintain the happiness they started with when they met at the altar.

However, there are some things — necessary and economical living equipment especially — that may with good reason be purchased on the installment plan or partly on borrowed money. Buying an electric refrigerator, for example, might be excusable even if part of the cost had to be paid on the installment plan. At least, it is often argued that an electric refrigerator is convenient and saves more in food than the cost of maintenance. Of course, in times of national emergency we must get along with what we have.

A good washing machine, if it can be had, is an example of a money-saving household device, for it is much less expensive to do the washing at home with good equipment than to have it done elsewhere. Labor-saving and money-saving devices that are frequently used represent investments that may be made with borrowed money, provided the purchaser can meet all payments on interest and principal without neglecting more basic needs. Food, clothing, shelter, and a minimum of entertainment are, of course, the most basic needs. You cannot afford to scrimp on them too much without creating new problems, such as those caused by ill health and irritability.

Give loan sharks a wide berth. You cannot afford to pay 24 per cent, 36 per cent, or 42 per cent interest on any money you may borrow. It just isn't good business, no matter how easy it is to get the money lent to you. If you have to pay more than 7 per cent on the unpaid balance, think twice before you borrow, even if it seems imperative to have the cash. Keep your credit rating good by paying your bills regularly, and then, if you do have to borrow money, you will be able to get it at a bank for from 5 to 7 per cent on the unpaid balance.

Newspapers all over the country recently carried the story of a man in a western state who took his case to court because, although he had managed for nine years to make interest payments on a small loan of two hundred dollars and had paid the principal four times over, he was not able to reduce the principal itself, and he wanted the courts to help him out of his dilemma. He had been paying interest at the rate of 3½ per cent per month, or 42 per cent per year. When you stop to think of it, it takes only fifteen years to double the principal at 6 per cent.

"Oh, Mom, I'm glad he hasn't any money. Don't you think it's more romantic if we just face the world with our bare hands?"

Plan against poverty. Poverty is a thief of happiness. Everyone has certain minimum material wants that must be satisfied. A man and wife may carry on together in the face of want, but with the best of intentions they will continually feel insecure and afraid. With this undercurrent in their lives they do not feel at ease and truly happy, or meet adequately the problems of human relations arising between them. Many irritations arise when every little desire is thwarted; quarrels take place, feelings of guilt follow, and common understanding becomes more and more impossible. Poverty is given as one of the main reasons for divorce and desertion.

This is not to say, of course, that you will readily give in to all the evils of poverty if you cannot avoid it. Sometimes, as during the great depression some years ago, a man cannot find work and the family is up against it, perhaps for a long time. Under such conditions you and your wife will fight with all the courage you have not to let yourselves be overwhelmed by bitterness, and not to let your children's lives be ruined just because you are temporarily poor. Perhaps there is no greater test of the love between two people than such a period of hardship; and it is a tribute to human beings that so many surmount the test, and come through, sometimes, stronger than before. On the other hand, though you plan for security, you will not put an undue emphasis on money. Devoting all your time and energy to worldly success can be ruinous to marriage or any other decent human relationship.

FOR CLASS DISCUSSION

1. Genevieve R——, a sophomore in high school, seventeen years old, was very much in love. She tried to persuade her parents to let her get married; but they refused and insisted that she finish high school. During the summer months she continued to beg them to let her get married. They argued that she and Jim did not have enough money to begin married life, and besides, there was the high-school education unfinished. Genevieve said that she wasn't interested in school any more, couldn't study — wouldn't, in fact. She wanted to remain at her twelve-dollar-a-week job and save money. Then, as soon as she and Jim had enough to get started, they could get married. Her parents finally agreed to this plan. Genevieve did not return to school; she married at the age of eighteen; and she never completed high school. Three years later she had three children.

Do you think Genevieve was wise? Explain.

Were the parents right in consenting to let her work? Why?

How much money could Genevieve have saved in the year she worked?

Supposing Jim had saved as much, would they together have enough for a safe start in married life?

2. What are the advantages and disadvantages of marrying young? For a girl? For a boy?

3. There is some evidence to show that children of parents who "live in with their folks" more frequently get into trouble because of stealing, truancy, and recklessness than do children of parents who do not "live in with their folks." How could this be explained?

4. Is it all right for both husband and wife to be working outside the home during the first part of their married life? Why?

GROUP ACTIVITIES

1. Do parents generally approve of their children's delaying marriage as long as possible? How do you explain their attitude? What is the opinion of the members of your class?

2. Make a survey of student opinions in your class as to how much money a young couple should have before they get married.

READINGS

In Literature

SHORT STORIES

Cather, Willa. "The Bookkeeper's Wife"; in *Golden Book* (November, 1919).

It is an old story, marriage. And what an ending for a man who is poor with a wife who wants the things other women have.

Gale, Zona. "The Need"; in *Bridal Pond*. Knopf.

"Dear Abel: I am so sorry it will hurt you that I couldn't invite you to a party like the other women."

Yezierska, Anzia. "Hunger"; in *Hungry Hearts*. Houghton Mifflin.

A New York tenement is no place for love.

For Further Information

Friend, M. R. *Earning and Spending the Family Income*, Units 3, 7, and 8. Appleton-Century.

Trilling, M. B., and Nicholas, F. W. *The Girl and Her Home*, pp. 127-156. Houghton Mifflin.

HOME ENVIRONMENT AND MARRIAGE

How can an apartment be made homelike? How can the desire to be important influence a young married couple's choice of living quarters? Is housekeeping the task only of the wife? How can a husband satisfy his wife's desire to be important?

HOME ENVIRONMENT has an important, though subtle, influence upon personalities. Everyone has a number of likes and dislikes regarding such things as pictures, wallpaper, furniture, rugs, lights, dishes, and other equipment in the home. Preferences in these matters may have been determined by emotional patterns acquired in childhood or developed through training and study. Whatever the case may be, they differ from one individual to another. Some people, for example, like spacious rooms and many of them; some prefer small, cozy rooms compact like a modern apartment. Some prefer orchid-colored wallpaper, while others dislike it. Differences in taste are multitudinous. In your own home you can try to create an environment most satisfying to your particular taste, but even that requires compromises and adjustments between husband and wife, for, naturally, they differ between themselves on a number of likes and dislikes.

Though it is impossible to go into details, it is possible to consider a few general rules or hints that may be safely followed in every home. The purpose of this section is to make a few suggestions that may guide you, when your time comes, in creating a home environment most likely to favor success in marriage.

Take your time about building. It is sometimes said that fools build and wise men buy. Some people have a new home built for themselves before they know from experience what they want in a home, with the result that, after having lived in the new house for a few years, they find many features do not work out in practice as they were originally planned. Later, they decide to build another home more to their liking, and then they may have to sell the first one at a sacrifice.

Make your own decisions. Whether you build, buy, or rent, get far enough away from your parental home to be forced to make your own decisions. Mr. and Mrs. B—— did not do this. They were so fond of Mrs. B——'s parents that they decided to rent the bungalow next door. One day a terrible screech was heard at the bungalow, and the next instant Mrs. B—— was seen running out of the front door and across the yard to her mother, who was watering the flowers on the porch. "Mother! Mother!" she screamed. "Come quickly — a mouse in the living room!" Would the young Mrs. B—— always depend upon her mother for help in a crisis? What would she do if a pan of grease caught fire? Would she learn to take care of such problems herself as long as her mother was next door?

Brighten the corner. Wherever you live you will find that bright walls and furnishings and plenty of light have a lifting effect upon the disposition, whereas dark rooms have a depressing effect. If you live in a rented house or apartment, it may be impossible for you to change the wallpaper; but you can brighten the furnishings, let in more light through the windows, and provide better artificial lighting.

Keep up with your friends in housing, if possible. In selecting your living quarters, it is important to keep up with your friends if your budget allows. It is not necessary to have more than your friends, but your home should not make you feel inferior when you are entertaining your friends in it. On the other hand, you should not plan your home in order to show off or arouse envy among your friends.

Make home a place for comfort. The wife will make the home "homey" and comfortable for her husband, so that it is a place to which he gladly returns at the end of the day's work. If she notices that he favors a certain chair in the living room and certain papers and magazines for reading, she will plan the room accordingly, making it easy for him to have the chair where he wants it, with the magazine rack, radio, or bookshelf handy.

Home environment is a cooperative project. The husband should be interested in his wife's efforts. For instance, he may help her to adjust the furniture or make other changes or plans for changes in the home. There is a tendency among husbands to consider housework and home planning as less important than their own daily work. In homes where this is the case the wife gets a feeling that her work is not significant. She not only resents the lack of recognition, but will in time lose interest and find more of her happiness outside the home.

Make it your own. Add your own touches, and make your living quarters your own, different and distinct. Make your own choices in furniture, china, pictures, fixtures, flowers, and the like. Your home becomes your own as you do things to it and in it.

Keep a few books on hand. Every young housewife should have two or three books on subjects related to home-making to help her with ideas for enlivening the home environment. Making your home your own is an art, and it cannot be learned during the first week you set up housekeeping. A number of good books, easy to read and full of helpful suggestions, have been listed in the bibliography at the end of this section. Special chapter references call your attention to information on the subject of home environment. If you have two or three of these books ready at hand, you can refer to them from time to time and never quite go stale on housekeeping in that home of your own.

FOR CLASS DISCUSSION

1. When Mr. Jones came home from his day's work, his wife had dinner ready in a large, spotless kitchen. She had trained him to come home at the same time every evening, wash immediately, and sit down to dinner. She prepared his favorite dishes and regularly reminded him of the fact. After dinner she wanted him to rest in the living room while she did the dishes. Mr. Jones used to gravitate to a large chair near the bay window, overlooking the avenue. But his wife did not like to have any one piece of furniture show more

wear than the other pieces, so, after a year of training, Mr. Jones shifted from one chair to another.   Since his wife was very neat, he did not sit down without first changing his clothes, and when his hands were dirty, he was careful not to touch doorknobs or chairs before he had washed.   He simply called to his wife and she came running to open the doors for him as he passed through the kitchen into the bathroom.   There were three mats on which he scraped his shoes in succession, so no dirt was tracked in.

He had to be pretty careful at home.   It was a beautiful home, exceedingly clean, and when he became impatient about Mrs. Jones's ways, he argued with himself that she was only right.   No one should come in and undo her excellent housekeeping.

Three years after he was married, Mr. Jones began to have engagements after supper.   He took up hunting and fishing and spent a good deal of time with men.   Gradually he spent less time at home.   One day his wife asked, "Why do you go out so often and leave me here? Isn't this house a good place to be?"   Mr. Jones did not know how to answer her.

Why did Mr. Jones spend so much time away from his home?

What suggestions would you make to Mrs. Jones?

2. Mrs. Brown was not interested in her home, though she loved her husband.   Housework was a bore.   She spent several hours a day reading.   Preparing meals was a routine without variations. She did not enjoy cooking; therefore, she planned the simplest possible meals.

Her husband could see the dust on every level surface.   She maintained that dusting was mostly foolishness because all you did was to stir the dust loose in the room so it could settle again, and then you would have to dust all over again.   He liked paintings, but she could not see how a few paintings might liven their living quarters.   They were married three years before the original furniture arrangement was changed, and Mr. Brown did the rearranging.   He spent one week of his vacation redecorating the house while she read three of the latest novels and occasionally looked up from her book to say, "What a nuisance, George, to spend your vacation upsetting the whole house!"

How did Mr. Brown feel about his wife's housekeeping?

What was her problem?

What could she do in order to be a better housekeeper for her husband?

INDIVIDUAL ACTIVITIES

1. Make a floor plan of an apartment or a house in which you would like to live when you are married. Place the furniture in the rooms in such a way as to be comfortable, convenient, and interesting.

2. Make a list of colors for interior decoration that have a pleasing effect upon you; also a list of those that affect you unfavorably. Check these lists with your closest friend of the opposite sex and see how much agreement or disagreement there is between you.

3. Make a list of the things you think you could do to a four-room apartment in order to make it a nice place in which to live. Keep the cost down to twenty-five dollars, and plan to make the changes without hired help.

READINGS

In Literature

SHORT STORIES

Jenkins, Herbert. "Mrs. Bindle's Discovery"; in *Golden Book* (February, 1930).

A man finds a pretty girl crying on the street corner and takes her home to her mother. His own home is made happier when his wife becomes suspicious.

Sherwood, Robert. "Extra! Extra!"; in *Book of Modern Short Stories*, edited by Dorothy Brewster. Macmillan.

"You're just lazy, Roy Whidden," said Mrs. Whidden. "You sit there reading your paper — night after night."

For Further Information

Draper, Dorothy. *Decorating Is Fun.* Doubleday, Doran.

Friend, M. R. *Earning and Spending the Family Income,* Unit 7. Appleton-Century.

Koues, Helen. *How to be Your Own Decorator.* Good Housekeeping.

Shultz, Hazel. *Making Homes.* Appleton-Century.

Trilling, Mabel B., and Nicholas, F. W. *The Girl and Her Home,* Units 2 and 7. Houghton Mifflin.

RELATIONSHIPS BETWEEN HUSBAND AND WIFE

Who should be "boss" — husband or wife? Should a husband frequently say "I love you" to his wife? Are there any indications by which it is possible to tell in advance that a couple is likely to be happily married? If so, what are they? If you quarrel during your engagement, are you likely to quarrel after marriage?

THERE IS NO MAGIC in a successful marriage relationship. It is, after all, only a matter of common courtesy and decency between two people. When being decent and courteous is successfully worked out between husband and wife, it leads to more than ordinary happiness because they are closer together than people in other social relations. For the same reason, when common decency and courtesy are not successfully maintained between husband and wife, it leads to more than ordinary unhappiness.

Save the surprise element. In all instances of very close relations between people there is a tendency for one to take the other for granted. The basic urges of life are then not satisfied between them, for they do not receive recognition, encouragement, and understanding. Their good qualities are not noticed; their love is taken for granted as something that is to be expected. On the other hand, undue attention is given to shortcomings, and any temporary lapses in faithfulness or diligence or affection loom big.

One batch of burnt biscuits gets a wife more comment than a

"You never take me any place since we became engaged. Just like a married couple."

hundred batches of perfect ones. One evening of crankiness gets a husband more comment than weeks of uncomplaining labor. The old saying, "Familiarity breeds contempt," holds good in the marriage relationship if husband and wife take each other's virtues too much for granted. In your home you will want to avoid such a state of affairs by saving an element of surprise in what you do. Surprise him or her by doing the unexpected once in a while. Occasionally interrupt the daily routine with something novel, funny, or different, so that your husband or wife never gets into the rut of taking you quite for granted.

When Antony said of Cleopatra that, among other virtues, she had "infinite variety," he implied that much of her charm came from her ability to keep alive the element of surprise that prevents a man from taking a woman for granted. You will plan to manage your life with your husband in such ways that he will not always know just what to expect; then his original interest in you as a person never will die.

Each will avoid rejection of the other. Husband and wife may indicate in countless ways that they reject each other. Rejection is shown in such actions as turning away when spoken to, disagreeing with and refusing requests that could be granted, being too busy to listen, showing no interest in the events of the day, criticizing in-laws, disliking the other's friends, and failing to join in laughter or to sympathize in sorrow.

On the other hand, acceptance is also shown in countless ways, the reverse of those already suggested — listening with interest, agreeing to and granting requests if possible, taking time to listen, showing interest in the events of the day, speaking well of in-laws, showing a preference for the things preferred by the other, and sharing in emotions.

How a husband may show affection. A husband need not emphasize his affection in so many words. He need not say "I love you" every day or be constantly demonstrative. He will make his affection evident by many acts of acceptance, such as showing an interest in the work done by his wife in the home, the meals she prepares, her activities in the church and the community, and her friends; noticing and praising her clothes; discussing plans with her; asking her opinion, not only on questions concerning the home, but also on public affairs.

How a wife may show affection. Likewise, a wife need not emphasize her affection by words and demonstrations. She, too, will betray her feelings in many acts of acceptance, such as showing interest in her husband's work and confidence in his way of handling the problems that arise on the job, sharing his emotions, showing that she appreciates the value of the income he provides, taking an interest in his friends and helping to make them comfortable, and showing her respect for his opinion by consulting him on various purchases and many other questions.

Avoid the bad, keep the good in the parental patterns. Husband and wife usually repeat the parental patterns; that is, a husband tends to act toward his wife as his father did toward his mother, and a wife tends to act toward her husband as her mother did toward her father. This is not always the case, but there are not many exceptions. That the relationship of parents has a great deal of influence upon the success of their children's marriage has been shown by Professor L. M. Terman, of Stanford University. Professor Terman studied a large number of married couples and found that one of the most important factors in marriage success was the success of the parents' married life. Thus, if the parents of a young couple had achieved a successful marriage relationship, it was fairly certain that the young couple themselves would succeed.

It is true, however, that many young people desire to reverse the parental pattern in a number of respects, particularly as regards mistakes and faults. This desire is so strong in some people that they are actually able to avoid or solve in their own marriage relationships many problems that led to unhappiness between their parents. But it takes constant conscious effort to avoid bad habits and develop good ones.

Learning to be husband and wife in childhood. Peculiar as it may seem, girls and boys learn to be wives and husbands while they are too young to realize it. Children learn a great many habits from their parents by imitation and follow these in their own lives when they get married. The mother's reaction to the father is an example that the daughter will be likely to follow when she reaches the mother's stage of development. The same thing is true of the son in relation to his father's reaction. This is not always, but it is generally, the case.

Overcoming old habits by constant effort. If the parents on both sides have been quarrelsome, you and your wife will have difficulty avoiding the same quarrelsomeness in your marriage unless you make a constant and conscious effort over a period of years. Some people like to quarrel, it must be admitted. But if you do not like to quarrel, and if your parental background is a quarrelsome one, you will have to make a serious effort to change the habits learned in childhood.

Your home is not made to break up. You will, of course, plan
to make your marriage a successful one. You will not enter into
it, as some do, thinking that if it does not turn out right, you can
always go home or get a divorce. Divorce is tragic because of
what it means in the way of heartbreak for parents and children.
If you plan to make your marriage a lasting one, you must make
up your mind to solve problems as they arise in the relationship.

Your wife is not a piece of property. As a husband you will
avoid the mistake so commonly made — an attitude of possessive-
ness toward your wife. You will not regard your wife as property over which you have legal rights of life and death, not to
mention the right of making every minor decision in your own
way. Your wife is an individual. You will respect her individuality and give her freedom to be herself. The man who prided
himself on what he had made of his wife was giving himself a
most damaging criticism. Was she his wife or a piece of property? They had a marriage license, but were they married in
any real meaning of the word?

Cooperate without too much sacrifice. When you have a husband or a wife, you will both plan your life as a joint enterprise,
sharing joys and sorrows, and growing and improving together.
You will not, through too much sacrifice on the part of one, permit yourselves to grow apart.

This was the case with Mr. and Mrs. A——, who lived on a
ranch in the West. Ranching, however, did not fully satisfy Mr.
A——, and, with his wife's encouragement, he decided to go to college. Together they worked hard. During the school year Mrs.
A—— remained on the ranch, managing affairs there. After college Mr. A—— got a position as a teacher, and they left the ranch.
Still, Mrs. A—— urged her husband to continue his schooling, and
by constant scraping and saving it was possible for him to do so.

The couple had to go without many things, of course, such as
new clothes, an automobile, and the ordinary luxuries enjoyed by
their friends. Three children came, but still they managed
somehow to have Mr. A—— continue his education until he obtained his Master's and finally his Doctor's degree.

By this time Mr. and Mrs. A—— were well along in life, their
children were in high school, and Mr. A——'s circle of friends

among professional people had grown. After all these years of relative poverty and sacrifice, however, Mrs. A—— never learned to enjoy life, even when they had a comfortable income. She continued to be worried about financial matters, felt uneasy about buying a new dress, and was uncomfortable in the company of her husband's professional friends.

She had sacrificed too much too long to keep up with him in his thinking and in his social activities. She had devoted so much of her time all these years to managing the household at a minimum cost that she had not been free to develop her own personality. When the time came for her to play a part in a different social group, she still felt inferior and was unable to live up to her husband's position.

FOR CLASS DISCUSSION

1. Elaine and Jack had been childhood sweethearts. During high school both occasionally dated with others, but they were usually seen together at school affairs. After high school Jack went to college and Elaine got a job. When Jack came home for holidays, the two were again seen together, though it was known that they both had dated others during the semesters. Two years after college, Jack obtained a position as a chemist and the two were married.

People wondered about them because they had never shown keen affection for each other. Sometimes it had seemed as if they were not even loyal. But Elaine and Jack were happily married without the fire and exciting romance that usually continues during the engagement and briefly after marriage. People said they were more like older folks than like young couples.

Do you think they were in love? Why?

Would you expect them "to live happily ever after"? Explain.

2. Though it is often said that opposites attract one another, careful studies of thousands of marriages indicate that this is not the rule, but the exception. As a rule, persons who are alike attract one another. Blonds tend to marry blonds, and the same is true of brunets, of tall persons, of short persons. How can you explain this?

3. Why do many young couples before marriage say that they will not be like others in their marital relations; their romance will always continue?

4. If a couple frequently quarrel before marriage, will they be likely to quarrel frequently after marriage? Explain your answer.

5. Is it possible to be married without occasional quarreling or resentment between husband and wife? Explain.

INDIVIDUAL ACTIVITIES

1. Imagine yourself married to someone with whom you occasionally have dates and make a list of statements concerning his or her prospects as a person who would be able to get along well with you. List both favorable and unfavorable statements. (If you cannot think of any unfavorable ones, you probably do not know him or her well enough for marriage.)

2. Similarly, study yourself as a likely mate for someone with whom you occasionally have dates. List both favorable and unfavorable traits and decide how you could remove the unfavorable ones.

3. Observe a couple who get along happily. How does each one act to keep the other happy?

READINGS

In Literature

NOVEL

Buck, Pearl. *The Good Earth.* John Day.
> Husband and wife were happy together. Then the land made them rich.

PLAY

Barrie, James. "Ten Pound Look"; in *Plays of J. M. Barrie.* Scribner.
> Don't be fooled by the title.

SHORT STORY

Freeman, Mary Wilkins. "The Revolt of Mother"; in *New England Nun.* Harper.
> How one wife put her husband in his place.

For Further Information

Bogardus, E. S., and Lewis, R. H. *Social Life and Personality,* pp. 67-74. Silver Burdett.

Eastburn, L. A., Kelley, V. H., and Falk, C. J. *Planning Your Life for School and Society,* Chapter 10. Scribner.

Friend, M. R. *Earning and Spending the Family Income,* Unit 1. Appleton-Century.

CHILDREN

Do children keep parents from having entertainment? Do parents of nine children have as much affection for each of them as parents of two? Is life easier for an only child or for one who is a member of a large family? What do you think of the practice of having a two-year-old do somersaults and perform before guests?

WHY HAVE CHILDREN?

There are many reasons, but the most fundamental is that everyone shares in the responsibility of preserving the race, and the only way to preserve the race is to have children. It is as normal to have children as it is to be interested in the opposite sex, choose a mate, and marry. In fact, a home without children is not complete; it is not fulfilling its duty to help keep the race alive.

Many people who do not have children wish they had at least one or two. They give various reasons — their friends have children, and they feel out of it when the discussion turns to the subject of children; they would like to have someone carry on their name and inherit their property when they are gone; and (the best reason of all) they want someone to love. Children give parents daily opportunities for service, sacrifice, and affection. As human beings become truly grown-up, they want children because they want more opportunities to be of service and to show affection.

Children provide an opportunity for unselfishness. There is a great satisfaction, called emotional security, that comes from having an interest in others and doing things for them. In a home children become objects of affection and care; they require time, attention, and sacrifice, and interest is shifted to them and away from the adults. For emotional security everyone, in any walk of life, should seek opportunities for unselfishness. Nature fortunately provides these opportunities in the complete family.

Children need affection. Doctors who understand the importance of mother-love in an infant's life say that a baby needs a certain amount of fondling and caressing. He needs the warmth and nearness of his mother's body and the rhythmic cradling of his mother's arms. Years ago it was thought that the fondling of a baby by his mother was unnecessary or harmful, but it has since been learned that this is not true. Some doctors strongly recommend that a mother who rears her child with a bottle should not give the baby his bottle in the cradle, but should take him up in her arms during the feeding time and hold him in comfort. It has been found that such handling of infants, if done wisely, helps them to develop more normally than they do otherwise.

A baby can sense whether it is welcome. A baby seems to know whether it is wanted or not. Most parents are happy to have a baby arrive, and many who, for financial or other reasons, at first do not feel very happy about it, soon grow to love the youngster as much as if they had never worried at all about its coming. Babies born and reared under these conditions are "wanted" babies, and their life is normal, other things being equal.

Rejected children. Some babies, however, come into the world really unwanted. Perhaps there is not enough money to provide for a child, or the parents think it will keep them at home too much, or it is born out of wedlock or too soon to suit the parents. Various reasons may enter into the attitude of the father and mother toward the child even before it is born, and as a consequence it will not receive the love, tenderness, and caressing that are its natural right and daily need. Children born to parents who show them little or no affection do not have a fair chance to grow up in mental health and with a sense of being socially accepted. Such children frequently grow up to be misfits, criminals, or "lone wolves," unless they are lucky enough to have some close friend who gives them the affection they missed and helps them to understand the problems of life. The conduct of rejected children can best be understood in the light of their need for affection. They do what they do because they are not loved.

A child-centered home. Although you love children and plan to have them, you will not go to the other extreme and make your home a child-centered home. Too much attention spoils the child. You will allow the children as much freedom as possible to decide for themselves what to do and what not to do. You do not want them to grow up tied to their mother's apron strings, or depending on their father to fight all their battles. When the home centers entirely around the children, they do not grow up emotionally. They are constantly dependent upon parental love when they should become more and more independent and more and more able to solve their own problems at play, at school, and at work. If you lavish too much care and love on your children, they may never learn to get along with others who do not satisfy their every want as you do; they may become social misfits, selfish, conceited, and reckless. There is a happy medium in loving children. You will try to find it and follow it in your own home.

The only child. The average family in the United States consists of four persons, two parents and two children (the true average is a fraction over four). A study of the figures shows that the families who can least afford it have the largest number of children and those who could best afford it have the smallest number, or none at all. It is, of course, not always possible to have exactly the desired proportion of boys and girls in a family, or even to have the number of children you would prefer; but at any rate it is best to have more than one child. An only child tends to vie with the parents for their affection; that is, he vies with his father to get the mother's love and with the mother to get the father's love. The child is not aware of this struggle, but it does frequently exist.

As the child grows older, his effort to be first both in his mother's and in his father's affection may create much unhappiness between the parents. Furthermore, an only child who has consistently followed this pattern of behavior at home also uses it in his relations with others outside the home. He wants to be

"Dear, have you explained to the guests that we never have conversation at dinner because it interrupts the children's radio program?"

HINTS FOR DISCUSSING THE CARTOON

Should parents permit children's radio programs to interfere with conversation at mealtime? Why? What does Junior's behavior show about his consideration for others? How would the guests feel? Would they be justified? If you had a son, would you let him turn on the radio in the situation pictured here?

first in the affection and attention of his friends and finds it difficult even to share a friend with someone else unless he is sure
that he himself is number one.

Dominating parents. As a parent you will avoid dominating
your children by telling them at every turn what to do or what
not to do and making their decisions for them in their choice of
friends, entertainment, a school or college, and an occupation.
Even though you have an overpowering love for your children,
you will hold it somewhat in check if you notice that it interferes with their free development. Some parents make their children so much a matter of property that they try to have the
children do everything they themselves wanted to do in their
youth.

Old-fashioned parents. As a parent you will try to grow with
your children, thinking as they do and even being interested in
the fads that make so much difference to them. Some parents
are old-fashioned. They have seen fads come and go and know
that none of them lasts. Since they do not understand their
children's interests, they discourage or prevent the children from
doing many things that others of the same age are doing. In your
family you will try to remember that you were a child once and
that now your own children need the understanding of parents
who, though they are wiser, still live in the same world as the
younger generation.

Expecting too much of children. Your children will, of course,
be priceless to you, and you will not readily find fault with them,
as strangers may. You will see all their good qualities and help
them to develop as fast and as far as possible. You will not, however, make the mistake some parents make and expect too much
of your children. Some children do not have the mentality to get
A's in their school work even when they study as hard as they
can. In such a case, you will not show that you are disappointed.
A child who feels that it is impossible for him to live up to his
parents' expectations goes through his youth with a feeling of
guilt. He thinks there is something wrong with him; he must
in some way be inferior. While, on the one hand, it is good to
stimulate your children to do the best they can, it is necessary,
on the other hand, to realize fully what this best is for each indi-

vidual child.   Then it will be possible to give encouragement for
work accomplished in terms of the child's own ability and effort.

Your children should have a fair chance of success.   Children
are sometimes given tasks that are too difficult for them. Naturally
they fail.   If failures are frequent in childhood, it is probable
that the child will develop an abnormal sense of inferiority or
inadequacy toward everything he does.   Feelings of inferiority
are also brought on by the impatience of parents toward children.
It is much better for a parent to give the child plenty of time to
do something than to sit by and finally, with impatience, say, "Oh,
he can't do it! It takes him too long!" A child should have things
to do that he is able to do, and he should have time to do them,
so that he may develop a feeling of success.

A child should also complete what he begins.   If he is constantly interrupted in his activities and constantly reminded of
his slowness or inability, it is natural for him to develop a keen
feeling of inferiority that may remain with him in everything he
tries to do.

The family conference in your home.   You may plan to have
family conferences in your home.   Some of the most successful
families settle their problems at such conferences.   Parents and
children get together around the dining-room table or in the living room and talk things over.   Such important questions arise
as the family budget, plans for next year, changes in household
arrangements, and how late, and for how many nights a week,
John and Jane should be permitted to stay out.   During the discussions the children get to know more about the responsibilities
carried by parents and those they themselves should carry.   They
get to know the reasons behind their parents' decisions and take
an active part in the family life.

The family conference brings democracy into your own home.
Families that frequently confer in this way are simply bringing
democracy into the home. They are reasoning things out together.
At such conferences it is possible for parents to discuss their own
youthful experiences with children.   When children hold out
strongly for one extreme and parents for the opposite, the discussion frequently ends in a compromise, with both sides giving in a
little.   Why, indeed, should not children listen to their parents,

who have had half a lifetime of experience? And why should not parents listen to their children, who have important desires that should be met and understood?

The family conference provides practice in cooperation. The family conference provides an excellent way for parents and children to develop a home life of cooperation and understanding that can add a great deal to the development of the children. Even though it is possible to achieve social maturity without an excellent home life, young people who have the guidance and understanding of parents, brothers, and sisters have a distinct advantage over those who do not. The habit of talking things over at home is usually begun by thoughtful parents. Perhaps you will have family conferences in your own home.

Your home will be a place where children learn to grow up, to make decisions, to respect the rules of society, and to meet the problems of life with increasing courage and success. Gradually, as the child becomes a youth and the youth an adult, with your help he will become independent of you, yet full of love and respect for you.

FOR CLASS DISCUSSION

1. Mr. and Mrs. Brown had one child for whom they wanted the best of everything. He was a beautiful child with blond, tousled curls and a cherub face. They adored him and spent much of their time cleaning him, dressing him, and playing with his toys for him. Finding that when he went out to play with other children, he came back with his pretty curls full of dust or mud, his cherub cheeks all smeared, and his clothes sometimes torn as well as dirty, they decided that this would not do for their boy. They were both extremely neat and they wanted to bring up their child with the same virtue. So they often said, "No, Johnny," "Don't do that, Johnny," "You mustn't touch that, Johnny." When Johnny left the house, his mother or father always went along, holding him by one hand and keeping him from walking away. Johnny was very curious about the world around him and whined and tried to pull away from the restraining hand. But he was constantly admonished, "Don't get into that, Johnny," "Leave it alone, Johnny."

Would you bring up your child this way? Why?

How would you improve on the methods of Mr. and Mrs. Brown? How will his childhood upbringing influence Johnny's behavior when he begins to go to school?

2. Mr. and Mrs. Jones had two children, a boy and a girl. Betty, the older of the two, was not Mr. Jones's favorite, for he had wanted a boy. Mrs. Jones, however, gave Betty all the attention and affection she needed. Two years later, the second child came, and Mr. Jones was overjoyed that it was a boy. Nothing was too good for Warren. The father devoted himself to Warren; the mother devoted herself to Betty. Mrs. Jones argued that, since Warren got everything from dad, Betty should get everything from mother; somebody had to love Betty, and, since Mr. Jones apparently did not, she would. This relationship continued during the childhood and youth of the two children.

Why should Mr. Jones be disappointed because the first child was a girl?

Were these parents hurting their children by dividing their affection? How?

What difficulties are likely to have arisen in the family because the mother favored Betty and the father favored Warren?

3. Mr. X completed the eighth grade at the age of seventeen. He was inferior in school work, but superior in physical activities. When he was seventeen he took up boxing and soon decided to enter a local boxing contest. However, his father told him that if he did, he would have to leave home. After much useless coaxing, the son decided to give up the idea.

Mr. X is now married and has a son of his own. The child is only six months old, but already he shows remarkable strength. He can stand erect on his father's hand for twenty seconds. His little body is sturdy and muscular, and he enjoys the many feats of strength in which his father trains him. Mr. X wants his son to become a champion in the ring.

Why is Mr. X training his son to be a boxer beginning at the age of six months?

Should he do so? Why?

What should he do for his son?

4. When you marry, would you prefer to have your first child a girl or a boy? Why?

5. Mention a number of things that a child inherits from his parents and a number of things he learns from them after birth.

INDIVIDUAL ACTIVITIES

1. The United States Income Tax Law allows a certain annual exemption for each child under eighteen. Find out what the exemption is and then discuss whether that is enough or more than enough to cover the cost of rearing a child? What are the expensive items in rearing a child?

2. On visiting in a home where there is a small child, study the ways in which parents show their acceptance or rejection of him or her. Directly after your visit make a list of their actions from this standpoint. How could their actions be improved?

3. What are the mistakes, and what the correct actions, of your parents in rearing you? How can you avoid making similar mistakes when you have your own children?

READINGS

In Literature

SHORT STORIES

Hergesheimer, Joseph. "The Token"; in *Best Stories of 1922*. Dodd, Mead.

> A bear of an old man, a pretty girl. Shall he obey his father and marry her?

Morrison, Arthur. "On the Stairs"; in *Tales of Mean Streets*. Modern Library.

> The most thought-provoking story as well as the most real you have had a chance to read. Don't read it if you are afraid to face life.

Williams, Jesse Lynch. "Not Wanted"; in *O. Henry Memorial Award Prize Stories of 1923*. Scribner.

> An unwanted boy finds a way out.

For Further Information

Friend, M. R. *Earning and Spending the Family Income*, Unit 1. Appleton-Century.

Keliher, Alice V. *Life and Growth*. Appleton-Century.

de Schweinitz, Karl. *Growing Up*. Macmillan.

Trilling, Mabel B., and Nicholas, F. W. *The Girl and Her Home*, Unit 4. Houghton Mifflin.

❧ IF YOU WANT TO KNOW MORE ❧

Throughout Part Two we have been studying social relations, with special emphasis on questions that occur most frequently to high-school students. Each high-school student, however, has a number of problems that are peculiar to himself, that are not common to everyone. For information on these problems further study is needed. If you want to know more about getting along with others, you will find it helpful to turn to one or more of the books listed here. These books not only provide information on many questions which have not been studied; they go more deeply and more completely into many questions which have already been discussed.

Doing the right thing at the right time is, basically, a matter of ethics or morals, so, if you want to know more about why an act is right or wrong, read these books:

Calkins, Mary W. *The Persistent Problems of Philosophy.* Macmillan. See index for references on "Ethics and Morality."

Carrel, Alexis. *Man the Unknown,* Chapter 4. Harper.

Dorsey, J. M. *The Foundations of Human Nature,* Chapter 8. Longmans, Green.

Drake, Durant. *Problems of Conduct.* Houghton Mifflin.

Durant, Will. *The Story of Philosophy.* Simon and Schuster. See index for references on "Ethics" and "Morality."

Randall, John H. *The Making of the Modern Mind,* Chapter 15. Houghton Mifflin.

Rousseau, Jean J. *Emile.* Dutton.

If you want to know more about solving your own problems of manners and etiquette, consult some standard authority such as:

Eichler, Lillian. *The Customs of Mankind.* Doubleday, Doran.

Post, Emily. *Etiquette.* Funk and Wagnalls.

Vogue's Book of Etiquette. Doubleday, Doran.

Since personal problems frequently have their beginning in the home, life in the home and relations among members of a family have been the subject of a great deal of study. Psychologists, psychiatrists, and mental hygienists have gone deeply into questions about family relationships. If you want to know more about this subject, consult one or more of the following books:

Adler, Alfred. *Understanding Human Nature*, Chapters 3, 5, 7, and 8. Garden City.

Beverly, Bert I. *In Defense of Children*. John Day.

Blos, Peter. *The Adolescent Personality*. Appleton-Century.

Dorsey, J. M. *The Foundations of Human Nature*. Longmans, Green. See index for references on "Family."

Groves, Ernest R. *Personality and Social Adjustment*, Chapters 10, 11, and 12. Longmans, Green.

Mowrer, H. R. *Personality Adjustment and Domestic Discord*. American Book.

Williams, F. E. *Adolescence; Studies in Mental Hygiene*. Farrar and Rinehart.

Zachry, Caroline B. *Emotion and Conduct in Adolescence*, Part II. Appleton-Century.

More information about sex, marriage, and relationships between the sexes can be secured from the books listed below:

Adler, Alfred. *Understanding Human Nature*, Chapter 7.

Bell, Howard M. *Youth Tell Their Story*. American Council on Education.

Shaffer, L. F. *The Psychology of Adjustment*, pp. 527ff. Houghton Mifflin.

Starch, D., Stanton, H. W., and Koerth, W. *Controlling Human Behavior*, Chapter 12. Macmillan.

Zachry, Caroline B. *Emotion and Conduct in Adolescence*, Chapter 13.

These books, like all well-planned books, contain references to other books. Often a book referred to in a reading list or bibliography has just what you want on a particular subject. Get in the habit of looking over the titles in bibliographies of the books you consult. You may read one or more books listed in a bibliography, and these may lead you to still others; if you do this, you will soon have familiarized yourself with a body of knowledge that is both broad and deep. Fortunately, in the field of human relations, you can use much of the information in daily living.

PART 3

MAKING YOUR WAY
IN TIME OF WAR

What Is Morale?

IT IS A TRADITION of the stage that no matter what happens, the show must go on.

The comedian may know that his beloved young wife lies sick and near death in the hospital; but he plays his part with the same old gusto, and the laughing audience never suspects for a moment that under the slapstick he himself is sick with dread. The gay ingénue may have had notice that next week the show ends, and she will have to go the rounds looking for another part; but she gives no hint of her worry as she plays up to the gallant hero. If a fire breaks out in the theater, the players will stick to their posts and do everything possible to prevent a panic in spite of danger to themselves.

These people are imbued with the feeling that they have a duty to a houseful of strangers far more important than their own worries, illnesses, or tragedies. No matter what happens, no matter how hard the present or how dark the future, they must not let the audience down. The show must go on!

This is what is known as *morale*. It is the ability to take even the worst misfortune in our stride, keep the chin up, stiffen the backbone for the sake of a cause, an ideal much greater than ourselves — and especially for the sake of fellow human beings whom we must not let down.

Not only actors are imbued with this tradition. The doctor who answers calls at all hours of the night, though he is badly in need of rest; the reporter who risks his neck to get a good story for his paper; the mother who greets the family cheerfully at dinner after a day when everything went wrong — these people, too, are living up to an ideal and tradition. They also have high morale.

All of us are capable of this kind of reaction once we truly realize that we are challenged to give our best and do our best. In ordinary living we often forget that we are under such a challenge; we easily fall into a state of mind in which life seems commonplace and unheroic. In war, the challenge is all around us. Then if ever we must forget ourselves, keep our chin up, stiffen our backbone — not that the show but that the Nation may go on.

Maintaining high morale in the face of the uncertainties and tragedies of war, which influences every one of us deeply and personally, is perhaps the most important challenge young people face today. It will bulk large in Part Three of this book because high morale is the foundation of making your way successfully in time of war.

KEEPING YOUR CHIN UP

How does the ability to get along with others help the war effort? Does war increase or decrease a young man or woman's opportunities for the future? Why does war increase personal problems on the home front? It is sometimes said that fear is contagious. What is meant by this? Is it possible to keep one's chin up even when one is afraid?

FROM THE STANDPOINT of groups rather than of individuals, national morale is something like school spirit.

When Centerville loses its most important football game, a wave of dejection naturally sweeps over the student body. But on the following Monday everyone is saying, "We'll beat them next year!" On Tuesday plans are being made for a big pep rally to precede the game with Southville on the coming Friday. That student body has good school spirit. In spite of temporary dejection the students as a group keep their chins up and rally fast. They have confidence in their coach, their team, and their school. Their morale is high.

There is far more at stake in a conflict between nations than in a friendly game between rival teams. National morale is more completely defensible and more challenging than school spirit; and it is absolutely necessary.

1. WHY MORALE IS NECESSARY

Morale enables us to carry on. John Doe, who is the sole support of his family, has just received a communication informing

him that his son is missing in action.   This tragedy grieves him
so much that he is absent from his defense job in a bomber plant
the ensuing week.   When he does return, he is so listless and disinterested that some of his work is imperfect.   How will his attitude influence his fellow workers, not to mention the other members of his family?   The chances are they will sympathize with
him and to some extent share his dejection.   Hence the efficiency
of their own work may be affected.   Now suppose this one man's reaction to tragedy were multiplied many times throughout the
nation.   How would that influence national morale and the efficiency of the war effort?

Take an opposite case.   On the day that Professor Dwight L.
Dumond, of the University of Michigan, was scheduled to give
an address, he was informed that his son had been reported missing in Egypt.   Many people thought he would not appear to give
the address, but he was there on time, and his words had greater
significance because of his strength of character.   He had the will
to go ahead with his work in the face of a personal tragedy.   He
was able to resist the natural impulse of inactivity that comes
with grief.   He saw that his task, small as it seemed, was a part
of the whole nation's war effort.

The same attitude might have inspired Mr. Doe to face his
grief courageously and return to his job the day after he had received his shocking news.   He might have been able to bear his
grief better by working with even greater concentration than
usual.   He would at least have known that in his own way he
was carrying on as his son had done.   His conduct would have
been an inspiration to everyone, including his family and his
fellow workers.

This is easy to talk about and hard to live; yet in time of war
thousands upon thousands of people live it every day and so help
a nation win through to victory.   High morale is made up of
millions of cases in which individuals forget themselves and their
own feelings in the greater need of the nation.

The enemy attacks our morale.   This is exactly what the enemy
does not want us to do.   A large share of his effort is devoted to
psychological warfare.   He knows that by maintaining high
morale at home, it is possible to run the military machine more

efficiently. Through radio and newspaper propaganda and a great many other activities, he works to keep up his own morale on the home front. He is fighting a total war and wants the entire population to drive ahead with purposeful activity regardless of tragedy, poverty, and every hardship. At the same time he continually wages psychological warfare against us; he wants us to be weak. He wants to break down our morale, so that we will lose confidence in ourselves, our cause, and our leaders and will not have the heart to go ahead with our work. He does this by propaganda and by sabotage.

The very nature of the struggle waged against us forces us with greater determination to keep our spirits high in the face of enemy efforts to cast them down. Fortunately, we know that one of the enemy's weapons is subtle, treacherous propaganda aimed at destroying our morale at home. And because we know it, we are continuously on our guard against it.

National efficiency demands morale. The present great conflict is called total war because it involves whole populations as well as armies and because all activities, without exception — working, playing, resting, eating, producing, studying — must be fitted into the national effort. But this requires temporary sacrifices on our part, the giving up of many pleasures and luxuries, the changing of plans for the immediate future — including, perhaps, those for education and occupation — separation from friends and loved ones, much hard work, all kinds of economies, greater disciplining and ordering of our lives, a deeper understanding of the necessity of obedience. In short, it requires sacrificing individual freedom in order that the nation as a whole may have greater freedom to succeed in the task of winning the war for us as individuals. High morale among us will enable our nation to carry on with maximum efficiency. Total war cannot be waged without it. No matter what happens, we keep our chins up, because we do not want to interfere, even in the smallest way, with the efficiency of total war; in fact, we want to carry on in whatever purposeful activity ours may be so that our own morale and that of those around us may remain at its highest.

Our cause is right. We have good reason for high morale because we know our cause is right. We were attacked and are fighting to preserve the way of life called democracy for ourselves and for peoples oppressed by our enemies. We know that democracy cannot long endure while dictatorship and totalitarianism flourish on the earth.

The meaning of democracy. But what do we mean by democracy? It is more than a word. It is a reality that has rich meanings precious to us. For more than a hundred and fifty years our fathers have worked, struggled, and fought to save and improve democracy.

Democracy means that human beings should be morally equal simply because they are human beings. They should be equal before the law. They should have equal rights in sharing the fruits of progress. They should have equal opportunities.

Democracy means liberty. The individual should be free in his beliefs. With due regard for the wants and wishes of others, he should have freedom of speech, freedom of inquiry, freedom of petition, freedom of assembly, and freedom of the press.

Democracy means tolerance — acceptance of (though not necessarily agreement with) other groups, races, and creeds.

Democracy means that the individual should be protected against those who are more cunning and crafty than he and wish to use him to their advantage.

Democracy means that the people should be sovereign. The government should be for the welfare of the governed, and the people should have a right to decide in their own way what is to their own interest.

Democracy means that there should be no legalized class distinctions. The individual should have the right to improve himself and move from one social level to another.

Democracy means peace — the right to a peaceful settlement of disputes through reasoned discussion and compromise.

Democracy means education — the right of all men to an education according to their abilities. This means free education for all — education for personal improvement, for the solution of social problems, and for the continual betterment of society.

Democracy means progress — improving the general welfare. It means not only that the general welfare *can* be improved, but that, through reasoned discussion and cooperation, it *will* be continually improved. We hope that eventually democracy — ours and that of other nations — can guarantee to all men the highest type of civilization.

These are some of the meanings of that way of life the preservation of which now finds us engaged in war. Although we recognize that our democracy has not been perfect, we believe that its direction has been toward improvement, and that this progress will continue. Americans shudder to think of giving up the ideals for which democracy stands. That is why a struggle aimed at preserving our way of life challenges us and why we are willing to make every sacrifice in order to save it. Such a challenge makes high morale readily possible in our nation in wartime. We know that our cause is right!

We were attacked. It will continue to be an important factor in our national morale that the enemy attacked us. We were forced to fight to preserve our democracy. We were attacked because we helped people who had been unjustly attacked by aggressor nations. In so doing we interfered with the plans of the aggressor nations. Then they attacked us. After they attacked, we took up arms to defend ourselves. We need never accuse ourselves of aggressive or conquering intentions. History has shown that nations who strike the first blow do not necessarily win the last battle. The treachery of our enemies fills us with confidence in our cause and stiffens our will to carry on to final victory through whatever difficulties arise at home, at school, at work, or on the battlefield.

2. HOW TO MAINTAIN MORALE

Fear and dejection weaken morale. Of the seven emotions discussed in Part One, two are especially responsible for interrupting or weakening the will to carry on with purposeful activity. These are fear and dejection, because fear tends to make us act in a confused and irrational manner, and dejection is accompanied by an impulse to inactivity. Is it possible to maintain high morale in the face of these emotions? Let us consider what causes them and what we can do to master them.

Wartime incidents leading to fear. It is quite natural to respond with fear to the thought of bombing. Experience in England indicates that children as well as adults had more fear in anticipation of an air raid than during the raid itself. Perhaps a general rule applies here, namely, that the fear of anticipation is greater than the fear of the reality itself.

You will recall from your study of this emotion that danger or lack of security gives rise to the emotion of fear. When a country is in danger, it is normal for all to share in this emotion in a general way, even though this does not interrupt the war effort. Naturally, everyone is seriously concerned about the progress of the conflict and the future security of the nation. A person may feel confident that eventually his country will be victorious, yet quite naturally experience a deep concern, somewhat mixed with fear, as an undertone to his daily living. This is a general fear common to people in time of war and is accepted as a problem that goes along with the terrific struggle in which everyone shares while the outcome is in the balance.

In addition to this general undercurrent of fear, individuals experience varying degrees of fear in response, for example, to the thought of losing a friend or loved one in the armed forces or the merchant marine. Enemy propaganda, aimed to misinform us about our own strength, may give us a feeling of insecurity and fright. The prospect of physical harm, as when we undergo an air raid or an attack by land, quite naturally inspires the feeling of fear. Acts of sabotage and treachery in our midst would have a similar influence. Delay in receiving word from someone at the front may keenly disturb us with fear or dejection or both.

Though it is not abnormal to experience fear in these instances, we must realize fully that its effect upon the personality is disintegrating. Fear tends to break us down and interrupt our concentrated efforts, whether we are studying, working, or playing.

What to do about wartime fears.

1. *Face the facts.* The fears discussed are experienced by everyone, are not abnormal, and should not make us feel ashamed. By force of will and habit we can learn to keep our chin up and go on with our work, even though fear sickens us at the pit of the stomach. It is only when fear masters us that its effect keeps us from carrying on and gives us cause to feel ashamed or guilty.

1-15

"*Well, it can't be good news every day! If it makes you that mad why don't you go out and buy another war bond? That always seems to help you.*"

The first step toward mastering our fear is to face it and honestly admit that we feel as we do. Then we are ready to do something about it.

If we want to keep going, we cannot kid ourselves along by using some mechanism of defense or escape. This is done by the person (1) who tries to cover up his feeling of shame about fear by bragging how frightened he is, or (2) who flatly denies that he has any fear whatever in the face of either national or personal danger, or (3) who becomes irritable and refuses to read the war news, listen to the radio, or discuss the war with others. These people have not yet taken the first step in the mastery of fear. Though they try to give us the impression that they are not afraid, we know they are using a mechanism to cover up the feeling of fear and the shame which they permitted to accompany it.

2. *Do something to help the war effort.* Fear is usually lessened when we get busy with some worth-while work. In wartime, this work will prove most relieving if it is related to the war effort. Among the many possible activities might be listed writing letters to men and women in the services; U.S.O. or Red Cross work; participation in War Bond campaigns or rallies; civilian defense jobs; gathering scrap metal, rags, paper, rubber, fats, silk, and so on; and studying to prepare for some necessary war work. In England — London in particular — everyone, except infants under the care of governesses or mothers, is given something to do. Experience there has shown that responsibility and a share in the war effort helps to lessen fear of bombing, fires, falling buildings, and other dangers.

3. *Take part in group activities.* Since it is known that being alone increases mental and emotional strain in times of danger, it is helpful to plan activities with others. Working or playing with others will transfer your thoughts and actions to them. The effect is to lessen your fear and rebuild your self-confidence and morale.

4. *Put faith in your leaders.* Trust in leaders and willingness to obey them in time of danger, as in an air raid, or fire, helps you to master your own feeling of fright. When you are concentrating on how to carry out an air-raid warden's instructions as quickly and correctly as possible, you will have less time to think about your own safety. In wartime there is naturally a great need for obedience in order that whatever must be done may be done as quickly as possible. Furthermore, with complete obedience, the leader's plans will undoubtedly be carried out with greater safety for all. To be able and willing to obey also gives us a feeling of confidence that we have done our part as it was asked. The responsibility for our safety is not left entirely to us as individuals, but rests in part with the leader; our responsibility is to cooperate immediately and quickly. Obedience in time of war at school, at home, in the community, or in the services makes

for high morale and either eliminates the possibility of fear or modifies it to such a degree that we can go ahead with our job.

5. *Let off steam.* Occasionally it would be well to let off steam by vigorous exercise or noisy games. Another way to reduce the tension of fear is to talk with some person in whom you have confidence, a teacher, friend, or parent. Some people keep a diary; writing about their feelings takes the keen edge off their fear.

How can panic be avoided? Panic occurs when a group of people feel themselves in danger and do not know what to do about it. Schools throughout the country have taken steps to prepare pupils and students for air raids and any other dangers that may occur, in order that they will have leadership and will know what to do in case of emergency. In fact, the fire drill has always been a device to avoid panic. Every effort is made to protect the school against panic by teaching the students an organized plan of action in case of danger. Carefully planned arrangements have been made and practiced in every community. These preparations are absolutely necessary to insure the safety of civilians. A few specific suggestions which you may follow in order to avoid panic are given here:

1. *Pair yourself off with someone.* If you feel the need of help, try to select someone in whom you have confidence. On the other hand, if you know of someone who needs a more calm and collected partner than he himself is, and you are such a person, pick him out and take him in hand during the time of crisis.

2. *Make yourself responsible for taking something with you.* Panic might be avoided by concentrating on some small responsibility, such as carrying school equipment or some valuable trophy to safety with you.

3. *During the raid in the shelter cooperate to the fullest extent* in activities such as singing, telling stories, or resuming studies.

4. *Give your air-raid warden or teacher, as the case may be, immediate and complete obedience.* It has already been pointed out that this will insure your safety. Responsibility will be transferred to the warden, and your mind will be occupied with the carrying out of instructions. Then you will not be confused about what you are going to do in the face of the present danger.

Wartime incidents leading to dejection. The feeling of dejection, like the feelings of fear and anger, may be shared by all in a general way because of temporary losses on the front or because all share to some extent in the grief of others. Because dejection is accompanied by an impulse to give up, it is closely related to national morale, and the enemy plays upon it through propaganda and sabotage. When national morale is high, however, the general undercurrent of dejection is accepted as an inescapable consequence of war, and each one carries on with his work, fully determined to reach the final goal.

The feeling of dejection can be caused by many things — delay in receiving eagerly expected letters, bad news of someone in service, the departure of a friend or loved one. Some young people of high-school age experience a keen feeling of dejection when they find it necessary to change their plans for the immediate future. Others, eager to enter the service of their country, may be dejected when they discover that they are physically unfit. Dejection in these and all other instances is normally accompanied by an impulse to give up; hence it is likely to weaken our morale.

What to do about wartime dejection. War brings grief; grief tends to make us give up; giving up will lessen the war effort; therefore, we want to be prepared to face dejection and master it.

1. *Busy yourself with something, preferably helping others.* You may find it impossible to put your heart into your work at first. Gradually you will come to understand that many others are carrying on as you are, and that it is more unselfish to keep a stiff upper lip than to give in to dejection.

2. *Talk it over with someone.* A good friend, through sympathy, may share your grief and to some extent help you to bear it and go on with living.

3. *Keep fit.* When you are physically fit, you have too much energy to be inactive. Physical health, then, serves as some insurance against the inactivity accompanying dejection. In fact, since physical and mental health are very closely interrelated, the former is one of the most important factors in high morale. It helps us to control the emotional tensions brought about by war.

Anger should not lead to intolerance. The emotion of anger is quite necessary in fighting. In fact, as all people may experience a mild fear in wartime, so all may experience a feeling of anger toward the enemy, his actions, and the principles on which he is trying to destroy us. This may, indeed, be a very helpful emotion in so far as it adds to our determination to win. However, when anger is transferred to naturalized citizens, or others who originally came from enemy lands, it interferes with high morale. Anger should not become intolerance, for through intolerance dissensions arise between groups in a nation that should be completely unified. Unless we have evidence to the contrary, we should take it for granted that naturalized citizens are loyal to the country of their adoption. To vent our anger upon them would have the effect of destroying their confidence in our nation, hence their loyalty to its cause.

Wartime incidents leading to elation. Events of war naturally play upon all emotions and stimulate the keenest feeling of elation as well as fear, dejection, and anger. When a great battle is won, spirits rise to heights of happiness. When a friend or a loved one in the armed service is promoted or rewarded for heroism, you feel elated because of his success. When you finally receive a long-awaited letter from someone in the service, you feel elated. When, on the home front, people around you show great force of character by keeping their chins up and doing their part in the face of danger, discouragement, and tragedy, you have a feeling of pride and elation because of them. Indeed, it is fortunate that in time of war there is cause for great happiness, for it provides a balance against the sadness that also accompanies war.

To get the most out of this happiness, we should be careful to restrain our actions when we feel elated. As a matter of fact, we should try to cling to this feeling of elation as long as possible and avoid dissipating or wasting it by going to extremes in joyous behavior. The longer we cling to it, the longer it will help us to weather those moments of fear and dejection when we need all the drive we can muster to keep going. The new surge of energy that comes with elation should in wartime, if ever, be used in useful work rather than be quickly wasted in gloating over the success of ourselves or of someone else.

War is a challenge. The rightness of the cause, the greatness of the task, and the sweep of the consequences, both for individuals and for the nation as a whole, make war a great challenge to us. The history of our nation is high-lighted with stories of heroism on the field of battle, on the home front, and in the quiet progress with which small children and young men and women do their part from day to day "keeping the home fires burning," hoping in that tomorrow when victory is won and the cause is vindicated. Though spirits may be temporarily toned with fear and dejection, still we carry on, the great national cause inspiring us to forget individual feelings and to keep the national morale at its highest. War tests the mettle of men and women, shows what we are made of, inspires us to do what in normal times we hardly thought possible. Indeed, war can bring out the best in us. By taking stock of the situation, by understanding how each one of us fits into the whole picture, by following certain techniques, we are able to carry on and help those around us to carry on despite the fears and griefs that must be brought under control.

FOR CLASS DISCUSSION

1. Myrtle, a junior in high school, had always maintained a high scholastic record until her favorite brother, Jack, arrived in Reykjavik, Iceland. Though she wrote him frequently, his letters to her and to the family came through irregularly. She worried a great deal for his safety and became exceedingly anxious as days passed without mail from him. Almost daily she and her mother broke into tears while discussing Jack and his life in the army. At school she day-dreamed, found it difficult to concentrate on her studies, and dropped out of club work. Her report card showed D's and E's.

What is Myrtle's problem?

What can you suggest that might help her keep her chin up?

If she followed your advice, how would that affect her school work?

2. Martin R—— surprised the United States History class one day during a current events discussion when he suddenly burst out with, "What's the good of all this discussion, anyway!" The class argued, however, that by discussing current events regularly it could keep informed of the state of the war and the international situation; that topics now discussed actually had historical meaning; and that discussing the war itself, if not carried to extremes, might tend to help everyone let off steam. Martin remained silent and sullen throughout most of this discussion, but finally he spoke again, and then with

the same annoyance that characterized his first outburst: "Well, I can't see it. I get sick and tired of all this war talk wherever you go. All you hear on the radio is news about the war. Same thing in the papers. What's it good for? I don't listen to it or read it. We're going to win the war, so what? Let's cut out all this war talk and get back to the book."

Is Martin sure we are going to win the war? Explain.

Why should he be annoyed by discussion of war subjects?

What mechanism is he using?

Does his attitude improve the morale of those around him?

3. In a certain war of fairly recent date, it was necessary for the farmers and ranchers to serve in the armed forces. The invaders, who greatly outnumbered them, gradually drove them back. As the farms and cattle lands were overrun, the women and children were seized and placed in concentration camps. Here they died by thousands from starvation and disease. When the defending farmers and ranchers learned of the fate of their wives and children, they lost heart. It is said that this factor led the country to an early capitulation.

Did the defending army have high morale? Explain.

4. In what ways do schools help to maintain high morale in the entire community?

5. What might be the enemy's object in bombing school buildings?

6. One soldier wrote home from Cairo that this war is going to be won as much by the number of letters the boys receive at the front as by the supply of guns, tanks, and planes. Discuss this statement.

7. How much of Lincoln's Gettysburg Address applies today?

GROUP ACTIVITIES

1. Make a list of the various acts of sabotage that could be committed in a school and suggest ways of preventing or counteracting the effects of each.

2. List the names and addresses of former students of your school now serving in the armed forces. Divide this list among the members of your class and let each member correspond with those on his list. In case you are in doubt as to what to write to the boys at the front, you may be sure they are interested in the ordinary things that go on at home, in the community, and especially at school. Little details that seem insignificant to us on the home front are extremely interesting to the boys in the service.

READINGS

In Literature

NOVELS

Lohrke, Eugene Wm. *Night Raid.* Holt.

> All through one night of terror an American doctor living in England goes on his rounds through the village, attending patients, keeping up their morale even after he has lost his medical supplies.

Steinbeck, John. *The Moon Is Down.* Viking.

> A portrayal of the value of morale on the home front.

Struther, Jan. *Mrs. Miniver.* Harcourt, Brace.

> This story gives you a picture of how much easier it is for a person to live through a war if he keeps going about his daily business.

SHORT STORIES

Bierce, Ambrose. "The Occurrence at Owl Creek Bridge"; in *In the Midst of Life.* Modern Library.

> A civilian sees a chance to destroy a military objective and does his duty like a soldier.

Daudet, Alphonse. "The Last Lesson"; in *Works*, Volume 20. Little, Brown.

> When the Germans conquered France in 1870, a school teacher and his class showed how to face conquest with courage.

Singmaster, Elsie. "The Battleground"; in *Gettysburg.* Houghton.

> This Civil War story portrays vividly the horrors of war in one's own community and the necessity for keeping one's chin up.

For Further Information

Nash, J. B. *Building Morale.* Barnes.

Pardue, A. *Your Morale and How to Build It.* Scribner.

Self-Discipline in War Time, a pamphlet published by Massachusetts Department of Mental Health and Massachusetts Society for Mental Hygiene, Boston.

TAKING PART IN WARTIME ECONOMIES

*Is it wasteful to be afraid? If so, what is wasted?
Why does a person feel better when he is taking an
active part in the war effort?   Is it unselfish to leave
the car at home and walk to the grocery store? What
future would you have, if the armed forces failed for
lack of equipment? Is the collecting of fats, metals,
rags, and other salvage materials more suitable work
for grade school children or high school students?*

IT MUST NOW BE CLEAR that the keynote of high morale is participation, taking part and sharing in the great war task. Participation is the result of high morale, but it also produces and maintains high morale. This principle must be applied to individuals in order that the nation as a whole may achieve the highest degree of useful effort.

We have already discussed what morale means in terms of the individual's ability to meet emotional crises. We shall now turn to the question of how you can contribute to the war effort by adjusting yourself to a new standard of living and taking part in the economies — at home, at school, in the community — required for the successful prosecution of the war.

Why has our standard of living changed?

1. *War needs.* Thrift and saving have become necessary because our standard of living has been changed. All efforts, all energies must be diverted to the war effort. Our armies must win the war, and for this they need great quantities of war materials. Production and transportation facilities must be diverted from civilian to military needs. We realize that there are not

enough raw materials to provide equipment for our armed forces and at the same time meet normal civilian demands; not enough transportation facilities to ship war materials to the places where they are needed and also transport civilian goods; not enough buildings and machines to manufacture necessities for the armed forces and also for civilians. And quite aside from materials and equipment, there is not enough labor to do all that is necessary for the war and at the same time meet normal civilian needs for goods and services.

If we civilians do our part, consuming a minimum of food, clothing, and equipment, all the manufacturing and transporting facilities usually in operation to make items for civilian use — clothing, shoes, electrical appliances, musical instruments, cameras, sewing machines, refrigerators, furniture — can be put to manufacturing and transporting war equipment and the machines with which to make it. For example, companies making electrical appliances for household needs in peacetime can be released for making optical instruments, telescopes, and bombsights for the armed forces. Textile manufacturers engaged in peacetime in spinning, weaving, bleaching, and dyeing fabrics for civilian clothing, sheets, towels, and linens, in wartime can make sheets and towels for army camps, shirting for soldiers, aprons for army cooks, shoe linings for army shoes, and flannels for outside dressings of wounds.

Iron and steel are basic metals. They are needed for ships, guns, aircraft, tanks, and trucks, and for machines and machine tools with which to make these things. During wartime, civilian use of these metals must be reduced. They must not be used for new metal beds, metal office furniture, stoves, lawnmowers, golf clubs, ice skates, pleasure boats, grandstands, and stadiums. Unnecessary civilian construction must be halted. Steel must not be used for large girders in office buildings, or even, unless it is absolutely necessary, for buildings put up for wartime production, or for hangars. Large timbers, now treated against decay, are used in many new factories and hangars. Wood is needed for ships, airplane propellers, as a substitute for cork in army equipment, and other war uses; therefore, civilians must postpone the building of new homes and the making of new furniture.

"My folks have had to economize and move into a four-room apartment. Must be pretty cramped, huh?"

HINTS FOR DISCUSSING THE CARTOON

Do you think these boys feel as cramped as parents back home who have to economize by living in a four-room apartment? Who make the greater sacrifice, the soldiers or their parents? What do you think of the morale of these soldiers?

Wool is needed for army, navy, and merchant marine uniforms and blankets; therefore, civilians must get along with what woolen clothing they have. Old wool, which can be rewoven into civilian clothing, should be saved in order that virgin wool may be released for military purposes.

Great quantities of leather are needed for soldiers' shoes — five to ten pairs per soldier per year. Aluminum is needed for airplanes. Immense amounts of rubber are needed for armored trucks, airplane landing wheels, helmet padding, oxygen masks, and so on. Molasses, otherwise made into sugar, is used for ethyl alcohol, needed for explosives and synthetic rubber.

These are only a few examples of the most common transfers made from production for civilian consumption to production for military needs. The lack of the civilian goods we could buy in normal times forces us to forego luxuries, unnecessary food, clothing, and automobiles, making us get along with what we have and do without many things we want. Consequently, our standard of living is temporarily reduced.

2. *War costs*. It goes without saying that the huge quantities of materials required by the military program can be provided only at tremendous expense. In normal times it is expensive to equip an army, but it is even more expensive in wartime. The increased production for military needs increases the opportunities for employment, while, at the same time, the increased need for man power in the armed forces decreases the number of workers available for the plants. The law of supply and demand aggravates the problem of costs so far as labor is concerned, because the price of labor increases. This is one of the reasons why the nation is faced with a problem of how to finance the extremely expensive wartime program.

Where is the Government going to get the money? From taxation, of course. While it is true that the worker is more highly paid than in normal times, two factors operate against the possibility of his enjoying more luxuries or more of the fruits of his labor than he would normally: the scarcity of the materials he would like to buy, and increased taxation. The Government also expects every earner to invest some of his money in war bonds. This is required for at least two reasons: so that the Gov-

Taking part in wartime activities is worth while and helpful, whether it be working in a victory garden, collecting scrap, or learning first aid. Activities like these not only help the war effort but also give emotional security to those who do their part.

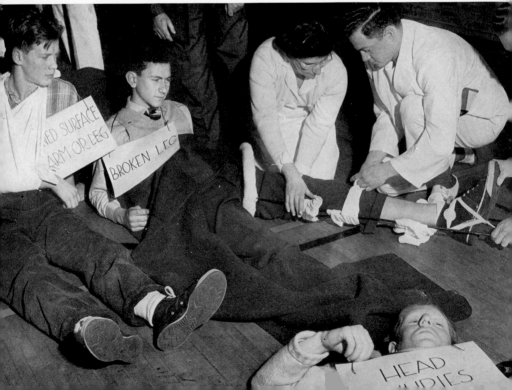

Morale is the spirit of willingness to make whatever sacrifices are necessary and to take whatever part you can in the prosecution of the war. When students serve as O.C.D. messengers (*above*) and as War Bond sellers and purchasers (*below*) they are doing their part on the home front.

Bradford Jr. College, Bradford, Mass.

ernment will have funds with which to pay industry for materials, and so that the citizens will have less money to squander on goods that are not absolutely necessary for existence.

Four factors tend to reduce our standard of living. First, there is the necessary shift of production from civilian to military goods. Second, the taking out of circulation of as much money as possible to meet war costs. The loss or reduction of imports, such as rubber, bananas, sugar, coffee, and tin, is a third factor. Finally, the increased demand for goods that cannot be supplied tends to raise prices, so that a given amount of money will buy less than it did formerly.

Though there may be individual exceptions to the rule that war reduces the standard of living, in general it holds true. You may be able to think of some family that, because of increased income, is able to buy a number of articles they formerly did without, but cases like this will be more and more exceptional. The stocks of civilian goods, such as furniture and electric appliances, which are available at the beginning of a war are eventually depleted, and no amount of money can replace them until the war is over and production for civilian needs is resumed.

It is clear, then, that thrift and saving are the order of the day on the home front. They are both possible and necessary for everyone. As a high-school student, you are not as yet directly participating in the war by serving in the armed forces or by working full time in a war plant, but you can participate in wartime economies at home, at school, and in the community. You yourself can help the President and the Secretary of the Treasury to prevent dangerous wartime inflation by not spending money, but putting it into savings instead.

Participation at home. Some suggestions for wartime economies that may be practiced at home will be made in the following paragraphs, grouped for convenience under the headings of food, gardening, clothing, personal effects, and household equipment and maintenance.

1. *Food.* In normal times many Americans have had too much to eat, perhaps not well-balanced diets, but overbalanced diets. Today it should be considered definitely unpatriotic to overeat, because overeating is wasteful and does not favor good health.

On the other hand, it is more important than ever to be properly fed. A well-balanced diet is required for abounding physical health and high morale. Many newspapers, magazines, and books nowadays contain good dietary advice. Better still, up-to-date material, based on the best modern knowledge of nutrition, can be obtained free from the Office of Defense Health and Welfare or the United States Department of Agriculture, Washington, D.C. It is a patriotic duty today to know how to be properly nourished.

Here are a few suggestions that will help you to avoid waste of foods and get the maximum benefit from them.

Throw nothing away. Study cook books and newspapers to find out how to use left-overs. Experiment yourself and suggest successful recipes to your friends.

Keep foods well covered and store perishables in the refrigerator to prevent spoiling.

Cook foods so as to get the greatest nourishment possible from them. Vegetables should be cooked in as little water and for as short a time as possible, to retain food values. Use the vegetable water, if any, in gravies and soups.

Study nutritive values so as to get the most for your money. For example, brown rice has eight times as much iron as highly polished rice. Many inexpensive cuts of meat are as nourishing as the expensive cuts.

Buy fruits and vegetables as much as possible when they are in season locally; out of season, they are more costly and require transportation that should be available for other purposes.

Buy food that the Government wants to distribute because there are temporary seasonal surpluses. Information concerning this can be obtained by reading government reports kept on file and up-to-date in libraries everywhere.

Save all tin cans. Clean them, cut out the ends, and stamp them flat for shipment. When a call is made for tin cans, you can deliver yours to the collection center.

Save all fats after getting full use from them at home. All such waste fats should be kept in a cool place until delivery to your meat store. They should not be kept in a glass container because that might break in handling.

2. *Gardening.* If you live in the country or in a village or town where space is available, raise as many vegetables as you can; if you do not have a garden of your own, it may be possible to use a plot of ground belonging to someone else. In many places community gardening is encouraged.

It is especially worth while to raise vegetables of which there is a scarcity, as indicated in government reports in the newspapers. In 1917 there was a scarcity of potatoes and people were urged to plant potatoes in their gardens and terraces. As a result of extensive potato planting, in 1918 this country had one bushel more per person than it had the previous year.

All gardens should provide an abundance of leafy vegetables, like lettuce, cabbage, Swiss chard, spinach, endive, and kale.

Tomatoes, rich in vitamin C, and many other vegetables may be canned if you raise too many for your immediate use. In fact, if you have enough space, you should plan to grow vegetables for a winter as well as a summer supply.

If you do not can or store vegetables and have more than you can use fresh, make a definite plan to give away the surplus so that nothing goes to waste.

3. *Clothing.* Buy only necessities. If you are a young woman, don't buy a handbag or pair of shoes to match every ensemble. Buy a color that will go well with the few dresses you have; it is not patriotic to have a dozen.

When it is necessary to buy clothes, get durable ones that will wear a long time and can stand rain, snow, and sunshine.

Make your own clothes, if possible, to release labor for the war effort.

Wash clothes often to insure longer wear; perspiration fades and rots fabrics.

Mend your clothes, darn your socks; have your shoes resoled.

Give special care to woolens and furs to protect them from moths.

Save cotton and woolen rags. Cotton rags are needed for machine-wipers. Woolen rags are rewoven into fabrics for civilian use. Save worn-out silks. These can be rewoven into gunpowder sacks.

4. *Personal effects.* Save lipstick holders, hairpins, bobby pins, hair curlers, toothpaste tubes, shaving cream tubes.

Be economical with soaps, soap powders, shampoo liquids.

Do not lose or give unnecessary wear to fountain pens, penholders, cameras, and sporting equipment.

5. *Household equipment and maintenance.* Avoid breakage of dishes, windowpanes, glass jars, and bottles.

Do not mislay or allow your garden tools, lawnmower, or sprinkler to rust.

Keep garden hose and all rubber equipment out of the sun, free from grease or oil, and in a cool place.

Keep all electrical appliances — refrigerator, sewing machine, toaster, vacuum sweeper, washing machine — clean and well oiled.

Do not run the vacuum sweeper over pins and other articles that will damage it. Clean it often, to put less strain on the motor.

Cool the iron before storing it away.

Avoid damage and unnecessary wear of kitchen utensils, especially those of aluminum and tin, which cannot be replaced.

Polish and otherwise take good care of furniture to prevent warping, cracking, and loosening of glued joints.

Make repairs as soon as necessary (if possible, make them yourself) to screen doors, window screens, garden hose, household linens, and so on.

Save on fuel. Buy coal during the summer months, or when recommended by the Government.

Save on electricity through thrifty use of power devices, radio, and lights.

In some communities it is directly helpful to the war effort to save on the use of water because of special wartime demands on the water supply.

Steel, iron, aluminum, and other metals — and rubber — needed for the war should be gathered from attics, basements, and elsewhere in the house and yard and made available to collection agencies.

Save paper. Newspapers, magazines, and wrappings not needed at home should be saved and sold to the junk dealer or delivered to the local collection agency.

Save your car. Use it only when absolutely necessary. Parents realize keenly that the car is becoming a luxury; naturally they are somewhat hesitant about giving it to the children for dates and other purposes. More and more people are reaching the point where they can no longer use the car at all. When you do use one — if you are that lucky — observe the following rules:

(1) Drive under thirty-five miles an hour.
(2) Don't let your speed force you to skid the tires at stop streets.
(3) Take curves and turns slowly.
(4) Rotate the tires every thousand miles. (This includes the spare.)
(5) Keep tires properly inflated and wheels aligned.
(6) Keep the car in the shade. Sunshine makes rubber tires, as well as the finish of the car, deteriorate.
(7) Keep the motor well-oiled and the brakes equalized.

Participation at school. Stocks of school equipment are either low or completely exhausted; many of the replacements normally provided will have to be postponed, and present equipment must do for the duration. Besides, some of the money formerly available for education has been diverted to the war, and many schools do not have the money to purchase school equipment even if it were available. You can help the war effort, therefore, by protecting school desks, tables, and typewriters.

In some schools students undertake to repair all their own equipment. Vocational classes refinish and repair wood and metal equipment; home economics classes clean and repair athletic equipment and make school letters, pennants, and backdrops for the stage.

Power tools, lights, and public address systems should be used sparingly because the power is needed in industry. Repairs and maintenance on many electrical devices may be made by students and teachers in order to get the longest possible use out of them and at the same time avoid robbing man-hours from industry.

Paper should be used on both sides. Many teachers customarily return all written work in order that students may do another assignment on the same paper.

When going to school by automobile is absolutely necessary, the car should be shared with others in order to save wear and reduce gasoline and oil consumption. Walking to school has become a patriotic duty.

Schools generally serve the national morale by organizing defense or conservation councils that plan and supervise the collection of materials which in normal times are likely to go to waste. In these plans every student should take an active part. A few high-school students think they are too grown-up to bother with such a little matter as collecting scrap metal, rags, fats, and the like, but the majority have vision enough to understand that millions of small contributions by schools throughout the nation actually make a huge contribution together.

Every school child in the nation should buy war stamps if he can get the money. High-school students should go into this in a bigger way than those in the lower grades because they understand more fully what the national problem is and have more money to spend.

All waste within the school should be eliminated. Home economics classes, for example, will observe the economies suggested under "Participation at home." Similarly, vocational classes will put every stick of wood, every scrap of metal to use.

Participation in the community. There are a number of ways for young people to cooperate with the community in wartime economies. A few suggestions are given here:

Do your shopping on foot even if gasoline rationing does not force you to do so. On your trips to the grocer and butcher leave the car at home even if you are permitted to use it. Others will take their cue from you.

If deliveries must be made by the butcher, baker, grocer, or cleaner, get your order in early enough so that a special trip does not have to be made to deliver it.

Save on paper bags by telling the grocer that he does not have to put every article in a separate bag.

Share your automobile with others by planning to have a full car whenever possible.

Encourage walking by telling others that you are walking. Show them that you approve of walking.

Adjust yourself to the appointment schedule of the doctor and dentist by making appointments several days in advance if possible.

Avoid making long-distance telephone calls. You may be causing delay in an important message that has to do with the war.

Plan hiking trips and picnic lunches as a substitute for driving to a neighboring town for a theater party.

Some communities provide community gardens. If you do not have a garden of your own, it may be possible to join a garden club.

Raise rabbits for food. It has been estimated that rabbit meat enabled Germany in 1918 to hold out against the blockade several months longer than would have been possible if this article of food had not been available. At present it is reported that Germany has more than twenty million breeding does, some in private hutches and some in hutches arranged on a community club plan. As every high-school student knows, rabbits mature and multiply rapidly, though they require no food necessary to the human diet. Raising rabbits, therefore, is an economical way to provide meat. The pelts, of course, are valuable also as lining for garments worn in extremely cold climates or at high altitudes.

Help save the farm produce. Since there is a great shortage of farm labor during wartime, there are many opportunities for boys and girls of high-school age to help with farm work, particularly in the harvesting of perishable crops such as fruits and vegetables. Offer your services at the United States Employment Office for this purpose, or, better, go right to the farms and orchards ready to work when you learn of the need.

Go berrying. A great variety of berries grow wild and in abundance. It may be that berrying expeditions are worth while in the countryside around your community. Dewberries, June berries, huckleberries, blueberries, red and black raspberries, gooseberries, blackberries, and strawberries are some of the most common wild berries excellent for canning, for jams and jellies, and for eating fresh. Gathering wild berries keeps them from going to waste, provides an economical product rich in vitamins, and also is good fun.

What is morale? A summary. All your personal problems — especially those that have to do with the future — are now intimately related to the future of your country. To the degree that

your country succeeds in the war, your future is secure. If the
war is won quickly, efficiently, and completely, your chances for
a happy and successful adult life are assured. If it is prolonged
or indecisive, your future is correspondingly darker. Morale and
efficiency on the home front have an enormous bearing on the
conduct and final outcome of the war.

The problem of making your way, therefore, is first of all a
problem of making sure that the war is carried through to a complete victory. Such a victory is impossible without high morale;
hence our study of morale and how every student has a part in it.
Let us briefly restate what has been said:

1. *We must understand what we are fighting for:* democracy,
what it is and may become for ourselves and for those oppressed
by the enemy.

2. *We must understand what the material and spiritual needs
of the nation are:* abundance of material for our armed forces and
uninterrupted zeal to keep our chin up and carry on.

3. *We must be familiar with specific ways in which we can
help:* materially, in thrift, saving, and hard work; spiritually, in
helping others, at home, at school, and wherever we are, to carry
on.

4. *We must accept the war:* through understanding of its
causes, we must believe in it and for the time being willingly sacrifice all personal desires that do not help the war effort.

5. *We must learn obedience:* for efficiency's sake we will not
stall any program by arguing some technicality or interfering
with the plans of our leaders.

6. *We must will to win:* through every hardship and disturbance we must drive on to complete the job we have to do,
small or great, heroic or unnoticed and apparently insignificant.

Morale, so conceived, will make defeat an impossibility.
Through victory, it will insure us the right and opportunity, as
individuals, to plan a brighter future in accordance with our
abilities.

FOR CLASS DISCUSSION

1. Thirty-five boys aged fifteen to eighteen were pulling weeds in a large field of soybeans. They stood in groups of four and five along the soybean rows. Occasionally someone pulled a weed. Several busied themselves switching each other with weeds. It is a known fact that the boys were well paid.

How does their work in the soybean patch fit into the program of wartime economy?

Do these boys fully realize their part in the war effort? Explain.

Are they old enough to understand?

2. A convalescing soldier was permitted to spend four weeks with his family back home. There he found many things that annoyed him. One of his acquaintances, deferred for essential war work, was earning huge wages and spending the money foolishly; his own girl friend was dating another man; his seventeen-year-old brother kept late hours and rarely studied; the radio and newspapers daily told of strikes and war stoppages; the community was engaging in an hilarious night life. All around him he saw reckless waste of time and energy, of gasoline, rubber, paper, food, and money.

Would you expect him to be eager to return to the front? Why?

How would his findings at home affect his own morale?

3. Discuss the following statement: "Jim won't help with any of these salvage campaigns until he learns that his brother is missing in action. Till then he'll let his kid sister do all the saving. Right now Jim's too grown-up; he's got senioritis."

4. A defense worker, when talking about men wasting time in the plant, said: "Well, what can you expect? They treated us pretty raw during the depression. Why should we cooperate now?"

Discuss his argument in the light of war.

INDIVIDUAL ACTIVITIES

1. Participate personally in the wartime economies and activities suggested in this section.

2. Help to organize for the class or school group projects that will help in winning the war.

READINGS

For Further Information

BOOKLETS AND PAMPHLETS

The following may be obtained from the Bureau of Home Economics, United States Department of Agriculture, Washington, D.C.:

Fight Food Waste in the Home, Bulletin No. AWI-3.
Reclaim the Family Wardrobe.
Rubber in Wartime.
Save Your Clothes.

The following may be obtained by writing the Bureau of Home Economics, Agricultural Marketing Association, Washington, D.C.:

Dried Beans and Peas in Low Cost Meals.
Dried Fruits in Low Cost Meals.
Egg Dishes at Low Cost.
Green Vegetables in Low Cost Meals.
More Milk for More Children, Miscellaneous 493.
Potatoes in Low Cost Meals.
Root Vegetables in Low Cost Meals.

The following may be obtained by writing to the publication addresses given in each case:

Be a Victory Planner, Bureau of Home Economics and Consumers Council, Superintendent of Documents, Washington, D.C.

Consumers Prices, Consumer Division, Office of Price Administration, Washington, D.C.

Consumers Research Annual Cumulative Bulletin; also monthly *Reports*, Consumers Research, Inc., Washington, N.J.

Consumers Union Buying Guide; also monthly *Reports*, 55 Vandam St., New York City.

Drying Food for Victory Meals, Farmers Bulletin No. 1918, United States Department of Agriculture, Washington, D.C.

Hidden Values, Sears Roebuck Company, Chicago, Illinois.

War Against Waste, Office of Emergency Management, Washington, D.C.

Wartime Recipes and Menus, Michigan Defense Council, Michigan State College, East Lansing, Michigan.

What's New in Home Economics, Harvey and Howe, Chicago, Illinois.

The War Effort and Your Future

YOUR FUTURE is not separable from the war effort. Whether you plan to get a job, continue your schooling, or enter the armed forces of your country, your plans must fit into the nation's war. The slightest notion on your part that you can live a life apart from the war, or the slightest effort to do so, will soon be blasted by events that interfere with purely selfish plans and also by the unhappiness that comes from withdrawing, not doing your part, being a slacker.

In times of peace we all have more freedom to plan individual careers than in times of war, when our plans are disciplined by the order of the national task. In fact, the Government may find it necessary for the duration to tell you where you are to work, because production cannot go on efficiently with bottlenecks here and there. If this is done, undoubtedly a serious effort will be made to find out just what you are suited for. The Government would then select your job for you, place you in it, and require you to deliver the goods. Similarly, the Government may, as England is doing, draft some for higher education, because the vast postwar readjustment and rebuilding will require a large number of highly trained specialists, many of whom have been taken out of universities for service in the war.

And, of course, the Government will require millions in our armed forces. Great care is taken to use the various skills men and women have for the many jobs that must be done in the armed forces. The job to which a person is assigned does not depend so much upon what he wants to do as upon what the military leaders need to have him do. A number of suggestions may be followed with advantage in making our way even during these times.

SERVING IN THE ARMED FORCES AND AUXILIARIES

> *Does military service provide opportunities for a future career? Is a person who is afraid of military service necessarily a coward? Should girls plan for auxiliary service? Who serves his country better, a soldier or a war-plant worker? Why should all plans for the future turn on plans for participation in the war now?*

ALL THOUGHTS about the future now begin with the question, "How can I serve my country best?" Lucky are the able-bodied, both men and women, who can enter the armed forces and auxiliary services and willingly surrender all their time, energy, and ability, and life itself if necessary, to their country. It is their duty, yes — deeply repaid in self-respect and the respect of their country today and throughout history; but it is a privilege, an opportunity, to be able to give so much for others, for home and country.

Not the old, but the young, are needed, because they are able to learn quickly and can stand up to the rigors of the service. They can take it. The old and the weak at home, though they do what they can to provide the weapons and keep the home fires burning, would soon be overrun by the enemy were it not for the young and the strong who stand between them and disaster. The great challenge, therefore, is to those who are able to serve their country on or near the battle line.

Get ready for it now. There are a number of things you can do now, while you are still in high school, to get ready for mili-

9-26

"I get a real kick out of studies since I found out how much of this stuff a bomber pilot has to know."

tary service. If you follow the suggestions given here, you will be more likely to put your whole heart into it and serve in the capacity for which you are best suited.

1. *Finish high school first.* A person with a high-school education has a better chance than one without. Because of the intensely technical nature of warfare and the extremely great variety of jobs to be done, modern armies must be made up of highly intelligent and well-trained personnel. For this reason high-school students are urged to complete their high-school education before they enter the service. Boys are encouraged to

specialize in mathematics, science, modern languages, and vocational subjects. Girls who look forward to joining auxiliary services of the army or navy are encouraged to specialize in commercial subjects, modern languages, and science. A great many high schools have introduced Spanish and Portuguese; some now offer Japanese and Chinese. Thorough preparation in any of these fields gives the high-school graduate a distinct advantage over someone not thus prepared.

2. *Get a physical check-up.* From a physical examination you will learn whether you now meet the standards of the branch of service you hope to get into, whether you have certain defects which may be remedied by the time you graduate from high school, or whether you will be definitely disqualified and will have to plan some other way to be of service to your country. Many high schools are intensifying their physical-education program with exercises designed to build up and toughen physical stamina. In addition, you can plan your own body-building program to include regular strenuous exercise at work or at play, plenty of sleep, and proper diet. And if, as a result of your physical examination, you learn of some defect, say in vision or teeth, it may be possible for you to correct it. Vision, for instance, can sometimes be improved by eye exercises or a change in diet; consult your doctor or physical-education director for information about corrective measures. Similarly, many dental defects can be corrected by the dentist if you get dental care right away.

3. *Study the opportunities in military service.* The variety of occupations in the armed forces and auxiliaries is as broad as in civilian life. From time to time branches are added to the services, but among those most commonly referred to are the Army, Navy, Air Corps, Marines, Coast Guard, Merchant Marine, Naval Reserve, Army Reserve, Red Cross, Women's Auxiliary Army Corps, and Women's Auxiliary Volunteer Enlistment Service. Each of these branches includes a great variety of occupations. The army, for example, needs every kind of worker from barber to photographer. Information about the various occupational opportunities may be obtained from your principal, the school guidance director, or the local draft board, or by writing to the

Selective Service Headquarters, which is usually located in the capital of your state.

Experience in the first World War has shown that thousands of men "found themselves" while in military service and remained there to carry on their life careers. There is no reason to believe that the situation will be different in the present war. Many thousands will find themselves most satisfied in military life and will remain there until pensioned or retired. Furthermore, if peace is worth fighting for, it is worth keeping a standing military organization to maintain it. The indications are that our country will do so. This means that many more men and women will plan their entire future in the armed forces or the auxiliary services.

4. *Find out about your interests and abilities.* In order to assist the military personnel in placing you most advantageously, you should know what your interests and abilities are. This will be discussed in more detail in the next section. The tests referred to on page 365 will help you to find out what kind of work you are naturally suited for and whether you should plan to continue your schooling in a military classification, as a Red Cross nurse, or in preparation for some other work. It is, of course, to the advantage of the war effort to have everyone doing the kind of work for which he is best suited. In fact, every effort is made to place men and women according to their abilities and choices. If you have information of this kind at your fingertips, you will have a better chance to obtain the kind of assignment or classification you would like to have.

5. *Make yourself emotionally ready.* With your conviction about the rightness of this war based upon the knowledge of why we are fighting, you can accept the war as yours and make yourself willing to do your part in it. Further, by looking ahead, you can plan for success in the service by making up your mind now to adjust yourself to your officers and fellows, to cooperate, obey, and fall in line. Get yourself emotionally ready now, and when the time comes it will be easier for you to change from civilian to military life.

Reasons for not entering the service. There are a large number of people of military age who, for one reason or another, do not join the armed forces in time of war. Let us consider some of the most common reasons.

1. *They are physically unfit.* It is possible for many persons to join the armed forces for limited service, even though a physical defect precludes their taking part in long marches and other strenuous exercise. These people are able to do some less strenuous but equally necessary work in camp in order that others may be released for combat duty. Persons who are rejected from all military service have a good reason to stay home. As a rule, they keenly regret it; but they make the most of their misfortune by doing their part on the home front, either in defense plants or in other necessary civilian duties.

2. *They have dependents.* Some are deferred from military service because others depend upon their income. In 1942 our Government made arrangements to help the dependents with monthly financial aid. This aid is not enough to maintain a luxurious life, but it does insure the dependents against dire poverty.

3. *They are engaged in essential war work or in farming.* Many of these deferments will be discontinued as the women of the nation become able to do the work of those deferred.

4. *They are engaged in essential study.* Because of their superior ability and skill some people must go on with their education either in non-professional schools or in colleges, for they will be needed for the war when they complete their work; or, if the period of study continues throughout the duration of the war, they will be needed to serve in peacetime. You can readily see what a serious problem would arise in the postwar period if our colleges and universities did not continue to train doctors, nurses, dentists, engineers, economists, and certain research specialists.

5. *They do not want to change their plans.* A few persons go to great lengths to avoid military service because they do not like to have their plans changed or interrupted. They try to get pull, suddenly begin to support someone, or get into a defense plant and try to have their employer request deferment. They may even seriously neglect their health, at the time they are to take a physical examination, in order to be rejected. It goes without saying that they are the slackers in a nation at war.

6. *They are conscientious objectors.* Persons in our democracy who are deeply convinced that it is wrong to bear arms are not forced to do so. They may serve their country, however, in non-combatant services. There are only two kinds of conscientious objectors — the phonies, who are afraid and object as an escape mechanism or like to make martyrs of themselves and by so doing get attention; and the sincere objectors, who really find it hard to take their stand amidst ridicule and criticism. These are in the great minority. A conscientious objector should look inside and ask himself whether he really is conscientious.

7. *They are afraid.* Fear — fear of hard work, fear of discipline, fear of not being able to give a good account of oneself, fear of danger — these are some of the fears that make a few persons go to great lengths to evade military service. These are not abnormal fears, however; a person is not a coward who experiences them. He need not feel guilty or ashamed because he has a sinking feeling in the pit of his stomach — unless this fear makes him a slacker.

Problems you have to face if you stay out. Whatever your reasons may be for not joining or not preparing to join the armed forces, if they are not sincere and sufficient in your own mind and heart, you lose your self-respect, and this loss of self-respect cannot help but haunt you and sicken your happiness ever after. On the other hand, if your reasons are sincere and sufficient, you still have to face the problem of social pressure. Others will wonder why you are not in uniform. You will find yourself continually explaining why you were deferred. Oftentimes you may wish that your lot had been thrown with those who were called or who enlisted. It will take character on your part to keep your chin up in the face of these problems occurring frequently for the duration.

FOR CLASS DISCUSSION

1. Don was having a discussion with his father about plans after graduation from high school. He wanted to join the Marines. His father reminded him that before the war he had always talked about studying law, that his school record and his ability indicated a successful future in the legal profession, and that he should plan to go to

college right after graduation. Don argued that he could get a great deal of education in the Marine Corps. Besides, he did not want to go to college while we were at war.

What should he do?

What would be the easier decision for Don? Why?

Was the father's advice correct? Explain.

2. Shirley thought being a housewife, a salesgirl, stenographer, or clerk was not very exciting. To her these jobs seemed not essential in time of war. She wanted to be of greater service to the country, perhaps as a Red Cross nurse or as a member of the Women's Auxiliary Army Corps. But her family needed financial help, especially because the two oldest boys were in the navy.

Are housewives, salesgirls, and so on, necessary to the war effort?

What do you consider to be Shirley's first responsibility?

Would she be of greater service to the war effort as a member of the WAAC or as a salesgirl or stenographer?

3. At the beginning of the German invasion of Russia, long lines of people stood waiting at the Blood Transfusion Institute in Moscow to offer their blood for wounded soldiers. A group of boys aged fourteen and fifteen also reported to give their blood, but they were turned down because the minimum age for donors was eighteen. They were keenly disappointed and wondered what they could give since they were also too young to join the army.

What does their attitude indicate as to their morale?

Are there any things they could do to help the war effort?

4. Discuss the pros and cons of the following statement: War requires the complete reversal of all peacetime standards of right and wrong in relationships with the enemy.

5. What factors operate in the present war to bring it close to the people on the home front?

READINGS

In Literature

NOVELS

Crane, Stephen. *The Red Badge of Courage.* Appleton.

Why does a man volunteer? What does war do to develop character? Here is a story which rings clear and sincere.

Erickson, Curtis L. *Army in Review.* Dutton.

This book tells of the experiences of two high-school boys who were assigned to write a paper on army life and, upon invitation of the commander, spent a week at an army post near by.

Innes, Hammond. *Attack Alarm*. Macmillan.

This author, a veteran anti-aircraft gunner, gives a description of air raids, air fighting, and bombing in an excellent story.

Nordhoff, Charles B., and Hall, James N. *Men Without Country*. Little, Brown.

Five convicts escape from a penal colony in French Guiana and after many hardships finally reach England and are able to join the Free French forces.

SHORT STORIES

Garland, Hamlin. "Return of a Private"; in *Main-Travelled Roads*. Macmillan.

This soldier did not regret his experience. He knew that he had fought for a worth-while purpose.

Henry, O. "The Moment of Victory"; in *Options*. Harper.

This excellent story-writer, in a very easy manner, gives various reasons why boys go to war.

For Further Information

Baldwin, H. *What the Citizen Should Know About the Navy*. Norton.

Baumer, Wm. H. *He's In the Army Now*. McBride.

Baumer, Wm. H. *How to Be an Army Officer*. McBride.

Craige, John H. *What the Citizen Should Know About the Marines*. Norton.

Ford, Harvey S. *What the Citizen Should Know About the Army*. Norton.

Hartney, Harold E. *What the Citizen Should Know About the Air Forces*. Norton.

Lane, C. D. *What the Citizen Should Know About the Merchant Marine*. Norton.

Powell, H. *What the Citizen Should Know About the Coast Guard*. Norton.

Spencer, Lyle M., and Burns, Robert K. *Military Training and Jobs*. Science Research Associates.

Tuthill, John T. *He's In the Navy Now*. McBride.

GETTING AND KEEPING THAT JOB

*Mention any occupation the pursuit of which might
well be postponed till after the war. Does a person
need pull to get a job? Are standards higher at
school or on the job? What is the more common
reason for discharging a worker, inability to do his
work or inability to get along with his fellows? Does
a person win friends because he receives a promotion?*

1. SELECTING YOUR JOB

IF YOU ARE NOT DRAFTED for war duty or for industry immediately
upon graduation, and you plan to get a job, here are a few suggestions that may well be followed. They will also come in
handy in case your Government drafts you for employment or
for military service, because, having carefully considered the kind
of work for which you are suited, you will be better able to assist
the agencies in placing you properly. Besides, if for the duration
you are not able to do the type of work you had hoped to do, you
can make plans to do it right after the war.

What are your interests? You know how hard it is to do good
work in a school subject that does not interest you. It is no
easier in a job that does not interest you. If you are interested
in your work, you get much of your recreation right on the job,
because the work is satisfying. In selecting the occupation you
want to follow permanently, therefore, you should ask yourself
whether it is likely to be and remain interesting.

If you are interested in your work, it is a continual satisfaction
to you. This contributes a great deal to morale and to your

ability to get along well with fellow workers and employers and to meet whatever difficulties arise in the work itself.

Many people who are not interested in a certain job at first become interested in it later. This may happen if you have the ability to do the work, if you work hard at it, if you become expert in it, if you earn good wages, if you can see future advantages, or if you realize that your job is necessary to the war effort. Generally speaking, however, it is better to choose an occupation in which you are keenly interested than to try to develop interest later in "any old job" you happen to get.

Interest tests. You probably have some idea what your interests are. Fairly accurate tests are now available to help you to know more about your interests and about how they line up with certain types of work. A test of this kind, easy to take and score, is the *Vocational Interest Inventory,* prepared by Glen U. Cleeton and published by McKnight and McKnight, Bloomington, Illinois. Another interest test is the *Preference Record,* prepared by G. Frederic Kuder and published by Science Research Associates, Chicago, Illinois. It is worth your while to get the help of these tests. But remember, they are tests of interest, not ability, and if you rate high in interest for certain occupations, do not jump to the conclusion that you have the abilities required for success in them. Consult your teacher or counselor if you want to take one or both of these tests.

What are your abilities? Most of the work people do requires a combination of the abilities, mental, mechanical, and social, discussed in Unit III. A stenographer, for example, should have mechanical ability, but should also be able to meet the public. A plumber, whose work is largely mechanical, should be able to deal with housekeepers, storekeepers, and so on. A lawyer should have keen mental ability, but should also be able to give advice in a way that makes it acceptable; and if he is a trial lawyer, he should be able to understand the members of a jury and convince them in his argument. Maid service requires mechanical ability in the use of various household appliances, but it also requires ability to get along with the family and with visitors.

Tests of abilities. When you choose your occupation you

should know whether you have the abilities it demands. From previous experience — school work, sports, extra-curricular activities, hobbies, and jobs previously held — you get some notion as to what your abilities are. Confidential talks with older people who know you will furnish additional understanding. You can get still more information from specially prepared tests, referred to in Unit III. The *Minnesota Occupational Rating Scales and Counseling Profile*, prepared by D. G. Paterson, Clayton d'A. Gerken, and Milton E. Hahn, and published by Science Research Associates, Chicago, Illinois, gives ratings of social, mental, mechanical, and other abilities needed for a great many specific vocations. Your teacher or counselor should be consulted if you want to take any of these tests.

Do your interests and abilities agree in your choice of occupation? If, as you study your own job problem, you find that you are keenly interested in aeronautics, say, and your ability is average or below average in mathematics, you had better change your mind about aeronautics. You cannot make your way successfully in an occupation for which you are not suited, and aeronautics requires a great deal of ability in mathematics. There are, however, a large number of occupations connected with aviation. Some are predominantly mechanical, such as that of aviation mechanic, and some predominantly social, such as that of stewardess. You may be able to choose one of these and succeed in it, provided your abilities meet its standards. By so doing you can work in the general field in which your interest lies and also make use of your particular abilities.

Do you have the health and physical strength for the job? Work always requires energy. You may be keenly interested in becoming a trouble-shooter on a power line, or a nurse, and have the ability to do the work, yet lack the necessary health and strength. Some jobs demand a great deal of strength and most of them demand good health. Nowadays many employers require that every prospective employee undergo a physical examination, because they have found it unwise to employ someone who does not have a physical condition that favors success.

Occupational trends. How can you find out about the supply and demand for workers in various occupations? During the past few years considerable information about occupational trends has been made available to high-school students, and this will continue to be the case. One of the most helpful things for you to do in selecting your occupation is to study these trends. Look up the occupation you have in mind in *American Job Trends,* written by H. D. Anderson and P. E. Davidson and published by Science Research Associates, Chicago, Illinois. Other sources of information about trends in employment are:

Vocational Guide. Science Research Associates, Chicago, Illinois. A monthly magazine which will give you up-to-date information about jobs.

Vocational Trends. Science Research Associates, Chicago, Illinois. A monthly magazine which will help you with the latest information about occupations in time of war.

Science, invention, and war continually bring about changes in occupations. Thus, hundreds of occupations that were common in horse-and-buggy days became unnecessary as the automobile replaced the horse and buggy. Gradually more and more young men chose auto mechanics for their life work. In the future, many opportunities will be open to young men and women to train for occupations in aviation, both military and civilian. Plastics is another coming field. The high-school student who plans carefully for his future will have to study the trends indicated by present conditions.

Getting information about a job. Pamphlets containing information about specific occupations, such as stenography, lens-grinding, and hundreds of others, are available. They usually tell (1) how many people are employed in a given occupation; (2) whether the trend is favorable for additional workers; (3) what the average beginner's and experienced worker's wages are; (4) conditions of work; (5) advantages and disadvantages; (6) opportunities for advancement; and (7) education and training required, and give additional information of particular importance regarding the occupation analyzed. Four pamphlet series are here listed:

American Job Series, Science Research Associates, Chicago, Illinois. A series of pamphlets giving information about trends, opportunities, and other pertinent facts. If your school does not have the series, you can write for a pamphlet on the job you have in mind.

The Occupational Index, Inc., Washington Square East, New York City.

A good reference to consult for present occupational opportunities.

Careers, Institute for Research, Chicago, Illinois.

Another series of pamphlets on a large number of occupations.

The United States Office of Education, Washington, D.C., will send you, free of charge, a pamphlet with this title, *80 New Books on Occupations.* For five cents each, you can get the pamphlets on individual occupations.

Is your chosen work difficult enough to challenge your best efforts and easy enough to make success possible? While on the one hand your desire to excel requires that you choose an occupation in which you can do good work and be of the greatest service to your country, on the other hand your self-respect requires that you choose one that is not too easy. You need the feeling that you are putting real effort into your job. Life becomes full of zest when the task in hand is difficult and challenging, but finally possible. You need the feeling of struggle and effort while you work, and even the uncertain feeling at times that you may not succeed; then with concentration and diligence you do the job anyway and feel elated when it is finished. Your occupation should give you many opportunities to feel that you have done well a job, difficult for you.

It is possible to get reliable information about the difficulty of a given occupation. If you have studied your own abilities and know what your potentiality is likely to be, you can find out whether the occupation you wish to follow is too hard or too easy for you. For information about the relative difficulty of occupations consult any of the sources listed in this section.

Can you finance the preparation required? Many occupations require more than a high-school education. If that is the case, what is the cost of the additional schooling or training? Can your family afford it? Can you afford it? In normal times young people are often advised to work a year and save money before they go on to the next step in their education, because there are many disadvantages to schooling under great financial stress. In the next section we shall consider problems related to further schooling in wartime. From the references already given you can get accurate information about the amount and kind of schooling needed for the job you want to get.

Is your favorite occupation in the family tradition? All other things being equal, if your answers to the questions raised in this section are favorable, and if you have relatively equal interests and abilities for more than one line of endeavor, the one in which your family happens to have a long tradition may prove to be the most satisfying for you. It is hard to explain this fact, because it depends upon so many subtle influences that you have had at home.

It always takes energy to break with tradition. Home-making, for instance, is traditionally a woman's vocation, and the girl who breaks with tradition and strikes out for a career — law, medicine, or business — has more obstacles to overcome on her way to success than the girl who follows in the tradition of her mother and begins her career with the many habits and attitudes by which she has been influenced during her childhood. A boy whose father, grandfather, and great-grandfather have been doctors might have fewer obstacles to overcome on his way to success in medicine than he would have in breaking with the family tradition and following a vocation for which his home experiences have not in any way prepared him.

In the present emergency, of course, thousands of girls will temporarily break with the family tradition and take jobs held by men in peacetime. Nevertheless, it will be necessary, at the conclusion of the war, for most of them to go back to home-making, in order that men returning from military service may resume the work traditionally theirs in normal times.

Summary. Making a careful study of the kind of work you should choose will help you to do your part, whether in civilian or military life. You can make a more thoughtful decision in selecting your occupation if you ask yourself the questions raised and explained in this section. If you select the right job for yourself, it will meet certain important requirements:

(1) It will be interesting to you.

(2) Your abilities will be equal to the job.

(3) Your interests and abilities will agree in the selection.

(4) You have the health and strength necessary for success in your work.

(5) Your occupation will provide opportunity to work.

(6) Your job will be neither too difficult nor too easy.

(7) You will be able to finance whatever training or education is necessary to prepare you for the job.

(8) Your choice will agree with the hopes and traditions of your family unless there is a good reason for changing.

READINGS

In Literature

ESSAY

Van Dine, S. S. "How I Got Away with Murder"; in *Philo Vance Murder Cases.* Scribner.

Van Dine tells how he came to write the Vance murder stories. It is catchy, like its title.

SHORT STORIES

Garland, Hamlin. "Up the Coolée"; in *Main-Travelled Roads.* Macmillan.

Farm life has its ups and downs. Mr. Garland plowed unbroken prairie grassland and knows his farm ways.

Grenfell, Wilfred. *Tales of the Labrador.* (Autobiographical.) Houghton Mifflin.

Missionary, minister, and doctor — Grenfell risked his life in snowstorm, on ice pack, and on windswept seas for his people.

Mansfield, Katherine. "The Singing Lesson"; in *Garden Party.* Knopf.

Teachers are human, though their troubles may not be shown.

Robbins, Leonard N. "Professor Todd's Used Car"; in *O. Henry Memorial Award Prize Stories of 1920.* Doubleday, Doran.

When behind the wheel of his car, Professor Todd became a new man.

For Further Information

Bliss, Walton B. *Personality and School,* Part 4. Allyn and Bacon.

Eastburn, L. A., Kelley, V. H., and Falk, C. J. *Planning Your Life for School and Society,* pp. 304-317. Scribner.

Fedder, Ruth. *A Girl Grows Up*, Chapter 8. McGraw-Hill.

Law, Frederick Houk. *He Got the Job*, Chapter 11. Scribner.

McLean, Donald. *Knowing Yourself and Others*, pp. 179-181. Henry Holt.

General References

Davey, Mildred A., Smith, Elizabeth M., and Myers, Theodore R. *Everyday Occupations*. D. C. Heath.

Filene, Catherine. *Careers for Women*. Houghton Mifflin.

Kitson, H. D. *How to Find the Right Vocation*. Harper.

Lingenfelter, Mary R. *Vocations in Fiction*. American Library Assn.

Proctor, Wm. M. *Vocations*. Houghton Mifflin.

Rosengarten, Wm. *Choosing Your Life Work*. McGraw-Hill.

2. HOW TO GET A JOB

It would be a good thing for the war effort if the largest possible number of high-school graduates were able to get the kind of jobs they wanted, for then there would be a minimum of unhappiness through temporary misplacement. You owe it not only to yourself, therefore, but to the nation, to find out what you are best suited for by interest and ability and then to cooperate in meeting national employment needs by trying to get into the kind of work in which you can be of the greatest service.

Learning about job opportunities. Information about jobs may be obtained in many ways, all of which should be tried if you want to get a job.

(1) The simplest, of course, is to learn of vacancies or opportunities through relatives and friends. Let them know you are looking for a certain kind of job; keep in touch with them. They will be more interested in you than they would be in a stranger and will let you know when they hear of an opportunity. It helps to "know the right people," though there is a certain snobbishness in the phrase as it is commonly used. However, if you get a job with the help of others, or through pull, as it is often called, you have to deliver the goods in order to keep the job and succeed in it.

(2) You may read about job opportunities in the Help Wanted

columns in newspapers. Some magazines also contain Help Wanted ads. Read these papers regularly as soon as they are issued and make application immediately if you see something that interests you.

(3) You may get help from school officials. Teachers, whose life work is dealing with students, are vitally interested in your welfare. Let them know what you plan to do and what your interests are. Give them a chance to help you. If you have an occupational counselor, be sure to visit with him every once in a while. He will probably know more about job opportunities for young people than any other person in your community, and he will try to help you get a job well suited to you.

(4) You may get help from local employment agencies. An employment agency is a clearing house for jobs, where information blanks about men and women who wish employment are kept on file. When the Government or private employers call for workers, the agency gets in touch with people suited for the work and sends them down to make personal application. Private employment agencies usually charge a sizable fee when they obtain employment for one of their applicants. City, state, and federal employment agencies do not.

(5) You may decide to write letters of application. These letters should be written by you, but you may get help in writing them. They should not be too long — one page is plenty; they should be neatly spaced and clean; they should be without mistakes in spelling, punctuation, and grammar; and they should show your interest in the particular job for which you are applying. Do not hesitate to get help in writing letters of application, but be sure to write them yourself.

Most adults rewrite application letters three or four times before they are satisfied to mail one. If you plan to look for job opportunities by using letters, you may wish to write similar letters to a number of concerns. In case you receive application blanks, fill them out completely and without mistakes and return them with a brief letter stating that you are enclosing the application which was sent you, you are still interested in a position, and you hope you will hear from them in the near future.

(6) You may be able to secure a position by making personal

interviews. It is not always necessary to wait for a vacancy or an advertised job opportunity. Many people obtain employment by making a list of various places where they would like to work and then systematically calling on employers.

The personal interview. In making a personal interview, there are certain things you should observe:

1. *Look the part.* If you are applying for a job in a machine shop, it would be better to come dressed as a machine-shop worker than to come dressed in your Sunday-go-to-meeting clothes. If you are applying for a typing position, it would be better to be dressed in tailored clothes than in chiffon scarves. If possible, come ready to go to work. Any peculiarities about your appearance, such as a little mustache or too much lipstick, hurts your chances of making a good impression with the employer.

2. *Be polite.* It is well to say, "Yes, sir," and answer questions in a soft tone of voice, not bragging, not afraid. Remain standing (not slouching) until you are invited to sit down.

3. *Show an interest in the job.* Let the employer know that you are interested in, even eager for, the particular job for which you are applying.

4. *Explain clearly what you can do.* Before an employer hires you, he must know what you can do and feel confident that you can do it. It would be well to plan your conversation in advance so that in explaining your abilities you state clearly what you can do and at the same time give the employer to understand that you do not know it all and are eager to learn more and improve on the job.

How it's done — Masculine. Warner B—— had just graduated from high school and planned to work in industry until called into service. He had taken an industrial course and had gained a little experience with wood lathes, machine lathes, shapers, and so on, but had never worked in a factory, and now he was trying to get a job. He had made the rounds of employment offices and factories in his community and was going around a second time when one employer told him that, although he himself had no vacancy, he had heard that one of the smaller manufacturing companies in town was in need of lathe operators.

"Thanks for telling me about that, Mr. Jones. I think I'll go right over there and see about it."

It was not a large concern at which Warner had to apply for this job. The owner did the hiring. Warner was dressed in overalls, ready to go to work, but he looked clean and healthy, wide-awake, and pleasant, as he went to the office and asked the telephone operator if Mr. Brown was in. After a few minutes Mr. Brown called him into his own office.

"Well, what do you want, young man?" he said as he took his chair behind the desk.

Warner remained standing and said, "I want a job, Mr. Brown. I just came from Jones Welding Company, and Mr. Jones told me that you needed lathe operators."

"He did, eh? Well, I don't know as I do. Let's see now, haven't you been in here before?"

"Yes, sir, I was here last week. I'm Warner B——."

"Oh yes, yes. I remember. Just have a chair there."

Warner said, "Thanks," as he took the chair.

"You're pretty young, aren't you, Warner — just out of high school?"

"I guess I am, but I'm not afraid of work, Mr. Brown."

"Well, maybe not. What can you do, my boy? I need a couple of lathe operators, but you can't operate a machine lathe, can you?"

"I operated the one in high school, and I took all the shop courses. I like that work, Mr. Brown, and I want to learn it."

"Well, you know, Warner, operating a lathe in school isn't quite like operating a lathe in the shop here. Were you good at it?"

"Yes, sir."

"Well, how good were you? How do I know you're good at it?"

"Would you care to telephone the principal, Mr. Brown? He can tell you about my marks at school. I always got A's and B's in shop courses."

"Well, I don't know. I think I'll have you go down and talk with Jim Black and look around a little bit."

When he had taken Warner down to the shop, Mr. Brown left him with Mr. Black and returned to the office, where he immediately telephoned the principal and gathered what information he could about the boy. Having decided to give Warner a chance, he called him back to the office. Warner again remained standing until he was told to take a chair.

"Well, what do you think of that dirty place down there, young man?"

"It looks good to me, Mr. Brown. It's the kind of work I always wanted to do. I'd sure like to have you give me a chance at it."

"Well, I don't know. Did you have a talk with Jim Black down there?"

"Yes, sir. He'd be a nice fellow to work with, too."

"Well, now, look here. How much do you figure you have to make at the start?"

"I don't know about that, Mr. Brown. I'd just as soon leave that to you if I could have the job."

"Well, let's see. When do you figure you could start?"

"Any time."

"Well, I'll give you a try. I'll take you down to Jim Black there and you do what he tells you."

"Thanks very much, Mr. Brown, I'm mighty glad to get started."

How it's done — Feminine. Helen D—— was applying for a typing job at the Merchants' Exchange Company. It was July. She wore a neat, tailored-style wash dress. As she entered Mr. X's office and saw him at his desk, she smiled and said, "Good morning, Mr. X," with a clear voice. When Mr. X motioned her to a chair, she took it and said, "I was glad to get your notice about the vacancy, so I came right over."

"You're Miss D——, aren't you?"

"Yes, sir. I filled out an application blank here some time ago."

"Yes, I see. I have it here. Of course, there are several applicants for this job, and we sent notices to some of them because we wanted to discuss the job with them further and then engage the one we think most suitable."

"I'm very happy I'm one of them, Mr. X. I'd certainly like to work at Merchants' Exchange."

"That's fine, Miss D——. We try to have a nice place for our

girls, and we think it's important for them to be happy in their work." Then, looking over her application blank, he continued, "I see you don't take dictation. The position we are thinking about doesn't require it at present, but it might possibly a little later."

"How soon, Mr. X? I'm working at shorthand in my spare time every day, and I think I'll soon be able to take dictation. The truth is, that's what I hoped to do eventually."

"Now about your typing. According to the blank here you can type sixty words a minute."

"Yes, sir, I can."

"Are you accurate, Miss D——?"

"Yes, sir, I think I can say I am."

"How about tabular work? Have you done much of that?"

"Not a great deal, but I feel sure I could learn it."

Having satisfied himself about Helen D——'s typing ability, Mr. X discussed with her at some length her ability to get along with people. Then he said, "The salary will be fifteen dollars a week, and there will be increases according to the progress you make."

"That sounds very good to me, Mr. X. And I think I can say that if I get the job I'll be able to take dictation after a month or two."

"That's fine. Now, that just about covers what I wanted to talk with you about. As you know, Miss D——, I'm calling in other applicants for the same position, and you'll hear from us in case we decide on you."

Miss D—— rose from her chair. "Well, I hope I'm the lucky one, Mr. X. And thank you for calling me in."

"You're welcome, Miss D——. Good-bye."

"Good-bye, Mr. X."

The next morning she was notified to report for work.

Summary. You can get information about job opportunities in many ways. As an up-and-coming young man or young woman you will make use of as many of them as you can.

(1) Keep in touch with the "right people" — those who are likely to know about jobs.

(2) Read the papers and trade magazines regularly.

The armed forces and auxiliaries provide youth an opportunity for service as well as for self-development. Above, soldiers in jeeps fording a shallow river. Below, a company of WAAC's on parade.

Applying for a job (*above*) requires, on the part of the applicant, proper dress, courtesy, interest in the job, and the ability to explain what he can do.

Getting along with fellow workers is necessary for success as well as for happiness on the job. This is especially true when men work closely together (*below*).

(3) Let school officials help.
(4) Visit employment agencies.
(5) Write letters of application.
(6) Make personal applications.

The most effective way to get a job is to make a personal application. Put your best foot forward and observe the following simple rules:

(1) Dress to suit the job, ready to go to work.
(2) Be courteous.
(3) Show vital interest in the job.
(4) Explain clearly what you can do.

READINGS

In Literature

ARTICLES

Giles, Ray. "They Group to Conquer"; in *Rotarian* (November, 1940).
> Contains information on how one may work with others to learn how to find the job one wants.

Giles, Ray. "They Pick Their Jobs and Land Them"; in *Reader's Digest* (February, 1940).
> Ideas get the job, but so do organizations.

Tunis, John R. "Ideas Get the Job"; in *Review of Reviews* (January, 1935).
> More than efficiency is necessary to get a job. Mr. Tunis gives a number of definite approaches that got results.

PLAY

Law, Frederick Houk. *He Got the Job,* pp. 1-13. Scribner.
> An interesting one-act play that reveals techniques of applying for a position.

For Further Information

Eastburn, L. A., Kelley, V. H., and Falk, C. J. *Planning Your Life for School and Society,* pp. 317-323. Scribner.

McLean, Donald. *Knowing Yourself and Others,* pp. 178-179. Holt.

Scharmer, F. M. *Boys' Guide to Living,* Chapter 6. Allyn and Bacon.

General References

Gardiner, G. L. *How You Can Get a Job.* Harper.

Maule, Frances. *Your Next Job: How to Get It and Hold It.* Funk and Wagnalls.

Lewis, E. E. *How to Land a Job and Get Ahead.* Harrison and Company.

Lyons, Geo. J., and Martin, Harmon C. *The Strategy of Job Finding.* Prentice-Hall.

3. GETTING ALONG WITH OTHERS ON THE JOB

Playing an active part in upholding national morale requires the ability to get along with others. On a job, of course, this will also improve your chances for success. In wartime, however, the first consideration is the war effort; hence anything that keeps it going smoothly is highly desirable. Here are a number of suggestions which apply directly to the problem of getting along with others on the job, but they may also be applied to getting along with others in the armed forces or in volunteer work.

Adjust yourself to the peculiarities of your employer. By constant conscious effort you can apply what you know about human nature to the problem of adjusting yourself to the personality of your fellow workers and your employer. Special efforts should be made to understand and satisfy the latter's peculiar likes and dislikes. One employer, for example, may want to be very quiet on the job, while another may like to exchange jokes with you. One may like to have you follow orders blindly, whereas another may prefer to have you assert yourself and make whatever changes you think are best. One may not wish to get acquainted with you personally while another may resent it if you are aloof. Study your employer and adjust yourself accordingly.

What are the demands of employers? In order to get along with your employers, you have to satisfy their demands, the most important of which are:

1. *They want you to do the work well.* They may like your personality, but if the work continually is unsatisfactory, sooner or later you will be demoted or discharged.

2. *They like to see that you are interested in your work.* They can tell whether you regard your work as an opportunity for service or as a necessary evil and the only way you can make your living. If they see that you like the work and put your heart and soul into it, it is easy for them to give you orders.

3. *They like to have you be prompt.* Employers are likely to take notice of workers who come a few minutes early and stay a few minutes late. At any rate, they will certainly notice it if you do the opposite. They can tell whether you are stingy or generous with your time.

4. *They like to have you look the part.* Employers take pride in the appearance of their workers. They feel embarrassed about one who dresses peculiarly or looks slovenly.

5. *They like to have you do an honest day's work and respond to wartime pressure.* In case rush orders come, as with war orders, they like to feel that you will make an extra effort to do the work more quickly than usual. Idling on the job should be outlawed for the duration, and of course it is bad at any time.

6. *They like to have you mind your own business.* They do not like to have you wander to someone else's office, desk, or machine with an air of sticking your nose into other people's affairs.

7. *They do not approve of practical jokes on the job.* Many workers have been discharged because of unnecessary foolishness and practical jokes. Employers are usually conscious of safety factors, and anything that disturbs the workers increases the possibility of accidents. Besides, while a worker is engaged in fun or foolishness, he or she is wasting time for which the company is paying.

8. *They like you to be open to suggestions.* Every employee occasionally needs suggestions and criticisms for improvement. If the employer can make these suggestions and feel that you are interested, his task is much easier.

9. *They like to have you get along with your fellows.*

What are the demands of your fellow workers? Getting along with your fellows on the job is in some respects different from getting along with your employers. You will find that they have certain likes and dislikes, the most important of which are:

1. *They like to feel that you like them.* The same oft-repeated problems of human relations — unselfishness and interest in the other fellow — are involved here.

2. *They like to have you able to take a joke and join in the fun.* If you are too sensitive to the gibes and sarcasm thrown your way by your fellows, you will be in misery all the time, because they will do it all the more. They like to have you able to take a joke, join in the fun, and be "one of the boys" — or the girls, as the case may be.

3. *They like to have you mind your own business.* Workers often develop a feeling that their particular job is something special. They like to feel that there are certain things they know about it that no one else knows, and they feel uneasy if others come nosing around.

4. *They do not like to have you speak evil about them.* It is a fatal mistake to make a damaging remark about a fellow worker to the boss or employer. A good rule to follow is, "Pass on the praise, but not the blame."

5. *They like to have you dress the way they do.* If you dress much better than they do, they will feel inferior and be jealous; if you dress much worse, they will feel that you do not fit in with them.

6. *They do not like to have you curry favor with the boss.* Most workers are looking for advancement, and if they see one of their fellows currying favor with the employer, they are afraid that he will get advancement before they do. They become jealous and can make life miserable for such a person.

READINGS

In Literature

NOVELS

Nordhoff, Charles B., and Hall, James N. *Mutiny on the Bounty.* Little, Brown.

A story of harsh, even cruel, leadership that results in mutiny. Here we can see how not to get along together.

White, Edward Lucas. *El Supremo.* Dutton.

A story of that strange country, Paraguay, which fought a war with its neighbors to the end — of its male population; a few hundred remained alive out of several hundred thousand.

SHORT STORIES

Detzer, Karl. "The Wreck Job"; in *Short Stories of 1926*. Dodd,
   Meade.
         An exciting story of working on the railroad in which a good
         wrecker boss gets fired and rehired.
Stephens, James. "The Boss"; in *Etched in Moonlight*. Macmillan.
         Here's how one man told off the boss.

For Further Information

Boykin, Eleanor. *This Way, Please*, Chapter 18. Macmillan.
Goodrich, Laurence B. *Living with Others*, Chapter 9. American
   Book.

4. MAKING THE MOST OF YOUR JOB

Whether or not your job is temporary, you should make the
most of it. Today your success, like almost everything else you
do, is bound up with the war effort. The suggestions given here
for achieving success are just as true during wartime as during
peacetime.

How can you clinch present and future success? Besides the
suggestions already made for success in your present employment, there are a number of other points that you should keep
firmly in mind if you are to continue moving ahead in the future.

1. *Take good care of your health.* As a rule, employers do not
approve if their workers are intemperate or careless about the
rules of good health. You may argue that your boss does not pay
for your spare time and has nothing to say about it, which is true
enough. On the other hand, though he probably will not say
anything about it, he will bear it in mind when there is a question
of advancement if he knows that you habitually dissipate. You
should not give him any cause to doubt your health and strength
for the job.

2. *Take part in the activities of your group.* If the office force
plans a beach party, be sure to go and help as much as possible.
If the gang plans a picnic, be one of them, taking part in the work
as well as the planning. If they will follow your leadership, do
not withhold suggestions. It is important for your fellow workers and your employer to know that you have leadership ability.

3. *Improve your skill in the present job until you become expert at it.* Make the most of your job now before you prepare for added responsibility. Some young people have one foot in their present job and one in the next. They are so eager for advancement that they do not devote themselves wholeheartedly to the work at hand. This is one sure way not to advance.

4. *But get ready for the next job.* When you have really made yourself expert at your present job, you can begin to prepare for a more difficult one. It goes without saying that this may require much hard work. You may need to take special training in night schools, study during your spare time, experiment with machines and operations after working hours if there is no objection. The more difficult the job ahead of you, the more hard work it will require if you are to take it on.

5. *Become familiar with the whole of which your job is a part.* If you work in a machine shop, get books and magazines on the particular types of machines used there so that you will know all about them from every angle. Get books on office management if you are a typist, stenographer, or bookkeeper. Make yourself familiar with procedures in similar working places elsewhere. You will get many ideas that may come in handy at any time. Study of this kind gives you perspective, a broader view of the meaning of your own work. It usually creates interest in other aspects of the work that formerly were unknown to you.

6. *Show initiative and responsibility.* If you can think of quicker and better ways of doing your job and you feel your employer would not object to the changes, go ahead. You should not be afraid to simplify the work if you are sure you can produce more for the company and have its interests at heart.

7. *Let your superiors know about your plans.* After having become expert in your work and prepared yourself for a more difficult job, talk with your employer about what you have been doing and what you are planning for the future. Show him that you are interested in being of greater service to the company and are willing to take more responsibility and work even harder. There is no harm in this; most employers will not resent it — quite the contrary — if you have the qualities of a good worker.

8. *Wait patiently for advancement.* Try to make yourself

satisfied and happy in your present job while you have it.   Keep your enthusiasm under control, and though you look forward to advancement, bear in mind that it will come in time, either in your present place of employment or elsewhere.   One of the most common problems of young men and women is an undue impatience for a promotion.   An employer can usually tell whether you are ready for advancement, and if you push him too hard he is likely to feel that he is being managed.   Do your work and more, and ask no favors.   If, after a reasonable length of time, it appears that your present position does not hold promise of the advancement for which you have prepared yourself, look elsewhere for a better job.

What shall you do about jealousy?   If you devote yourself to the job and get ready for a more responsible one, some of your fellow workers may be jealous of you.   Most workers are looking for advancement, and some of them may resent it if you are moved on over their heads.   Sometimes this resentment is justified, if there has been unfair competition.   An overambitious young man or woman may, for example, curry favor with his or her employer or talk unfairly about fellow workers.   Naturally this will cause jealousy.

It is possible to improve yourself on the job without the ill will of the majority of your fellows, but you will have to be careful not to make a show of your ambitions, or to make any fellow worker feel inferior, or to get the better of him in any way. Whenever possible, you should go out of your way to help and speak well of your fellows, even those who are jealous of you.

You can't avoid all jealousy.   The jealousy of some people is, of course, unfounded.   They want advancement, but have not received it because of their own shortcomings.   Perhaps they do not get along with their fellows or employers and have not become expert in their present job.   They have a strong desire for advancement, but not enough determination to earn it.   When another person, perhaps a younger one, comes in the office or the shop and succeeds in the very thing in which they failed, they feel inferior and envious.   There is very little you can do in such cases.   Everyone who rises to a position of importance meets a certain amount of jealousy on the way.   The best you can do is not to return it or hold it against anyone, but go quietly about your business.

Summary. Make the most of your job, for any present or future success you may achieve contributes to the war effort because it involves high morale and maximum service on your part. It is largely a matter of hard work and good human relations. Some of the keys to success are:

(1) Take good care of your health and avoid excesses.
(2) Take part in the activities of your group.
(3) Improve your skill in your present occupation until you become expert at it.
(4) Get ready for the next job.
(5) Become familiar with the whole of which your job is a part.
(6) Show initiative and take responsibility.
(7) Let your superiors know about your plans.
(8) Wait patiently for advancement.
(9) Try to avoid giving cause for jealousy, but do not let jealousy make any difference in your honest efforts toward improvement.

READINGS

In Literature

ARTICLE

Lodge, John E. "Learning to Remember"; in *Popular Science Monthly* (September, 1936). Also in *Reader's Digest* of same month.

> Can you learn to memorize 372, 623, 422, 767, 231 in 4.37 seconds? This article tells, too, how an ice man doubled his pay by learning to memorize.

NOVELS

Deeping, Warwick. *Sorrell and Son.* Knopf.

> A story of how slights on the job were turned to advantage.

Giles, Ray. *Turning Your Imagination into Money.* Harper.

> You need ideas on the job if you wish to be promoted.

Kyne, Peter B. *The Go-Getter.* Farrar and Rinehart.

> The boss said to a young man, "If you want to be promoted, get me that certain blue vase." He won the promotion.

General References

Fancher, Albert. *Getting a Job and Getting Ahead.* McGraw-Hill.

Lewis, E. E. *How to Land a Job and Get Ahead.* Harrison and Company.

Sherman, Ray W. *If You Want to Get Ahead.* Little, Brown.

FOR CLASS DISCUSSION

1. When Mary Andrews finished high school, she had three opportunities for work. Since she came from a well-mannered, though not well-to-do home, she was offered a good maid service job with a beginning salary of ten dollars a week, room and board included. This position was with a highly respected family and would provide better living quarters than Mary had at home.

A second opportunity available to Mary was that of typist and receptionist at fourteen dollars a week. Mary had taken a commercial course in school; her four-year average placed her in the upper ten per cent of the class.

A third opportunity was assembly work in the local brass factory at twenty dollars a week. Work in the brass factory required speed in assembling the various parts of door locks and similar articles produced there. She had to sit at a bench and perform the same manual operations again and again all day long. This job promised considerable overtime work which might raise her income to twenty-five or thirty dollars a week.

Mary Andrews chose the job in the brass factory. What might her reasons be for this choice?

Do you think she chose wisely? Explain.

Rank the three jobs from best to worst for her and explain why you rank them thus.

2. Harry W—— was the only graduate of the industrial course at Centerville High School ever to take valedictory honors. He was expert in mechanical work, having a record of straight A's in all shop subjects. He was also superior in mathematics, science, and history. As a freshman he had known what he wanted to do after high school. He wanted to become a foreman in the Centerville Implement Works.

Harry's parents had not required that he work on part-time jobs during high school, and they were pleased that he was faithful in his school work. But it was understood that Harry would begin to make his own way after graduation.

On the Saturday following commencement Harry went to apply for a job at the Centerville Implement Works. He put on his good clothes and strode into the general office. There were three men ahead of him, but as soon as Mr. Jones, the superintendent, entered, Harry said, "Hi, Mr. Jones," and walked past the other men to shake hands with the superintendent.

Mr. Jones took his hand, and quietly said, "Hello, Harry. How's your pa?" and turned to the men who had arrived first. He spent fully twenty minutes with these men, during which time Harry interrupted the switchboard operator with many comments about himself, his intention to work there, and his ambitions for the future.

Finally Mr. Jones called to have Harry come into his office. Harry beamed as he entered, "As I was tryin' to tell you, Mr. Jones, Dad's O.K. Told me he was talking to you a coupla weeks ago. Now whadyou say about a job?"

"Is that arthritis all gone now?"

"You mean Dad's? No, he's all bent up with it. But I'm fit as a fiddle myself, and I can sure make some money for you."

When Mr. Jones asked him just what he could do, Harry said nothing to the point, but bluffed his way. He was not discouraged by anything Mr. Jones said. He had unbounded confidence that he would be an asset to the company. At one time in the interview he said, bending over Mr. Jones's desk, "I'll let you in on a secret. I'm planning to be foreman here some day."

Mr. Jones repressed a laugh. Finally he said, "Harry, I think you've got a lot to learn, but ——"

"Nobody knows that better'n I do."

"I think you've got a lot to learn, but I'm going to give you a chance."

"I knew you would, Mr. Jones. I'll start in an hour, as soon as I can get into some other clothes and get back."

Mr. Jones rose from his chair and sternly said, "No, you won't, Harry. If you want the job, you start now."

"With these clothes? I couldn't do that, you know."

"If you want the job, you can. It's up to you."

"Okay, okay! Where do I start?" He was beaming again.

Fifteen minutes later one of the shop men came in to ask, "What did you send me that cocky kid for anyway?" Mr. Jones smilingly explained, "I know his old man pretty well, Rawley, and I know the kid's really got something. Right now the kid thinks he's got everything. Just take that idea out of his head and he'll be all right maybe."

What do you consider is the biggest problem for Harry to solve now that he has a job? Do you think he will solve it? Why?

Did Harry choose the right occupation?

What are his chances for future success?

What are the mistakes Harry made during the interview?

3. Gerrit S—— wanted to learn the greenhouse gardening business. He was a bright boy, quick-witted, and full of the Old Nick. Gerrit liked to play practical jokes on the greenhouse workers, and they, of course, played jokes on him. His boss put up with this foolishness for a long time because Gerrit readily learned a great deal about the heating plant, sprinkling schedule, transplanting methods, and so on. But when the tomatoes were ripening, and Gerrit again and again started tomato fights, the boss told a few of the men to "let him have it." Consequently, Gerrit found himself attacked by four men at the same time from different directions. He was a sight when, accidentally, he met the boss at the end of the rows. After the smashed tomatoes had been picked up, Gerrit was given his choice: either pay for the tomatoes at ten cents a pound (there were about thirty pounds) or get his "time" and go.

If you were Gerrit what would you choose? Why?

Did Gerrit's employer do the right thing? Explain.

What was Gerrit's main problem?

4. When Mark W—— first began to work at Amalgamated, he was very happy and a good worker. He was always prompt, pleasant with his boss and his fellows; he worked hard, and satisfied the requirements of the job. He also spent a good deal of time studying the machines on which he did not work, and he read about the company's business. A year passed. During this time he received three increases in wages. During the months that followed, however, Mark did not receive any more increases because his wage was the top for shop workers at Amalgamated. He wanted a promotion, but no vacancy occurred. After a while he became disinterested in his work; he was occasionally irritable with fellow workers; he stopped studying and working with other machines; and he frequently came to work after the whistle blew.

Was the company at fault in not promoting Mark?

Explain the changes in his behavior.

What should Mark have done?

5. Why do some people feel embarrassed or self-conscious when they apply for a job?

6. If two applicants of equal qualifications apply for a position, will an employer be likely to choose the one whose friends are also his friends? Explain.

7. If a mistake has been made and you are not to blame, would you say so, even if you know another person will have to take the blame? Explain.

8. Can a gruff, blustering employer be a good boss?

9. Discuss the following statement: The trouble with most young fellows is that they have one foot in one job and the other in the next.

10. Is there any truth in the remark that "you have to have the breaks or you'll never get anywhere"?

INDIVIDUAL ACTIVITIES

1. Make arrangements with a teacher, vocational counselor, or some school official, to take an interest test and ability test and discuss the results with him.

2. Does your chosen occupation meet all the requirements listed in this section? Check yourself with the aid of the summary given on pages 369 and 371.

If you have not decided finally on your occupation, select any one that interests you at all and apply the same requirements to that occupation; assume for the time being, that you have chosen it for your life work.

3. Make a list of your personality traits that may interfere with success on the job. What can you do to overcome each of these unfavorable traits?

FURTHER SCHOOLING IN WARTIME

Why does the government encourage high-school graduates of high standing to continue their education? Mention kinds of further schooling that might well be postponed until after the war. Are skilled workers or professional persons in greater demand during wartime? Did people in by-gone centuries require as much training for their life work as people do nowadays? Why?

1. *SHOULD YOU PLAN FOR FURTHER SCHOOLING?*

IF YOU ARE UNABLE to continue your education because you are soon to be drafted, try to get into a branch of the service that will give you the schooling needed later for your life work. Occupations in military service, for both men and women, are so broad and varied that in most instances it is possible to choose the kind of work you want to do. Information about this subject is available at your local draft board. You may find that, instead of facing an interruption to your plans for education, military service will provide a greater opportunity.

We hope, though we cannot know, the war will at worst be only a temporary interruption to our plans. When it is over, we should be ready to make the most of the future. If further schooling is a part of your plan for the future, and the war interrupts the plan, you should not despair of getting more education eventually. Many a man resumes interrupted schooling and actually profits by his greater maturity and the hard knocks he has had during the interruption. For many high-school graduates, however, it will be possible to go on with educational plans now; but, of course, these plans will have to be in line with what the nation needs. Approximately seventy-five per cent of the officers in the army are college graduates; other branches of the service have a similiar or even greater percentage of college graduates among their officer personnel. Further schooling, of one kind or another, is needed for many wartime occupations and also for those that must be filled after the war is over.

Your schooling should primarily have a vocational aim. Going to college to get a four-year literary and cultural education is definitely out of the picture in time of war, at least for men; and probably fewer women will go in for this kind of education. Your schooling will have to be related to the war effort in one way or another if you are to be allowed to continue it. Even women may be drafted for war work when the need becomes urgent enough.

Does your life work require further schooling? If you have selected your vocation according to the principles explained in the previous section, you know what preparation the work requires. If advancement depends entirely on the training you get while on the job, you will not need further schooling before you begin. And if you do need it, your best move is to get your first job immediately, whether it is in civilian or military life.

Do you like the idea of going to school? Be honest with yourself and see whether you like the idea of going to a trade school, a business school, some other special school, or college; or whether you would like to go to night school while working. If you do not like studying, it may be better for you to work a year and make up your mind after you have had further experience. Often a year of work will give a person a much better understanding of the advantages of more training. If you go to school without being interested in it, you will have a hard time. You ought to know by now that learning is easiest when you like to learn, hardest when you dislike it.

If you like the idea of going to school to prepare yourself well for civilian or military life, you have the advantage of beginning with an attitude that helps to make learning easy and pleasant; further schooling will be a pleasure in itself.

Do you have the ability to succeed at school? From various sources, many of which were given in the previous unit, you can determine what level of ability is required for success in your chosen vocation. If you have taken any ability tests listed in Unit III and have talked with some reliable older person about your chances for success, you already know whether you have the ability to succeed in the schooling required. It is not wise to tackle a job or further schooling unless you like it and are able to succeed in it. Tackle the thing in which you have a fair chance of success; then you can put your efforts into it with a will and with confidence that you can make good. Going to any kind of school without the mechanical, social, or mental abilities needed for success there would be like going to bat with two strikes against you. Therefore, be reasonably sure in your own mind that you have the ability to make good at a certain kind of school before you decide to go.

When should you get the needed schooling? In time of war, many young people find it necessary to postpone further schooling for the duration; others feel duty-bound to go on with their education if they can. For some there is a definite advantage in working a while before going on to school, because on the job — as in the service — they get to meet the world outside of school. Good schools do try to organize activities as nearly as possible according to life in the world outside, but experience there is generally more theoretical, while experience on a job is more practical.

Can you afford it? Before you go on with your education, you should know how much it will cost and whether you can afford it. If you cannot afford it, you may have to work until you have saved enough to see yourself through. It is not wise to go to school unless you have at least half the money needed to complete the course, or at any rate enough to complete one year. If you do not have enough to see you through the first year, it would be much better to wait until you do. It is hard to get the most out of school when you are constantly worried by lack of funds and have to undergo too much hardship because of extreme poverty.

What kind of schooling should you have? It has already been pointed out that your education should have a vocational aim and be related to the war effort. There are schools for every vocational need, prepared to train you for occupations that must be filled as quickly as possible — colleges, trade schools, night schools, and business colleges. Your choice depends upon a careful study of the job you want. If you have chosen your vocation and have studied it, you are not likely to make the mistake of going to college when you should go to a trade school.

Where should you go for further schooling? Needless to say, there are many schools offering similar education and training, but there are also great differences among them in quality, reputation, cost, and convenience. For example, you might be able to take a secretarial course at any one of several business colleges. Which one should you select? The same question could be asked about any other kind of school.

1. *Go to the school that has the best reputation.* Find out about a school's reputation from persons who have attended it and are now at work, and from other adults who know the school. Your teachers and school officials would also be likely persons to consult on this subject.

2. *Go to the school that specializes in the particular training you need.* Many schools offer similar courses, but each has certain ones that stand out as superior to the same courses in other schools. This may be because of superior teachers or superior equipment or both — perhaps even superior students. Go to the school that is known for training of high quality in your particular field of interest.

3. *Go to the school that has a high percentage of placements for its graduates.* But check up on this, and beware of the school that guarantees you a job, for most of them, even in wartime, do not place as many graduates as they say they do.

4. *Go to the school that is conveniently located.* All other things being equal — reputation, quality of training, and prospects of placement — choose the school most convenient for you to attend.

5. *Go to the school you can afford to go to.* The last consideration should be cost. In most instances it is, of course, better not to let the money question influence your choice of school. Unfortunately, it often must. Do not give up an education just

because you cannot go to the best — and perhaps the most expensive — school in the country. Others may be nearly as good.

Summary. We have been trying to find a sound basis for deciding whether to go on to school after high-school graduation. Assuming that your plans are not to be canceled in the near future by military service, you will be safe in your decision if you can satisfactorily answer the following questions:

(1) Does your plan for further schooling have a vocational aim related to the national emergency?

(2) Does your vocation require further schooling?

(3) Do you like to go to school?

(4) Have you the ability to succeed in it?

(5) When should you go to school, now or after the war?

(6) Can you afford it?

(7) What kind of schooling should you have?

(8) Where should you go to get it?

Coming to a decision about whether you need more schooling, what kind it should be, and where you should go to get it is a problem that requires careful thought, especially when so many people around you are entering their country's service. Solving your problems by thinking them through in advance is the grown-up way to solve them. In the following parts of this section you will get information about various kinds of schools. As a thinking person, you may be able to use the information to solve the problem of further schooling in time of war as it applies to you.

READINGS

In Literature

ARTICLES

Detzer, Karl. "From Campus to Dinner Pail"; in *Kiwanis Magazine* (December, 1940). Also in *Reader's Digest*.

> For the student who wants to fit into the business world and get practical experience and earn a living while going to college.

Johnson, Thomas M. "We Buy New Students"; in *Reader's Digest* (September, 1935).

> Do not fall for the college field representative's line.

Seabrook, William. "They Find Out What You're Fit For"; in *Forum* (August, 1938). Also in *Reader's Digest*.

> Read this article and make your own decisions.

For Further Information

Bliss, Walton B. *Personality and School,* Chapters 12 and 13. Allyn and Bacon.

Bogardus, E. S., and Lewis, R. H. *Social Life and Personality,* pp. 195-199. Silver, Burdett.

Eastburn, L. A., Kelley, V. H., and Falk, C. J. *Planning for School and Society,* pp. 316-317. Scribner.

2. AT NON-PROFESSIONAL SCHOOLS

Let us assume that, after due consideration of wartime problems as they affect your future, you have decided to get more schooling. In making your plans, then, you should know something of the multitude of possibilities now available for further education or training. Maybe you will be approached by an agent who wants to have you sign up for a correspondence course. There may be night-school classes in or near your community. You may have thought about entering a trade school or attending business college or junior college.

What do you know about the education or training offered in these various schools? How do you begin? How much will it cost? How long will it take? These questions and many others have to be answered before you decide upon where to go to school.

First, we shall see what the non-professional schools have to offer. Among these the most common are (I) correspondence schools, (II) night schools, (III) trade schools, (IV) business schools, and (V) junior colleges.

I. Correspondence Schools

A large variety of courses may be taken by correspondence or the home-study plan. You sign for a certain course, make a down payment, get your books and study materials by mail, make additional payments, and so on, until you complete the course. You can go as fast or as slowly as you like. You can get further schooling by the home-study method for many commercial occupations and trades, and even for some professions.

If you read some of the correspondence-school advertisements appearing in magazines, you may get the idea that the easiest, quickest, and least expensive way to get your further schooling is by home study. Does this prove to be the case in actual practice?

The hardest way is by correspondence. Actually, for most people the hardest way to get further schooling is through home study. Although it is true that many people who cannot go to school do obtain further education by taking correspondence courses, it is, nevertheless, a difficult method. There are several reasons for this, and we may as well face them.

1. *The guidance and inspiration of teachers cannot be fully carried over to you by correspondence.* Personal contact between learner and teacher is missing when you do your work by correspondence. Most people need this contact in order to do their best work.

2. *You are entirely on your own.* You do not have to do a certain amount of studying every day, go to classes, or match wits with fellow students. You are on your own. You study when you want to and send in your written work when it is ready. This is good training if you can do it, but, just because they are on their own, few young people are able to continue their study by means of correspondence courses.

3. *Your studying must be done in spare time.* You have to have excellent study habits and a keen determination to succeed with a correspondence course. The home-study plan has been more successful with adults than with graduates fresh from high school, because adults who enroll in correspondence schools do so after experience on the job gives them a strong desire to better their position.

4. *Correspondence-school training is narrower than training in a regular school.* It is narrower for the reason already mentioned — that it does not provide the social contacts available in other schools. Daily relationships with fellow students and teachers help you to develop abilities in addition to those which you are developing from study itself.

5. *Only a few succeed.* The advertisements refer to those who succeed. By far the larger number who begin a correspondence

course do not complete their study and do not obtain employment in the work for which they planned to prepare themselves. The advertisements, of course, do not refer to the large majority of failures and uncompleted courses.

Use great care in selecting the school. Notwithstanding these reasons, a number of graduates fresh from high school do enroll in correspondence courses. If it is your plan to do so, make sure that the school in which you enroll is a *bona-fide* correspondence school. You can make sure about it by following a few worth-while suggestions.

1. *Talk it over with your counselor, high-school principal, superintendent of schools, or other school officials* who have had experience in advising graduates about further schooling. They may be able to give you the names of people in your community who have taken work by correspondence.

2. *Talk it over with someone who has taken work by correspondence.* Such a person can tell you his own first-hand experience — how much it cost him, how successful he was, how valuable the study has been for him, and many other bits of information you ought to know before you sign your name on the dotted line and make a down payment.

3. *Write to the Department of Public Instruction* in the capital of your state for information about correspondence schools. Many states have their own lists of accredited correspondence schools and you can tell at a glance whether the school you have in mind is accredited. If a school is on an accredited list, it meets certain important requirements with respect to its advertising methods, teaching personnel, financial condition, placement facilities, and so on.

4. *Consult the Home-Study Blue Book,* which is a directory of private home-study schools and courses, published annually by the National Home-Study Council, Washington, D.C. The 1943 edition gives the requirements which must be met by the schools and lists about fifty approved correspondence schools and some five hundred different courses offered by them.

Home-study plans with supervision. Some high schools have special arrangements for providing teacher supervision for students who want to take certain courses by correspondence not offered in the high-school curriculum. Schools having arrangements of this kind usually schedule daily periods of study in school and provide a teacher to guide the students in their work. Correspondence-school work pursued under such conditions is much more successful than that pursued entirely on the initiative of the student himself.

It is also possible in some states for people who have not been able to go to college, but who wish to continue their education, to take college courses by correspondence and with local supervision. Students who enroll in such courses must have a plan for meeting regularly with a teacher or supervisor approved by the college, though the work is done in writing and submitted to the college.

Getting your further schooling by the home-study plan is difficult, especially when it is not supervised; but it does give you a chance to forge ahead if you cannot leave your job, yet are determined to prepare for increased responsibilities in the future.

II. Trade Schools

No doubt there is a trade school in your community. If you have chosen a trade for which there are local employment opportunities and also preparatory training courses, your problem of further schooling is fairly simple. If you have selected a trade for which you must attend a trade school or technical school elsewhere, however, you will have to give it careful thought before you decide to go.

Most trade schools get aid from the Federal Government. A fairly complete list of such schools and the courses they offer is contained in the *Directory of Federally Aided All-Day Trade and Industrial Education Programs.* This is Miscellaneous Bulletin No. 2375, published by the United States Office of Education in Washington, D.C. It contains a list of schools offering all-day programs, the trades taught, and the names and addresses of the schools. In this excellent directory you will find listed courses in plumbing, electricity, dressmaking, auto mechanics, boat construction, commercial art, chef's training, and many others, in schools from Madison, Maine, to Miami, Florida, and Honolulu, Hawaii.

A small sampling of trades taught. The following list of trades taught, besides those already mentioned, includes only a few of those contained in this directory:

Air-conditioning
Aircraft mechanics
Baking
Barbering
Beautician
Body and fender repairing
Bricklaying
Carpentry
Commercial art
Cooking
Costume designing
Dental assistant
Dressmaking
Household service; management, maid service, servant training
Janitor service: building maintenance, custodian, engineer
Jewelry making and design
Landscaping
Lumbering
Machine shop
Masonry
Meat cutting

Medical secretary
Millinery
Neon tube lighting
Oil refining
Painting
Photography
Power machine operation
Printing
Radio
Restaurant, tea-room, and cafeteria service
Shoe repairing
Soda fountain dispensing
Stagecraft
Table service
Tailoring
Tool and die work
Trade sewing
Waiter and waitress training
Weaving
Welding
Woodworking

Corporation technical schools. These are trade schools organized and operated by various corporations, such as the Ford Motor Company, General Motors Corporation, Chrysler Corporation, and others. Though it is fairly difficult to gain admission to schools of this type, once you get in and complete the course successfully, you are sure of a job. The main purpose of the corporation's technical school is to train its workers in the special skills required in the company's plants. Attendance at a school of this type has several advantages: it gives you specialized training, pays you while you study, and assures you of a position.

Part-time study. Arrangements may sometimes be made for a part-time job and part-time schooling. This is more frequently done by women in various types of office work than by men. A dental assistant, for example, may be able to work half a day and go to junior college for courses in chemistry, bookkeeping, typing, or what not the other half. Such courses would have a direct bearing upon her work in the dentist's office and would increase her ability to be of service to her employer. A garage worker who wishes to make a more careful study of automobile wiring and electricity may arrange to take a certain number of hours off each week to get the specialized instruction in a local junior college or trade school.

A trade school is not a finishing school. The trade school aims to prepare students in cosmetology, table service, air-conditioning, costume designing, or whatever the trade may be, for useful employment in that trade. It does not aim to turn out fully trained workers. Trade schools plan to give students many opportunities to develop some of the skills and acquire some of the information needed for success. After trade school, the test is the job.

III. Night Schools

Another way for you to get further schooling is by attending night school while you hold a full-time job.

Many communities provide a variety of night-school classes giving courses in business, trades, or professions. Night schools are usually arranged to satisfy the demands of the community, and classes are held in the buildings used during the day for regular school attendance.

Public and private night schools. There are public and private night schools. The former are organized primarily as a service to the community and the fees charged are small, provided you reside in the community. As a rule, private schools are operated for profit. They also satisfy community demands, and render a service in doing so, but the fees are, of course, much larger than those charged in public schools. It is sometimes possible for a private school to provide better-trained instructors than are provided in public night schools, but this is not always the case. You should consult your school advisers regarding the conditions in your community.

Fees. Private schools usually charge approximately the same fee for a certain course — say Stenography I — whether it is taken in the evening or during the day. Also, the fees are the same for those who live elsewhere as for those who reside in the community.

Public schools usually charge local residents a small fee that does not nearly pay for the cost of instruction or housing. There may be a laboratory or breakage fee if the equipment used in the class is expensive and subject to depreciation and maintenance charges. Nonresidents who do not live within the corporate limits of the city usually pay a sizable tuition. Information about night-school fees can be obtained by writing to the principal, registrar, or director of the school you have in mind.

Night-school offerings. The principles underlying public school evening classes are: (1) a person is never too old to learn; (2) he should have an opportunity to learn what he wants to learn; and (3) public schools should provide training facilities to supply the wartime demand for workers to replace those drawn into the armed forces. You may find people of all ages, sixteen-year-olds or sixty-year-olds, in night-school classes, depending upon the demand. You may also find a great variety of classes, but in times of national emergency training for war jobs takes precedence over everything else as a rule.

If you want to continue your schooling, but cannot give up your job, you should find out what the schools in your community offer during evening classes. Information of this kind is easy to get. Just write to the superintendent of schools, or to the principal, director, or registrar of the school you have in mind. Better still, call in person.

IV. Business Colleges

Opportunities for employment in business — military as well as civilian — range from the simplest office work to the most difficult and complex accountancy and administration. Some positions can be filled only by brilliant young men and women who have completed four years in a school of business at a university. Business colleges not connected with a university are not as a rule able to provide adequate training for positions of this kind. Some stenographic and bookkeeping positions require four years of high school, two or three years of schooling in business college, and superior mental ability. Some positions in general office work, involving less difficult typing, bookkeeping, and stenography, can be held successfully by graduates of a high-school commercial course or by students who have completed from six to twelve months in a commercial college. Commercial colleges try to meet the requirements of most occupations in the business world.

The business college operates for profit. The commercial college is privately owned and operated for profit. Tuition fees are the only source of income; such schools do not receive endowments or governmental aid. Hence commercial colleges are fairly expensive as compared with city- or state-owned colleges and universities.

Business colleges aim for early completion of course. Commercial colleges depend for their success upon tuition collected from those who attend, but this very fact has forced them to develop courses of study that satisfy the demands of students. Students are willing to pay for commercial training if they get commercial training. As a rule, they want to complete their course as quickly as possible and get a job. They do not wish to spend time in a commercial college studying cultural subjects, such as foreign language, history, science, and mathematics, which they could get at a regular college or university at less cost.

How long does the course in a commercial college take? A bookkeeping and accounting course may be completed in five to twenty-four months, depending upon the extent to which you want to carry your study in this field. A secretarial course may be completed in six to twelve months and a stenographic course in five to nine months. A course that combines the essential features of the bookkeeping and secretarial courses may be completed in ten to eighteen months.

How much is the tuition? Approximate costs for these courses are as follows:

Course	Low	High
Bookkeeping and accounting	$ 95	$450
Secretarial	100	250
Stenographic	95	175
Combined course	150	300

It is possible in some commercial colleges to shorten the time required by completing units ahead of schedule.

As previously mentioned, almost all commercial colleges also provide a schedule of evening classes.

Placement service in commercial colleges. A commercial college depends for its success, not only upon offering courses of study that satisfy the wants of students, but also upon its success in placing students in occupations. It is generally known that a large number of commercial college graduates are placed in employment during wartime. If you need further schooling in commerce and are thinking about attending a commercial college after high-school graduation, your best sources of information and guidance are your school officials.

V. *Junior Colleges*

Junior colleges vary considerably from community to community, each having sprung up in answer to local needs. Although most of them provide courses in business, trades, and professions, there is no uniformity among them. If you plan to attend a junior college, you should get complete information about the courses offered by careful study of the catalogue and by making a personal call.

Costs. The enrollment of a junior college is made up largely of high-school graduates in the community and near by. If you plan to get your further schooling at a junior college in your own city, you can do so by paying a small tuition fee; or perhaps there will be no fee. A student from outside the community would have to pay more than a resident. Living costs and books would comprise the major part of your expenses, and this would amount to considerably less than half the annual cost of attending a commercial college or a private trade school. The period of training, however, would be longer, though the training would be broader.

Business education in junior colleges. About eighty per cent of all junior colleges offer courses in business education. The occupations for which they train students are similar to those for which commercial colleges give training. They include bookkeeping, accounting, stenography, secretarial work, clerking, filing, billing, salesmanship, advertising, banking, administration, and others. Business courses in the junior college are generally not limited to vocational subjects, however; there are usually additional required subjects of a cultural nature. These would include psychology, English composition, history, and other subjects intended to give the student, in addition to vocational skills, a broader knowledge of life and the world.

Training for trades in junior colleges. Most junior colleges also provide courses in the various trades most common in the community. As is the case with business training in junior colleges, the period of training is usually longer than that prescribed in a trade school, because the program of studies would include cultural subjects.

Professional training in junior colleges. Academic courses pursued in junior colleges are acceptable for credit in regular colleges and may be used in a military classification. You can, for example, begin a pre-medical or pre-law course in junior college. Many high-school graduates attend junior college for two years before entering college, because, if the junior college is in their own community, they have very little tuition to pay and can live at home while pursuing studies equivalent to two years of college work.

READINGS

In Literature

ARTICLES

Benjamin, Roy, Jr. "The South Blazes a New Trail for Youth"; in *Forum* (March, 1940).

To success by way of the trade school.

Knudsen, William S. "If I Were 21"; in *American Magazine* (June, 1939).

"Go West, young man, go West" was the old call to success. The new frontier is described by the former president of General Motors who is now active in our war program.

MacEvoy, T. P. "Youth, Get Your Toe in the Door"; in *Reader's Digest* (April, 1941).

Mr. MacEvoy says that typing and shorthand are essentials to success and does a good job of substantiating his statement.

McDermott, William, and Furnas, J. C. "Floodlighting the Job Market"; in *Survey Graphic* (April, 1940). Also *Reader's Digest*.

Where are the best jobs now?

For Further Information

Directory of Federally Aided All-Day Trade and Industrial Education Programs. Miscellaneous Bulletin No. 2375, United States Office of Education, Washington, D.C.

Home Study Blue Book, National Home Study Council, Washington, D.C.

National Teachers Commercial Federation, Sixth Year Book; the Business Curriculum. Bowling Green, Kentucky, 1940.

3. AT COLLEGE

Going to college in time of war is not necessarily unpatriotic. England, for example, has drafted men to go to college, and the United States Government also has appropriated federal funds for a large number of students in college. Why? Because we shall always be in need of university-trained men, not only for the duration, but for the postwar period as well. A large number of specialists have been taken out of the universities for war work, and the armed services have taken many students. Many who might have planned to go to college, and who by virtue of their abilities should have gone, have joined the army, navy, or marines. As a result, the number of college and university students has fallen off and a shortage of doctors, dentists, engineers, economists, and other university-trained men is bound to occur. To offset such a shortage, young men and women of promise are not discouraged from continuing their education. When they graduate from a college or university their country will need them, either in military service or in postwar reconstruction. Meanwhile, they contribute to national morale by doing their part as students.

Suppose you have decided upon a career that requires a college education. You have well above average mental ability; your high-school record is very good; you have a keen desire to go to college, and you feel this is what your country wants you to do. Having come to a decision on these basic questions, and on those discussed earlier in this section, you now have to decide where to go and how to finance your course.

One of the best sources of information is *American Universities and Colleges,* a directory published by the American Council on Education, 744 Jackson Place, Washington, D.C. It contains information about the location of colleges, scholarships, courses, instructors, enrollments, and tuition. Most high-school libraries have a copy of this handbook.

Factors influencing your choice. You choice of a college should take into account the five factors governing the choice of any school. These were discussed in the first part of this section and include the reputation of the school, its field of specialization, opportunities for placement after graduation, convenience of location, and cost.

The college catalogue. College catalogues usually contain most of the information needed by a prospective student. They contain information about expenses, including tuition fees, board and room, books, and the like; the minimum amount of money you need in order to begin; scholarships; living conditions at the school and in the community; dormitories; opportunities for part-time employment and for entertainment; the departments, the courses offered, including specially arranged military courses, and the teaching personnel; and finally, suggested curricula. If you have catalogues from several colleges, you can compare them and gain impressions that will help you to decide where to apply for admission.

How to get a catalogue. College catalogues may be obtained by sending a letter or postcard asking for them. The following form is acceptable:

1234 Main Street
Centerville, M——.
Jan. 6, 19—

Registrar
Grand Lane College
Grand View, Indiana

Dear Sir:

Please send me your college catalogue and any other helpful information for freshmen. I am planning to study in the School of Engineering.

Respectfully yours,
John R. Doe

You should send a letter or card to the registrar of each college and university you have under consideration, indicating the department (such as the School of Engineering in the example given) in which you are interested.

When should you apply for admission? Some students begin to gather information about colleges during the latter part of their junior year and make application for admission early in the second semester of the senior year. If your application is tentatively accepted, pending the outcome of your last semester's work, you may take other definite steps.

Getting a part-time job in your freshman year. For instance, if you have to work part time, you can plan a trip to the college to have a personal interview with the appointment or employment officer. By making a personal application at an early date, you have a much better chance to get a job, and one of the kind you prefer, than if you wait until you arrive at college in the fall.

Arranging for a room. Another advantage of receiving an early admittance letter from the registrar is that you will have more time to make arrangements for living accommodations. Rooms in dormitories must be spoken for well in advance. This is the case also with conveniently located rooms in private homes.

In case you cancel college plans. If circumstances later in the senior year force you to cancel your plan to go to college, you are free to do so, and if you notify the registrar sometime during the summer, it will be possible for you to have the dormitory deposit refunded.

Obtaining admission at more than one college. Students sometimes obtain admission at one college and then go to another. This is not quite fair to the first college, because after the officials spend time evaluating your record, deciding to accept your application, and corresponding with you, they count on your coming unless something unforeseen prevents you. Besides, your high-school office spends considerable time on your application to make your case successful. Before you apply for admission to a particular school, you should be reasonably certain of attending it if you are admitted.

Be sure of finances for one year at least. It is generally recommended that high-school graduates should not enter college unless they have a definite plan for completing at least the first year. There are, of course, various possible sources of income — scholarships, part-time employment, money from home, funds from an educational insurance policy, trust funds, war bonds used in lieu of tuition, or funds in a savings bank. The following table will give you some idea of what it costs to go to college:

ONE YEAR — 36 WEEKS

	Low	High
Books	$ 20	$ 40
Tuition	100	500
Board	250	400
Room	100	180
Clothes and laundry	72	150
Entertainment	72	150
	$614	$1420

Scholarships. Many colleges offer scholarships to freshmen; in fact, some of them seem to vie with each other in their efforts to increase enrollments. One method of building up enrollments is to offer a large number of small scholarships covering tuition or part of it. Do not let a scholarship of this kind make you decide to go to a college that does not give good training in the field you have chosen. It is worth more to go to the right school than the small amount saved by the scholarship. If, because of your superior record or for some other reason, you get a scholarship in the school of your choice, your financial burden will, of course, be reduced.

Plan some time for recreation. If you plan on a part-time job as a source of income during your first year, you should get one that will not take all of your spare time. You need time for study, of course, but you also need some time for recreation. It is not advisable to work so many hours that you cannot do your school work properly, make social contacts with fellow students, and attend special lectures, convocations, music programs, or other activities — especially those connected with the war, such as United Service Organizations entertainments or Red Cross and other war relief work. If possible, a college education should include more than grinding at books and a job.

Saving for college. Before you go to college, you should if possible have some fund, either in a bank account or in war bonds, set aside exclusively for your education. Saving this money yourself will enable you to carry habits of thrift into college life and manage your finances successfully while you are there. It will also give you something now to look forward to and perhaps help you to be more diligent in your high-school studies.

Loneliness in college. One of the most common problems of college freshmen is loneliness. Most of them manage to solve the problem or endure the loneliness, but there are always a few who go back home before the year is over. It will help you to know about this problem in advance, so that you can plan to meet it when it comes. Precautions can be taken. You can plan to attend some of the dances, teas, or social affairs provided. Keep in touch with old friends, make it a point to acquire new ones, and spend some time with the latter regularly.

A part-time job often prevents loneliness because it gives balance to college life and makes a student too busy to think about himself and home all the time. Jobs also provide opportunities for contacts, sometimes important ones, with other people. Hard work of a physical nature, exercise, or athletics may help to keep you from the loneliness experienced by many freshmen in college. Contributing to the war effort in one or more ways also helps one to forget himself and keep his chin up.

College is not a snap. A college education requires hard work and diligent application. It takes more than average mental ability to succeed. If you have the ability and interest to continue your education in college, there is the satisfaction of meeting new and more difficult problems and planning over a period of years to prepare yourself for a life of service.

READINGS

In Literature

ARTICLES

Fowler, Bertram. "Cooperating Their Way Through College"; in *Survey Graphic* (June, 1939).
> This is an article worth reading.

Tunis, John R. "Men of Harvard — 25 Years After"; condensed from the book, *Was College Worthwhile* (Harcourt, Brace) in *Reader's Digest* (December, 1936).
> A stimulating analysis of the value of college training.

NOVELS

Johnson, Owen. *Stover at Yale.* Little, Brown.
> Stover loved football, but he went to college for other reasons.

Perry, Lawrence. *The Fullback.* Scribner.
> When a good athlete quits the team because he is working his way through college, he is apt to become unpopular.

Tunis, John R. *The Duke Decides.* Harcourt, Brace.
> Would it be athletics or work? What is a college for?

For Further Information

American Council Directory, American Council on Education, 744 Jackson Place, Washington, D.C.

Bulletin No. 2, 1933, "Statistics of Universities, Colleges, and Professional Schools, 1931-1932," Federal Office of Education, Department of Interior, Washington, D.C.

College Blue Book, H. W. Hurt, De Land, Florida.

FOR CLASS DISCUSSION

1. John Doe will be graduated in June. He has been thinking about a vocation but he cannot make up his mind definitely. He is interested in many things. His high-school record is superior in all respects. It will be easy for him to secure admission to college. Besides, his family is well-to-do.
What should he plan for next fall?
What could he do to become more certain about his future work?

2. Bill M—— had always wanted to go to West Point. The prob-

lem of making his way in life had been settled long ago and had centered in a military career. There were indications that he might not be able to pass the entrance examinations, for his high-school record was only average; but he never doubted that he would eventually go to West Point. During his senior year he tried to get an appointment through the Congressman in his district, and when at last he learned that he was to be second alternate, his heart sank. He spent two anxious months wondering how he would ever get there, and then he learned that one of the candidates had failed to pass the entrance examinations. Bill became first alternate.

About this time he had a chance to enter an industrial trade school. He enrolled, reserving the intention to drop out as soon as the appointment to West Point came through. But, much to his own surprise, he found work in industry very interesting. He became deeply absorbed in it and forgot about West Point. Three months later the appointment actually came through, but Bill was so enthusiastic about the success he was having in trade school that he declined the appointment.

Did he do the right thing?

Were there indications that Bill was not suited to the rigid study of West Point?

Would he have been as happy if he had gone to West Point? Explain.

Which of the two types of further schooling would be likely to help him more in making his way in life?

3. When Geraldine N—— was a junior in high school her adviser asked why she did not change from the college preparatory course to the commercial course, since she definitely intended to become a stenographer or a secretary. Geraldine said she had talked it all over with her mother and had decided to get an academic high-school training first. Her mother had told her that four years of English, two years of a foreign language, three years of history, three years of science, and three years of mathematics would serve as a good foundation for any girl who went into a business office. After graduation Geraldine was going to business college and complete her course in one year.

Was Geraldine's mother right?

What do you think Geraldine's adviser said about this plan?

4. Arthur E—— was a brilliant boy of sixteen when he was graduated from high school. There was a junior college in his town, but he applied for admission at the state university. One or two people

told his parents that Arthur was pretty young to be going off to college alone, but their doubts made no difference in the final plans. In October, Arthur was taken to college by his father and mother. When they said good-bye and he saw their car turn the corner, he suddenly felt quite alone. The university campus looked strange, imposing, impersonal. He was afraid, deep down. But he had always been a good student and now he decided to forget himself in his books. That night, however, he did write a long letter home. And the next night, too. And the next. He found it impossible to study as he used to do, and he went home the first week-end. From that time on his school work suffered because of his loneliness, letter-writing, and week-end trips. When the mid-semester examinations had been taken and returned, he found, for the first time in his life, a series of D's and E's.

At the end of the semester he left the university in what he secretly considered a disgrace. He enrolled in junior college at home, however, and again completed his school work with superior grades.

Why did Arthur at first decide to go to the university when he could have gone to junior college at home?

Why did he fail at the state college?

Will he ever be able to go back to the college? When?

5. What chance of success at college is there for each of the following?

    a. A brilliant boy who never studied diligently in high school and who was graduated among the lowest 25 per cent of his class.

    b. A brilliant girl of excellent study habits, who was graduated among the upper 5 per cent of her class with an all-A record.

    c. A boy of average mental ability, who had to work for his grades and was graduated thirtieth from the top in a class of one hundred.

    d. A brilliant boy who received barely passing marks in all of his subjects except five in which he received A's.

    e. A well-to-do, charming girl of average mental ability and superior social ability.

    f. A boy who is considered most promising for success in college, but who has recently shifted his interest from further education to service in the navy.

6. If a person does not know what occupation he plans to follow for life, and if he has enough money, is he justified in going to college for a general literary course not leading toward teaching or engineering or any vocation?

7. Some people recommended that although a college student should not be required to earn all of his expenses, he should be required to earn part or half of his expenses. On what grounds do they make this recommendation?

INDIVIDUAL ACTIVITIES

1. Send to the superintendent, principal, director, or registrar of the nearest school that provides training for your life work for complete information about courses offered.

2. Talk with a person who has attended the school to which you would like to go.

3. If possible, call in person, see the school officials, and spend an hour looking at the buildings and grounds.

4. Begin a savings account for future school needs. You can begin with a very small amount set aside regularly. The important thing is to keep at it faithfully and keep hands off!

Conclusion

SO FAR IN THIS BOOK you have been studying the problems of understanding yourself, getting along with others, and making your way in time of peace and in time of war. The upshot of the discussion is that *you can solve these problems.* But there are three provisos. You can understand yourself, get along with others, and make your way, if:

(1) You are honest with yourself, face the facts, and don't kid yourself along.
(2) You are courteous and considerate and observe the Golden Rule.
(3) You make the most of your abilities and the opportunities around you.

In the final pages, let us see what happens when you do solve your own personal problems. We can anticipate the conclusion by saying that you just naturally become a likable person and a successful person; and the latter means that you become a leader in some things and a good follower in others.

A LIKABLE PERSON

Does a woman have to be beautiful or a man handsome to be likable? Why do you like your best friend? What are the traits of a person who has many friends in school? What makes a likable person likable?

IT IS AN ODD FACT that you become a likable person when you solve your personal problems; for these problems represent the things that disturb your personality and your relations with others. As you understand yourself better and solve your problems, you gradually acquire certain traits that other people like in you. The changes that take place as you grow toward your ideal self may come unconsciously, or by constant conscious effort, or more likely by a little of each.

What makes a likable person likable? A person is not likable just because he or she is the best pianist, soloist, track man, or fullback in school, or has plenty of ready cash, or is the best-dressed boy or girl in the group, or has a record of excellent scholarship, or never disagrees with others. What, then, does make a person likable? Doctor Donald A. Laird, one of the many psychologists who have studied this problem, suggests that all likable people, as a rule, have certain personality traits in common. Some of these traits and certain others will be discussed here briefly.

A likable person tries to like other people. It is possible to find some good in your worst enemy. When you study the reasons for his faults, you are also able to see his virtues and feel kindly, perhaps even cordial toward him. A likable person makes an effort to like others. In time this becomes a habit, or what is called second nature.

A likable person is interested in others. If you want to be likable, you will try to understand the desires of other people and their ways of doing things. You will share their happiness and their grief. In conversation you will listen attentively and ask questions that will bring out the other fellow's point of view. What he says and does will be interesting to you.

A likable person is unselfish. As you become likable, your own wants and wishes gradually mean less to you, and the wants and wishes of your fellows mean more. Your actions are governed more and more by the wishes of others instead of by purely selfish considerations.

A likable person knows how to accept favors. A likable person is willing to receive kindnesses from others and is appreciative in accepting such favors. Many people do not like to accept favors because they feel that this obligates them to the giver, and they do not want to be obligated. A likable person, on the other hand, is willing to give up a certain amount of his own independence in order that others may be pleased by giving to him; in other words, he is willing to be obligated because he likes others. A great deal has been said about graceful giving, but graceful receiving is just as important.

A likable person is not moody. Friends do not flock around the moody individual. A person who has long periods of despair, sulkiness, or irritability does not attract others because his personality tends to check the happiness of those around him. To be a likable person, you will avoid moodiness.

A likable person is not self-conscious. Self-consciousness, as explained in an earlier chapter, implies egotism, concentration on self rather than on others. People may not be able to explain why they do not respond favorably to a self-conscious person, but they instinctively feel that his self-consciousness means that he is not interested in them. When you become interested in those around you and in the things they are doing, sooner or later your self-consciousness will disappear.

A likable person is a good cooperator. Good followership is essential to likableness; it is a form of cooperation, which is necessary in all walks of life. Examples at school are teamwork in athletics, helpfulness in the classroom, and participation in extra-curricular activities. You will find the likable student cooperating with his fellows.

A likable person does not dominate his friends. As a likable person, you will not force your ideas upon the group by talking all the time or by talking louder than everyone else. Nor will you force your leadership upon the group by insisting that your suggestions be followed.

A likable person helps others to feel important. If you want to be likable, you will be willing to modify your own desire for superiority to let the other fellow satisfy his; you will be willing to let him be in a superior position. You will satisfy your desire for power primarily by making and keeping friends.

A likable person has faith in his fellows. Suspiciousness is one of the characteristics of a person who does not have many friends. To be liked, you must learn to be confident that others can do things, besides yourself, and that they will be fair with you.

A likable person speaks well of others. Obviously you do not go around flattering others, but you will frequently speak well of them to their friends.

A likable person likes to be of service. You will think of your job as an opportunity to be of service, and, in your relations with people away from work, you will be helpful as a matter of habit. It is a habit you will enjoy once you acquire it.

These are the traits you develop when you solve your personal problems and keep your ideal self in action. They help you to realize the best that is in you wherever you are, at school, at home, on the job, or in military service. These traits lead to success, and inescapably they enable you to become a good leader in some things and a good follower in others. But it is all a gradual process.

Making improvements is a gradual process. Every young person tries to improve himself or herself at times, doing away with bad habits and setting up good ones; but all too frequently he gives up too soon and does not try again for a long while. His impatience for success actually stands in the way of succeeding, for personal improvement comes only with constant effort. Young people want to get things done quickly; they do not like to think of keeping at even as difficult a job as rebuilding the personality for years and years. Perhaps you have had the experience of making a fine start, and then having something discouraging turn up so that you give way to a sudden feeling of hopelessness, thinking, "What's the use? I can't change, anyway. That's how I am, and I can't do anything about it." A healthier attitude in these circumstances, which occur frequently, would be to grit your teeth and try right over again.

You should remember that every gain, no matter how small, is going to make it easier to prolong the better habit during the next trial. Rebuilding the personality cannot be done all at once or without failures. It is impossible to remove habits of long standing without much persistent and renewed effort. Do not let your impatience retard, interrupt, or cancel the process.

Are you able to criticize yourself? If you have the ability to criticize yourself, you may become a sort of master mind making observations on yourself, like a scientist at a microscope. It has been said that our most severe critics are our best friends; often our own improvement is made possible through the excellent criticism of these friends, and we ought always to welcome it. But genuine criticism among friends is very rare, and we learn more and more that it is necessary for us to study ourselves — to see ourselves as others see us — so that we may make ourselves better liked by our fellows. Self-criticism involves an awareness of virtues as well as faults, gives you a picture of yourself in relation to others, and helps you to avoid unbalanced points of view, such as you find, for example, among those who permit themselves to become conceited or melancholy.

Do you talk about your personal problems with some friend? An important step in the direction of removing or correcting a fault is securing a complete understanding of it. It is as if by dividing the evil into the parts that make it up — dissecting it under the microscope — you are actually preventing it from growing together again as strong as it was before. The process of self-examination helps you to know just what is wrong and why. There are various ways of analyzing faults, but any method that brings about a complete understanding will help you to correct or remove the fault. One way is to discuss it with someone, preferably a friend who can sympathize and understand. With such a person you can talk very frankly about the habit, discussing the various little gestures or feelings or thoughts that make it up. After all, it is our own self-interest — or supposed self-interest — that keeps us from facing the facts. We do not wish to admit to ourselves or to anyone else that we are imperfect. Why not use this self-interest to make ourselves better?

Talking confidentially with a sympathetic person has several possible advantages. It relieves your mind to talk about something that is troubling you and enables you to face the facts rather than suppress them. It will probably lead to a better understanding of yourself and help you to take a scientific instead of an emotional attitude toward the problem. Finally, and most important of all, it may provide suggestions for improvement.

READINGS
For Further Information

Bliss, Walton B. *Personality and School*, Chapter 29. Allyn and Bacon.

Fedder, Ruth. *A Girl Grows Up*, Chapter 5. McGraw-Hill.

Goodrich, Laurence B. *Living with Others*, Chapters 1 and 12. American Book.

Laird, Donald A. *Why We Don't Like People*. Glaser.

Morgan, John J. B. *Keeping a Sound Mind*, Chapter 13. Macmillan.

Webb, Ewing T., and Morgan, John J. B. *Strategy in Handling People*, Chapter 2. Garden City.

Wright, Milton. *Getting Along with People*, Chapters 1 and 5. McGraw-Hill.

LEADERSHIP AND FOLLOWERSHIP

Does a leader work harder than a follower? Is a superintendent in a factory more important than one of his workers? Could a good follower also be a good leader? In a group of five or six students meeting in committee, is the chairman necessarily the leader? Who is?

ABRAHAM LINCOLN had millions of followers — people who thought with him and cooperated with him in his leadership of the nation. But he himself was also a follower. As President, he followed the advice of his cabinet members and other specialists who gave him information about national and international problems, which involved the interests of his millions of followers. A President leads the millions, but he also follows them. He keeps attuned to their desires and their thinking, and, although he may sway them to some extent, they sway him to a large extent as well.

Similarly, a senior class president uses his leadership to direct the plans of the class for various projects such as field days, proms, excursions, plays, and class memorials. But what would happen if he tried to direct the members of his class against their interests? What would happen if he did not understand how to get along with people? If no one in the class agreed or cooperated with him, he might still be called the senior class president, but he would not be a leader. To be a leader, he too must keep attuned to the sentiments of his followers, find out what the class members want, redirect their interests to some extent, and in his leadership follow the best and strongest and most generous interests of his group.

Leadership always involves followership, and a well-adjusted personality develops both. This is the natural result when personal problems are solved or on the way to being solved. Although popular interest usually centers on leadership, followership is equally necessary in society. A true democracy depends upon both. There is a real glory in good followership, and it represents high achievement in the mental health of the personality.

What leads to leadership? There are, perhaps, two types of leaders. One type is represented by Napoleon, who had so keen a feeling of inferiority that he wanted to show himself and everybody else that he really was somebody. The other type is represented by President Lincoln, who naturally understood people's wants and found them following him. The former type of leadership springs from an unsolved personal problem, the latter from good personal adjustment coupled with a gift for dealing with people.

No one is a "born leader." A man who becomes a leader may have been brought up in a home environment favorable for the development of social abilities, but leadership itself requires a good deal more than social ability. Many people who are good mixers can never be leaders in the sense of having a large following. There are a number of other qualities that are absolutely necessary, and their development requires hard work, constant effort, and great patience. After a long time, when a person has trained himself successfully, he may become very smooth and persuasive, and people will say that "he is a born leader." Little do they know of the devotion he gave to improving himself.

The foundation of true leadership is self-control. If you want to control others, you should first be able to control yourself.

A teacher who has difficulty in controlling her class usually has difficulty in controlling herself. The same is true of a boy who has difficulty in controlling his younger brother, or a senior class or a club president who has difficulty in controlling his group.

Controlling a group or even one other person requires planning, thinking things through in advance, being prepared for questions or problems that may arise. The person who does not do this planning does not have his own thinking in control and is not respected by those he is supposed to lead. When emergencies come up, he is not ready to meet them, and his followers lose confidence in him. Any show of anger, fear, or confusion indicates a personal problem that is not solved. This is sensed immediately by the group, and they instinctively react unfavorably. The leader does not have himself under control; how can he control others?

The basis of ability to control others is the ability to control yourself. If you want to become a leader in anything, you will plan your actions carefully and try to control yourself according to the plan. Self-control, however, is only one of the qualities of leadership.

Have you the will power for leadership? A leader should have a great deal of will power and a strong desire to go ahead with plans that seem to him to be important. He may find many obstacles in the way of getting things done, but he will drive ahead with a will, never stopped by difficulties that make others give up in despair or disgust. A strong will keeps him fighting for the successful completion of a worth-while plan.

Leadership in a school situation. This can be illustrated by the case of a certain high-school student, Bill M——, who thought it would be a fine gesture on the part of his class to leave a memorial to the school. He was not the president of the class, but in this particular project he showed leadership. He talked with the president about his plan; then he approached a number of other seniors. He found a few in favor of the idea, but many were against it because they wanted to spend all the money in the treasury for a grand splurge on field day. He was not discouraged by the sentiment of the majority, however, for he was convinced of the value of his idea.

Slowly Bill M—— secured the support of first one student, then another. Soon he began to search out a few of the more influential members of the class and promoted the plan with them. Finally the matter was brought up at a class meeting, and Bill spoke in favor of it after two other students had discussed it. The class was not very enthusiastic, and a long discussion followed. The meeting ended in failure, except that a large number of students talked with each other about the proposal that day and during the week. At the next class meeting it was brought up again. The class was more sharply divided than before, and it was again impossible to get final action.

Another week of heated informal discussions followed. An English class and a history class in which Bill was a member spent an hour in debate on the subject. At the next class meeting the motion was put to a vote. Bill called for a secret ballot because he was afraid a showing of hands would defeat the plan. The motion was carried 34 to 26. He had had the will power to carry the fight to a finish.

Have you the intelligence for leadership? A leader should have not only a great deal of knowledge about facts and men, but also understanding, so that he will be able to use what he knows in any new situation. He should be quick to see what must be done, and the ability to do this is what is known as intelligence. Leaders usually know a great deal about the facts of any situation in which they are interested as leaders. If they do not already know, they find out.

The president of a high-school club, for instance, will probably know more about the problems related to putting on a prom than any other member of the class. If he does not, he must bring into play his understanding of human nature by selecting committees that will be especially able to get the necessary information; and after they have studied the question, he will try to learn all he can from them. The information he gains will help him to see what steps should be taken. If the information is not complete, he will look farther by digging into records of former club activities and talking with the principal, the teachers, and former students who may be able to give him additional facts. When he has found out all he can and has thoroughly studied present needs in the light of this knowledge, he is ready for a meeting of the club. If he is a good leader, he will not dare to call a meeting before he has a great deal of knowledge about the question to be discussed and a great deal of understanding about the steps to be taken.

One of the differences between a leader and a follower is that the leader "burns the midnight oil" in an effort to gain a great deal of knowledge about a situation in which the group needs his leadership.

Are you enthusiastic? You may have heard the old saying, "Enthusiasm is contagious." People have found it contagious because in the leader's enthusiasm they can see the success of his plan before the work is finished. Enthusiasm is a strong feeling of hope and of excitement over the importance of a cause. With enthusiasm vibrant in a leader's personality, he radiates confidence to the group. They share his enthusiasm and his confidence in the success of the project to be undertaken, and with this attitude they are able to give him complete cooperation. A leader who is not enthusiastic over a cause cannot expect his followers to be enthusiastic.

At the same time, he must exercise a certain amount of restraint, for if his enthusiasm is too strong, too far ahead of that of others in the group, there is danger that they will have a feeling of inferiority. For this reason a clever leader usually first approaches individual members of the group, planting in them the seeds of his own enthusiasm for a cause and letting them work with the others while he remains occasionally in the background, quietly studying the group's acceptance of the idea.

Are you self-confident? Self-confidence and enthusiasm go hand in hand, except that self-confidence should continue during those periods when enthusiasm is not needed to fire the imagination of the group. Enthusiasm is not necessary, for example, for the successful management of routine activities. Self-confidence, on the other hand, is a necessary requirement of leadership at all times.

A leader should be confident of his ability to deal with individual members of the group and with a group as a whole. He should be confident of his plans and of the general direction in which his leadership takes the group. He may be wrong, but he should be confident that he is right. Like all men, leaders make mistakes. Sometimes they fail to see the mistakes or the inevitable future results of their present actions. A leader who knowingly takes a wrong step is, of course, betraying his group. He should at all times be confident that what he is doing is right. This inspires such confidence in his followers that they will cooperate with him, whether he is right or wrong.

Have you the energy for leadership? A leader must have a

great deal of energy. People marvel at the amount of work done
by a great public figure. He is busy all day and a large part of
the night, yet he is full of pep the next day. Some leaders, it is
true, burn themselves out and die at an early age because their
tremendous energy output exceeds their physical endurance.
They go to extremes.

A leader should be careful to plan his time in such a way as to
provide variety. He should exercise, play, take vacations, and
be able to relax quickly and completely so that within a short
time he can rebuild both body and mind. He spends most of
his energy in dealing with people. Through social relations he
seeks to accomplish many of his aims for the benefit of the group.
This activity is a constant drain upon his nervous system. Hence
it is very helpful to him to have a relaxing hobby. Perhaps a
hobby that requires physical exertion is especially suitable, because it balances mental activity and helps to maintain a healthy
body.

Can you shoulder responsibility? When the question is asked,
"Who is to blame?" a leader should be willing to say, "I am." He
should take the responsibility for the actions of the group, because it is through his leadership that the group does its work.
Even though a certain person in the group has failed, the leader
will be reluctant to permit blame to fall upon that individual.
He knows that if he had handled that person in a different way,
he might perhaps have forestalled failure. A leader is usually
much more willing to take responsibility than a follower is. He
is not afraid to go ahead, and, by showing his willingness to take
responsibility if the project should fail, he convinces those who
may be somewhat hesitant that they need not fear to do their
part.

A leader is modest. Of course, a leader gets a great deal of
credit for the successes achieved by the group. But he will be
modest in accepting this credit. He knows that the achievement
depended upon the cooperation of the group, and it is easy for
him to say, "We have to thank Bill and Jack for that. Those
fellows did a fine piece of work."

The attitude with which followers tackle a given task is to a
large extent determined by the quality of leadership inspiring

them in their work. When the leadership is poor, the cooperation of the group is usually poor also. Conversely, when the leadership is excellent, the followership is usually excellent also. A good leader assumes responsibility in securing the whole-hearted cooperation of his followers. If he is not able to inspire them with confidence in the work they have to do, enthusiasm for it, and a desire to cooperate, he should not be the leader of that group. It is his responsibility to win them over to a cause and obtain the greatest possible measure of cooperation.

Have you the necessary courage? Every new undertaking contains an element of danger because it may fail. A leader must have courage to carry it out in the face of that danger. Although he knows that every failure will damage his leadership and that certain failures may destroy it entirely, he carries on with firmness and boldness. He is fearless in taking the chances that must be taken for the good of the group and the cause.

A leader can take criticism. He must also have courage in the face of another important danger — the ill will of people who oppose his ideas, plans, and leadership. If he were afraid of his critics or his enemies, he could not serve as a leader, for fear would destroy the qualities of leadership in him. A leader will not ignore his enemies or opponents — in fact, he will study them and learn from them; but he will not respond to them with fear. He will not permit his enemies to damage his own personality or the work of his group. He needs courage to continue in the face of hostility as well as in the face of doubt or possible defeat.

There is leadership in all walks of life. If you want to become a leader of a large or a small group, at school, in church, in the community, in the factory, or anywhere else, you must develop the qualities we have discussed. You will begin with self-control, for the control of others begins with the control of self. Along with self-control, you need an ever-increasing measure of will power, intelligence, enthusiasm, self-confidence, energy, willingness to take responsibility, and courage. It is possible for you to develop these qualities in your personality just as others have. Remember that no one is a born leader. Every leader works hard, long, and patiently to develop his leadership, and, if you want to, you can begin that hard, long, and patient effort yourself.

Leadership is sometimes based upon false principles. Many leaders, especially political leaders, build a huge following by crusading for some widespread hatred. Thus, one may hold his people because he leads a crusade against the Jews, another because he leads a crusade against the rich. If a leader secures the cooperation of his followers mainly because they are in agreement with him on one or more hatreds, he is building his leadership upon false principles. In the long run he is bound to fail. Good leadership and followership must be built upon affection, respect, and confidence — in general, upon constructive qualities rather than upon destructive ones such as fear, anger, and hate.

Followership is needed in a democracy. In a democratic country intelligent followership is extremely important because the follower is the one who governs. This idea runs through all our thinking, in government, business, school, church, and other groups. According to our theory, the average man has an important place in the management of the whole activity in which he plays a part. Followership then comes to mean, not only intelligent thinking, but also intelligent working — not only intelligent cooperation in planning things, but also intelligent cooperation in doing them.

No one is at all times a leader or at all times a follower; hence it is well for everyone to study the qualities and techniques of both leadership and followership. A good leader will be interested in improving his followership because to be an excellent leader he must at times be an excellent follower.

Though we lead at times, we follow most of the time. Followers constitute the majority in any group anywhere. It is in the nature of a social group that, soon after they get together, someone becomes the leader and the rest become followers. The success and efficiency of every group depends upon three things — the quality of the leadership, the quality of the followership, and the value of whatever the group is trying to accomplish.

What are the qualities of followership? Although not every follower need have a great deal of vision, initiative, and intelligence, there are certain qualities he must have. The first of these is the ability to cooperate.

Cooperation. A good follower can work with his fellows and derive happiness from doing something that is of value to the majority, even though at the moment it does not seem to be of value to himself. He can take orders without resentment and work in harmony with others for a common cause. The advantage that comes to the group as a whole is more important to him than any personal momentary gain. One of the most valuable qualities of any worker is this ability to cooperate. If you ever ask for a letter of recommendation, the person who writes it will pay you the highest compliment if he says that you are an excellent cooperator.

Loyalty. Loyalty is perhaps the greatest of all virtues. A leader should be loyal to the group and the group to him. It is not always possible for the individual members of a group to see as clearly into the future as the leader does. They cannot always visualize the final success of the work they are doing. This is sometimes the case with children, who follow the leadership of parents. In order that they may work with pleasure and confidence, followers must have faith that their leader is directing them rightly so far as essentials are concerned.

In a democracy we do not want blind, unreasoning faith. We believe that every follower has a right to study the whole plan in which he is taking a part. If his study convinces him that he is wrong in cooperating, and the matter is an important one, he should not continue against his own convictions. However, if his differences of opinion with the leader have to do only with minor details, nonessentials, he should remain loyal to the leader and the group.

Ability to get along with one's fellows. Since the accomplishments of a group depend upon the combined efforts of a number of individuals working together, it is extremely important for them to be able to get along well with each other. The less friction there is, the better. A person who can get along with his fellows is an extremely valuable member of any group; one who cannot, interferes with his own progress as well as that of others. He himself is discontented and does not do his best, and he also increases the discontent of others. The failure of many worth-while projects in school, church, and community can be traced to a few such individuals.

Diligence. A good follower is diligent in the routine tasks required by a group project. Inventing, planning, and carrying out plans is not always required, but the ability to work stead-fastly at a given task is extremely important. Many workers are known for their leadership in diligence itself. Millions of people are not exceptionally brilliant, but, if they have developed habits of faithfulness and diligence in routine tasks, they are rendering a service necessary to the group.

Ordinary jobs are important. Most work is in itself rather uninteresting and dull, yet every task can be thought of as both interesting and valuable because it is part of a more important whole. Washing dishes, for example, may be considered unin-teresting in itself, but millions of women might find more satis-faction in it than they do if they saw its larger meaning as a serv-ice in the lives and activities of all the other members of the family.

The leading-on value of work. All work, no matter how sim-ple, monotonous, or drudging, has a leading-on value; that is, it has a meaning in relation to bigger things and other people. A charwoman whose daily duty it is to scrub the library floor is rendering a service of value to the people who use the library every day. If she can do her work diligently from day to day with contentment, she is rendering an important service in the whole scheme of life. Who knows but that it is just as impor-tant as the work of the scholar? Both the scrubwoman and the scholar can be leaders in their own field of service and their own way.

The solution of personal problems ends in better leadership and followership, and these qualities are both present to some extent in every well-adjusted personality. What you have learned from this book may help you to attain the kind of leadership and fol-lowership that suits your own abilities and interests. Merely knowing a little more about the causes that underlie your actions and those of others is bound to make some difference, even if you do not actively do something about it.

The adventure of personality development, however, depends upon what you do about it. A book may inspire you, but it cannot make you take action. Personality development can be the great adventure in which you find your true self and build yourself according to the best that is in you. But, after all, you are the one to do it. It's up to you.

READINGS

In Textbooks

Bogardus, E. S., and Lewis, R. H. *Social Life and Personality*, pp. 27-41. Silver, Burdett.

Eastburn, L. A., Kelley, V. E., and Falk, C. J. *Planning for School and Society*, Chapter 13. Scribner.

Goodrich, L. B. *Living with Others*, pp. 146-147. American Book.

Law, F. H. *He Got the Job*, pp. 177-179. Scribner.

Wright, Milton. *Getting Along with People*, Chapters 18 and 19. Garden City.

INDEX